APPLEWOOD
MILITARY HISTORY
SERIES

The Life of General Daniel Morgan

Of the Virginia Line of the Army of the United States

James Graham

APPLEWOOD BOOKS
Bedford, Massachusetts

The Life of General Daniel Morgan
was originally published in
1859

ISBN: 978-1-4290-2133-3

- -

APPLEWOOD'S MILITARY HISTORY SERIES

Thank you for purchasing an Applewood book. Applewood reprints America's lively classics—books from the past that are still of interest to modern readers. This facsimile was printed using many new technologies together to bring our tradition-bound mission to you. Applewood's facsimile edition of this work may include library stamps, scribbles, and margin notes as they exist in the original book. These interesting historical artifacts celebrate the place the book was read or the person who read the book. In addition to these artifacts, the work may have additional errors that were either in the original, in the digital scans, or introduced as we prepared the book for printing. If you believe the work has such errors, please let us know by writing to us at the address below.

For a free copy of our current print catalog featuring our bestselling books, write to:

APPLEWOOD BOOKS
P.O. Box 365
Bedford, MA 01730

For more complete listings, visit us on the web at:
awb.com

Prepared for publishing by HP

LIFE OF GENERAL DANIEL MORGAN.

THE LIFE

OF

GENERAL DANIEL MORGAN,

OF THE

VIRGINIA LINE

OF THE ARMY OF THE UNITED STATES,

WITH PORTIONS OF HIS

CORRESPONDENCE;

COMPILED FROM AUTHENTIC SOURCES.

BY JAMES GRAHAM.

"QUISQUE FABER SUÆ FORTUNÆ."

NEW YORK:

DERBY & JACKSON, 119 NASSAU ST.

1859.

W. H. TINSON, STEREOTYPER.   GEO. RUSSELL & CO., PRINTERS.

PREFACE.

When a writer puts forth a book, the subject of which has pre-engaged public sympathy, he is more than ordinarily obligated to furnish such explanations regarding its origin and character, as may give it a claim to public confidence. The chief, if not the only recommendations of this work, will be found in the motives which suggested it, and in the truthfulness of its details. However well-founded may be my fears, that I shall fail of success in all other respects, I cherish the hope that in these I shall prove more fortunate. Satisfaction to the reader and justice to myself, equally require, then, that in presenting these sketches to the public, the considerations with which they originated, and the circumstances under which they were completed, should be briefly stated.

At the death of General Morgan, his papers, correspondence, &c., went into the possession of his son-in-law, General Presley Neville. During the fifteen or twenty years which succeeded, many of these papers were lost or destroyed. What remained of them at the termination of this period, however, were collected, arranged, and bound into two large volumes, by the general's grandson, Major Morgan Neville, to whom, at the death of his father, they were left. When he died, these volumes became the property of his widow, who submitted them to my perusal, with the object of ascertaining whether the publication of a select portion of their contents would be advisable or not.

This collection is a very valuable one, embracing as it does, letters hitherto unpublished, from Washington, Greene, Lafayette, Wayne, Gates, Jefferson, Hamilton, Henry, Rutledge, and many other distinguished men of the revolutionary era. It was with no little pleasure that I perused and re-perused these interesting relics of men and times associated with such glorious recollections. They furnish an epistolary history of the war, from the pens of its leading spirits; and abound in facts and circumstances,

which the historian has either failed or feared to notice.   But what chiefly
attracted my attention, was the additional light which they shed upon the
private character and military services of General Morgan, and upon the
details of his long and eventful career.   Until I saw these papers, I labored
under the common error of assigning to him a position among the worthies
of the revolution, far below that which ħe not only deserved, but actually
occupied.   My curiosity to learn all that was attainable of his history was
now aroused.   After examining all the sources of information within my
reach, I became convinced that few, if any, of the heroes of that day furnished
larger contributions than he did to the glory of our arms, or surpassed him in
the amount and value of their services.   Nevertheless, I found that beyond
a few brief, and generally incorrect sketches, and a short paragraph in a
biographical dictionary, almost everything regarding him, not incidental
to the history of the revolutionary struggle, existed only in a tradition,
already distorted by the operations of time, and soon to be merged into
an irreclaimable oblivion ; that his character and conduct had been mis-
conceived in some cases, and misrepresented in others; and that from
these causes, many of our revolutionary historians had been betrayed into
statements at variance with facts, and injurious to his fame.   The absence
of full and correct information regarding a man whose name and deeds
furnish so rich a source for national pride, has, besides, tempted Fiction to
make him the theme of her legends.   But the fanciful pictures which she
has drawn, though recognizable, are not likenesses, while they fall far
short of the spirit and dignity which invested the reality.

The American people hold in especial reverence the memory of those
whose patriotism and valor were rendered conspicuous in the revolutionary
war.   The day is far distant, if, indeed, such a day will ever arrive, when
they will cease to regard with interest everything in relation to that band
of heroes and sages.   I felt that the merit of good intentions would at
least be accorded him, who would essay to rescue so distinguished a name
from the fate with which it was threatened ; and that if he should succeed
in adding to the stock of correct information, regarding some of the most
important events of the war, he might hope for a more gratifying indica-
tion of public approval.   Yet, the original, and other sources of information then in my possession, furnished ample means, not only to compass
these ends, but to vindicate his spotless reputation, to restore him to the
high position which he occupied among the heroes and patriots of the war,
and to win him a more enduring, if not a more favorable hold upon the
memory of posterity.   With reflections like these, originated the determi-

nation on my part, to collect and arrange all the information concerning the general, that was attainable at so late a day, and while drawing from this a detailed narrative of his eventful life, to obtain for his fame all the benefit which its testimony afforded.

But ample as were the materials furnished by Gen. Morgan's MSS., and the published memorials of the revolutionary war and of its leading spirits, much was yet to be gathered before a complete and connected chain of events could be formed. My efforts to supply this deficiency led me into an extensive correspondence, and resulted in a great addition to my original stock of information. And here a proper occasion presents itself to make my acknowledgments to the gentlemen who so promptly responded to my calls for aid. To a large number of these, it would be but echoing the suggestions of my gratitude to express my thanks in connection with their names; but the fear that such a return would be distasteful to them, counsels me to be silent. A few, however, have contributed so largely and so valuably to my collections, as to render acknowledgments a duty as well as a pleasure. The first of these is the late Dr. Wm. Hill, of Winchester, Virginia. This gentleman, who died about three years ago, was one of Morgan's personal and intimate friends. He attended the general during the illness which terminated his life, and preached the funeral sermon which was delivered over his grave. To him I am indebted for a large collection of facts, anecdotes, &c., in relation to Gen. Morgan, which run through his entire career, and which are recorded from his own lips. It would be difficult to estimate the advantages I derived from this valuable contribution. Besides the intrinsic information which it yielded so largely, it served as an index, whereby the reduction of a chaos of facts into order was facilitated, and it explained circumstances, which, without it, would have remained inexplicable. Whatever of merit may be accorded to the connection of events, as displayed here and there through the work, will in a great degree be owing to the assistance I received from Dr. Hill. To P. H. Skipwith, Esq., a grandson of Gen. Greene's, I am greatly obliged for copies of a number of letters, written by Gen. Morgan to Gen. Greene; among others, the original report of the battle of the Cowpens, and the letters following that event up to the time when the American army reached Guilford Court House. These contributions were exceedingly valuable, as they added largely to the mass of testimony, proving that the statements of many historians, in relation to the operations of the adverse armies, before and after the battle of the Cowpens, are erroneous. My acknowledgments are likewise due to T. M. Nightingale, Esq., also a descendant of Gen. Greene, for portions of Morgan's correspondence, little less valuable and interesting than those received from Mr. Skipwith. I am also under obligations to Gov. Johnson, of South Carolina, not only for the valuable information which he caused to be prepared and sent to me, but for the lively interest which he manifested in the progress and object of my labors.

In the compilation of these SKETCHES, recourse was necessarily and frequently had to such published authorities as yielded the description of information I sought. I have had frequent occasion to profit by the details of works of this character; but in no case have I knowingly done so, without making the usual marginal reference. Should any instance to the contrary be discovered, however, I hope it will be attributed to inadvertence rather than to design. From this general acknowledgment, I must, however, make an exception in favor of Judge Johnson's Life of Gen. Greene, to which work I am indebted for much and valuable information regarding Gen. Morgan's connection with the military operations in the South, during the years 1780 and 1781. The assistance I derived from Judge Henry's narrative, in describing Morgan's sufferings and services during the memorable expedition to and assault upon Quebec, and from Gen. Wilkinson's memoirs, in giving his participation in the campaign which terminated with the surrender at Saratoga, also deserve especial notice.

I will now close by declaring that if the result should prove in any degree an acceptable offering to the memory of the man whose life and services it purports to record, and whose fame it essays to preserve, I shall feel myself amply rewarded.

JAMES GRAHAM.

NEW ORLEANS, *May*, 1856.

CONTENTS.

―――――◆◈◆―――――

CHAPTER I.

CHAPTER II.

CHAPTER III.

i *   ix

CHAPTER XVII.

CHAPTER XVIII.

CHAPTER XIX.

CHAPTER XX.

CHAPTER XXI.

THE LIFE

OF

GENERAL DANIEL MORGAN.

————◆◆◆————

CHAPTER I.

The Ancestry, parentage, and early history of General Daniel Morgan—The impressions created by his first appearance in Virginia—His first employment—Superintends a mill —employed as a wagoner—Purchases a wagon and horses, and becomes a wagoner on his own account—His great and rapid improvement, physical and mental—Glance at the country and its population—He begins to attract notice—The opening of the seven years' war—Morgan engaged as a wagoner in the train of General Braddock—The army advances—The difficulties which it encounters in its march—Morgan fights and conquers a noted pugilist—Braddock's defeat—The retreat to Fort Cumberland—Measures of defence taken by the Virginia Assembly—Morgan employed as a wagoner in the service of the colony.

REGARDING the ancestry, the parentage, and even the early history of GENERAL DANIEL MORGAN, but little is known. The writer deeply regrets the necessity, thus imposed upon him at the very outset of his labors, of disappointing, if not disgusting the reader : for generally, there is no part of a great man's career which is regarded with more interest than that with which it commences. But the deficiency should, and we feel assured will be, ascribed to the causes about to be stated, and not to any want of pains or perseverance on the part of the writer.

The only source of information on these points was General
Morgan himself. Yet for reasons which remain unexplained, he
was studiously uncommunicative regarding them. When ques-
tioned concerning his parents or family, or the days of his
childhood, he either evaded a direct answer, or replied in a
manner that put a stop to further inquiries of such a nature. It
was only at rare intervals, and in the warmth of friendly conversation, that these subjects were broached by him, and then only
incidentally. On such occasions he would hastily resume the
main thread of his discourse, evincing, even to casual observation,
that he had betrayed himself into an allusion to recollections
that were either painful or disagreeable. To these occasional
and involuntary revelations we are, therefore, indebted for everything that is known concerning him, previous to his first appearance in Virginia.

General Morgan was of Welsh extraction. Between the years
1720 and 1730, many emigrants from Wales arrived at Philadelphia, and, proceeding thence up the Delaware, settled on its
banks. Among those emigrants were his parents. He was
frequently heard to declare that his father and mother were
Welsh, and that they had emigrated to this country about the
above-mentioned period.* It appears that after residing on the
Pennsylvania side of the Delaware for a year or two, they
removed to the opposite shore, in New Jersey, where they lived
in a small clearing, cultivated by the father, until all trace of
them is lost. What their circumstances were, how they lived,
and when and where they died, are facts that were never
revealed by General Morgan ; and, perhaps, after his removal to
Virginia, remained unknown even to himself. Whether they
had any children besides the subject of this notice, is a question
equally involved in mystery.† He was never heard to speak of

---

* MSS. of Dr. Hill.

† A biographical sketch of General Morgan, published many years since, in a work,
entitled, " The Glory of America," states that he had a brother. " On the northern fron-

brothers or sisters, however; and the impression is, either that he never had any, or that having had either or both, they died before he had attained a distinguished position.

In relation to the events and circumstances of his life, up to the period, when, in 1753, and at the age of seventeen years, he made his first appearance in Virginia, he was equally reserved Rogers, in his Biographical Dictionary, and a few other writers, state that he was a native of Durham township, Bucks County, Pennsylvania. All other authorities, however, including his descendants, concur in assigning to New Jersey the honor of his birth, and it is believed, correctly so. He was born in Hunterdon County, in that State, in the winter of the year 1736.

The details of the succeeding seventeen years of his life would furnish little to interest the reader, even were it in our power to give them. When first known in Virginia, it was but too evident that he had derived but little advantage from the teachings of the schoolmaster, for he could read but indifferently, wrote a hand barely legible, and had but an imperfect knowledge of the fundamental rules of arithmetic. His manners were rude and unpolished, and his appearance and conversation did not distinguish him from the humble order of men to which he seemingly belonged. From the time he was able to labor, he must have been kept actively employed by his father, in clearing land, spliting fence rails, and in performing other tasks incidental to the

tier of New Jersey," the writer goes on to say, "his brother resided, whom he had not seen for many years, and who, he learned, was in extreme indigence. On his return from Saratoga, he left his troops a few days, and went twenty miles out of his way to see him. During this visit, he slept on the bare floor, his brother having but one bed in the house, which he refused to occupy on account of the indisposition of his sister-in-law. He offered his brother a good farm if he would remove with him into Virginia, which, from strong local attachment, his brother declined." We have looked around in vain for a confirmation of this story; and, all the circumstances being duly considered, we cannot accord to it our belief. It is much more probable that such an offer was made by a rich and generous brother, than that it was declined, for the reasons assigned, by a poor one. But if this statement is correct, the brother must have died soon afterward, or the fact of his existence would have become generally known, as was everything else in relation to General Morgan, subsequent to his brilliant exploits during the War of Independence.

improvement of a new farm. This was the only occupation he
understood at that period, and in this only he sought employment.
Everything regarding him, in fact, gave token of the great disadvantages which must have surrounded his boyhood.*

The cause which resulted in his abandonment of the home of
his parents, and his settlement in Western Virginia, was briefly
stated by him to be a disagreement between his father and himself. His departure was without the knowledge or consent of his
parents. He travelled through Pennsylvania during the winter
of 1753, stopping for a few weeks at Carlisle, where he obtained
some employment. In the spring of that year he crossed into
Virginia, and reached a small settlement in Berkeley County
(since Jefferson), called Charleston. Here, soon after his arrival,
he obtained employment from a Mr. Roberts, who cultivated a farm
in the neighborhood.

Young Morgan proved to be very industrious, and capable of
performing a large amount of labor. The first task at which he
was set was to grub a piece of ground in a rough, primitive state,
for which he was to be paid by the acre. The work was done so
much to the satisfaction of his employer, that he received a succession of jobs of the same kind, and at length was engaged to
superintend a saw-mill, which had just been erected by Mr.
Roberts.† He was employed in this manner for the greater part
of a year, when a Mr. Ashley, steward to Nathaniel Burwell, Esq.,
of Frederick County, offered him a situation as a wagoner.‡ At
this period, and for many years afterward, supplies for the region
west of the Blue Ridge were transported in wagons, from Fredericksburg and the older settlements east of that range of mountains. The business of the wagoner had not then to contend with
the rivalry of the steamboat and the railroad; it was, in consequence, a profitable and an important one. The wages offered to
Morgan by Mr. Ashley, were much better than those he had been
receiving at the saw-mill. Besides, the business recommended itself

---

* MSS. of Dr. Hill.   † MSS. of Dr. Hill.   ‡ Lee's Memoirs, 428.

to Morgan, as being less continuous and confining than the labor in
which he had been up to that time engaged; and moreover, it favored
a design he had already formed, of becoming a wagoner on his own
account, as soon as he could command the means of purchasing a
wagon and horses. He accordingly accepted the situation, and for
about six months drove a wagon between the estate of Mr. Burwell,
on the Shenandoah, and the principal market towns east of the mountains. He was subsequently employed in the same capacity by
John Ballantyne, Esq., the owner of a plantation on Opequon
Creek.*

A little more than two years had elapsed since Morgan arrived
in Virginia, when his accumulated earnings enabled him to purchase a wagon and team. He now became a wagoner on his
own account. During this period, the favorable change which
had taken place in his circumstances, was not more remarkable
than that which his person and manners had experienced. The
half-formed boy had developed into a man; and one, too, of such
proportions and vigor as are seldom to be met with, even in persons above twenty years of age. His mind had experienced a
corresponding improvement, and already displayed those qualities
which seldom fail to confer on their possessor a distinction more
or less marked, according to the circumstances by which he is
surrounded. His strength and spirit, his frank and manly bearing, his intelligence and good-humor, set off by a rich fund of
natural wit, which he kept in constant exercise, rendered him a
favorite among the people, and contributed to give him a great
influence over his associates.

At this period, the settlements in this as in every other part of
Virginia, west of the Blue Ridge, were few and far between,
thinly inhabited by a people who, for the most part, were as
rough and uncultivated as the country they occupied. Winchester
was a small settlement, and Berrysville was in the womb of time.†
Beyond Winchester, in a westerly direction, the country was

---

* MSS. of Dr. Hill.   † Sparks's Writings of Washington, vol. ii., pp. 151, 2.

uninhabited, save by the aborigines, and by a few pioneers, more than ordinarily adventurous and daring. The perils by which the inhabitants were surrounded, and the hardships and privations which they were occasionally called upon to endure, gave a dash of intrepidity and recklessness to their character, and made them regard courage and other soldier-like qualities as those entitled to the highest praise and honor. The habits and manners, feelings and impulses, of Morgan, harmonized with those of the people with whom he was then in association. He therefore not only assimilated readily with them, but soon became popular in their eyes. It was not long after this period, when his immense strength and indomitable spirit, qualifications which, above all others, captivate the humbler order of minds, gave him the undisputed position of a leader among them.*

Morgan was pursuing his occupation of a wagoner, when important events gave a new and advantageous turn to his energies.

The rival claims of Great Britain and France to the fertile regions west of the Alleghanies having been productive of bloodshed, were now about resulting in war. A short time before hostilities broke out, Captain Trent was obliged to surrender the fort he had established at the confluence of the Alleghany and Monongahela rivers. Subsequently, Col. Washington surprised the detachment of French under M. Jumonville; while he, in turn, was obliged to succomb to the French and Indians, at the Great Meadows.† Instances of savage incursion and murder had been of common occurrence. They now increased to such a fearful extent, as to threaten the depopulation of the country west of the Blue Ridge. The people of the provinces, and particularly those of Virginia, were in a state of great excitement; and from New York to North Carolina, the preparations for war were everywhere observable—in the enlistment and organization of

---

* MSS. of Dr. Hill.   † Marshall's Washington (Second Edition), vol. i., pp. 4–6.

troops, and the collection of military stores, wagons, horses, &c.
General Braddock having been sent from England with a fine
army for the conquest of the country west of the mountains, had
arrived in the Potomac, and was awaiting the opening of the
spring to commence operations.*

The contemplated advance of so large an army through such
an extent of wilderness, called for extensive means of transportation, but it was with the greatest difficulty, that the necessary supply of horses and wagons could be obtained.† One so full of the
spirit of a warrior as was Morgan, needed not offers more tempting than those which were made him to join the expedition with
his wagon and horses. He relinquished his peaceful pursuits, and
commenced his military career in the humble capacity of a
teamster.

The army under Braddock, consisting of two British regiments,
with a train of artillery, and the necessary supplies of provisions
and military stores, was put in motion early in April, and concentrated at Fort Cumberland, the designated base of future operations, about the middle of May.‡ Here it was joined by a provincial force of about twelve hundred men, and a body of teamsters, camp-followers, &c., to the number of five hundred more.
In the beginning of this month, Morgan proceeded to Fort
Cumberland with a wagon-load of supplies; and there, with
a large number of troops, regular and provincial, and teamsters,
and others engaged in the service, awaited the arrival of the
army. The object of the British general was the capture of Fort
Duquesne; and, to effect this, he intended moving forward without delay. But, from the want of a sufficient number of wagons
and horses to transport the artillery and supplies, it was found that
an immediate advance was impracticable. After three weeks
had been consumed in supplying this deficiency, the army was at

* Marshall's Washington (First Edition), vol. i., p. 384.
† Ibid, vol. i., p. 390.
‡ Spark's Writings of Washington, vol. ii., p. 469.

length put in motion. But so slow and difficult was the advance, that, upon reaching the Little Meadows, it was found necessary to adopt new measures to expedite the progress of the army. A body of twelve hundred men, composed of the greater part of the regular forces, and several companies of provincial troops, commanded by Braddock in person, was accordingly pushed forward. The remainder of the army, having in charge the artillery, baggage, and supplies, was left under the command of Colonel Dunbar, who had orders to follow the advance by easy marches.*

The first division moved from the camp at Little Meadows on the 19th of June, leaving Colonel Dunbar and his command at that place. With the latter, the nature of Morgan's duty compelled him to remain. The country through which they had to advance was rugged and uneven, and the road was intersected by swamps and creeks; they consequently moved forward but very slowly. The horses at length became so fatigued as to threaten a stop to further progress. Among the expedients resorted to, for the purpose of accelerating the advance, one was to detach from one-half of the wagons and artillery-carriages the horses belonging to them, and attaching double teams to the rest, to move forward in this manner for half a mile or so. The horses were then brought back, and attached to the remainder of the baggage-train, when they again moved in advance of that already thrown forward.

It was during this march that the circumstances occurred which are related in the following anecdote. A difficulty arose between the captain of a company of Virginia troops (to which Morgan was attached in his capacity of wagoner, his wagon being laden with their baggage), and a powerful fellow who accompanied the army, and who had the reputation of being a skilful pugilist, and a bully. It was agreed between the disputants that upon the first halt the matter should be settled by a fight. As soon as the

---

* Marshall's Washington, vol. i., p. 391.

company halted for dinner, the captain stepped out to meet his antagonist, when he was accosted by Morgan—

" Captain," said he, " you must not fight that man."

" Why not ?" inquired the officer.

" Because," replied Morgan, " you are our captain, and if the fellow was to lick you, we should be all disgraced. But, I will fight him, and if he licks me, it will not hurt the credit of the company."

The captain remonstrated ; but disliking the necessity of placing himself on a level with a blackguard, and perceiving that his antagonist was perfectly willing to accede to the arrangement, he consented. Morgan, stripping himself, at once engaged the bully, and in a very short space of time, gave him so severe a beating that he was unable to rise from the ground. The prowess displayed by one so young, against a man of mature years and vigorous frame, and who, moreover, was celebrated as a pugilist, gave Morgan high consideration among his associates.

From the 19th of June, the day on which Braddock moved forward with the advance, until the 10th of July, the troops under Colonel Dunbar followed slowly and with great difficulty. On the evening of the 10th, while lying encamped at a point about seven miles west of the Great Meadows, the disastrous news of Braddock's defeat reached them. During the succeeding two days, fragments of the discomfited detachments continued to arrive, and soon the contagion of their fears spread through the camp. Numbers of the provincial troops immediately turned back towards home ; and many of the wagoners, after disencumbering their wagons, drove off to the settlements, leaving the helpless sick and wounded to escape, as they best could, the savage enemy, who, it was supposed, were in hot pursuit.*

On the morning of the 12th of July, General Braddock was brought into the camp upon a litter. An order was soon after

* Sparks's Writings of Washington, vol. ii., p. 86.

given to retreat to Fort Cumberland; and on the 13th, the artillery, stores, baggage, &c., having been destroyed, the wagons remaining, among which Morgan's was included, were filled with the sick and wounded, and started in that direction. The troops under Colonel Dunbar remained on the ground until the next day, in order to check the expected pursuit of the French and Indians, and to await the arrival of such of the fugitives as were still behind unhurt. During the night of the 13th, and when the retreating forces were within a mile of the Great Meadows, General Braddock expired.* He was buried in the middle of the road, to prevent the discovery of his body by the Indians. Morgan's wagon drove over the grave, as did all the wagons which followed him on the route to Cumberland. On the 17th, the sick and wounded, with the fugitives, arrived at Cumberland. Colonel Dunbar, with the remainder of the army, also, soon after, reached that place.

The news of the disastrous result of Braddock's campaign was received throughout the British provinces with the greatest astonishment. On the frontiers of Pennsylvania and Virginia, it created the liveliest apprehensions. The fears of the inhabitants of those exposed situations, that the enemy would profit by their successes, and renew their robbing and murdering incursions, were speedily realized. The exigencies of the case required the application of all the means of resistance which the British officers, or the colonial authorities, could command. But, Colonel Dunbar, notwithstanding the defenceless state of the frontier, and the expected advance of the enemy, soon after put his troops in motion for Philadelphia, where they went into winter quarters.†

The government of Virginia met the emergency with promptitude and vigor. It authorized an additional regiment of sixteen companies to be immediately raised, and appointed Washington as

* MSS. of Dr. Hill.
† Marshall's Washington, vol. i., p. 395.

its commander. One of the minor consequences of this and other measures, having in view the defence of the Virginia frontier, was the continuance of Morgan in the service of the colony. He, with his wagon and team, was attached to the quarter-master's department.

CHAPTER II.

Morgan is engaged in transporting supplies—The attack of a band of Indians repulsed—
He strikes an officer, and receives five hundred lashes—Anecdote—Inroad of the
French and Indians—Surprise and destruction of Captain Mercer and his command—
Morgan joins a body of militia sent to reinforce the garrison at Edward's fort—In an
attack upon the fort, Morgan distinguishes himself—Receives commission as ensign—
Falls into an ambuscade, is desperately wounded, but escapes—Remarks upon his character, habits, &c.—The meetings at Berry's tavern—His fights with Bill Davis—Anecdote—Morgan marries—Establishes himself at "Soldiers' Rest"—Pontiac's war—Morgan takes the field, and advances to Fort Cumberland—At the close of the war, returns
home—His daughters—His moral and intellectual improvement—Is commissioned a
captain.

DURING the eight years which succeeded the defeat of Braddock, we have only occasional glimpses of Morgan's career. This
is unfortunate, for the period was full of terrible incidents, a
knowledge of his participation in which, it is believed, would furnish us with instances of heroism as brilliant as those which
afterwards rendered him famous. There is no doubt of the fact,
however, that he shared in nearly all the principal military
events of the war, and that he was frequently a member of the
small parties of woodsmen which so often went in pursuit of predatory bands of the French and Indians. Such of these, and other
remarkable events of his life during this period as have survived
the wear of time, will now be given.

During the fall of 1755, and the winter and spring of the succeeding year, Morgan was engaged in transporting supplies to the
troops which were posted at various points along the Virginia
frontier. In the performance of this duty, he was constantly sub-

jected to the greatest danger from the lurking foe; and on two
or three occasions, narrowly escaped being killed. On one of
these, he contributed so essentially to the repulse of a band of
Indians, who waylaid the small party which accompanied him
and some other wagoners, on the road from Fort Cumberland to
Winchester, as to have accorded to him the credit of the victory.
In the spring of 1756, he was sent with a wagon-load of stores
to Fort Chiswell, one of the posts which had been established along
the Virginian frontier, and situated on the head waters of New
River. While at this place, a terrible disaster befell him. A
British lieutenant, taking offence at something which Morgan had
said or done, abused him in violent terms, and at length struck
him with the flat of his sword. Morgan's indomitable spirit could
not brook this outrage. Forthwith clenching his fist, he struck
the officer so heavy a blow as to extend him senseless on the
ground. This was regarded as an offence so grave against military
law, as to call for summary and exemplary punishment. A drum-
head court-martial sentenced Morgan to receive five hundred
lashes. Being immediately stripped and tied up, he received all at
once the allotted number of lashes, save one. When the terrible
punishment was over, it is said that the flesh on his back hung
down in tags.* None but one possessing unusual powers of
endurance, and an iron constitution, could have survived an act
of cruelty so extraordinary, even in the British army of that day.
But he soon recovered from its effects. The officer, sensible upon
reflection that he had been in the wrong, and regretting the consequences which had followed, afterwards made Morgan a public
apology. This was a slight atonement for so deep an injury; yet
it was deemed sufficient by Morgan, who, from that moment, mag-
nanimously discharged his mind of all resentment towards the
author of his sufferings and disgrace.

In the summer of 1790, at Old Fort Chiswell, the tavern-keeper
at that place pointed out to our informant† the white oak tree

* MSS. of Dr. Hill.   † MSS. of Dr. Hill.

to which Morgan was tied when he received this unmerciful lashing.

In after life, and when among his friends, Morgan frequently alluded to this event; but seldom without humorously remarking that there was one lash of his sentence remaining unpaid. As an instance of this kind, the following anecdote is related of him, when, in after years, he was confined by his last illness to his bed. "Upon one occasion," says our informant,* "while assisting in changing his linen, I discovered his back to be covered with scars and ridges from the shoulders to the waist. 'General,' said I, 'what has been the matter with your back?' 'Ah!' replied he, 'that is the doings of old King George. While I was in his service, upon a certain occasion, he promised to give me five hundred lashes. But he failed in his promise, and gave me but four hundred and ninety-nine; so he has been owing me one lash ever since. While the drummer was laying them on my back, I heard him miscount one. I was counting after him at the time. I did not think it worth while to tell him of his mistake, and let it go so!'"

During the spring and summer of 1757, the French and Indians, descending in great numbers into the country east of the mountains, and penetrating to the base of the Blue Ridge, spread death and destruction among the intermediate settlements. All the minor forts were attacked, and even forts Cumberland and Loudon were menaced. Among other disasters which befell the Virginians during this period, was the surprise and destruction of Captain Mercer and thirty-six of his men, by a large body of French and Indians. This officer, with fifty men, garrisoned Edward's fort, a post situated on the south side of the Cacapehon river, and at a point about twenty miles northwest of Winchester. A large body of French and Indians having committed several murders in the vicinity of the fort, Captain Mercer, at the head of the greater part of his garrison, sallied out in pursuit of the enemy. The latter, anticipating this step, scattered meal along

* Dr. Hill.

the line of their retreat, and adopted other expedients to draw their pursuers into the ambuscade which was subsequently pre-pared for them, under the abrupt bank of a small stream. Mer-cer's men were passing the fatal spot, when the Indians opened a destructive fire upon them, sixteen falling dead at the first dis-charge. The others, attempting to save themselves by flight, were pursued and slaughtered in every direction, until, out of forty men, but six reached the fort in safety.[*]

Edward's fort forming an important link in the chain of fron-tier defences, it was necessary to supply without delay the loss which its garrison had sustained in the late disastrous affair. All the troops at Winchester at this time were about fifty recruits, who formed the garrison of Fort Loudon. None of these could be spared, for even that important post was menaced by the enemy. In this emergency, the militia were called out.[†] Among the rest who promptly obeyed the call, was Morgan. With about fifty others, he marched to Edward's fort, and remained there for some time.

This is the first occasion that we have any knowledge of, on which Morgan appeared in the ranks of an army. What his position was in the garrison is unknown. It is believed, however, to have been one of command.

A short time after his arrival at Edward's fort, it was attacked by a formidable body of French and Indians. On the morning of the second day after the fort was invested, the enemy made a sudden and furious assault upon the works. But chiefly owing to the brave example set the garrison by Morgan, who, it is said, killed four of the savages in as many minutes, they repulsed their assailants with great slaughter. As the latter were seen retiring, Morgan shouted out at the height of his powerful voice, " Let us follow the red devils !" The garrison sallied forth as one man, and soon overtook the retreating foe. After a short, but desperate

[*] Kercheval's History of Virginia, p. 146.
[†] Sparks's Writings of Washington, vol. ii., p. 142.

conflict, the Indians fled in every direction, leaving a large num
ber of their killed and wounded on the field.

The courage and prowess, as well as the judgment and presence
of mind which Morgan displayed on this occasion, attracted
general notice, and won him the meed of universal applause. He
was no longer the obscure and unobserved wagoner or militia man,
but was regarded as one who had given unequivocal proofs of his
fitness to command. He was now fairly on the road to distinction. His acquaintance with Washington commenced about
this time, and was one of the consequences of his meritorious
conduct.

In the spring of 1758, great preparations were made for the
campaign which resulted in the evacuation of Fort Duquesne, the
expulsion of the French from the valley of the Ohio, and the
extortion of a temporary peace from their Indian auxiliaries. The
Provincial Government exerted itself in raising and organizing
troops, and in otherwise aiding the efforts of the commander of
the British forces, General Forbes.* The soldiery qualities which
Morgan had so frequently exhibited, caused him to be recommended to the governor by several of the leading men of Western Virginia, for a captaincy. But from that perversity of disposition which seems to have constantly influenced, if not controlled, Governor Dinwiddie's official conduct, he refused the solicited promotion. Notwithstanding it was represented to the
governor, that Morgan, besides his high military qualifications
possessed great influence among the people in Frederick, and the
adjoining counties, and that his advancement to a captaincy
would have the effect of swelling the ranks of the Provincial
troops; all that could be obtained for him was an ensign's commission. This he accepted; and in the capacity of an ensign, he
was stationed, first, at Edward's fort, and afterwards at other
forts on the western frontier of Virginia. It was while engaged
in this way that an event occurred, which nearly cost him his

* Marshall's Life, vol. i., pp. 488-441.

life, and suspended for a time his military career. The details are as follows :—

He was sent with an escort of two soldiers from one of these forts, with dispatches to the commanding officer at Winchester. About a mile from the place where this fort formerly stood, is a remarkable precipice called the Hanging Rock. A part of the road, along which Morgan and his companions had to travel, lay between the fort and this precipice, and the margin of a watercourse, leaving an intervening space, just wide enough for a man to pass. The place was rendered memorable from being the scene, years before, of a terrible encounter between contending parties of Catawba and Delaware Indians, and was admirably adapted for an ambuscade. For this purpose it appears to have been selected by a party of Indians and a few Frenchmen, who were then prowling about, seeking an opportunity for plunder and slaughter. Fully aware of the vicinity of the fort, they were not disapointed in their expectations of surprising some party going to, or coming from it. The enemy hid themselves among the rocks above the road, and lay quietly until Morgan and his escort came under them, when, taking deliberate aim, they fired, killing the escort, and desperately wounding Morgan himself. The men fell instantly from their horses, which the Indians had taken care not to injure. The ball which struck Morgan entered in at the back of the neck, grazing the left side of the neck-bone; then passing through into the mouth, near the socket of the jaw bone, came out through the left cheek. In its passage, the ball knocked out all of the teeth on the left side, without, however, otherwise materially injuring the jaw. Although terribly wounded, Morgan kept his seat. The blood ran in a stream from the fearful wound, and he became helplessly weak; yet he preserved his senses until he had secured himself from further harm. The animal upon which he was mounted, a fine young filley, was so frightened by the unexpected discharge, that for a few moments she stood motionless, as if spellbound. At length, leaning for

2*

ward, and grasping her neck with his arms, he urged her into motion. Fortunately for her rider, she took the direction back to the fort. The Indians, supposing him to be mortally wounded, left him to be followed by one of their party only, and turned to scalp the two who had fallen, and to catch their horses. Morgan, in the mean time, feeling certain that he had but a short time to live, was only anxious to get beyond the reach of his pursuers, before he died, that he might prevent his body from being mangled. He urged on his mare with his heels, and the noble animal, putting forth her utmost strength, bore him beyond the reach of the Indian, never slackening her speed until she reached the fort.

The late Morgan Neville, Esq. (a grandson of Morgan), in a biographical sketch of the general, written by him, remarks on this fortunate escape as follows:—

"I well remember, when a boy, to have heard General Morgan describe, in his own powerful and graphic style, the expression of the Indian's face, as he ran with open mouth and tomahawk in hand, by the side of the horse, expecting every moment to see his victim fall. But when the panting savage found the horse was fast leaving him behind, he threw his tomahawk, without effect, and abandoned the pursuit with a yell of disappointment."

Morgan was taken from his horse perfectly insensible. For a long time his case was a critical one; but with care and judicious treatment, he recovered, after a confinement of more than six months. It may be remarked here, that notwithstanding the numberless perils which he encountered, as well before as after this event, during his long and active military career, this was the only wound he ever received.

Morgan was now about twenty-three years of age. His appearance at this time was remarkably imposing, and indicative of great strength and activity. In height he was upwards of six feet; his form was symmetrically put together, muscular and massive;

and, although unencumbered with an ounce of superfluous flesh, he weighed nearly two hundred pounds. Upon his return to Frederick, he renewed his intimacy with his old associates. His fine military appearance, no less than his courage, and the general manliness of his conduct, gave him a high position among them ; while the superior traits of character he displayed, and the sufferings he had so manfully endured, secured him the regard and sympathy of a better class of people.

But his morals had suffered by the life he had been leading. His associates in the army had not been of the best description, and his habits had consequently experienced a change for the worse. Card-playing is a common refuge of the soldier from the tedium of inaction ; and, in those days, many, even of the higher rank of military officers, furnished indifferent examples of sobriety to the men in the ranks. Morgan had become addicted to drinking and gaming. But his strength of constitution enabled him to bear excess in liquor, without appearing intoxicated : indeed, in such a state he was seldom or never seen. He thus escaped being regarded as a drunkard. His skill as a gamester had the effect of increasing, rather than of diminishing, his resources. These and kindred habits, necessarily threw him into the company of the very worst description of people, and led him, besides, into numberless broils and difficulties.

Yet, although for a time addicted to habits of the most demoralizing character, and which generally lead their victims to destruction, the judgment and prudence which ever stood forth prominently in his character, prevented them from exercising more than a limited control over him. He was still industrious and saving. He longed to be above a condition of dependence ; and, even amid the wild orgies which filled up so large a portion of his time, he never lost sight of this laudable ambition.

When we duly consider the times in which he lived, the loose code of morals which then prevailed, and the unfavorable circumstances which had, from his boyhood, surrounded him, much may be educed in extenuation of his faults. These, his after life triumphantly proved to be fortuitous deviations from the walks in life which his unbiased inclinations prompted him to follow. But it must be admitted that his conduct at this period furnished anything but a presage of the distinction which he was yet to achieve. Would that we could draw a veil over this portion of his life, without at the same time doing violence to truth and justice.

It was the custom at this time for all the athletic young men who resided in the country, between Winchester and the Shenandoah river, to assemble every Saturday afternoon, at a tavern, about midway between the river and the town, kept by a man named Benjamin Berry. Here they boxed, wrestled, and practised other athletic exercises during the daylight, while drinking and gaming generally occupied the night. Morgan was a constant attendant at these meetings, and in trials of strength and agility, almost invariably carried off the palm of superiority from his competitors. These exercises, though always commenced in a friendly spirit, would sometimes produce angry feelings, and end in a fight. Morgan's superior vigor drew on him the envy and ill-will of many whose pride he had humbled in this way; and his fiery disposition bursting into flame on sufficient provocation, he had his full share of serious encounters.*

In the mountain, on the east side of the river Shenandoah, resided three or four brothers by the name of Davis, all of whom were men of extraordinary size and bodily strength. One of these, Bill Davis, as he was called, was the strongest and most active of them all. He was reputed to be the champion of the neighborhood; and he and his brothers kept the whole country around in awe of them. It happened, at one of the Saturday evening gatherings at Berry's tavern, that Morgan had a difference with this champion Bill Davis, which produced a tremendous fight between them. Morgan, in speaking of this battle many years

* MSS. of Dr. Hill.

afterwards, acknowledged it as his belief that Davis surpassed him
in strength, but that he made up for this deficiency in superior
dexterity, tact, and management. After a long and terrible fight,
Davis was obliged to yield, and Morgan, amid the triumphant
shouts of his friends, was proclaimed the conqueror. This event
was a source of great joy to the neighborhood. While it gratified
the resentment of those whose pride had been humbled by the
Davises, it added much to Morgan's popularity and reputation.*

Under the chagrin of this defeat, Bill Davis threatened vengeance, and announced his intention of trying conclusions with
Morgan again. Afraid, however, to venture on this experiment
single-handed, he induced his brothers, and a few other moun-
taineer bullies, to the number of half a dozen or more, to unite
with him for the purpose of taking possession of the play-ground
at the tavern, and of driving Morgan and his friends from
the premises. Morgan, being apprised of this design, selected
from among the latter an equal number of the stoutest men
he could find, when he repaired with them to the tavern, and
awaited the arrival of his foes. Soon Davis and his friends
appeared, and a severe battle ensued, which resulted in the
discomfiture of the assailants. For a year or so afterwards, these
factions contended with each other; and, before the contest
ended, many a fierce and protracted battle was fought between
them. Chiefly through the skill and management of Morgan, if
not from his courage and strength, and his superiority as a
pugilist, his party always came off the conquerors. They finally
drove the Davises and their friends from the tavern, and kept the
play-ground to themselves.†

This tavern was situated at a place about ten miles east of
Winchester, and six miles west of the Shenandoah river. Around
the spot has since sprung up a thriving village, which is popularly known as *Battletown*—a name it derived from its site being

* MSS. of Dr. Hill.   † MSS. of Dr. Hill.

the scene of those numerous encounters to which we have just adverted. The present inhabitants are, it is said, very anxious to have the place called by its proper name, Berrysville, a name which was given to it by Mr. Berry, the proprietor of the tavern, and the former owner of a part of the land on which it is built. It is, nevertheless, called Battletown by everybody in that part of the country, excepting the inhabitants of the village themselves.*

In connection with the account just given of Morgan's fight with Bill Davis, the following little anecdote, communicated to the writer by Dr. Wm. Hill, who attended and nursed Morgan during the closing scene of his life, may appropriately be introduced here : " While helping the general out of his bed," observes Mr. Hill, " I discovered one of his toes lying upon the top of his foot. ' General, what is the matter with this toe of yours ?' I inquired. 'I got that many years ago,' he replied, 'in a fight I had with Bill Davis, and in kicking him, at Battletown. I broke that toe, then, and I never could get it to lie in its right place since.' "

This was certainly the most unfavorable and unpromising epoch of Morgan's life. The dearth of particulars regarding it is the less to be regretted, from the belief that were it otherwise, an unpleasant duty would devolve on his biographer. We may confidentially say, however, that his faults were those of an imprudent, and not of a vicious disposition. They were the results, not of an innate depravity of heart, but of a defective education, and bad associations, operating on a mind as yet unformed, and pregnant with the wildest impulses.

Happily, as he advanced in years, he became more and more sensible of the impropriety and folly of his conduct. Before he

* Berrysville is now the county seat of Clark County. It was established, Jan. 8, 1798, on twenty acres of land, belonging to Benjamin Berry and Sarah Strebling, and the following gentlemen appointed trustees: Daniel Morgan, Wm. McGuire, Archibald McGill, Rawleigh Colston, John Milton, Thos. Strebling, Geo. Blackmore, Chas. Smith, and Bushrod Taylor.

attained his twenty-seventh year, he had gradually reformed his habits, and adopted a discreet and orderly way of living.

How far this gratifying change was contributed to, by the great master-passion, Love, it would be difficult to say. Certain it is, however, that about this time he became enamored with a young and lovely woman, named Abigail Bailey, who soon afterwards became his wife.

Mrs. Morgan, like her husband, was indebted for the distinction that attended her after life, to none of those considerations which the admirers of high connections and a remote ancestry always include in their estimates of personal worth and respectability. She was the daughter of poor parents, who resided on a small farm in Berkeley County, and who cultivated the soil for a subsistence. Like thousands of the matrons of those days, the mothers of our heroes, sages, and statesmen, the circumstances of the times and of the country denied her the advantages of an education. She possessed a person and mind that were formed by nature to adorn the most brilliant circle of beauty and talent; and what is of greater consequence, her heart was full of every virtuous and elevating principle. Long before the period when the fortunes of her husband gave them both a position in the first rank of society, her susceptibility of improvement was evinced in the lady-like ease and grace which she had acquired, and the good sense, not to say elegance, which her conversation displayed.

Some time before his marriage, Morgan purchased from a Mr. Morton, a handsome two-story dwelling, and a valuable piece of land, situated at a short distance from Berry's tavern, which he named "Soldier's Rest." Here, with his wife, he established himself, and commenced his domestic career.

Shortly after Morgan's marriage and settlement at "Soldier's Rest," peace was concluded between the French and English governments. This event was almost immediately followed by the combined and terrible onslaught on the forts and the inhabitants along the whole Western frontier, from the Lakes to North Carolina, rendered memorable as Pontiac's War. To give anything like an adequate idea of the fearful ravages which were committed by the Indians on this occasion, would occupy a space greater than can be spared to events which are fully detailed in history, and which have but a partial relation to the subject of this work. The surprise and massacre of the settlements at Muddy Creek, and Big Levels, aroused the Governor and Council of Virginia to the necessity of prompt measures of defence, if they would save the region west of the Blue Ridge from being laid waste and depopulated. One thousand of the militia were, accordingly, called into service, in aid of the regular forces already on the frontier.* Of these, five hundred were draughted from the Northwestern counties, and placed under the command of Colonel Stevens. Morgan took the field on this occasion, and held the post of lieutenant in one of the companies of this regiment.

A short time after the organization of this body of men, Colonel Stevens advanced a number of small detachments in support of those points which most needed defence. It was found, however, that the savage enemy had suddenly decamped. This unexpected and unaccountable movement was subsequently explained by the fierce and protracted attack which was made by the Indians on the forces under Colonel Bouquet, while on their march to Fort Pitt. This officer was dispatched, with five hundred men and a supply of military stores, for the relief of that fort. The Indians, on hearing of his march, concentrated from every quarter, in the hope of surprising and destroying him. They attacked his troops, on the 5th of August, in a defile near the head waters of Turtle Creek. But after a bloody encounter, which lasted the greater part of one day and the morning of the next, Colonel Bouquet practised a stratagem which secured him

* Sparks's Writings of Washington, vol. ii, p. 341.

the victory.* He was then permitted to proceed to Fort Pitt without further molestation. On finding that the Indians had disappeared, Colonel Stevens, suspecting some such design as that which they had in view, advanced to Fort Cumberland with two hundred and fifty of his command. The remainder were stationed in the vicinity of Winchester. Morgan, with a detachment from this latter force, was posted for some weeks at a place since known as Pugh's Town. But after the defeat sustained by the Indians in their encounter with Colonel Bouquet, they did not give the militia an opportunity of engaging them, but soon after retired to their towns, north and west of the Ohio. The subsequent advance into their country of General Bradstreet and Colonel Bouquet, forced them to conclude a peace, the terms of which were afterwards arranged at the "Treaty of the German Flats." The militia were accordingly disbanded, and Morgan returned to his home.

Here, with his wife, and the two daughters with which she subsequently presented him, he passed the succeeding nine years in domestic pursuits. A life of this kind seldom affords many interesting incidents, nor does it tend to develop distinguishing traits of character. During this period he was diligently employed in the cultivation of his farm, and the extension of its limits, and in adding the usual appurtenances of a complete country residence. He paid considerable attention to the raising of stock, in which he was very successful. By his military grants for the services he had rendered during the previous wars, he had acquired a considerable quantity of valuable land. The result of all this was, that about the year 1771, his resources were very much increased, and he began to be regarded among his neighbors as a man of substance. He had long since abandoned his former loose associates, and was now exclusively the companion of the worthy and intelligent Mrs. Morgan, who was a very pious lady, and exercised a happy influence over him. There is no doubt that she contribu

* Sparks's Writings of Washington, vol. ii, p. 334.

ted largely to the amendment which his manners and morals displayed about this period.*

Morgan's mind had in the meantime experienced a corresponding improvement. For some time previously, and during his after life, his leisure hours were chiefly occupied in reading, and in otherwise improving his defective education. He took a lively interest in public affairs, and his discussions on this subject indicated an independent mind and a sound judgment. On those vital questions, which already arrayed the people against their rulers, and which eventually set the ball of revolution in motion, the opinions he held and avowed were equally indicative of the freeman and the patriot.

Their two daughters profited by the pious training of the mother, and the solicitude of the father for their education. None are so conscious of the advantages of mental culture as those who experience the daily mortifications arising from a want of it. The children of such people are generally as well educated as the means of their parents will admit.

Between the years 1764 and 1774, we have but one incident of a military nature to record, having reference to the subject of this work. In the year 1771, he received a commission† from Wm. Nelson, Esq., the acting Governor of Virginia at the time, as Captain of the militia of Frederick County.

* MSS. of Dr. Hill.

† WILLIAM NELSON, ESQ., PRESIDENT OF HIS MAJESTY'S COUNCIL, AND COMMANDER IN CHIEF OF THE COLONY AND DOMINION OF VIRGINIA,

To DANIEL MORGAN, GENT,

By virtue of the power and authority to me given, as President of His Majesty's Council, and Commander in Chief in and over this Colony and Dominion of Virginia, with full power and authority to appoint officers, both civil and military, within the same, I, reposing especial trust in your loyalty, courage, and good conduct, do, by these presents, appoint you, the said Daniel Morgan, Captain of the militia of the county of Frederick, whereof Adam Stephen, Esq., is Lieutenant and Chief Commander: You are therefore to act as Captain, by duly exercising the officers and soldiers under your command, taking particular care that they be provided with arms and ammunition, as the laws of the colony direct; and you are to observe and follow such orders and directions from time to time, as you shall receive from me, or any other superior officers, according to the rules and discipline of war, in pursuance of the trust reposed in you.

Given at Williamsburgh, under my hand, and the seal of the Colony, this fourth   , and in the eleventh year of His Majesty's reign, Anno Domini, 1771.

WILLIAM NELSON.

SEAL

CHAPTER III.

For several years after the termination of Pontiac's War,
but little occurred, in the Valley of Virginia, at least, to check
or interrupt the advancement of the peaceful arts, or to call into
action the arms of the province. The chief features of the times,
and of those which followed, in this quarter, until the commencement of what has been called "Lord Dunmore's War," were,
the rapid increase of the population and resources of the country;
the immense tide of emigration which flowed thither, and to the
region beyond, as far even as the banks of the Ohio river; and
the rage for speculating in public lands. These circumstances
were regarded by the Indians with undisguised dissatisfaction;
they had already caused much bloodshed in Kentucky; and it
was easy to perceive that sooner or later, they must produce similar results in Virginia.

The crisis at length arrived. Under apprehension (whether
real or feigned is still a question in dispute). that the Indians

were about commencing a general massac.'ʋ of the frontier inhabitants, a party of land speculators, headed by Captain Michael Cresap, shot two Indians, while the latter were descending the Ohio in a canoe, a few miles above Wheeling. The same party, learning on their return that a number of Indians were encamped at Captina Creek, a small stream which emptied into the Ohio, a short distance below Wheeling, at once proceeded thither, and killed and wounded several of the band. But the crowning act of atrocity was yet to be perpetrated. A party of thirty-two men, headed by a man named Daniel Greathouse, proceeded to an Indian camp, near Yellow Creek, and under circumstances of the grossest treachery, murdered all the Indians that could be decoyed across the stream from their camp, by the temptation of liquor. The murders perpetrated at Captina and Yellow Creeks, included the whole family of the generous and unfortunate Chief Logan, who became famous in the war which followed.*

Hostilities immediately commenced. The Shawanese were the first to take up the hatchet; they were soon after joined by the warriors of the Northern and Western tribes. Most of the traders and white men who were found within the Indian territory were murdered; and all the innocent families on the frontier, from the sources of the Monongahela to the Kanhawa, were obliged to flee towards the mountains or to the forts, to escape the general massacre.

Intelligence of these disastrous events reaching Williamsburg, Lord Dunmore at once took measures for the defence of the frontier, and the invasion of the Indian country west of the Ohio. He issued orders for the organization of a large force from among the inhabitants of the Northern counties west of Blue Ridge, to be led by himself in person. General Andrew Lewis was ordered to raise four regiments of volunteers and militia from the South-

* American Pioneer, vol. i, p. 8. Doddridge's Notes, pp. 226—229. Butler'sHistory of Kentucky, pp. 53, 54.

western counties. While these forces were in process of organization, for the purpose of invading the Indian country, steps were
taken for the immediate defence of the frontier. Major Angus
M'Donald was directed to raise, as speedily as possible, a body of
four or five hundred men, and with this force to throw himself
between the settlements and the Indians.* Under directions†
from this officer, Morgan took the field. In a very short space of
time, he raised the necessary complement of men to form a company, and with it, and one or two other companies, which were
raised under similar circumstances, he marched to Wheeling
Creek, the point of rendevous for McDonald's command. Towards
the end of June, a force of upwards of four hundred volunteers
assembled at this point.

Finding that the Indians had not appeared in any considerable
numbers on the Virginia side of the Ohio, Major McDonald now
resolved to abandon the defensive operations he had been directed
to carry on, and to invade the Indian territory. He accordingly
embarked his forces, and descending to the mouth of Captina
Creek, landed there, and advanced westward to the Indian towns
on the head waters of the Muskingham River. After a few days'

---

* Doddridge's Notes, pp. 243–244.

† "11th June, 1774.

"DEAR SIR:—I have received accounts from the Ohio that there are eight persons
killed. I think that you ought to get fifty or sixty men, in order to set out next week. Therefore, get what you can of your own company, and send or go to the other companies to
get and make up your number; for I expect orders from the Governor about Monday,
or Tuesday next, and I do not want to draught any, but to get volunteers. As the pay
will be very good, you can get good men; and I beg you to take none but such as can be
depended upon, that we may do service to our country and gain honor for ourselves.

"I have sent to Captain Alexander and Captain Lewis, and will send to Captain Allan
this day, to call a muster and to know what men can be got. I have no expectations
from the town companies, therefore you must exert yourselves in the country.

"I am, Sir,
"Your obedient servant,
"ANGUS McDONALD.
"CAPTAIN DANIEL MORGAN, Frederick Co."

march, and when within six miles of the Wappatomica Town, the advance, commanded by Captain (afterwards General) Wood, fell into an ambuscade which had been laid for the invading forces, by about fifty Indian warriors. When the fire of the Indians opened upon the troops, they were marching forward without the caution necessary on such occasions, not apprehending an attack. For a moment they were disconcerted; Wood's company fell back; but, being quickly joined by Morgan's—the next in the line of march—the Indians were speedily driven from their lurking-place, leaving behind them one warrior killed and several wounded. McDonald's forces sustained a loss on this occasion of two killed and eight wounded.

They now advanced with more circumspection towards the Indian town, which, on their arrival, they found abandoned. The Indians, deeming it useless to attempt defending their town, and rightly judging that their invaders intended crossing the river towards the next town, retired to the opposite shore, and there lay in wait for their approach. This scheme was fortunately discovered in time to prevent McDonald from thereby suffering a severe loss, if not a complete defeat. Small parties were hereupon sent along the river bank, above and below the town, to observe the Indians, and to give notice should they attempt to come across.*

Some days thus elapsed, during which a few skirmishes took place, when the Indians sued for peace. This was promised them by McDonald, on condition that they should surrender to him five of their chiefs as hostages. The chiefs were accordingly placed in his hands. But it was represented by the latter, that peace could not be made without the presence of the chiefs of the other towns. Two of the hostages were successively sent to bring in those chiefs; but not returning, after a considerable lapse of time, McDonald moved against the upper town, which, after a slight skirmish, was taken by his troops.

* Butler's Kentucky, Introduction, p. 57.

48   THE LIFE OF

It was then discovered that the Indians had employed the time
which was vainly spent in the negotiation, in removing their
women and children, old people and effects from the upper towns,
and in concentrating their forces. It became plain that their professions of desire for a peace were insincere, and that they would
resume hostilities the moment they could do so with the hope of
advantage. McDonald, observing this, and finding, besides, that
his provisions were running short, resolved upon a retreat. After
burning the towns which he had taken, and destroying all the
corn which he could not carry away for the use of his troops, he
took up his line of march for Captina Creek, on his route to
Wheeling.

As soon as the retreat became known to the Indians, they
assembled in large numbers, and burning with the desire of
revenge, soon overtook the Virginians. Along the whole line of
march, from the Muskingum to the Ohio, an almost unceasing
conflict was maintained between the adverse parties. In this protracted contest, the Indians suffered severe losses; but numbers of
the Virginians were killed and wounded, and several who were
captured were reserved for a terrible fate.* For several days
before McDonald reached the Ohio, his troops were forced to subsist on one ear of corn each per day. Although Morgan and his
company took a prominent part in the contest with the Indians
during the retreat, he lost but few of his men.

A short time after the return of McDonald's regiment to
Wheeling, Lord Dunmore, with the northern division of the main
army, arrived at that place. The plan of the campaign first
determined on, contemplated a junction of the forces under Lord
Dunmore and General Andrew Lewis at the mouth of the
Kanawha. His lordship here announced a change in his plan of
operations. He had now determined to descend the Ohio to the
mouth of the Hockhocking, and ascending that river to the falls,
to cross thence to the Shawanese towns on the Scioto. Messen-

* Doddridge's Notes, pp. 241-243.

gers were accordingly sent to General Lewis, who with much difficulty had reached the appointed place, with his command, announcing to him the change of plan, and directing him to join the main army with his division, near the lower Shawanese towns on the Scioto.

The motives of Lord Dunmore, in taking measures which threatened not only the success of the campaign, but the very existence of the division under General Lewis, have never been satisfactorily explained. They were generally believed at the time to have originated with the royal government, and to contemplate the speedy effectuation of such a peace with the Indians as would secure their co-operation with the British authorities, should the existing difficulties with the colonies ultimately require an appeal to force.

A few days were spent at Wheeling in making some final arrangements for the campaign, when Lord Dunmore embarked his forces in a fleet of keel-boats, pirogues and canoes, and descended the Ohio to the mouth of the Hockhocking. His army, which had been augmented by Morgan's and other companies of Colonel McDonald's regiment, numbered at this time over twelve hundred men. Having erected a stockade fort at this point for the protection of his sick, and as a dépôt for his stores, he ascended the Hockhocking to the falls, and thence marched across the country westward towards the Scioto.*

In the mean time, a fierce and bloody battle had taken place near the mouth of the Kanawha, between the forces under General Lewis and the Indians. In obedience to Lord Dunmore's orders, General Lewis was about advancing towards the Scioto, when he was attacked in his camp by a large force of Indians, under the leadership of Cornstalk, the great sachem of the Shawanese. The battle was obstinately contested for ten hours, when by a skilful manoeuvre on the part of General Lewis, which induced the Indians to believe that an attack, which, by a diver-

* Atwater's Hist. Ohio, p. 115.

3

sion, he made on their rear, proceeded from a reinforcement sent by Lord Dunmore, they retired from the conflict, and crossing the Ohio soon after, retreated to their towns on the Scioto. This is generally admitted to have been one of the most sanguinary and well-fought battles which mark the annals of Indian warfare in the West. On the part of the Virginians, twelve commissioned officers were killed and wounded, seventy-five men were killed, and one hundred and forty-one were wounded. What the force of the Indians was, and what their loss in this battle, have never been ascertained. It is believed, however, that they had a great superiority in numbers, and it is highly probable that their loss was little inferior to that of their opponents.*

While Lord Dunmore was on his march to the Scioto, and before the result of Cornstalk's designs against Gen. Lewis became known, the Indians met his lordship's offers of peace with delays and evasions. But as soon as they discovered that they had sustained a defeat at "the Point," and that the chances of war were against them, they made repeated overtures to his lordship to put an end to the contest. He continued, however, to advance, and at length established himself at "Camp Charlotte."†

The division under Lewis, desirous of revenging the loss it had sustained, was now rapidly approaching Lord Dunmore's camp. The Indians, hopeless of success against the united forces of an army, one division of which had already beaten them with great loss, and apprehensive of the consequences of another contest with their late opponents, renewed their solicitations for peace. At length, when a number of their towns had been destroyed, his lordship consented to an armistice, preparatory to a treaty of peace.

Messengers were hereupon sent to Gen. Lewis, announcing the armistice, and directing him to halt. It was with great difficulty that the General and his troops could be restrained from disregarding measures, which they considered as not only

* Doddridge's Notes, 231.   † Atwater's Ohio, p. 115.

defrauding them of their revenge on the Indians, but as having that very object specially in view. It was only when the order to halt was given for the third time, and by Lord Dunmore in person, that it was reluctantly obeyed by the indignant Lewis and his command.*

Lord Dunmore having signified his willingness to treat, runners were accordingly sent to all the Indian towns, to summon the chiefs, most of whom appeared in due time. The chiefs of two or three of the towns higher up the country not appearing, however, and his lordship having predetermined to crush every manifestation of Indian hostility or resistance, it was resolved to send a force against these places, and to destroy them. Major Crawford, with a body of about four hundred men, which included Morgan and his company, advanced against the hostile towns, which they destroyed without opposition, the inhabitants having fled at their approach.†

The terms of peace were soon afterwards satisfactorily arranged. The Indians stipulated, among other things, to observe peace and amity towards the whites, to deliver up all the prisoners held by them, and to recognize the Ohio river as the boundary between the contracting parties. The brave and magnanimous, but unfortunate Logan kept aloof, and took no part in the treaty. It was on this occasion that his speech, so celebrated as a model of eloquence, was delivered.

Thus terminated "Lord Dunmore's war." After the Indians had delivered their prisoners, and presents were distributed among them, the army was put in motion for Fort Pitt.

When the division to which Morgan was attached reached the mouth of the Hockhocking, they were there informed of those startling public events which had taken place during their absence in the campaign; and which, it was manifest to the dullest of comprehension among them, threatened to lead to hostilities between the colonies and the mother country. Here

* Butler's Kentucky, Introduction, p. 63.　　　　† Ibid.

they learned, among other exciting incidents in the progress of public affairs, that by act of Parliament, the port of Boston had been closed, and other disabilities inflicted on the inhabitants of that city; that the House of Burgesses of Virginia had, in consequence, passed an order, deprecating this despotic measure, and appointing a day of fasting, humiliation, and prayer; and that a congress of delegates from the different colonies had assembled at Philadelphia, with the object of taking measures to resist the tyrannical encroachments of the British government on the liberties of the American people. "Upon learning these things," Morgan remarks, in a sketch of a portion of his military career, written by himself, "we, as an army victorious, formed ourselves into a society, pledging our words of honor to each other to assist our brethren of Boston in case hostilities should commence." Faithfully did they fulfil their pledge.*

The winter and spring of the year 1775 was spent by Morgan at home with his family, and in attending to his domestic concerns. He was, however, an attentive observer of the great political movements then going forward. In the difficulties between the colonists and their rulers, he was a firm and zealous supporter of the cause of the former. He made no secret of his opinions upon this subject, nor of his readiness, should the result be an appeal to force, to take up arms in defence of his country. The bold and decided tone in which he denounced the tyrannical proceedings of the British government, had a salutary effect in bringing many of his neighbors to his own way of thinking.

The difficulties between Great Britain and the colonies were now rapidly approaching a crisis. On the 19th of April, the first blood of the war was spilled at Lexington. On the 17th of June, the glorious struggle on Breed's Hill occurred. On the 10th of June, the second Continental Congress assembled; and on the 14th of the same month, it made provision for raising and equip-

---

* MSS. of Dr. Hill.

ping an army of twenty thousand men, and appointed Washington the commander in chief of its forces.

Among other results of these proceedings of Congress, was one calling into its service ten companies of riflemen, to be raised in the States of Pennsylvania, Maryland, and Virginia.* Of the two companies for which Virginia was called upon, Morgan was selected as the captain of one, by the unanimous vote of the committee of Frederick County.†

* Sparks's Writings of Washington, vol. iii., p. 100.

† FREDERICK COUNTY:

In Committee, June 22, 1775.

In obedience to a resolve of the Continental Congress, dated 14th of June, 1775, viz.: "That six companies of expert riflemen be immediately raised in Pennsylvania, two in Maryland, and two in Virginia; that each company, as soon as completed, shall march and join the army near Boston; to be there employed as light infantry, under the command of the chief officer of that army—" this committee, reposing a special trust in the courage, conduct, and reverence for liberty under the spirit of the British constitution, of Daniel Morgan, Esq., do hereby certify that we have unanimously appointed him to command a Virginia company of riflemen, to march from this county.

He is hereby directed to act, by exercising the officers and soldiers under his command, taking particular care to provide them with the necessaries, as the 1st Resolve of Congress directs; and that he is from time to time to follow such directions as he shall receive from the commander-in-chief, or any other of his superior officers of the continental army.

Signed by order of the Committee,

CHARLES MYERS THURSTON, *Ch. F. C.*

The above was confirmed by the following commission from Congress:

IN CONGRESS.

The Delegates of the United Colonies of New Hampshire, Massachusetts Bay, Rhode Island, Connecticut, New York, New Jersey, Pennsylvania, the Counties of New Castle, Kent, and Sussex on Delaware, Maryland, Virginia, North Carolina, South Carolina, to Daniel Morgan, Esquire:

We, reposing especial trust and confidence in your patriotism, valor, conduct, and fidelity, do, by these presents, constitute and appoint you to be Captain of a company of riflemen * * * * * * * * * * * * * in the army of the United Colonies, raised for the defence of American Liberty, and for repelling every hostile invasion thereof. You are, therefore, carefully and diligently to discharge the duty of captain * * * by doing and performing all manner of things thereunto belonging. And we do strictly charge and require all officers and soldiers under your command to be obedient to your orders as captain.

And you are to observe and follow such orders and directions from time to time, as you shall receive from this or a future Congress of the United Colonies or Committee of Congress for that purpose appointed, or Commander-in-Chief, for the time being, of the

Morgan, burning with ardor, lost no time in delay. In less than ten days after the receipt of his commission, he raised a company of ninety-six young, hardy woodsmen, full of spirit and enthusiasm, and practised marksmen with the rifle. John Humphreys, who was killed in the assault on Quebec, was his first lieutenant. William Heth, afterwards a colonel, who greatly distinguished himself in the subsequent events of the war, was his second lieutenant. His ensign was Charles Porterfield, afterwards a colonel, and an officer, who, by his many brilliant and daring achievements, had earned a proud name among the defenders of his country, and was rapidly rising to distinction when he fell on the bloody field of Camden. A finer body of men than those who composed the company were seldom seen. One that rendered better service, or that shed a brighter lustre on the arms of their country, never had existence.

Early in July, Morgan started from Winchester at the head of his company, and in twenty-one days reached Boston, having travelled a distance of six hundred miles without losing a man by sickness or desertion on the route.

The rifle companies were the first which were ordered to be raised by Congress; they were the first to obey the summons of their country; and Morgan's company was one of the first, if not the very first, of the number to reach Boston.

When Morgan arrived in the vicinity of Boston, he found the British army, under General Howe, occupying the city, Bunker's Hill, Cope's Hill, an entrenchment on Roxbury Neck, and other minor positions. A strong naval force was also stationed at commanding points. The American army lay on both sides of Charles river, on the left to the Mystic, and on the right to

army of the United Colonies, or any other, your superior officer, according to the rules and discipline of War, in pursuance of the trust reposed in you. This commission to continue in force until revoked by this or a future Congress.

June 22, 1775.   By order of the Congress,
                                        JOHN HANCOCK, *President.*
Attest, Charles Thompson, *Secretary.*

Dorchester, closely investing Boston on the land side.* Washington had taken the command about a month previously, and was then busily engaged in organizing his forces. Since the battle on Breed's Hill, no conflict of a nature more important than one between small parties of the opposing forces had taken place. Both armies were sedulously occupied in strengthening their respective positions, and in making provision for an attack which was mutually expected.

Before the month of August expired, all the companies of riflemen had arrived, and were encamped at Cambridge. For six weeks Morgan's company remained inactive at this place, save in perfecting itself in discipline, and in occasionally assisting in the construction of the works. This state of inglorious repose was becoming very irksome to Morgan and his men, when an opportunity for service at length presented itself. It was intimated by the commander-in-chief, that he had in contemplation an expedition, the nature of which could not be revealed, which would require the services of three of the rifle companies. Morgan, at his own earnest request, was detached with his company, as a part of this expedition. The offers to join it of Captains Smith and Hendricks, each commanding a company of the Pennsylvania riflemen, were also accepted.

The nature of this expedition, the events which attended it, and its result, will form the subject of the succeeding chapter.

* Spark's Writings of Washington, vol. iii., pp. 26–28.

CHAPTER IV.

Invasion of Canada—Arnold's expedition to Quebec—Joined by Morgan—Dispute in relation to command—Letter from Washington—Expedition moves up the Kennebec—Its
progress, and the difficulties it encounters—Morgan's capacity for command, illustrated
—Difficulties encountered by the expedition—It crosses the " height of land "—Morgan
and his company attempt to descend the Chaudiere—Lose all their bateaux, and narrowly
escape destruction in the rapids—Expedition suffers dreadfully from hunger, cold and
fatigue—Reaches the settlements at the river de Loup—Subsequently advances to Point
Levi—Reflection—Sympathy of the inhabitants in the objects of the expedition—Morgan
captures midshipman McKenzie—The humanity he displayed on that occasion—Preparations for crossing the St. Lawrence, and assaulting Quebec—The river crossed.

In the month of June, 1775, Congress took measures for the
invasion of Canada. A resolution was passed, appointing General
Schuyler commander of the projected expedition against that
province, and directing him to take the steps necessary to promote
its success. Three thousand men from New England and New
York were designed for this service, to the expenses of which,
fifty thousand dollars in specie were voted. Attached to this
command were Generals Wooster and Montgomery.

General Schuyler repaired to Ticonderoga, where the succeeding
two months were spent in collecting and organizing his forces,
and in preparing for a general movement. In the month of
September, the army moved, and after an ineffectual attempt to
capture St. Johns, took a position on the Isle Aux Noix. Here
General Schuyler, who had been for some time much indisposed,
became so ill as to be unable to leave his bed. His recovery
being very slow, the command devolved upon General Montgomery. Under the direction of this officer, Fort Chamblie and

the town of St. Johns were successively taken; Governor Carleton, with about one thousand men, was defeated by Colonel Warner at Longueisle; and this event was succeeded by the surrender of Montreal. The British fleet, consisting of eleven sail, with a large quantity of military stores were captured. General Prescott and a number of his officers and men were taken prisoners; Governor Carleton, and about two hundred men, with difficulty escaping to Quebec.[*]

While these operations were in progress, General Washington, at the instance of Arnold,[†] set on foot an expedition, designed as a scheme of co-operation with the army under Montgomery, which was as remarkable for its novelty and boldness, as for the dangers and difficulties which it involved. These overcome, however, and a brilliant and speedy issue to the struggle in Canada was rendered almost certain. As Morgan occupied a prominent position in this expedition; and as the result, although disastrous, enabled him to display on a broader field of action, those great military qualities which he possessed, and to win, even in defeat, the applause and admiration of his countrymen; we may count upon pardon in dwelling with some minuteness over its thrilling details.

The subject of this expedition was first broached by Washington in a letter addressed by him to General Schuyler, dated at Cambridge, 20th of August, 1775. "The design of this express," the general goes on to say, "is to communicate to you a plan of an expedition, which has engaged my thoughts for several days. It is to penetrate to Canada, by way of the Kennebec river, and so to Quebec, by a route ninety-six miles below Montreal. I can very well spare a detachment for this purpose of one thousand, or twelve hundred men, and the land carriage by the route proposed is too inconsiderable to make an objection. If you are resolved to proceed, as I gather from your last letter is your intention, it

* Marshall's Washington, vol ii., pp. 301-313.
† Maine Historical Society, vol i., p. 341.

would make a diversion that would distract Carleton, and facilitate your views. He must either break up and follow this party
to Quebec, by which he will leave you a free passage, or he must
suffer that important place to fall into our hands, an event that
would have a decisive effect and influence on the public interests.
There may be some danger that such a sudden incursion might
alarm the Canadians, and detach them from that neutrality which
they have hitherto observed; but I should hope that, with suitable
precautions, and a strict discipline, any apprehensions and jealousies
might be removed. The few whom I have consulted upon it,
approve it much; but the final determination is deferred until I
hear from you. You will therefore, by the return of this messenger, inform me of your ultimate resolution. If you mean to
proceed, acquaint me as particularly as you can with the time
and force, what late accounts you have had from Canada, and
your opinion as to the sentiments of the inhabitants, as well as
those of the Indians, upon a penetration into their country; what
number of troops are at Quebec, and whether any men-of-war,
with all other circumstances which may be material in the consideration of a step of such importance. Not a moment's time is
to be lost in the preparations for this enterprise, if the advices
from you favor it. With the utmost expedition, the season will
be considerably advanced, so that you will dismiss the express as
soon as possible.*

The scheme having met the approval of General Schuyler,
measures were at once taken by the commander-in-chief to put it
into operation.

The active and fearless spirit which Benedict Arnold had
evinced, particularly in the taking of Ticonderoga, had attracted
towards him the notice of Washington; and pointed him out as
one eminently fitted to conduct an expedition, so daring and
adventurous as that determined upon. The command was accordingly given to him, and with it, a commission as colonel in the

* Sparks's Writings of Washington, vol iii., p. 68.

continental line. The force detached on this service consisted of about eleven hundred men, divided into ten companies of infantry, three of riflemen, and one of artillery. Attached to the command were Lieutenant Colonels Christopher Green, and Roger Enos, and Majors Timothy Bigelow and Return J. Meigs. The rifle companies were commanded, that from Virginia by Morgan, and the other two from Pennsylvania by Captains William Hendricks and Matthew Smith. The artillery company was under the orders of Captain Lamb. The staff consisted of Christian Febriger, adjutant; David Hyde, quarter-master; Dr. Senter, and another gentleman, whose name is not recollected, doctors; and Mr. Samuel Spring, chaplain. Several enterprising individuals, among others, Colonel Aaron Burr, Matthew Ogden, and John McGuyer, joined the expedition as volunteers.[*] The wives of two of the Pennsylvanian riflemen, Mrs. Grier and Mrs. Warner, accompanied their husbands, and even assisted them during the toilsome and difficult march. Although these poor women had their full share of the sufferings, from hunger, cold, and fatigue, which were experienced alike by officers and men, and from the effects of which a number died on the way, they displayed as much fortitude, and as great powers of endurance, as the strongest of the army, with which they ultimately arrived, safe and in good health, at the St. Lawrence.[†]

The necessary preparations for the expedition had all been made. Arnold had received his instructions from the commander-in-chief. These enjoined him, after assuming his command, to exercise the utmost diligence and prudence in prosecuting the march to a speedy and successful termination; upon all occasions to treat the Canadians as friends, and by every means in his power to conciliate the good will of the Indians. He was commanded to protect the property, and to respect the religion and customs of the people through whose country he passed, and to repress

[*] Collection Maine Historical Society, vol. i., 383.
[†] Judge Henry's Account, 65–66.

violence and plundering under the severest penalties. The details of his instructions were carefully drawn up, and nothing calculated to contribute towards a fortunate issue of the expedition was left unnoticed.* A letter to Arnold accompanied these instructions, charging him to regard the Canadians as friends, and to conduct himself towards them accordingly ; directing him to punish every violation of this command with the utmost severity ; and repeating in more emphatic terms all the principal points in the instructions. He was also furnished with a large number of manifestoes, intended for distribution among the people of Canada, which explained the nature of the contest between Great Britain and the colonies, and urged them to co-operate with the latter in resisting the comon oppressor of both. About one thousand pounds in specie were placed in his hands to defray contingent expenses.†

Everything was now in readiness for a movement. A general knowledge of the route had been acquired by Arnold, from the journal of a British officer, who had travelled over the ground some fifteen years before. The expedition was suggested by a perusal of this journal.‡ Intelligence had likewise been derived from several St. Francis Indians, who had recently visited Washington's camp, and who were familiar with those interior regions. Arnold had likewise been furnished with a manuscript map of the country watered by the Kennebec, and the journal of a tour through that region, by a gentleman long a resident in its vicinity.§ Two persons had been sent forward to explore the country to be traversed, and to ascertain the disposition of the inhabitants. Eleven transports were then lying at Newburyport, ready to convey the troops thence up the Kennebec river to the town of Gardiner, where two hundred bateaux had been constructed for the further transportation of the army. The provisions, baggage, ammunition, &c., had all been provided,

---

* Sparks's Writings of Washington, vol. iii., 86-89.   † Ibid.   90-91.
‡ Maine Historical Society, 341.   § Sparks's Arnold, 28, 29.

and nothing remained undone which might facilitate the operations of the detachment, or add to its efficiency and confidence.

The troops left Cambridge on the 13th of September. Having marched to Newburyport, where they encamped and remained for three days, they embarked on board the transports and sailed for the Kennebec on the 19th. In compliance with the directions of the commander-in-chief, several vessels had been previously dispatched eastward, to ascertain if the coast in that quarter was clear of British cruisers. The next day the fleet reached the mouth of the Kennebec without accident or molestation, and the wind being fair, it found no difficulty in sailing up to Gardiner, the point of debarkation.*

The arms, ammunition, baggage, and provisions, having been removed from the transports to the bateaux, the detachment moved up the river, and, on the 23d, rendezvoused at Fort Western, a place opposite to that where the town of Augusta now stands.

Five or six days were spent at this place, in completing the necessary preparations. A party of eleven men, including their commander, Lieutenant Steel, and two guides, were sent forward from this point, to explore and mark the Indian paths at the carrying places along the route; and to cross the high lands to the Chaudiere river, and ascertain its course.†

While the army lay at this point, a misunderstanding occurred between the field-officers, subordinate to Arnold, and Morgan, in relation to a claim of command which they asserted over him and his division. Morgan contended that the rifle companies, having been raised by a special act of Congress, and being, moreover, intended as the advance of the expedition, were subject to the command of Col. Arnold only. In this opinion he was sustained by Captains Smith and Hendricks, the officers com-

* Sparks's Arnold, 27. Maine Historical Society, vol. i., 890.
† Judge Henry's Account, p. 17.

manding the other two rifle companies. The difficulty was at
length referred to the commander-in-chief, who decided in favor
of the field-officers. As the letter on this subject is the first of
the long series which subsequently passed between Washington
and Morgan, and which evince to the close a progressive increase
in the friendly feelings with which they mutually regarded each
other, it is invested with no common interest, and may be very
appropriately introduced here :—

" CAMP AT CAMBRIDGE, Oct. 4, 1775.

" SIR: I write to you in consequence of information I have received,
that you and the captains of the rifle companies on the detachment against
Quebec, claim an exemption from the command of all the field officers,
except Col. Arnold. I understand this claim is founded upon some expressions of mine ; but, if you understood me in this way, you are much mistaken in my meaning. My intention is, and ever was, that every officer
should command according to his rank. To do otherwise would subvert
all military order and authority, which, I am sure, you could not wish or
expect.

" Now the mistake is rectified, I trust you will exert yourself to support
my intentions, ever remembering that by the same rule by which you
claim an independent command, and break in upon military authority,
others will do the same in regard to you, and, of consequence, the expedition must terminate in shame and disgrace to yourselves, and the reproach
and detriment of your country. To a man of true spirit and military character, further argument is unnecessary. I shall, therefore, recommend to
you to preserve the utmost harmony among yourselves, to which a due
subordination will much contribute ; and wishing you health and success,

" I remain, your very humble servant,
" GEORGE WASHINGTON.

" To CAPTAIN DANIEL MORGAN."*

In relation to the difficulty thus decided, it is worthy of
remark, that notwithstanding the earnest and somewhat unnecessary desire which the field officers referred to displayed at this
time, to extend their control over Morgan and his command

* Sparks's Writings of Washington.

an emergency subsequently arose, as will be seen in the sequel, wherein they felt it expedient, not only to yield the point in dispute, but to place themselves and their commands under his direction.

The season being far advanced—too far, indeed, as the event proved—to allow of a successful issue to the expedition; and an essential element of success being the secrecy of the movement, which was endangered by delay, but little time was lost in making the necessary dispositions. Colonel Arnold formed his forces into four divisions. The riflemen, being the first, were to lead the van. Morgan was appointed their commander. His duty was, " to follow the footsteps of the exploring party, and to examine the country along the route ; to free the streams to be ascended from all impediments to their navigation, and to remove all obstructions from the road ; to ascertain all the fords which intersected the line of march ; to examine the numerous portages over which it would be necessary to move, and to take such measures as would facilitate their passage." Besides these, his position imposed on him the duties incidental to an advanced guard. For, although the expedition experienced no opposition until it arrived on the north bank of the St. Lawrence, the disposition of the Indians who inhabited the country between the head waters of the Kennebec and the Chaudiere, was stated by the scouts to be hostile ; it certainly was but partially known. And even were the representations regarding their sentiments ever so favorable, the proverbial fickleness and treachery of the Indian character must have led an old Indian fighter like Morgan to consider an attack from them as a probable contingency. Thus was imposed upon him the necessity of an untiring vigilance in guarding against the chance of a surprise—a duty which added heavily to those already enumerated, which his corps was required to perform.

His men were armed, each with a rifle, a tomahawk, and a long knife. They were dressed with flannel shirts, cloth or buckskin

64   THE LIFE OF

breeches, buckskin leggins, and moccasins. Over these clothes
they wore hunting-shirts, made, for the most part, of brown linen,
some of buckskin, and a few of linsey woolsey. These shirts
were confined to the waist by belts, in which they carried their
knives and tomahawks. Morgan's company wore caps, on which
appeared the words "liberty or death." For himself, he appears
to have adopted the Indian dress on this expedition. When met
by the exploring party on their return from the head waters of
the Chaudiere, he wore leggins, and a cloth in the Indian style.
His thighs, which were exposed to view on that occasion,
appeared to have been lacerated by the thorns and bushes.*

The second division was composed of three companies of infantry, under Lieutenant Colonel Green and Major Bigelow. The
third consisted of three companies of infantry, and Captain Lamb's
artillery company, with one piece, commanded by Major Meigs.
The rear guard, under Lieutenant Colonel Evans, was formed of
the remainder of the infantry, consisting also of three companies,
and a body of teamsters, carpenters, &c.

These dispositions having been made, on the 25th of September,
Morgan's command embarked in bateaux and canoes, with orders
to proceed with all speed to the Great Carrying Place. The next
day, Colonel Green and Major Bigelow, with the second division,
were sent forward. The third and fourth divisions, under Major
Meigs and Colonel Enos, respectively, were put in motion, each a
day after that which preceded it.†

On the fifth day after leaving Fort Western, Morgan and his
corps reached the falls of Norridgewock. During this part of the
journey, the riflemen experienced great fatigue and discomfort.
As the bateaux had to be pushed forward against a strong current, the men were almost continually mid-deep in water. Two
portages on the route were crossed with much labor. Upon
arriving at Norridgewock, many of the bateaux were found to be

* Judge Henry's Campaign, p. 15-51.
† Collections of Maine Hist. Soc. vol. l, p. 397.

so leaky, as to have already destroyed a considerable part of the stores, and to require repairing before proceeding further. They were, however, speedily discharged, the necessary repairs made, and the toilsome and difficult task of transporting them and the baggage over the rough and difficult portage above the falls, a distance of a mile and a quarter, was at length effected. These operations, and a halt, to enable the rear to come up and cross the falls, occupied a week's time, during which all but the rear division had collected at and about this place.

On the 6th of October, Morgan again moved forward, and towards the close of the next day, reached the Carratunc Falls. These having been passed without any unnecessary delay or accident, he pushed ahead against a rapid current, and on the evening of the 9th, arrived at the Great Carrying Place.

The divisions of Green and Meigs arrived the next day. A few hours after their arrival, Colonel Arnold, with an Indian guide and a few followers, in canoes, reached this point. He had seen the last division embark from Fort Western, when he pushed forward to the front of the line.*

The difficulties which had thus far been encountered were great indeed. The men had been nearly half the time in water; and this, together with the hardships and fatigues which they had undergone in bearing their bateaux and effects across the numerous portages, had seriously dispirited them. Already their numbers had experienced a heavy reduction by sickness and desertion. They were cheered somewhat by the delusive belief that the principal obstacles in their way had already been surmounted. But formidable as these obstacles had proved to be, they were as nothing to those yet to be encountered.

On the morning of the 10th of October, Morgan and his command commenced crossing the Great Carrying Place. From the point of starting to that on the Dead river where they intended to re-embark, was fifteen miles, with three small lakes intervening.

* Sparks's Arnold, p. 32.

66   THE LIFE OF

Over this extensive space, which embraced precipitous ascents,
yawning ravines, thick, entangling woods, swamps, and water
courses, the riflemen were obliged to carry the bateaux, baggage,
provisions and arms. Numerous were the journeys from one end
of the Carrying Place to the other, before their herculean task
was accomplished. By dint of the greatest labor and perseverance,
the bateaux were transported on the men's shoulders, over the
different portages and intervals of land, from lake to lake, laden
and unladen, until at length, on the 19th, they were once more
afloat on the waters of the Dead river, the effects embarked, and
everything ready for a fresh start.

As the troops advanced, their difficulties, perils, and hardships
constantly increased. In the despondency which thus became
general, their ignorance of the country yet to be traversed served
but to magnify its actual terrors. While crossing the Great Carrying Place, they were met by Lieutenant Steel and his exploring
party, on their return from the head waters of the Chaudiere.*
The representations of the difficulties and dangers of the route
which were made by these men, found ample corroboration in
their haggard appearance and helpless condition.† Indeed, the
prospect at this time was well calculated to shake the resolution of any man, less determined and adventurous than was
Arnold, and to palsy the efforts of any corps, less brave and hardy
than that he commanded.

During the succeeding three days, Morgan and his command
lay encamped on the Dead river, recruiting the men, and waiting
for the rear divisions to come up. At this time the commands
of Green and Meigs were well advanced. That of Enos, however,
had only proceeded a short distance across the Great Carrying
Place. In the meantime, a block-house was erected at the second
portage, for the reception of the sick and disabled, which had

* Collections of Maine Hist. Soc., vol. v. p. 398.
. † Judge Henry's Campaign, p. 50.

now become fearfully numerous. The commissary of Norridg-wock was directed to send one hundred barrels of provisions to the Great Carrying Place, near the Kennebec, where another block-house was erected to receive them.

Morgan's high qualifications for command were fully displayed on this celebrated march. He is described by a member of the expedition as " a large, strong-bodied personage," with a " stento-rian voice," and one, " whose appearance gave the idea history has left us of Belisarius." " His manners " were characterized as " severe," but " activity, spirit, and courage in a soldier procured his good will and esteem," and " where he became attached, he was truly kind and affectionate." * The rules which he adopted for the safety and guidance of his men, were marked by that judgment and prudence which distinguished his after career. Although he met with much opposition from the refractory spirit of a portion of his command, the energy of his will enabled him generally to enforce obedience to his orders. With the men composing his own company, he was popular as a commander, and beloved as a friend. Confiding implicitly in his judgment and discretion, they obeyed with alacrity his directions, regardless of the labor or the self-denial which they involved. With the Penn-sylvania companies, however, the case was somewhat different. Although it would be difficult at any time to collect a finer body of men than that these companies composed, yet, in common with almost all newly organized bodies of troops, they were opposed to the restraints, as they were insensible to the advan-tages of discipline, and a due subordination. The local prejudices which existed at this time between Pennsylvanians and Virgi-nians, and the belief among the Pennsylvania riflemen that one of their captains, Hendricks, was entitled by rank to the position which Arnold had conferred upon Morgan, contributed to the difficulties with which the latter had to contend in exercising the command.†

* Judge Henry's Campaign, p. 16.   .   † Ibid., p. 196.

The principal of Morgan's rules were, that there should be no straggling from the camp, and that no one should fire off his piece without permission. Reasonable as these orders were, they met with opposition from the men of the Pennsylvania companies under the countenance which their officers afforded them. While the riflemen were encamped on Dead river, a man named Chamberlain, belonging to Captain Smith's company, proceeded a short distance from the camp, and discharged his piece. On approaching the camp, gun in hand, he was confronted by Morgan, who accused him of the breach of orders in firing. Chamberlain, who is represented as "an arrant liar," promptly denied the charge. Morgan, convinced that he was correct, and provoked at the cool mendacity of the man, sprang to a pile of wood, snatched up a stick, and turning upon Chamberlain, declared that he would knock him down, unless he confessed the fact. At this juncture, Captain Smith, who was present during the altercation, interposed; and picking up another stick, swore he would strike Morgan, if he attempted to put his threat into execution. Sensible that the step he was about to take was not strictly military; apprehensive, besides, that by pushing the matter further, a difficulty about rank might grow out of a quarrel among the officers of the riflemen, Morgan receded from his purpose, and walked away. Morgan's life furnishes few instances of such forbearance as he displayed on this occasion. Among the motives which induced him to relinquish his purpose, and to disregard Captain Smith's threat, fear of that officer cannot be included—a man of whom it is said, that "this was the only spirited act known of him during the campaign.*

On the 21st of October, Morgan advanced, followed by the commands of Colonel Green and Major Meigs. At this time, Colonel Enos was approaching the Great Carrying Place. The boats, which were heavily laden with the baggage, provisions, &c.,

* For further particulars of Captain Smith, see Henry's account of the Expedition to Canada, pp. 221-222.

had on board only the men necessary to navigate them. The main bodies of the different divisions marched by land, following the meanderings of the river.

Among the difficulties with which the troops had to contend, was that arising from their ignorance of the country. The bateaux were frequently led away from the main stream into its branches, proceeding sometimes for miles before the mistake would be discovered. The troops on shore, guided by the boats, generally fell into the same error. Thus, in some instances, an entire day was consumed in moving up and returning on a wrong course. One instance of this kind may be mentioned. A short distance above the place where the cabin of the Indian chief Natalis stood, a stream from the westward empties into the Dead river. All of Morgan's boats and men proceeded up this stream about seven miles, before they were apprised of their mistake by the boat which was sent after them for that purpose. In the mean time, they discovered an Indian settlement, which proved to be that of the chief Sabatis and his family. The Indians were all absent. Their property, consisting of venison, corn, kettles, &c., were enclosed in a species of cages, made of birch bark, which were placed in the forks of some trees in the vicinity. Sabatis and his adherents being considered at this time as the friends of the British, their effects were considered the rightful spoils of war. Such of them as were not made subservient to the wants of the riflemen, were destroyed; after which, they returned to the Dead river.*

The country along the Dead river was more favorable to an advance than any through which the troops had hitherto passed ; and for many miles that stream presented a smooth surface and a gentle current, interrupted at intervals, however, by falls, over which it was necessary to " carry." The troops pushed forward with accelerated pace. At this time, it was confidently believed that the Chaudiere would be reached in two or three days.

† Henry's Campaign, p. 84. Maine Historical Society, p. 398.

But these expectations were doomed to a fearful disappointment. During the preceding two or three days, much rain had fallen. On the evening of the 22d, the riflemen encamped on the bank of the river, in the neighborhood of a lofty mountain, since called Mount Bigelow. The stream had already commenced swelling; and before daylight the next morning, it had inundated the encampment, which was abandoned in haste for higher ground. When morning came, the river presented a frightful aspect. It had risen during the previous night eight or nine feet, and flowed with great rapidity.

These circumstances, however discouraging, were not permitted to delay the advance. The boats, having been placed in charge of the most active and skilful of the men, were put in motion ; the main body of the troops, in the mean time, proceeded by land up the south bank of the river. The meandering of the stream, with the inundation of the low lands in its vicinity, and the rapidity of the current, prevented both boats and troops from making much progress. After a very fatiguing march, they arrived on the evening of the 23d at a fall of four feet, where they encamped for the night.

This was a day fraught with more disasters than any one which had preceded it. With great difficulty the boats had been brought up to the neighborhood of the four-feet fall. The central current at this point ran with immense velocity, forming eddies of corresponding swiftness on each side of the river. As the boats approached, they were caught by the eddies, the strength of which rendered them entirely unmanageable. Ascending the stream with great rapidity, a number of them were forced against the shore, where, with much difficulty, they were secured. Seven of them, however, were caught by the current, which speedily engulfed two or three, and dashed the remainder to pieces against the shore below. Unfortunately, these boats contained the greater part of the remaining provisions, all of which, together with a considerable sum of money, a quantity of baggage, and the arms of the boatmen, were lost, the men with great difficulty escaping with their lives.

To the causes of distress and discouragement which had pre viously been experienced, a scarcity of food was now added. This threw such a gloom over the future, that the bravest among them were almost ready to despond.* The advance was still thirty miles from the head of the Chaudiere river. Short as that dis tance was, comparatively, it was uncertain, from the difficulties presented by the swollen river and the inundated land, in what time it could be accomplished. The number of sick and disabled had greatly increased during the last few days; and the remain der were rendered incapable of ordinary exertions from hunger, cold, and fatigue. A council of war took the state of affairs under consideration, at which it was resolved to continue the advance, to send all the sick and disabled back, and to bring forward from the rear a fresh supply of provisions; and that while one strong party would return to carry these resolutions into effect, another would proceed with all speed to Canada, and send thence supplies to meet the advance.

Accordingly, a party of ninety men of Major Meigs's command, under Major Bigelow, were sent with the sick and disabled to the rear, from which they were to bring the required provisions, then in charge of Col. Enos. This officer and Col. Greene received directions at the same time to advance with as many of the best men of their divisions as they could furnish with fifteen days' pro vision; and to send the remainder, with the sick and disabled from the front, to the post at Norridgewock.† Arnold soon after wards embarked with seventeen men in five bateaux, and pro ceeded towards Canada.

At this time, Col. Greene was crossing the Great Carrying Place, and Col. Enos had reached that point on the Kennebec.

On the morning of the 25th, the troops moved forward. The

---

* Sparks's Arnold, p. 36.
† Collections of Maine Hist. Soc., p. 364; Sparks's Arnold, pp. 36, 37.

succeeding two days passed without the occurrence of anything remarkable. Yet such were the embarrassments which impeded their progress, that during this time, they advanced only twenty miles.

On the 28th, the eyes of the adventurous band were gladdened with a sight of the elevated ground which interposes between the waters of the Kennebec and the Chaudiere. Cheered by an object which seemed to promise a speedy termination of their toils and sufferings, they pushed manfully on. The bateaux remaining were transported across two wide portages this day; and at night-fall, the troops in advance, which at this and all other times included Morgan and his riflemen, encamped on the bank of the pond, where the portage across the " height of land," commenced.*

The succeeding day was employed in transporting the boats and baggage across the portage, a space of four miles and a quarter, to the waters on the other side, which emptied into the Chaudiere. In the absence of accurate information regarding this river, Morgan supposed that it would prove as favorable to navigation as the streams which had been ascended. In this event, the transportation of all their boats across the portage was recommended by many reasons. The advantage afforded by the current would greatly facilitate the progress of the troops; and, while saving them from the fatigue of marching, enable them in some measure to recruit their exhausted strength. The measure, besides, would compensate for the great labor necessary to carrying it into effect, by furnishing the prompt and certain means of transporting the troops across the St. Lawrence, on their arrival at that river. Accordingly, Morgan gave orders to this effect. But Captains Smith and Hendricks refused to take over the carrying-place more than one boat for each of their companies. Morgan determined to carry over all the bateaux belonging to his company. With incredible labor the task was performed, and on the morning of the 29th, the advance of the army was in readiness to descend.†

* Judge Henry's campaign, p. 62.   † Ibid

GENERAL DANIEL MORGAN. 73

At this point, it became known that Col. Enos, with the whole of his division, a large quantity of provisions, and the medicine chest, had abandoned the expedition at the Twelve Mile Carrying Place, and returned to the Kennebec.

The provisions were now nearly exhausted. There was no meat of any kind left. The flour, which alone remained, was divided among the men. It yielded five pints to each, which were baked the same day into as many cakes. Upon this scanty amount of food they were to subsist until they reached the settlements at Sertigan, then distant nearly ninety miles.*

So gloomy was the prospect at this time, that were it not much more hazardous to retreat than to advance, the former alternative would have been adopted. Before a movement took place from this point, however, fresh encouragement was derived by intelligence from Arnold. This officer, having proceeded with his party to the head of the Chaudiere, wrote back to the officers of the detachment, that the French inhabitants were rejoiced to hear they were coming, and were ready and willing to assist them ; that there were few or no regular soldiers at Quebec, and that the place could be easily taken ; that he would advance without delay, and send back provisions as soon as possible ; and that the troops could go most of the way by water.†

On the morning of the 30th, the riflemen set forward, Hendricks and Smith's companies on foot, along the margin of the lake, and Morgan's in their bateaux. The advantage which, by extraordinary labor, Morgan had thus secured his company, made a deep impression upon the men whom he now left behind. In the course of this day, he entered Lake Megantick, and pushing forward, in the evening encamped for the night on its eastern shore.

The rain, which had fallen during the whole of the 30th, was succeeded at night by snow, which on the following morning, lay on the ground to the depth of several inches. Though suffering greatly from

* Judge Henry's campaign, p. 63.　　† Collections of Maine Hist. Soc. vol. i., p. 367.

the effects of cold, hunger, and fatigue, the men did not despond, but, cheered by the example of their commander, exerted themselves with resolution. Early on the 31st, they embarked, and pushed for the outlet of the lake, which forms the head of the Chaudiere river, reaching that point in the evening of the same day.

The next morning, they commenced descending the Chaudiere. For some time after entering this river, they proceeded gently on without any accident. But as they descended, the current constantly increased, until at length it carried them along with great rapidity. Soon, every succeeding minute added to the difficulties and dangers of their situation. First one, and then another of their bateaux were sunk and swept away, the men with difficulty reaching the land. Morgan now determined to make for the shore and land his men; and to examine the river for some miles below, before proceeding further in the bateaux. But before this determination could be carried into effect, the bateaux entered a series of rapids, and became entirely uncontrollable. In the lapse of a few minutes, all the remaining boats were dashed to pieces, and their contents scattered over the boiling tide. The men with difficulty struggled to the shore with their arms—all but one, who was drowned. Morgan's life was in imminent peril for some time; but he succeeded at length in reaching the shore, and in preserving the money which Arnold had placed in his hands for the use of his men.* Lieutenant McClelland, of Captain Hendricks's company, being sick, had embarked in a boat which his men brought over the "height of land," and accompanied Morgan and his company when they started on the lake. He and his boatmen were providentially saved from destruction, by their boat lodging against a rock, a short distance above a perpendicular fall of from twelve to twenty feet.†

Here Morgan and his riflemen, weary, wet, cold, and hungry, encamped for the night. By this last disaster, they had lost the remains of their clothing, provisions, everything, in fact, which

*MSS. Henry's Campaign, p. 67.   †Ibid, p. 69.

might have served to mitigate their sufferings. With a few exceptions, they had saved their arms and ammunition. The pangs of hunger were too keen to be resisted ; yet there was nothing to appease them. A dog that followed the company was killed and devoured, not even excepting the entrails. Moccasins, leather breeches, and cartouch-boxes, were minced up and boiled, and eaten with voracity.

On the morning following, the men scattered abroad for a mile or so from the camp, some in the hope of meeting with game, and others to gather such roots and berries as the country afforded. Their success was very meagre. Previously to this, the riflemen, being for the most part practised hunters, frequently killed moose, deer, and other animals, on the line of march. They thus enjoyed an advantage over their fellow soldiers, the infantry, which frequently made amends for the unsavoriness or scantiness of their rations. Early in the day, and when about moving forward, they were joined by the Pennsylvanians. These companies had lost, by starvation and fatigue, three or four men in the preceding three days. They were in a famishing condition. The rifle companies, now reunited, resumed their march along the bank of the river.

The distress of the men at this time was too great for description. Another day's suffering must have deprived them of all power to proceed. But during the afternoon, a boat was discovered ascending the stream ; and, soon after, several head of cattle were perceived coming up the shore. This proved to be the supply promised by Arnold, who, having reached Sertigan on the 31st, immediately sent back all the provisions that could be obtained there at the moment. The joy of the men was evinced in feeble huzzas, and in their advance with a quickened pace. Towards evening they reached the wished for supply. This consisted of a quantity of flour and oatmeal, and two small oxen, which had already been killed and cut into pieces for instant use. The remainder of the provisions had been dispatched to the

relief of those who were still behind. Such was the voracity
of the hungry men, that in an inconceivably short space of time,
all the meat was consumed. Even the entrails of the bullocks
were eaten by those who arrived too late to 'obtain a less objectionable portion of the animals. Some who came up at the close
of the feast, consoled themselves with a mixture of flour or meal,
and water, which they ate with evident satisfaction. The troops
encamped at this place for the night.

On the morning of the 4th, they started early. Having travelled some miles, they at length reached the river de Loup,
a stream which empties into the Chaudiere from the eastward.
A few hundred yards beyond this river, stood " the first house " in
Canada. Crossing the river in bateaux which had been left
there for the purpose, they approached the house with the rapture
of men, now assured that they should not perish by famine.*

Here the hungry soldiers found a plentiful supply of beef, fowls,
butter, and vegetables. Wild with the desire to stay the gnaw-
ings of a hunger, which, with most of them, was intolerable, they
instantly fell upon the provisions. The consequences which
would certainly follow excess, were foreseen by most of the
officers, and a number of the more prudent of the men; and,
as far as their influence and example would go, were guarded
against. But to a large number, the pleadings in behalf of mode-
ration were unheeded. Hunger had rendered them furious, vora-
cious, insatiable, deaf to every consideration. Death itself was
defied in the enjoyments of the moment. Morgan's company
avoided a course so imprudent. Most of his men had served their
military novitiate on the Virginia frontier, where they had
frequently experienced the want of food for days together. Such
men needed no admonitions to guard them against an over-indul-
gence of their appetites. Those of them, however, who were so
disposed, were checked by the authoritative interference of Morgan and his officers. A considerable number of the infantry and

* Collections of Maine His. Soc., vol. i., p. 401 ; Judge Henry's Campaign, p. 72-73.

the Pennsylvania riflemen, died from the effects of their imprudence on this occasion.*

Here were found Natalis, Sabatis, and about forty other
Indians, whom Arnold had induced to co-operate with him.
They subsequently marched with the army, and fought at the
assault on Quebec.

On the 5th of November, those of the army who were in
a condition to move, advanced still further down the country.
Among these, and still in the front, was Morgan's company.
More accustomed to the toils of war than their fellow soldiers,
and being under the command of an officer of much experience,
who had husbanded all their resources, the men of this company,
notwithstanding the march imposed on them, an equal share of
its hardships, and more than a share of its labors, were less
fatigued at its termination, than any other company in the expedition. But one man was lost during the march, and he was
drowned when the rapids of the Chaudiere engulfed their boats.
The other companies lost large numbers by sickness, desertion,
starvation, and repletion. Let it not be understood by what has
been said here, however, regarding Morgan's men, that their condition, upon arriving at Sertigan, was anything less than distressing in the extreme.

The troops, advancing as fast as their feeble state would permit,
arrived on the 7th at St. Henry's, four leagues from the St. Lawrence. Before night, the detachment, to the number of nearly
six hundred men, reached this place and encamped.

On the 8th, the entire force marched in compact order to a
small hamlet, situated about a mile from Point Levi, in which
they quartered themselves. They were joined on the march,
and at this place, by a number of armed Canadians.

Thus terminated one of the most extraordinary marches on record.
In the course of eight weeks, a journey of six hundred miles was
performed, much the greater part through an unexplored wilderness, which presented nature in her roughest and most forbidding

* Collections of Maine His. Soc. p. 102; Judge Henry's Campaign, p. 73--74.

aspect. Civilization has has since done much to soften the features of this rugged region. At the time in question, however, the terrors of the scene were unrelieved by the presence of a civilized being, and but few of the aborigines were willing to dwell in a region so inhospitable. Exertions almost superhuman were required to overcome the difficulties of the route. Powers of endurance, beyond those usually vouchsafed to man, were taxed to the uttermost. It is true, the health and strength of this gallant body of men yielded beneath their toils and sufferings. But their courage remained uncooled, even by the rigors of a Canadian winter, which added its terrors to their manifold distress. Pressing on with a fortitude superior to every obstacle, not famine staring them in the face, nor the desertion of faithless friends, nor the uncertainties attending their advance into an enemy's country with numbers so reduced, could check their progress. Inspired by a love of their country, and of the glorious cause in which they were engaged, death alone could have put a period to their exertions.

The march at length performed, the sufferings of the past served but to inspire them with a greater reliance on the future. And, in truth, the appearances of the moment were auspicious of a brilliant termination of their efforts. From the first the inhabitants received them with kindness, and evinced a friendly eagerness to supply their wants. They were open in the expression of their hatred of the British rule; and while many of them joined the expedition in arms, nearly all the remainder evinced a warm sympathy in its objects. The troops in Quebec were few in number, and short of provisions; while the inhabitants of the city and the vicinity were generally disaffected. News had been received by Arnold of the advance of Montgomery into Canada, and his capture of Fort Chamblée.* These encouraging circumstances, and a few days' repose, soon restored to the Americans their wonted courage and confidence.

The Canadians regarded with wonder and awe, a body of men

* Collections of Maine Hist. Soc., vol. i, .

who had descended into their country through a wilderness, which
they had hitherto considered impassable. They could not realize
to their satisfaction the accomplishment of an undertaking so
desperate. The strength and courage which could overcome such
fearful obstacles, were, in the estimation of these people, equal to
the achievement of almost any undertaking. An event which so
severely shocked their notions of probabilities, gave rein to their
imagination. Among other reports regarding the riflemen which
spread abroad soon after their arrival, it was said that they were
encased in iron. This arose from a mistake, originating in the
sound of a word. The Canadians who first saw the riflemen, in
their peculiar costume, noticed particularly their linen hunting
shirts; and afterwards spoke of them as *vêtus en toile*. As the
intelligence spread, the word *toile* (*linen*) was changed into *tôle*
(sheet iron).*

On the morning of the 11th, a report reached head quarters,
that the British were landing at a mill on the bank of the river,
about a mile distant. The riflemen, seizing their arms, instantly
proceeded at a run towards the point indicated. Morgan and the
Indians were foremost in the race. Upon reaching the brow of
the precipice which overlooks the river, they observed a boat
belonging to a frigate lying at anchor about a mile below,
approaching the shore. The boat soon struck the bank, and a
midshipman, a lad named McKenzie, brother to the captain of the
frigate, sprung ashore. The tide ebbing at the time, the boat's
crew were ordered to shove off, and go higher up to a deeper
landing-place. While obeying this order, they discovered the
Americans on the bank above, and immediately pulled off shore,
leaving their officer to his fate. Morgan, frustrated in the
design he had formed to surprise and capture the boat's crew, now
opened a fire upon them. The midshipman, comprehending at
once his situation, plunged into the river, in the hope of being able
to regain his boat. But being deserted by the boat's crew, who

* Sparks' Arnold, p. 46–47.

pulled out still further from the reach of danger, and noticing the balls which now struck the water around him in fearful proximity to his head, he turned towards the shore, and otherwise signified his willingness to surrender. The firing hereupon ceased, and the midshipman approached the shore, when the Indian Sabatis, scalping knife in hand, suddenly sprang forward, with the evident intention of murdering and scalping the prisoner. Morgan and Humphreys, from the impulses of a humanity common to both, instantly flew to the rescue. Morgan's superior strength and activity enabled him, not only to outstrip his lieutenant, but to overtake and pass the Indian. Rushing into the river where the boy stood, observing the scene just described in a state of irresolution, Morgan brought him to the shore, and assured him of his protection. The Indian, with a menacing look, was ordered to relinquish his purpose, which he did, but evidently with an ill grace.

The troops, wet and hungry, now returned to their quarters. Marching along the shore, a sloop of war, which had warped up the river while the events just described were occurring, suddenly opened a fire of ball and grape-shot upon them. Although the fire was very heavy, and at a short distance; and although it took the men a considerable time to ascend the steep and craggy bank beyond the reach of danger, no one was injured.[*]

During the five days which the Americans spent at Point Levi, Arnold was actively employed in conciliating the good will of the inhabitants, and in making preparations for an early movement against Quebec. The manifesto to the Canadian people, with copies of which Washington had furnished Arnold, was published. The bolder portion of the people were encouraged to arm and embody themselves; and the alarm which was manifested by a few upon the advance of the army, speedily yielded to the assurances that it came to protect and not to plunder them. The troops were engaged, some in putting their arms and equipments

* Henry's Campaign, p. 80-83.

in order, and others in making scaling-ladders. About forty canoes and skiffs had been collected for the transportation of the troops across the St. Lawrence. But before these necessary preparations were completed, a violent gale arose, which continued for nearly three days, rendering the river impassable during this time for skiffs and canoes, such as Arnold had obtained. Two days passed after the troops were in readiness for action, before the storm abated. At length, on the 13th, the wished for moment arrived, the events subsequent to which will form the subject of the succeeding chapter.

CHAPTER V.

Vigorous preparations of the enemy—Americans cross the St. Lawrence—Morgan proposes an immediate assault upon the town—Capture of Caldwell's house—Demonstration before the the town—Altercation between Morgan and Arnold—Americans retire to Point aux Trembles—On the arrival of Gen. Montgomery, they return and lay siege to Quebec—It is at length resolved to assault the town—The dispositions with this object, and the attack—Arnold, struck down, is succeeded in the command by Morgan —His intrepid conduct during the assault—Captures the first barrier—Advances against the second barrier—Encounters a body of the enemy—Morgan shoots their officer— Bloody encounter at the second barrier—Americans repulsed—Are at length surrounded by the enemy, to whom they surrender—The progress of Montgomery's division—Reflections.

WHEN the advance of the expedition had reached Dead river, Arnold dispatched two Indians from that point to Canada, with letters, one to Gen. Schuyler, apprising that officer of the progress which had been made, and the probable time it would take to reach the St. Lawrence ; and the other to Mr. Mercier, a gentleman in Quebec, favorable to the cause of the colonists. These Indians are believed to have been in the interest of the Canadian authorities, for the letters never reached the persons to whom they were addressed, and were, probably, delivered, the one for Gen. Schuyler to Col. McLean, at the Sorel ; and that for Mr. Mercier, to Lieut.-Gov. Cramahé, commanding at Quebec, in the absence of Sir Guy Carleton. Certain it is, that about the time when the Indians could have reached their respective destinations, the authorities of Canada became apprised of their danger, and took instant measures to avert it. To this unfortunate step on the part of Arnold, may, with justice, be attributed the failures which attended the efforts to accomplish the main object of the expedition.*

No sooner was Col. McLean apprised of the movement against Quebec, than he determined to descend the river in all haste, to the defence of that place. On the third day after the Americans had reached the St. Lawrence, and while they were waiting for the storm to subside, to enable them to cross the river, Col. McLean, with one hundred and seventy men of his regiment of emigrants, passed down and entered Quebec. Lieut.-Gov. Cramahé had been equally prompt and energetic. When the approach of the expedition was announced to him, there was not a single soldier in the town. On the 5th of November, a vessel arrived from Newfoundland, bringing one hundred and fifty men, chiefly carpenters. These men were instantly employed in repairing the defences, and in making platforms for the cannon. A frigate, two sloops-of-war, and one or two smaller armed vessels, were lying at Quebec at the time. These vessels were anchored opposite the town, in positions to guard the river for some distance above Wolf's Cove, while between four hundred and five hundred of their crews were landed to man the defences. Armed boats were kept constantly on the move, to guard against a passage of the river; the more effectually to prevent which, all the bateaux, boats, and canoes, found on the south bank of the river, had been withdrawn to the opposite shore. The inhabitants were invited to embody themselves, and to assist in repelling the threatened attack. About one hundred and seventy residents, chiefly English and Scotch, responded to the call; but the Canadians evinced no inclination to follow their example. It was only upon the threat of being expelled, with their families, from the town, that about six hundred of them reluctantly took up arms.

On the afternoon of the 13th, the storm having subsided, Arnold gave orders to prepare for a movement. At nine o'clock that night, the troops paraded on the beach of the St. Lawrence,

* Marshall's Washington, vol. ii., p. 319; Sparks's Arnold, p. 34.

where the canoes lay ready to convey them across the river.
Morgan and his command of riflemen were the first to embark.
The river at this point is about two miles wide, and the current,
at ebb tide, very rapid. The course of the boats lay between the
frigate and one of the sloops-of-war. Had they been discovered,
the guns of the ships could have blown them out of the water
But, favored by the darkness of the night, they fortunately slipped
through unperceived, and, in about an hour, landed at Wolf's
Cove.*

Immediately on reaching the shore, Morgan dispatched Lieut.
Heth, with a few men, towards the town, to reconnoitre. Pickets
and sentries were sent to the plains above, and along the shore
above and below the landing place, to guard against surprise.
The remainder of the troops, finding a large uninhabited house on
the spot, entered, and having lit a fire, awaited the arrival of the
main body.

About one o'clock, the boats reached the place of rendezvous a
a second time, bringing over Colonels Arnold and Green, and
about one hundred and sixty men. Immediately returning, the
boats again approached the shore about four o'clock, freighted
with another division of the men, when they were discovered
by one of the enemy's guard-boats. A fire immediately opened
on both sides. It continued, however, only a few minutes; at
the lapse of which the enemy rowed off, with a loss of three men
killed.

At this time, about one hundred and fifty men of the detachment, and all the scaling-ladders, still remained to be brought
across the river. But, the discovery which had just been made—
the light of the moon, which, having risen, now shone brightly—
and the difficulties presented by the tide, which ran out with
gread rapidity, altogether rendered the passage of the river again,
on that occasion, a measure too hazardous to be attempted. A
boat was, however, sent to the men, informing them of what had

* Collection of Maine His. Soc., vol. i. p. 403-4; MSS. Henry's Expedition, p. 83.

occurred, and directing them to await a more favorable occasion for crossing.

During the period between the departure of the boats and their arrival for the third time, Morgan's party returned from their reconnoissance, and reported that everything was quiet near the city.* It became evident, then, that the enemy were not aware of the passage of the river by the Americans; and, consequently, that they were unprepared for any hostile measures which might now be taken against them. A state of things so favorable to the capture of Quebec, suggested to the active mind of Morgan the propriety of an immediate advance with that object, as soon as the detachment, then crossing the river, had landed. On making known his views in a council of the officers, only those of the riflemen, and a few others of subordinate rank, gave them any countenance. From the time Arnold learned that his advance against Quebec had been discovered by the enemy, he gave up all design of taking the place by surprise or assault. At this time, he contemplated nothing beyond investing the town, and cutting off its communications with the country, until the co-operation of Montgomery could be had.† The bold proposition was, there-fore, coldly received both by himself and the principal officers present. It was, however, still under consideration, when the dis-covery by the British guard-boat and the firing took place. It being naturally supposed, after these events, that the alarm thus occasioned would speedily spread to the town, an advance to the assault found few advocates, and was generally condemned. Notwithstanding the numerous reasons which existed for believ-ing that the enemy were on the alert, it appeared the next day, that they had been entirely unconscious of the passage of the river by the Americans, and of the conflict with the guard-boat, until several hours elapsed after the occurrence of these events. The entrance to the town, called St. John's Gate, had been open during the whole night, the only defence of which was a

* Judge Henry's Expedition, p. 86.   † Collections of Maine His. Soc., p. 371-372.

gun, guarded by a drowsy watch.* The impression soon became fixed, that had they, upon landing, marched immediately against the town, they might have captured it with the greatest ease.

Under the belief that there was nothing to gain by further concealment, Morgan was ordered to advance towards the town, and to make observations. At the head of his company, he proceeded about half a mile to a large pile of wooden buildings, with numerous out-houses, the property of Lieut. Gov. Caldwell. On approaching nearer, it was found that the premises were guarded by a body of soldiers. Advancing towards the main entrance, he was discovered by the guard, challenged, and fired upon ; but, rushing forward, he entered the house at the head of his company, and captured the guard without loss or injury.

The main body had, in the mean time, ascended from the bank of the river, and advanced in the direction of the town. Most of them took up their quarters in Caldwell's house, and the rest in some buildings in the vicinity.

During the morning, Arnold received information that Colonel McLean, with six hundred men, and some field-pieces, was coming out that day to attack him.† Preparations were accordingly made to receive the enemy. Pickets and sentries were posted at all the approaches, while the main body was held in readiness for instant action. One of Morgan's men, named George Merchant, having been placed on guard in a thicket near the suburb of St. John, was surprised and captured in the afternoon, by a party of the garrison, who sallied from the town for the purpose. By the time the alarm reached the American quarters, the occurrence had magnified into the expected approach of the enemy. The men were instantly under arms, eager to meet the threatened attack. But the British did not appear. Arnold now determined to approach the town, and to invite a conflict. Should the garrison decline the challenge, he was not without hope that his

* Henry's Expedition, p. 85.
† Collection of Maine Historical Society, vol. p. 874.

advance would evoke a demonstration in his favor by the inhabitants. As the troops drew near, hundreds of citizens were
observed on the parapet. A loud huzza arose from the citizens,
which was responded to by the Americans with three cheers. But
the hoped-for movement, either by the soldiery or the inhabitants,
did not take place. The time had not arrived for the people to
take a decisive part in the struggle; and if the British commander
ever felt an inclination to imitate the conduct of Montcalm,
on the same ground, and under similiar circumstances, the fate of
that gallant officer and his command furnished a salutary warning
against unnecessary risk, and, doubtless, quickly repressed the
feeling. The only response which he vouchsafed to the demonstrations of the Americans, was discharges of cannon from the
batteries. This scene lasted for about an hour, when the
Americans at length withdrew from the ground, and retired to
their quarters.

As the British party returned with their prisoner to the town,
they were pursued by the American guard into the suburb St.
Johns, where, the party being reinforced by the garrison, an animated contest commenced and was maintained for some time.
Fearing that the Americans might effect a lodgment in the
suburb, the enemy at length set fire to the houses, and retired
within their works.

The events of this day terminated with the transmission, by
Arnold, of a letter with an officer and a flag, to Lieutenant Governor Cramahé, summoning him to surrender the town. This
officer, deeming it prudent to avoid all communication with the
Americans, fired upon the flag as it approached.

The circumstance under which Merchant was captured, reflected
less upon the vigilance of the soldier than upon the judgment of
the officer of the day, who placed the man in a situation, unfavorable for observation, but well calculated to lead to such an event
as that which occurred. Merchant was a tall, handsome man,
and from his bravery and good conduct, a favorite with Morgan.

He was sent, a few days after, hunting-shirt, leggins, moccasins and all, to England, probably as a finished specimen of the rifle-men of the colonies.* It appears that Morgan was much dissatisfied with the progress of affairs up to this time. From information received during the day, it became apparent, that had his advice been followed, the town might have been surprised and taken. He was exceedingly angry at the capture of Merchant, and inveighed in a character-istic style at the officer, whose " stupidity " caused him the loss of a valuable man. The disappointment of his expectations of a conflict on the Plains, and the occurrence of what he conceived to be the senseless parade before the walls of the town, did not contribute to restore his good humor. He was in this state of mind when his men complained to him, that notwithstanding the large supplies of flour which had recently been received, they were still kept on the short allowance of a pint a day, which had been observed in the latter part of the march to the head waters of the Kennebec. Accompanied by Captains Hendricks and Smith, he waited on Arnold, and after representing the facts of the case, demanded redress. If the matter complained of could have been traced to its source, it probably would have proved a part of that system of peculation, which Arnold seldom lost an opportunity of practising. At first he evaded, and at length, bluntly refused a compliance with Morgan's request. A violent altercation ensued, during which Morgan appeared to be on the point of striking Arnold. Language of defiance passed from Morgan as he and his officers left head quarters. The next day, and thereafter, however, the riflemen were served with a full allowance of provisions.†

Nothing worthy of notice transpired during the 15th, save the transmission of another flag to Quebec, summoning the town to surrender. The bearer was treated as on the previous occasion of the kind, and narrowly escaped with his life.

* Henry's Expedition, pp. 86-87.   † Henry's Expedition, p. 98.

On the day following, the troops were disposed between the St. Lawrence and the St. Charles, so as to interrupt communication between the city and the country. The riflemen removed from Caldwell's house to one about half a mile in the rear, where they obtained excellent quarters. The nunnery near the St. Charles was occupied as an hospital. A large log-house between the nunnery and the city was taken possession of by the riflemen as a guard-house and post of defence. On this day, Sergeant Dixon, of Smith's company, while crossing the St. Charles with a few men in a ferry-boat, had his leg taken off by a cannon ball, fired from one of the guns at Palace Gate. He died the next day.* This was the first man of the expedition who fell by the hands of the enemy. Merchant was the first man captured.†

During the two days which succeeded, the troops, their arms, ammunition, &c., underwent an inspection. To Arnold's surprise, it was discovered, that nearly all the cartridges were spoiled, there not remaining, fit for use, more than five rounds to a man ; that the rifle powder had also suffered damage ; and that nearly one fourth of the muskets and rifles were unserviceable. All of the troops were deficient in the clothing necessary for the rigor of the season, and some of them were nearly naked.‡ Many of the men were sick, and the list was rapidly increasing. News was received on the 18th, that Montgomery had entered Montreal. But this cheering intelligence was qualified by the information, that Carleton, with two hundred men, had escaped, and was then descending the river to Quebec.§ At the same time, the rumor

* Although but a sergeant in the expedition, Dixon was a gentleman of education and good property. In illustration of the spirit which actuated the men of these times, an anecdote is related of this patriotic soldier, which is worth repeating. No American need be informed that a tax on tea contributed largely towards bringing about an appeal to arms between the colonies and Great Britain. The lady who ministered to the wants and comforts of the dying man, presented him, among other things, with a bowl of tea. The beverage was respectfully but finally declined, with the observation, "No, madam; it is the ruin of my country."—*Henry's Expedition, p.* 93.

† Henry's Expedition, pp. 90–92.
‡ Marshall's Washington, vol. ii., p. 323.   § Sparks's Arnold, p. 47.

of an intended attack from the town was renewed, with increased probabilities of its truth. Under these circumstances, Arnold resolved to retire to Point aux Trembles, a position beyond striking distance of the city, and where he could safely await the promised co-operation of the victorious Montgomery.*

On the 19th, the main body marched towards Point aux Trembles. The detachment which was left on the south bank of the river on the morning of the 14th, had crossed the day before, and now marched with their companions. Morgan and his riflemen remained on the ground for an hour after the main body had been in motion, when they also set forward, covering the retreat. About mid-day, as the troops were marching along the bank of the river, a large boat with sails, and soon afterwards, a scow were observed descending the stream under a press of sail. On their arrival at Point aux Trembles, they were informed that these vessels bore Gov. Carleton and his men to Quebec, and that they had left that place but a few hours before. The statement received an unusual confirmation, shortly afterwards, from the cannon which welcomed Carleton's arrival at Quebec, the reports of which were plainly heard at Point aux Trembles.

Here comfortable quarters for the troops were obtained. Tight houses and warm fires compensated in a degree for want of clothing, and good provisions were in plenty. The succeeding ten days were passed without the occurrence of any remarkable incident, when, on the first of December, General Montgomery arrived. This officer, having garrisoned Montreal, marched without delay with the residue of his army, amounting only to three hundred men, to join Arnold. Three armed schooners, laden with artillery, ammunition, provisions, and clothing for Arnold's command, left Montreal when the General moved towards Quebec, with directions to follow him down the river.†

The troops were paraded to receive the general, who addressed them with a brief but impressive speech, in which he praised the spirit they had displayed on the march through the wilderness;

* Henry's Expedition, p. 94.   † Henry's Expedition, p. 98.

expressed the hope that this spirit would continue ; and concluded by observing that he had ordered them a supply of warm clothing, which he expected to arrive in a few days. A new life was infused into the whole corps by this spirit-stirring speech, which was responded to by loud cheers.

The next morning, Morgan, with the riflemen, was ordered to advance towards Quebec. The main body followed the day after. Although the walking was exceedingly fatiguing, from the large quantity of snow which had fallen during the preceding week, the riflemen pushed forward with such activity, that before sunset, they reached a settlement in the parish of St. Foix, about three miles from Quebec, where they quartered for the night. The next morning, Morgan advanced, and took a position nearer to the city, where he remained until joined by the army.* The return of the Americans so soon was unexpected by the enemy ; and in consequence, one of their picket guards and a number of straggling soldiers were surprised and taken prisoners.

On the 5th, General Montgomery, with the army, arrived before Quebec. At this time, his whole effective force did not exceed nine hundred and seventy-five men. But, confident in himself and in the intrepidity of his men—reckoning, too, upon the fears or the privations of the garrison, and upon the disaffection of the inhabitants, he made immediate preparations for investing the town. Some days elapsed before the vessels, laden with the artillery, stores, and clothing, arrived. During this time, the garrison was summoned to surrender. The governor answered by firing on the bearer of the summons. A message of similar import, introduced through the agency of an inhabitant of the town, proved equally ineffectual. But the expected vessels at length arriving, their cargoes landed, and the troops supplied with warm clothing, the operations against Quebec were pushed with vigor.

The American lines extended across the peninsula on which the

* Henry's Expedition, p. 99.

town stands : the right, with Montgomery's troops, on the St.
Lawrence ; the centre, with Arnold's New England infantry ; and
the left, with Morgan's riflemen, on the St. Charles. At first, the
riflemen took post in a large stone house. But being within
range of the enemy's guns, it was speedily battered about their
heads. They changed their position the next morning to one
more secure, though nearer to the enemy's works.

On the morning of the 17th, Captain Lamb, with his artillery
company and a strong fatigue party, had succeeded in constructing
on the plains, distant from St. John's Gate about six hundred
yards, a battery of snow, in which were mounted five nine-
pounders and a howitzer. The work had been performed the
night previous. The earth was frozen so hard, that it was found
to be impossible to pierce it with the entrenching tools. The only
resort was snow, which, having been fashioned into the required
shape, was rendered comparatively solid by the addition of water.
The guns had opened on the city but a short time, however, before
the battery was pierced several times by the weightier metal of
the enemy. Yet the efforts of the Americans were persisted in
with manly resolution, although it was perceptible that the effect
of their fire was feeble. About two hundred shells were thrown
into the town at different times. At length a ball pierced the
battery, killing three men, when a further prosecution of the
bombardment was relinquished.

Every day, a skirmish, more or less serious, took place between
the riflemen and that portion of the garrison who were stationed
in the neighborhood of Palace Gate. In these encounters, the
riflemen did not escape loss; neither did they suffer unavenged.
They harassed the enemy constantly, few of the latter making
their appearance within gun-shot, that were not either killed or
wounded.

The affairs of the Americans had now reached a crisis, which
required, either an abandonment of the siege, or the adoption of
measures more prompt and vigorous. The men began to regard

the prospect of success as exceedingly gloomy. The snow was continually falling, and the weather grew colder as the season advanced. The hardships and fatigues which the troops were obliged to encounter, surpass belief, as they defy description. From these causes, a large number were in the general hospital. That nothing might be wanting to fill the measure of their afflictions to the brim, the small-pox broke out in the camp, and spread with great rapidity. An order was subsequently issued, that those who had contracted the disease, should wear a sprig of hemlock in their hats, that others might recognize and avoid them.* In spite of the patriotic feelings which warmed their hearts and nerved their arms, many of them looked forward with impatience for the period, then near at hand, when by the expiration of their term of service, they could escape such an accumulation of hardships and horrors. Many of those who remained for a longer period, looked with composure at death, if no other means availed to free them from their sufferings. Vain were the efforts of the officers to induce men to re-enlist. The patriotism of 1775 seemed almost extinguished amid the snows of 1776. The riflemen consented to remain with the general, even though he should be deserted by the Eastern men. But this praiseworthy example found few or no imitators among the latter.†

Under these circumstances, a council of war took into consideration the propriety of an early attempt to carry the town by assault. A number of the officers were opposed to such an attempt. But a majority of them, and among the rest, Montgomery, Arnold, Morgan, Febriger and the captains of the rifle companies, were warmly in favor of giving it a trial. Morgan, who was ever the advocate of decisive measures, spoke with warmth and force in favor of an assault. He reminded the officers of the opportunity which the first night of their landing afforded them of taking the city, had they but resolved to make the attempt. After adverting to the prospects of success which the circumstances of the adverse

* De Botta, vol. i., p. 124.   † Henry's Expedition, p. 113.

forces afforded them, he concluded by remarking upon the great amount of government property which was stored in Quebec, and upon the rights which the usages of war conferred upon those who storm a fortified town. These latter considerations had their due weight; and the proposition was at length unanimously assented to.

The plan of attack first adopted, contemplated a simultaneous assault, by four divisions, upon the upper and lower towns. Through the communicativeness of some of the officers, this plan soon became generally known to the men, one of whom deserted, and imparted it to the enemy. The general, prudently giving out that the man had gone under his instructions, to gain intelligence, conferred with his principal officers in forming a new plan of attack. It was now resolved, that two light divisions should make a feigned attack on St. Johns and Cape Diamond, the two important points on the upper town; while the main body, divided into two columns, were to make the real assault on opposite points of the lower town. It was further agreed, that the attack should be made by night, and on the occurrence of the first snow storm.*

It was not until the night of the 30th of December, that such weather occurred as was required in making the assault. The early part of this night was mild and clear, while the moon shed a bright light upon the snow-clad scene. But about midnight, the heavens became suddenly overcast, and soon after, snow began to descend upon the wings of a fierce and bitingly cold northeast wind. At the well-known signal, the troops silently assembled; and by two o'clock, they were accoutered and ready to advance to their respective positions.†

Colonel Livingston, with one hundred and sixty Canadians, and Major Brown, with a small detachment of Massachusetts troops, received directions to march against the upper town, the Colonel at St. Johns Gate, and the Major at Cape Diamond; and at the signal for a general movement, to advance and attract the atten-

---

* Henry's Expedition, p. 112.   † Henry's Expedition, pp. 113-114.

tion of the enemy in that quarter by noisy demonstrations.
Arnold's command, divided into two battalions, assembled at the
guard-house, at St. Roch.   In front was the colonel, and Brigade
Major Ogden, with a storming party of thirty men.   Captain
Lamb's artillery company, with a gun mounted on a sled, succeeded in the line; and next in order were the riflemen, with
Morgan at their head.   This force constituted the first battalion.
The second, composed of the New England infantry, under Colonel
Green and Major Meigs, brought up the rear.   The riflemen were
furnished with scaling-ladders,* and each man of Morgan's com-
pany carried a spontoon in addition to his rifle.   Arnold was to
advance along the river St. Charles, and to assault the barriers
at the northern and western extremities of the lower town.   Montgomery, with four battalions of New York troops, and a part of
Colonel Easton's regiment, formed on the plains near the St.
Lawrence.   He was to proceed along the margin of the St. Lawrence, by the way of *Anse des Mères*, around the base of Cape
Diamond, near which was a strong defence.   The general was
accompanied at the head of his storming party by Captain Cheeseman, Major McPherson, and Mr. Aaron Burr.*

The preconcerted signal having been given, at 5 o'clock on the
morning of the 31st, and in the midst of a terrific snow storm, the
divisions advanced intrepidly to the assault.

Col. Livingston and Major Brown executed the duties respectively assigned them with promptitude.   Owing, however, to the
nature of their orders and to the smallness of their forces, they
were unable to produce such an effect as, under the first plan of
attack, and with a force sufficiently strong, it became apparent
was practicable.   Relying with too much confidence on the simple
appearance of the strong works on these points, or divining the
true character of the assault, the garrison left them almost entirely
defenceless, and concentrated in the lower town.   Half an hour
had elapsed after Colonel Livingston had arrived opposite Cape

* Collections of Maine Hist. Soc., vol. i., pp. 406–407.

Diamond ; yet with all the noise which his men could produce, he was unable to attract the slightest notice from the enemy, so completely unprepared were they to resist an assault at this point.

Arnold's division moved forward along the road through St. Roch. Before the head of the division passed Palace Gate, the garrison became aware of their danger, as was evidenced by the ringing of the bells of the town, and the furious cannonade which was opened from the works above, in the direction of the assailants. The latter, however, with their arms secured under the skirts of their coats, from the effects of the snow, advanced in single file along the narrow and difficult way between the precipice and the frozen shore of the Bay of St. Charles. But for the impossibility of distinguishing objects at any distance, from the darkness of the night, and the heaviness of the snow-storm, the Americans could have been easily destroyed by the fire of the batteries. As it was, they lost a number of men from the random discharges of cannon and musketry. Proceeding rapidly, they at length arrived at the first barrier, from which, as they approached, was opened on them a smart discharge of musketry. Instead of rushing forward in disregard of this fire, the American storming party halted, and commenced a useless fusillade against the barrier. Before Arnold could correct the error, and put the front in motion again, he received a ball in the leg, which, shattering the bone, brought him to the ground. The momentary confusion caused by these events, brought Morgan to the front, just as Arnold was struck down. It was at this crisis in the conflict, that Morgan, at the instance and in compliance with the express wishes of all the field officers of the division who were present, assumed the direction of the assault. "They would not take the command," he observes, in a short sketch written by himself, of his early military career, " alleging that I had seen service and they had not, which reflected credit on their judgment." Morgan now raised his voice, always terrible in the hour of battle, and which was heard above the din of arms, ordering his riflemen to the front. They obeyed the summons with a cheer, and without a moment's hesitation or delay, rushed over the barrier, driving before them like chaff the enemy posted there. A short distance beyond the barrier, was a battery extending across the road, and flanked by the houses on either side, on which was mounted two twelve-pounders. As the riflemen advanced against this battery, the guns, charged with grape and canister, opened on them. The first gun was elevated too high, and did no injury; the other flashed without discharging, when the riflemen reached the wall, and planted their ladders. Morgan ordered a man near him to ascend one of the ladders. Perceiving that the soldier reluctantly obeyed, Morgan pulled him down, and stepping on the ladder himself, shouted to his men, "Now, boys, follow me!" The ladders were instantly manned. As soon as Morgan's head appeared above the wall, a platoon of musketry was fired at him from within. So close was the discharge, that the fire scorched his hair, and grains of powder were imbedded in his face. But this was the only injury he sustained, although one ball passed through the top of his cap, and another grazed the left side of his face, cutting off a lock of his hair. The concussion was so great, however, as to knock him from the top of the ladder down into the snow below. For a moment the ascent was checked, in the belief that he was killed. But he was instantly on his feet again, and had recommenced ascending the ladder. Another cheer rose from his men as they followed his example. Keeping his head down until he reached a step near the top of the ladder, he made a spring and bounded over the wall among the enemy. He was instantly followed by his men, among the foremost of whom were Cadet Porterfield and Lieutenant Heth. Morgan, in his descent, alighted on one of the cannon, under the muzzle of which he fell, severely hurt by a contusion on the knee. A dozen bayonets were instantly levelled at him; but the situation in which he fell created a delay, sufficiently long to enable his men, who now came pouring over the wall, to rescue him and attack his assailants.*

* Dr. Hill.

5

The enemy, daunted by the impetuosity of the assault, made but a feeble resistance, and at length fled into a building flanking the battery, from the windows of which, however, they renewed the conflict. They were speedily dislodged by the riflemen, who, by Morgan's orders, fired a volley into the house, which was followed by a charge with their spontoons. The enemy were driven through the building, and out at the rear into a neighboring street. Morgan ran through a sally port at one end of the battery, and thence round the corner of a building. Here, as he anticipated, he met the retreating British, whom he ordered, in a menacing tone, to surrender, if they expected quarter. Captain McCloud and about 30 of his men were thus made prisoners.

In the capture of this post, an important advantage had been gained ; and had the main body of the division but followed and supported the riflemen, its united strength could have easily made head against the panic-stricken foe, and captured the lower town. Only Morgan's company, a part of Captain Smith's under command of Lieutenant Steel, and a few bold spirits from different parts of the division, had advanced thus far. The remainder had either halted on the road, or lost their way. Morgan, nevertheless, pressed forward in the streets within the captured defences, and to the neighborhood of the second barrier and battery. But the darkness and his ignorance of the course to be pursued, and the defences to be encountered, rendered a further advance with so small a force, too hazardous to be attempted. He was now joined by Captain Hendricks and the remainder of the riflemen. But the force was still too weak in the opinion of most of the officers, to justify an immediate advance. " Here," Morgan observes in the sketch already quoted, " I was ordered to wait for General Montgomery : and a fatal order it was. It prevented me from taking the garrison, as I had already captured half the town. The sally port through the (second) barrier," he continues, " was standing open ; the guard had left it, and the people were running from the upper town in whole platoons, giving themselves up as prisoners, to get out of

the way of the confusion which might shortly ensue. I went up
to the edge of the upper town *incog.*, with an interpreter, to see
what was going on, as the firing had ceased. Finding no person
in arms at all, I returned and called a council of what few officers
I had with me; for the greater part of our force had missed their
way, and had not got into the town. Here I was overruled by
sound judgment and good reasoning. It was said, in the first
place, that if I went on, I should break orders; in the next, that I
had more prisoners than I had men; and that if I left them, they
might break out, retake the battery we had just captured, and cut
off our retreat. It was further urged, that Gen. Montgomery was
certainly coming down along the shore of the St. Lawrence, and
would join us in a few minutes; and that we were sure of conquest,
if we acted with caution and prudence. To these good reasons, I
gave up my own opinion, and lost the town."

The situation of affairs with Morgan grew every moment more
critical. The main body of the division had not joined him.
Nothing had as yet been heard from Montgomery. The firing
had ceased in every quarter; and this circumstance added to the
uncertainty which prevailed regarding the movements either of
friends or enemies, rendered the men uneasy, and filled their
minds with undefinable apprehensions. The piercing cold of the
weather was aggravated by the blinding snow; and standing
inactive, exposed to the rigors of the storm, they soon became
chilled to the bone; while from the same cause, their fire-arms
were rendered almost entirely unserviceable. Their situation was
one well calculated to make the boldest quail. Morgan was
among the few who resisted the growing panic. He revived the
drooping courage of his men by a few spirit-stirring remarks,
assuring them of complete success if they would but be firm.
He now hastened back on the route of the advance, to find and
spur on those who still remained behind. On the outskirts of
the town he found Colonel Green and Major Meigs, with about
two hundred of the New England troops, who immediately
pushed forward under his guidance to the first barrier.

It was here resolved, after a short consultation, to penetrate still further into the town, the riflemen in advance, supported by the infantry. Day began to dawn, as Morgan with his men moved towards the enemy's second defensive position. At this point was a barrier, eight or ten feet high, erected across, and near the termination of a narrow street, which led by a steep ascent into the *entre of the lower town. Behind this some yards, and upon *ground on a level with the top of the barrier, had been constructed a platform, on which were planted two twelve pounders. The position and strength of these defences were noted an hour before by Morgan, when he passed them to recon- noitre the upper town. They were then left defenceless, having been abandoned when the first barrier and battery were taken. But, in the meantime, Gen. Montgomery's division had been repulsed ; and the garrison in this quarter having been reinforced by the victors, they took heart again, and re-manned their works, which, unfortunately, had not been occupied by the assailants. Growing more confident, a party of the garrison, under Lieut. Anderson, sallied through the barrier, for the purpose of attack- ing the Americans, whom they expected to find dispersed, and probably plundering the town. They had just issued through the sally port into the street, when they suddenly encountered Morgan, advancing at the head of his men. Anderson, stepping forward, commanded the Americans to lay down their arms. Snatching a rifle from the hands of one of his men, Morgan replied by shooting him through the head, stretching him lifeless on the ground. The British hereupon hastily retreated within the barrier, when a fierce and bloody conflict commenced. From the windows of the houses on both sides of the street, and through the loop-holes in the barrier, was opened a murderous fire upon the Americans, who, cooped up in a street not more than thirty feet wide, hardly left space for a shot to fall harmless. Unshaken by the difficulties opposed to their progress, and by the loss they had already sustained, the riflemen prepared to assault the bar- rier. The few scaling-ladders which Morgan's company alone had brought thus far, were placed against the wall. On these, and on a mound which Lieut. Humphreys and a few men had hastily erected, a body of the men, headed by Morgan, Hendricks, Steel, Humphreys, Heth, and Porterfield, made a desperate attempt to scale the barrier. Their appearance above the wall was followed by a discharge of grape from the guns of the battery, and a heavy fire from the windows on each side; while beneath they beheld a double row of bayonets, ready to receive them should they descend. It was impossible, from the want of a sufficiency of ladders, for the few hardy spirits who had gone thus far, to proceed against such terrible obstacles, and the attempt was relinquished. The riflemen, and others who supported the storming party, had not been idle in the meantime. The accuracy of their aim compelled the enemy to desert their battery before they had fired three rounds. But the fire from the windows and loopholes could not be so easily checked or counteracted, while it was constantly adding to the number of their killed and wounded. It was about this period of the strife that Humphreys fell, mortally wounded. A large number of the men had also fallen. The survivors, dispirited by their want of success, now threw themselves into the houses on each side, which afforded them a shelter both from the storm and the enemy. From the windows of these houses, they renewed the contest; and it was during this time that the enemy suffered most severely. But, even here, some valuable lives were lost on the part of the Americans. Capt. Hendricks, while aiming his rifle at an object, was pierced through the heart by a random shot. Their fire, however, had caused the enemy at the barrier, as well as those in the battery, to retire under cover. Morgan, furious at his repulse, refused to retire into the houses; and, with a few of his bravest officers and soldiers, remained opposite the barrier. Perceiving that the moment was favorable for renewing the attack, he called, in a voice louder than the tempest, on those in the houses to come forth and scale the barrier. But he called in vain. Neither exhortations nor reproaches could produce the desired effect. The repulse, the loss, the severity of the storm, and weariness, with a hopelessness of success, had disheartened the most audacious. Being, at length, compelled to relinquish all present designs against the barrier, he ordered the few brave men who still stood by him to join their comrades in the houses, while he, accompanied only by Lieut. Heth, returned towards the first barrier, in order to concert with the field officers, some plan for drawing off the troops. At this point were Majors Bigelow and Meigs, who concurred with him in the expediency of an immediate retreat. A preliminary step in carrying this resolution into effect, being the withdrawal of the troops from the houses near the second barrier, Lieut. Heth was dispatched to perform this duty. Great as were the hazards to be encountered in proceeding to the troops in the face of the enemy, Heth met them manfully. But, notwithstanding all his efforts, only a few of the men could be prevailed on to expose themselves to the tempest of shot which must necessarily be encountered, in gaining the bend in the street, a short distance in front of the barrier. Once beyond this bend, there was no longer any danger; and, could they have shaken off the despondency which deterred them from promptly following Lieut. Heth, they and their companions at the first barrier might have effected their retreat. But, while the precious moments left them for escape were wasted in indecision, Captain Law, with two hundred of the garrison, and two field-pieces, sallied from Palace Gate; and Captain Dearborn, who, with his company, was held in reserve near this place, having surrendered, all retreat in that direction was completely cut off.

The Americans now found themselves encircled by enemies, far their superior in numbers, and confident from the favorable turn which their affairs had taken. Morgan's unconquerable spirit rose with the emergency. In a council of the officers then present, which took into consideration the desperate state of their affairs, he proposed to assemble immediately as many officers and men as could be collected, and to cut their way back out of the town. They were prevented from adopting this daring proposal, only by the hope that Montgomery, of whose fate they were still in ignorance, would succeed in his attack; and that in this event their co-operation would be invaluable, while a premature retreat might subject one or both of the divisions to destruction, and the assault to a failure. They accordingly resolved to maintain their position for a short time longer.

A desultory fire was, in the meantime, kept up between the opposing forces. Time, however, brought no hope to the beleaguered Americans. Being now evidently the sole object of attack, the whole disposable force of the garrison having gathered around them, they at length perceived that they were no longer masters of their own destiny, and on being summoned, surrendered themselves prisoners of war.

Such was Morgan's vexation upon realizing the hopelessness of his situation, that he wept like a child. On being summoned by some of the enemy's soldiery to deliver up his sword, he peremptorily refused a compliance, but placing his back against a wall, with the weapon in his hand, he dared any one of their number to come and take it. He persisted in this determination, notwithstanding the threats of the soldiers to shoot him, and the exhortations of his men, not to sacrifice his life in useless opposition. At length perceiving a man near at hand, whom he took by his dress to be a clergyman, he asked him if he was not a priest. Being answered in the affirmative, Morgan delivered his sword to the clergyman, observing, " Then I give my sword to you ; but not a scoundrel of those cowards shall take it out of my hands."*

Most of the accounts of this battle concur in stating the American loss at about sixty men killed and wounded. Arnold, in one of his letters, says, that " About three hundred were taken prisoners, and, as near as he could judge, about sixty killed and

* Dr. Hill.

wounded." Carleton, in his official account of the action, stated
that "the rebels lost six or seven hundred men, and forty or fifty
officers, while his loss was only one lieutenant and 17 men."*
Both these statements, and more particulary the latter one, are
believed to be very incorrect. The proneness of military men to
magnify their advantages, and to diminish their losses, renders
them questionable sources of information on such topics. Judge
Henry, in his interesting account of this assault, is probably as
far beyond the mark, in stating that the Americans lost, of non-
commissioned officers and privates, one hundred and fifty killed,
and fifty or sixty wounded. On the same authority, the enemy
had forty or fifty killed, and many more wounded, a statement
founded on information derived from the British soldiery themselves, on corroborating circumstances.† A medium between these
varying statements would probably approximate the truth, and in
the absence of further information, at once definite and reliable, we
are disposed to rest on this conclusion. Captain Hendricks, of the
Pennsylvania riflemen ; Lieutenant Humphreys, Morgan's first lieutenant, and Lieutenant Cooper of Connecticut, were among the killed.
Captain Lamb, Major Ogden, Captain Hubbard, and Lieutenants
Steel and Tisdale, were wounded. When Morgan's company landed
on the north side of St. Lawrence, it numbered nearly eighty men.
Yet from death in battle and by sickness, not more than twenty-five
of its members ever reached their homes.‡ Hendricks's and
Smith's companies, though each originally as strong in numbers
as Morgan's, were reduced in a like fearful ratio. When the
Americans advanced to the assault, they numbered over twelve
hundred men, including the Canadians and Indians. After the
repulse no more than seven hundred men re-assembled under
Arnold. This would leave five hundred to be accounted for
among the killed, wounded, prisoners, and missing. Of the American wounded, very few recovered. Falling in the deep snow,

* Collections of Maine Hist. Soc., vol. i., p. 410.
† Henry's Expedition, p. 120.   ‡ Ibid., p. 144.

and being unable to extricate themselves, they soon fe'l victims to the intensity of the cold, unless rescued from such a fate by some prompt and friendly hand. After the Americans surrendered, a number of their wounded were thus preserved by the humane activity of Governor Carleton.

The captives were not kept long in ignorance of the fate of the gallant Montgomery. He had advanced at the head of his column, accompanied by Captains Cheeseman and McPherson, and Mr. Burr, along the margin of the St. Lawrence, towards the enemy's defences at *Anse des Mères* under Cape Diamond. These con-sisted of two rows of pickets, planted a short distance apart, beyond which was erected a block-house. This was a square two-story log-building, with loop-holes for musketry below, and port-holes above, at which two twelve pounders, charged with grape and cannister, were pointed towards the narrow avenue by which an enemy must approach. The position was defended by a body of seamen and Canadians. The Americans were not discovered until they had penetrated through the first row of pickets, when the Canadians, delivering an ineffectual fire, abandoned the defences, and fled towards the town. The fugitives communicated their fears to the seamen, who manned the guns in the block-house, and they also fled. It afterwards appeared that for a considerable time, this important position was abandoned. Could the Ameri-cans have promptly advanced at this juncture in sufficient force, an entrance into the lower town would have been rendered com-paratively easy. But the difficulties of ascending the hill, and of penetrating through the pickets, had greatly impeded their pro-gress, and the precious moment was lost in waiting for the rear to come up. About two hundred men having at length collected, Montgomery moved forward at their head towards the block-house, exclaiming, " Push on, brave boys, Quebec is ours." These were his last words. When the column had advanced within forty paces of the block-house, one of the cannon was discharged by a sailor, who, having returned to see what it was that delayed the

5*

Americans, and observing them approaching, picked up a match, and before he again fled, fired the gun. By this discharge Montgomery fell, and with him Captains Cheeseman and McPherson, an orderly sergeant, and a private. Unfortunately for the issue of the assault, Lieutenant Colonel Campbell succeeded to the command. This officer has been justly described as one, quite deficient in the qualities necessary for such an emergency as had arisen. Instead of emulating the conduct of Morgan, under precisely similar circumstances, he delayed the advance in useless consultation, until the enemy returned to their works, when he ordered a retreat. The soldiery, disheartened by the death of their general, immediately retired at a pace which soon degenerated into a flight. Mr. Burr, placing Montgomery's body on his shoulders, hurried through the deep snow in the line of the retreat. The enemy sallied from their works after the fugitives. The pursuit became so hot, that Burr was forced to abandon his noble burden, which was found the next day, enveloped in the newly fallen snow, on the shore of the St. Lawrence. It was subsequently brought into the town, and buried with the honors of war.

Thus terminated the celebrated expedition to Quebec. This part of our subject will appropriately close with a few reflections, suggested by its thrilling details. The scheme of taking Quebec by assault was neither rash in design, nor hopeless of execution. The great strength and extent of the works of the city, which, if fully manned, could perhaps have been maintained against any force whatever—furnished embarrassments rather than advantages, to the small garrison which defended them. The forced coöperation of some 600 Canadians could not be regarded as adding materially to the means of defence. These, and the remainder of the inhabitants of French origin, were ripe for revolt, and ready to join the assailants, the moment they safely could. Leaving these people out of account, then, the strength of the Americans, both as it regards numbers and efficiency, was much superior to that of the garrison. The capture of Quebec would have completed the conquest of Canada; and a result so all-important, called for the adoption of any step, however hazardous, that furnished the remotest hope of its accomplishment. Many other considerations of weight were added, prompting, if not compelling, the American general to a resort to decisive meas-ures. The resolution, then, to assault Quebec, appears to have been fully justified by all the circumstances under which it was taken.

The preliminary arrangements for the assault, although compli-cated, appear to have all been carried into effect without accident or mistake. The troops marched to the attack, cheerful and con-fident. In the early stages of the assault, the enemy yielded on every hand. Nothing, it seemed, was wanting to crown the effort with complete success, but an ordinary share of courage and determination. It is here that we must look for the causes of the failure. While some of the troops exhibited a valor and perse-verance, seldom, if ever, equalled, others, it must be admitted, betrayed a want of those ennobling qualities. Had the efforts of Morgan's riflemen, and of the few brave men who rushed with them over the enemy's works, been supported by the rear of the column, the lower town would have been taken by Arnold's divi-sion alone. Had Montgomery not fallen, or having fallen, had he been as ably succeeded by Campbell as Arnold was by Mor-gan, his division would, doubtless, have been equally successful. With the united American forces in the lower town, embracing as it did the bulk of the city's wealth, the inhabitants, either from a desire to secure their property, or from disaffection to the British rule, would have coöperated with them in compelling the garrison, if necessary, to surrender.

Never, perhaps, was the discharge of a single gun followed by such important consequences, as the one which, though fired at random, struck down Montgomery at the moment of victory. It secured to Great Britain a province, greater in extent than all her other possessions together, and which was on the point of being wrested from her for ever. It gave a disastrous termination to a campaign, which, on the part of the Americans, had hitherto been a succession of triumphs. While the British government were thus encouraged to persevere in their efforts to bring the colonists to unconditional submission, the latter were proportionably dispirited at results, so contrary to their expectations, and so unfavorable to their cause. Thenceforward, the tide of war reacted on the Americans in this quarter, until at length, from being the invaders, they were made the objects of invasion. It may be safely asserted, that the consequences of this single discharge of grape were not wholly neutralized, even by the subsequent capture of Burgoyne at Saratoga.

CHAPTER VI.

Governor Carleton—His kind treatment of the prisoners—Their efforts to escape—Morgan
offered a colonelcy in the British service, which he rejects with indignation—Arnold
still invests Quebec—Arrival of the British fleet, with an army of twelve thousand men
—The British rule re-established over Canada—The prisoners petition Gov. Carleton for
permissions to return to their homes on parole—Their liberation—Morgan visits the
American head-quarters—At the recommendation of the commander-in-chief, he is
appointed colonel of the Rifle regiment—Recruiting for the new army—Morgan urged
to push the enlistment for his regiment—He marches to Morristown—Formation of the
regiment of Rangers—The instructions of the commander-in-chief.

THE Americans having surrendered, the officers were conducted to the Seminary, and the non-commissioned officers and
privates to the Jesuits' College, or Recollets, where they were
confined. Of this division, only about one hundred men succeeded in escaping.*

Sir Guy Carleton, Governor of Canada, was as much distinguished for courtesy and generosity, as he was for talents
and courage. Whether it was from policy, or from the suggestions of those better feelings which we have ascribed to him,
certain it is, that he caused the gallant band which the chances
of battle had thrown into his hands, to be treated with much
more kindness, than it was usual for British officers, either before
or after the affair at Quebec, to extend to American prisoners.
This kindness was observed to the privates as well as to the
officers, and induced the general belief, that a desire to alienate
them from the cause in which they had been engaged, if not
to draw them into that of their captors, would be found among

* Collections of Maine His. Soc., vol. i., p. 410.

the motives for its adoption. Subsequent events established the correctness of this impression.

Among the prisoners, a number were of English and Irish birth. These were left the alternative, either to enlist in Colonel McLean's regiment of emigrants, or to be sent to England to be tried for treason. Those born in America were offered their liberty upon enlisting. Accordingly, a large number, chiefly natives of Great Britain, entered the British service, with the intention of seizing the first opportunity which might offer to desert. A short time afterwards, several succeeded in escaping, some by descending the almost perpendicular sides of the snow-clad rock on which Quebec stands, others by jumping from the top of fortifications thirty or forty feet high, into snow from ten to fifteen feet deep, and a few by running the gauntlet through a fire of grapeshot and musketry. What remained of this class of recruits, after the lapse of a few weeks, being regarded as hopeless cases for conversion, were remanded to prison.*

About the beginning of March, the prisoners were removed from the college to Dauphin jail, an old French building, about three hundred yards from St. John's Gate. During this month, a formidable plot which they had formed, not only to escape, but to seize the works at St. John's Gate, and to admit Arnold and his force into the town, was discovered by the garrison, just in time to prevent it from being carried into effect. From some hoop iron, found in one of the rooms of the building, they manufactured swords and spear heads, handles for which were furnished by the fir planks, which formed the bottoms of their berths. By an ingenious device, cartridges were obtained from the soldiery without exciting suspicion. These were converted into matches, with which it was intended to fire the guns of the works upon the city. Joseph Aston, a private in Capt. Lamb's company, succeeded, by the aid of his companions,

* Sparks's Life of Arnold, p. 55.

in effecting his escape. He was to inform Arnold of the intended movement, and to obtain his co-operation. Everything was arranged, and the time for action fixed, when the imprudence of two of their number aroused suspicion. The partial investigation which followed would have failed to make any discovery, when, by the treachery of an English deserter, also a prisoner, the whole plot was betrayed. The prisoners were immediately loaded with chains, which they were compelled to bear for the succeeding two months. During this time, they suffered extreme misery from scurvy, and from a diarrhœa, occasioned by the water.* It was not until the arrival of the British army from England, and the retreat of the Americans from before Quebec, that the irons were struck from their limbs.†

All the captured officers were treated with marked kindness and consideration; but to none was this treatment displayed in so great a degree as to Morgan. The following anecdote, related by himself, will serve to illustrate, not only the implication of a design on the part of the British commander to seduce his prisoners from the cause of their country, but the high opinion which this officer had formed of Morgan's military talents, from the conduct of the latter during the assault. He was visited occasionally by a British officer, to him unknown, but, from his uniform, he appeared to belong to the navy, and to be an officer of distinction. During one of his visits, after conversing upon many topics, he asked Morgan if he did not begin to be convinced that the resistance of America was visionary. He endeavored to impress upon Morgan the disastrous consequences which must infallibly ensue, if the idle attempt were persevered in, and earnestly exhorted him to renounce the ill-advised undertaking. He declared, with seeming sincerity and warmth, his admiration of Morgan's spirit and enterprise, which he said were worthy of nobler employment, and told him,

* Collections of Maine His. Soc., vol. i., p. 410–411.
† Henry's Expedition, p. 146–163.

that if he would consent to withdraw from the American and join the British standard, he was authorized to offer him the commission, rank, and emoluments, of a colonel in the royal army. Morgan rejected the proposal with disdain, and concluded his reply by observing : " I hope, sir, you will never again insult me in my present distressed and unfortunate situation, by making me offers which plainly imply that you think me a scoundrel !"*⁄⁄

Notwithstanding the failure of the assault, and its unfortunate results, Morgan and his fellow captives were not without hope that their friends, who still menaced Quebec, would yet restore them to liberty. Arnold, who had succeeded to the command, encamped with the remains of the army before the town, and by cutting off all communication between it and the surrounding country, reduced it to great distress. He intercepted and captured all supplies intended for the garrison, cut off its detachments whenever they ventured abroad, and by repeated and bold attacks, rendered its situation extremely harassing and precarious. Congress had authorized the raising of nine regiments, and at the request of the commander-in-chief, the New England governments made provision for adding materially to this force, the whole being intended to operate in Canada, early in the spring. Encouraged by these and other indications of a determination to prosecute the war with vigor in that quarter, the assailants held their ground, awaiting only the arrival of the promised reinforcements, again to attack the town. These came in so slowly, however, as hardly to add anything to the effective strength of the army, the arrival of one body of men being generally neutralized by the departure of another. Sickness, and particularly the small pox, had, besides, reduced the nominal force nearly one half. Thus three months passed without producing anything decisive ; yet the season was rapidly approaching when the ice would break up, and the promised reinforcements from England might be expected to arrive. Under these circumstances, Arnold

* Lee's Memoirs, p. 429. Dr. Hill, Major Neville.

determined to resume the siege. Batteries were erected against
the town, and upon the shores of the river, which opened their
fire on the 2d of April.* His troops gained the suburbs, where
they set fire to several houses, and obliged the garrison to pull
down others to prevent the fire from spreading. Here, however,
they were obliged to pause; but they succeeded in withdrawing
without sustaining any considerable loss. The attempts to burn
the shipping in the harbor, by means of red hot shot and fire
ships, were not more successful, although prosecuted with all the
energy of which the numbers and the circumstances of the besiegers
admitted.

These events, which marked the passage of the month of April,
were regarded by the prisoners with no common interest. Besides
keeping them in a constant state of restless anxiety, they produced
on their minds rapid alternations of hope and fear. But their
prospects were soon destined to assume a fixed and gloomy coloring. On the morning of the 6th May, the frigates Isis and Surprise, with three transports, arrived at Quebec. These were a
part of the expected British fleet, which, it was now announced,
were working up the river, having on board 12,000 German and
English troops, with Generals Burgoyne, Phillips, and Riedesel.
The troops brought by the transports having been quickly landed,
Carleton, at the head of one thousand men, with six pieces of
artillery, sallied forth against the besiegers. At a council of war,
held the day previously, in the American camp, it was the unanimous opinion of the officers present, that the army was too feeble
to hope for success from an assault of the town. It was accordingly resolved to remove the sick, the artillery and the stores,
higher up the river, preparatory to a movement of the troops in
the same direction. While engaged in carrying these designs
into execution, Carleton appeared. General Thomas, who had
succeeded Arnold in command of the American forces, ordered a
retreat, which soon became a flight. He left behind him all his

* Marshall's Washington, vol. i., p. 61.

THE LIFE OF

THE LIFE OF

artillery and baggage, which, with a considerable number of his men, fell into the enemy's hands.*

From this time forth, our affairs in Canada were nothing but a series of disasters, relieved, it is true, by instances of courage and address, worthy of success, and which even gave glory to defeat. We therefore willingly take leave of matters no longer incidental to the object of our labors. Suffice it to say, that Gov. Carleton, having completely reëstablished the British rule over Canada, returned to Quebec about the middle of June.

The prisoners had long since given up all hopes of a speedy liberation, save through the success of our arms in capturing the enemy, thus offering facilities for their exchange; or, through the clemency of Gov. Carleton. Ignorant of the progress of events to the southward, their expections of being exchanged were faint and uncertain; and while the contest was yet undecided in Canada, the supposition that Carleton would comply with their desires, was out of the question. His return, however, elated with victory, induced Morgan, Green, and others among the prisoners, to believe that the favorable moment had at length arrived, when the magnanimity conspicuous in his general conduct might be successfully appealed to. Their confidence was strengthened by the fact, that the restraints which had previously been imposed on them were then somewhat slackened, the officers having recently received permission to walk in a large garden adjoining their quarters. A petition† was accordingly drawn up, and having been signed by the officers, was laid before the governor.

---

* Marshall's Washington, vol. i., p. 62.

† TO HIS EXCELLENCY, THE HONORABLE GUY CARLETON, ESQ., CAPTAIN GENERAL AND COMMANDER IN CHIEF OF ALL HIS MAJESTY'S FORCES IN NORTH AMERICA, ETC., ETC.

MAY IT PLEASE YOUR EXCELLENCY:

Impressed with a just sense of your Excellency's humanity and benevolence, and urged by the peculiarity of our present disagreeable situation, being destitute of both friends and money, we beg leave to request that your Excellency will condescend to take our case into consideration, and grant us relief, by permitting us to return to our respective homes, on our parole, which we shall ever deem sacred, assuring your Excellency

Although no immediate answer was returned to this petition, it i believed that it had the desired effect. On the seventh of A**gust following, all the prisoners in Quebec, then amounting to fifty-one commissioned officers, and three hundred and seventy-three non-commissioned officers and privates, were discharged on their parole.

The generosity of Carleton's character displayed itself on this occasion. The men thus discharged being mostly in a destitute condition, were furnished by him with clothing and such other necessaries as they stood in need of. An act of such extraordinary kindness towards enemies having drawn some expressions of surprise from his officers, he is said to have replied: "Since we have tried in vain to make them acknowledge us as brothers, let us at least send them away, disposed to regard us as first cousins."*

On the 10th of August, the prisoners were embarked on board of five transports, which sailed the next day for New York, under convoy of the Pearl frigate. On the 11th of September, they reached their destination. After being detained for some time in the harbor of New York, they were landed at Elizabethtown Point. It was ten or eleven o'clock at night, the moon shining brightly, when Morgan, standing on the bow of the boat as it approached the land, sprang to the shore, and throwing himself on the ground, as if to embrace it, cried out in a burst of patriotic feeling " Oh, my country !" They all seemed delirious with joy,

that we shall make it a point to surrender ourselves to any of his Majesty's officers, when and where your Excellency may think proper to direct.

Being likewise sensibly touched with the deplorable state of our men, who remain prisoners at present, we take the liberty to recommend them to your Excellency's consideration, earnestly soliciting that some measures may be taken for their relief, and we should be extremely happy if they could possibly return to their families, many of whom must be reduced to the greatest distress.

Your Excellency's compliance will be esteemed a singular favor, and ever gratefully acknowledged by

Your Excellency's most obedient and very humble servants

Seminary, Quebec, June 7th, 1776.   [Here followed thirty-four names.]

* Sparks's Writings of Washington, vol. iii., p. 268.

and the night was passed in singing, dancing, hallooing, and every wild expression of pleasure.*

Morgan repaired without delay to the American head-quarters, and communicated to the commander-in-chief the desire he felt to enter again into the service of his country, as soon as his liberation from his parole would permit. It is proper to observe here, that Washington had not been an inattentive observer of the events of the Canadian war, and particularly of those which marked the glorious but unfortunate career of the detachments he had sent thither from Cambridge. Nor was he unmindful of the rights of those who survived the struggle in that quarter. Congress having passed a resolution, directing the exchange of prisoners which had been agreed upon between the respective commanders of the contending armies, to be made from the officers and soldiers taken on Long Island, Washington remonstrated against the injustice which would thereby be done the troops captured in Canada,† and succeeded in getting that body to direct, that in the exchange, the latter should have the preference. He also counteracted the inclination evinced by General Howe, in negotiating an exchange, to pass over the prisoners in Canada. His correspondence with the President of Congress and the governors of the States, showed that the claims to remembrance and reward of the officers who served in Canada, had not been forgotten by him.‡ In the organization of the new army, he was enabled to carry out his just and generous inclinations towards those brave but unfortunate men.

Morgan met with a flattering reception from the commander-in-chief. The assault on Quebec had spread his name throughout the country, and in the estimation of Washington, placed him among the foremost of those who had so greatly distinguished themselves on that memorable occasion. Before Morgan left the camp for his home in Virginia, the views and wishes of the com

---

* Henry's Expedition, p. 183–186. Collections Maine Historical Society, vol. 1., 413.
† Sparks's Writings of Washington, vol. iv, pp. 140–141.   ‡ Ibid. p. 150.

mander-in-chief regarding him, were transmitted to the President
of Congress in the following letter :—

HEIGHTS OF HARLEM, 20th Sept. 1776.

* * * * * * * * * * * *

SIR: As Colonel Hugh Stephenson, of the rifle regiment, lately ordered
to be raised, is dead, according to the information I have received, I would
beg leave to recommend to the particular notice of Congress Captain
Daniel Morgan, just returned among the prisoners from Canada, as a fit
and proper person to succeed to the vacancy occasioned by his death.
The present field officers in the regiment cannot claim any right in preference to him, because he ranked above them, and as a captain, when
he entered the service. His conduct as an officer, on the expedition with
General Arnold last fall, his intrepid behavior in the assault upon Quebec,
when the brave Montgomery fell, the inflexible attachment he professed to
our cause during his imprisonment, and which he perseveres in, and, added
to these, his residence in the place Colonel Stephenson came from, and his
interest and influence in the same circle, and with such men as are to compose such a regiment, all, in my opinion, entitle him to the favor of Congress, and lead me to believe that in his promotion, the States will gain a
good and valuable officer for the sort of troops he is particularly recommended to command.

Should Congress be pleased to appoint Captain Morgan in the instance
I have mentioned, I would still beg leave to suggest the propriety and
necessity of keeping the matter close, and not suffering it to transpire
until he is exonerated from the parole he is under. His acceptance of a
commission under his present circumstances might be construed as a violation of his engagement ; and if not, the difficulty attending his exchange
might be increased. The enemy, perhaps, would consider him as a field-
officer, of which we have but very few in our hands, and none, that I
recollect, of that rank.

I am, sir,
Your very humble servant,
GEO. WASHINGTON.*

Morgan's return once more to home and friends was signalized by the display towards him of an affection and regard,
which went far in repaying him for the toils, the perils, and the

* Sparks's Writings of Washington, vol. iv., pp. 124-125.

sufferings he had experienced. He found his wife and children in good health ; and, thanks to the forecast, which, even amid the excesses of his earlier career, made him provide for the future, learned, that they had suffered no privation nor unhappiness, save that arising from the absence of their best friend and natural protector. His old associates and neighbors gathered around him, and in return for their hearty congratulations upon his re-appearance among them, safe and uninjured, made him repeat, again and again, the adventures which had marked the period of his absence. A month was speedily passed in recruiting his health and strength, and in arranging and bringing up his private affairs. But he was destined soon to return to a nobler field of action. Towards the close of November, he was informed that Congress had determined to act upon the suggestion of the commander-in-chief, and confer upon him a colonel's commission.* He was also advised, that in a short time he might expect to be exchanged, when he would be required at once to take the field. Before the year closed, he was notified of his release from his parole, had

* IN CONGRESS.

The *Delegates* of the *United States* of New Hampshire, Massachusetts Bay, Rhode Island, Connecticut, New York, New Jersey, Pennsylvania, Delaware, Maryland, Virginia, North Carolina, South Carolina, and Georgia. To Daniel Morgan, Esq.:—

We, reposing especial trust and confidence in your patriotism, valor, conduct and fidelity, do, by these presents, constitute and appoint you to be Colonel of the Eleventh Regiment of Virginia—— in the army of the United States, raised for the defence of American Liberty, and for repelling every hostile invasion thereof. You are, therefore, carefully and diligently to discharge the duty of colonel, by doing and performing all manner of things thereunto belonging. And we do strictly charge and require all officers and soldiers under your command to be obedient to your orders as colonel. And you are to observe and follow such orders and directions, from time to time, as you shall receive from this or a future Congress of the United States, or committee of Congress for that purpose appointed, or commander-in-chief for the time being of the army of the United States, or any other your superior officer according to the rules and discipline of war, in pursuance of the trust resposed in you. This commission to continue in force until revoked by this or a future Congress.

Dated the Twelth day of November, 1776, seventy-six. By order of the Congress.

Attest, CHARLES THOMPSON,   JOHN HANCOCK,
              Sec.   *Pres.*

received his commission, and was instructed to commence recruiting for the ranks of his regiment.

Congress had now made arrangements for raising an army on a more permanent footing; and the commander-in-chief was making the greatest exertions to carry out their designs. The untoward turn which affairs had taken had dispirited the people. The recruiting service progressed so languidly, and yielded results so unexpectedly small, as to excite the most alarming fears for the future. From the outset of the struggle, Washington had been unceasing in his exertions to induce Congress to adopt this course; and his predictions of the fearful crisis in the public affairs which otherwise would sooner or later ensue, were but too faithfully verified. "Reinforcements come up so extremely slow," he says, in a letter to the President of Congress, written about this time, "that I am afraid I shall be left without any men before they arrive. The enemy must be ignorant of our numbers, or they have not horses to move their artillery, or they would not suffer us to remain undisturbed. I have repeatedly written to all the recruiting officers, to forward on their men as fast as they could arm and clothe them; but they are so extremely averse to turning out of comfortable quarters, that I cannot get a man to come near me, though I hear from all parts that the recruiting service goes on with great success. It would be well if the board of war, in whose department it is, would issue orders for all officers to equip and forward their recruits to head-quarters with the greatest expedition."*

Morgan had entered earnestly into the business of recruiting. Yet, even with his general acquaintance among the people, and his popularity as a commander to aid his efforts, they were but partially successful. Some time before his discharge from his parole, the officers, then scattered all over the country on recruiting service, had picked up every available man; and, as he required those who were accustomed to the woods, and to the use of the rifle, his difficulties were increased. While thus

* Sparks's Writings of Washington, vol. iv., p. 30-302.

employed, he received a letter from Richard Peters, Esq., at that time Secretary of the Board of War, inclosing a resolution of Congress, adopted in conformity with the suggestions of the commander-in-chief. The resolution and letter are subjoined :—

In Congress, February 24, 1777.

Resolved—That the Board of War be directed to send letters to express to the colonels or other commanding officers of the several regiments now raising and recruiting in the States of Pennsylvania, Delaware, Maryland, and Virginia, ordering them immediately to march the *troops* enlisted under their command, by companies and parts of companies, to join the army under General *Washington ;* proper officers being left behind to recruit the companies or corps that are not yet complete, and to bring up the recruits.

Extract from the minutes,

CHAS. THOMPSON, *Secretary.*

WAR OFFICE, *Baltimore, Feb.* 24, 1777.

SIR : Congress having received intelligence of the enemy's being reinforced in New Jersey very considerably, it becomes absolutely necessary, both for the preservation of the army under General Washington, and to check the progress of our cruel and remorseless invaders, that he be joined immediately by all the forces which can possibly be procured. You have the resolve of Congress on that head enclosed, by the direction of the Board of War, with which they request you will instantly comply, by sending all the men raised in your regiment. Let them bring what arms, blankets, and clothes they have, or can by any means obtain, and the deficiency will either be supplied at Philadelphia or at head-quarters. Let nothing delay your immediate march, either by companies or parts of companies, as you can get them together, as the safety of our country much depends upon the exertions of its army at this trying period; and it is hoped no care or pains of yours will be wanting, when all we hold dear and valuable demands them.

I have the honor to be, your very obedient servant,

RICHARD PETERS, *Secretary.*

To COL. MORGAN, *Winchester, Va.*

Although Morgan had succeeded in enlisting a number of such men as he desired, they were yet too few, in his opinion, to come under the directions of the resolution and letter just quoted. These men besides, were scattered about at different points, embracing an extent of more than forty miles of country; and some further time would be required to collect and organize them, before they could be sent forward as directed. The urgency of the case, no doubt, was great, and few, perhaps, were more strongly impressed with this fact than Morgan himself. He had some time before been addressed by Governor Henry, who called upon him to lose no time in filling the ranks of his regiment, and marching to New Jersey. A few days elapsed, and another letter from the same quarter was received. This letter, although not material to the matter in hand, is yet so characteristic of its distinguished author, that we cannot resist the temptation to give it a place in our narrative :—

WILLIAMSBURG, *March* 15, 1777.

SIR: I must once more address you on the subject of marching your regiment to join Gen. Washington. There is a more pushing necessity for your aid than you are acquainted with, or I can with propriety explain in detail. You will, therefore, surmount every obstacle, and lose not a moment, lest America receive a wound that may prove mortal.

I am, sir, &c.,

P. HENRY.

COL. MORGAN.

Long before the glorious struggle terminated, Patrick Henry learned to appreciate Morgan as a man, who, in the labors of patriotism, needed no spur " to prick the sides of his intent," and to regard him as one in whose breast dwelt a spirit kindred to his own.

Having raised a force of about one hundred and eight men, Morgan took up his line of march, and reached the camp at Morristown about the beginning of April. Up to this period, with the exception of a few hundreds from Pennsylvania, New Jersey, and Virginia, there was nothing in the American camp to indicate that Congress, months before, had made provision for the

6

enlistment and organization of a new army. Of the sixteen regiments ordered to be raised the preceding December, but five
or six hundred had arrived at head-quarters. The commander-in-
chief was bitterly disappointed. He found himself not only
unable to carry into effect the offensive operations he had meditated, but unequal even to defensive warfare. Nay, more, he was
indebted to his preservation from destruction, either to the supine-
ness or the want of information of his opponent.* But, affairs
assumed a more promising aspect during the succeeding two
months. Recruits having come in pretty rapidly, preparations
were made for opening the campaign with a vigor proportionate
to the means supplied to carry it on. The camp at Morristown
was broken up, the detachments called in, and the army moved
to Middlebrook. The effective force at this time was only five
thousand, seven hundred and seventy-eight men.

On Morgan's arrival at head-quarters, he was received by
the commander-in-chief with marked kindness and consideration.
He entered at once on the duties of his station. But, the situation of affairs in the camp at this time, when one army was about
disbanding, to be succeeded by another not yet assembled, much
less organized, imposed on him an inaction but ill-suited to
his temperament. This was, however, destined to be short lived.
The early military career of the commander-in-chief had taught
him the value which might properly attach to a select corps of
sharp-shooters, composed of hardy, active men, accustomed to the
woods, and skillful in the use of the rifle. The preceding
campaigns had presented many occasions, forcibly suggesting the
want of such a corps, when its presence might have turned
the tide of battle. He determined no longer to defer its formation. A body of five hundred picked men was accordingly
formed from the different regiments composing the army. The
command of this corps was given to Col. Morgan; Richard But
ler, of Pennsylvania, an officer admirably qualified for the post,

* Sparks's Writings of Washington, vol. iv., p. 302.

received the lieutenant-colonelcy ; and the gallant but unfortunate Morris, of New Jersey, who fell gloriously a short time afterwards at Chestnut Hill, was appointed major. The captains for the eight companies, into which the regiment was divided, were appointed by Morgan. His selections displayed that knowledge of human nature, and that soundness of judgment, which formed such conspicuous features in his character. They were Captains Cobel, Posey, Knox, Long, Swearingen, Parr, Boone, and Henderson. Amidst all the severe tests to which these officers were subsequently subjected, not one of them failed to realize the expectations of his commander, nor to distinguish himself on one or more occasions.

On the 13th June, the corps being completely organized and ready for service, as the events of a few days signally proved, the following letter of instructions was received by Morgan :—

INSTRUCTIONS

To Col. Morgan—

Sir : The corps of Rangers newly formed, and under your command, are to be considered as a body of Light Infantry, and are to act as such, for which reason they will be exempted from the common duties of the line.

At present you are to take post at Van Vechten's Bridge, and watch, with very small scouting parties (to avoid fatiguing your men too much under the present appearance of things), the enemy's left flank, and particularly the roads leading from Brunswick towards Millstone, Princeton, &c.

In case of any movement of the enemy, you are instantly to fall upon their flanks, and gall them as much as possible, taking especial care not to be surrounded, or have your retreat to the army cut off.

I have sent for spears, which I expect shortly to receive and deliver to you, as a defence against horse. Till you are furnished with these, take care not to be caught in such a situation, as to give them any advantage over you.

Given under my hand at head-quarters, Middlebrook, the 13th of June, 1777.

George Washington

CHAPTER VII.

ON the morning of the 13th of June, the day on which Morgan
assumed the command of his regiment, Sir William Howe, leaving
2,000 men at New Brunswick, sent two strong columns of his
forces, under Generals Cornwallis and De Heister, in the direction
of the Delaware. The purpose of this movement was to induce
Washington to quit his fortified camp at Middlebrook, and risk
an engagement in defence of the quarter threatened. The front
of Cornwallis's column reached Somerset Court House by the
dawn of day, when it was discovered by one of Morgan's detached
parties.* Intelligence of this movement of the enemy having been
communicated to head-quarters by Morgan, he at once advanced
with his regiment to the neighborhood of Somerset.

Being secured on their flanks by the Raritan and Millstone, the
enemy were found too strongly posted to be approached without
danger. But during the five or six days that they occupied this

---

* Writings of Washington, vol. iv., p. 468.

position, several spirited encounters took place between small parties of their force and detachments of the Rangers, in which the latter were invariably victorious. Finding that Washington was not to be drawn into a disadvantageous engagement, and not daring to prosecute his seeming purpose of crossing the Delaware, the British general returned to New Brunswick on the 19th of June.*

Morgan, in conformity with the instructions† he had received from head-quarters, kept a vigilant eye upon the enemy. Their return to New Brunswick was signalized by several spirited attacks on their flanking parties by the Rangers.

On the morning of the 22d, General Howe evacuated New Brunswick, and retired towards Amboy, setting fire to every building on his line of march. Washington, on being apprised of the retreat, detached three brigades (one of which was Wayne's), under Gen. Green, to fall on the enemy's rear, while Sullivan and Maxwell were ordered to co-operate upon their flank. The main body, in the meantime, paraded on the heights, ready to act as occasion might require.

As Morgan was posted in the immediate neighborhood of the enemy, he was first apprised of their movements, and thereupon he immediately pushed forward to annoy them. He first encountered a strong picket of Hessians, who were soon driven in upon the main body. The latter were at this moment in full retreat across the bridge, a strong division of their forces being drawn up to cover the movement. Against this body, Morgan immediately

* Marshall's Washington, vol. i., pp. 147, 148.

† HEAD-QUARTERS, 15th *June*, 1777.
SIR:
His Excellency desires you will continue to keep out your active parties carefully watching every motion of the enemy; and have your whole body in readiness to move without confusion, and free from danger. He likewise requests that you make your men be particularly careful of their provision, or they must often suffer.

I am, Sir,
Your most obedient servant,
RICHARD R. MEADE, A. D. C.
COL. D. MORGAN.

directed the fire of his regiment; and after a fierce struggle of a few minutes, the enemy were forced to give way, and to seek the shelter afforded by some redoubts which they had previously constructed on that side of the river.* The advantage afforded them by the redoubts subjected Morgan to a momentary check; but Gen. Wayne's brigade arriving at this juncture, the contest was renewed with greater spirit than ever. After a short struggle, the British abandoned their redoubts, and retreated precipitately along the Amboy road.

Morgan, followed by Wayne, kept close to the heels of the enemy; and before he gave up the pursuit, forced their rear guard, on several occasions, to face about, and exchange several sharp fires with his riflemen. For more than an hour, the contest was maintained with severe loss on both sides; and it was not until Wayne and Morgan had advanced in the pursuit as far as Piscataway, that they ordered a halt.† They had reckoned with confidence on the co-operation of Sullivan and Maxwell, in which event they felt assured, that the day would prove a disastrous one to General Howe. But this not being obtained, they paused awhile at Piscataway, to refresh their men, and then returned to New Brunswick. The opinion prevailed in the army after this battle, that had Maxwell arrived at the post assigned him, in time to take a part in the contest, the enemy's rear guard of 1500 men would have been cut off and captured.

In this action, Morgan greatly distinguished himself. His corps had fought with extraordinary valor; and, although it suffered severely in its repeated encounters with the enemy during the preceding few days, the loss of the latter was far greater. Morgan and Wayne, as well as their officers and men, were made the subject of very commendatory remarks in the letter which Washington addressed to the President of Congress, after the action. Honorable mention was made of "their conduct and

---

*Sparks's Writings of Washington, vol. iv., p. 471.   † Ibid

bravery on this occasion,* and the fact was specially noted, that
"they constantly advanced upon an enemy far superior to them
in numbers, and well secured behind strong redoubts."*

The new and somewhat exposed situation of the main body of
the American army, in its advanced position at Quibbletown,
offered temptations to the British commander to make a fresh
attack. The object of his first movement was to draw Washington from his entrenched camp, and bring on a general action.
He now thought that a rapid movement of his force might enable
him to turn the American left, and gain the heights in its
rear, thus forcing Washington to fight at a disadvantage.
Accordingly, on the night of the 25th, he recalled the troops
which had crossed to Staten Island, and early next morning
made a rapid movement, in two columns, towards Westfield.
The right, under Cornwallis, took the route by Woodbridge
to Scotch Plains; and the left, led by Howe, marched by
Metucking meeting-house. In addition, four battalions, with
six pieces of cannon, were detached to Bonhamstown, in order to
cover Amboy. Howe was to attack the left of the American
army at Quibbletown, while Cornwallis was to gain the heights
on the left of the camp at Middlebrook.†

After the action of the 22d, Morgan took post in advance
of the main body, and in the neighborhood of Woodbridge.
On the morning of the 26th, the advance of Cornwallis was
discovered, and soon after vigorously attacked. The conflict
was maintained with spirit for half an hour, and with a severe
loss on the part of the enemy. But, their main body coming
up to the support of the advance, Morgan commenced retiring
towards the camp. Washington, as soon as he heard the firing,
comprehended how matters stood. He ordered a retreat to
Middlebrook, after having detached a strong corps under Ster
ling, to secure the mountain passes on his left. Cornwallis

* Sparks's Writings of Washington, vol. iv., p. 472.
† Marshall's Washington, vol. i., p. 149.

continued to advance, and at length encountered Sterling, who, after a warm engagement, was obliged to give way with the loss of three pieces of cannon. Cornwallis then pressed forward as far as Westfield. Here finding that his object had been foreseen, and provided against, he halted for two days, and then commenced a retreat to Amboy.*

When it became known that Cornwallis had halted at Westfield, Gen Scott's brigade and Morgan's corps were thrown forward to observe and annoy him. As soon as the retreat commenced, he was immediately attacked by these officers. Along the whole way to Rahway, a continued skirmish was kept up with the flanks and rear of the enemy, who lost a large number of their force in killed and wounded.† They marched, however, in a compact body, and, leaving no opening for a serious attack, kept their assailants at bay. They reached Amboy, and crossed over to Staten Island by the 30th of June.

For some time previous to this period, the designs of the enemy baffled conjecture, and had been a source of great disquietude to Washington. It was now believed that a junction between Burgoyne and Howe was contemplated. Measures were at once taken by the commander-in-chief to counteract such a scheme. Nixon's brigade was sent to reinforce the northern army under Schuyler; Generals Parsons and Varnum were ordered to march with their brigades to Peekskill; the division under General Sullivan was pushed forward to Pompton; and the head-quarters, with the remainder of the army, were successively removed nearer to the Highlands and to the Hudson; first to Morristown, then to Pompton, and afterwards to the Clove.‡

Morgan, who, since the retreat of the British to Staten Island, had been posted at Chatham, was early advised of the movements of the army, and had received the necessary instructions

---

* Marshall's Washington, vol. i., p. 149.
† Sparks's Writings of Washington, vol. iv., p. 475.
‡ Sparks's Writings of Washington, vol. i., p. 149–150.

to guide him.* He remained at this place for about a week; when the impression gaining ground that the enemy were about moving up the North river, he received orders† to march north-ward. He accordingly pushed forward as directed, and reached Hackensack on the second or third day following.

Everything, at this time, indicated that a conflict was at hand; and Morgan and his corps were eager for a better opportunity than had yet offered to distinguish themselves. But, again all was doubt and uncertainty as to the real object of the enemy's active and extensive preparations. Their fleet, having taken on board a large number of troops and stores, had dropped down the bay, encouraging the presumption that it was about putting to sea. The orders, which originated in a belief that the enemy intended moving up the Hudson, were accordingly counter-

---

* MR. LOTT'S FARM, 11th July, 1777.

DEAR SIR: Upon a presumption that the enemy intend to move either up the North or East river, our army marched this morning from Morristown, and will proceed leisurely towards the Clove, unless we have some certain intelligence that they intend southward.

Colonel Dayton, who is at Elizabethtown, watching the motions of the fleet, will give you immediate information which way they go. If up the East or North river, you will follow directly, keeping upon the right flank of the main army. The road is rather better than the one we march. You need not harass your men, but come on leisurely: if there is any occasion to hurry, we will send an express to you.

I am, dear sir, your most obedient servant,

TENCH TILGHMAN, A.D.C.

COLONEL MORGAN, at Chatham.

† HEAD QUARTERS, NEAR CLOVE, 19th July, 9 o'clock, P.M., 1777.

DEAR SIR: We have received your letter of this date. From the intelligence received this afternoon, we have every reason to believe that the enemy are about to move up the North river. It is, therefore, his excellency's orders, that upon receipt of this, you march your corps to the bridge, at the great falls, from thence to Paramus, thence to Kakegate, and thence to Haverstraw; there to observe the motions of the enemy; and, if they land on the west side of the river, below the Highlands, you are to take possession of the road to the forest of Dean Furnace, and oppose their penetrating that way. But, if the enemy push up the river, you are to get over the mountains into Fort Montgomery, and there wait for further order. Your baggage (except what you think necessary for the men to carry), is to be sent by the nearest route towards this place, and from here to whatever place the army is, under a small guard.

I am, dear sir, your most obedient servant,

JOHN FITZGERALD, A.D.C.

COLONEL MORGAN.

130 THE LIFE OF

manded; and Morgan, on reaching Hackensack, received directions* to halt until further orders.

He, accordingly, halted at this place for a few days. The
intentions of the enemy still remained unknown, yet their great
preparations rendered it certain that they meditated some important expedition. The only resource left the commander-in-chief
in this emergency, was to dispose of his force in such a manner as
to be in some measure prepared for the enemy in whatever quarter they might appear. In the meanwhile, he exercised an untiring vigilance in watching their movements, and in guarding
against a surprise.

A few days elapsed, when news was received, which, for a
time, seemed to furnish a certain clue to the enemy's designs.
The fleet had left New York, with a very large force on board,
and stood out to sea. Apprehending now that Philadelphia was
the point threatened, as it subsequently proved to be, the commander-in-chief put the greater part of his army at once in
motion towards that city. The orders which reached Morgan on
this occasion, were as follows :—

CAMP AT KAMAPAUGH, *July* 24, 1777.

SIR : The enemy's fleet having left Sandy Hook and gone to sea, you
are immediately, on receipt of this, to march with the corps under your
command to the city of Philadelphia, and there receive orders from the

* CLOVE, *July* 21, 1777, 7 *o'clock, A.M.*
DEAR SIR : Since I wrote to you the night before last, we found out that the intelligence which occasioned the order to you, was premature. His excellency, therefore,
orders me to direct, that if you have marched to the northward of Paramus, you return
and take post there. If you have not got so far on receipt of this, you are to occupy some
place near you which you may find most convenient for the reception of your men. If
your baggage has not got far from you, you had better order it back immediately.
I am, sir, your most obedient servant,
JOHN FITZGERALD, A.D.C.

P.S.—You will let us know where you are as soon as you have fixed upon a place. As
it may be probable that the enemy may make an incursion from Staten Island, you will
require no instructions from head-quarters to march and oppose them.
J. F.
COLONEL MORGAN, *Rifle Corps.*

commanding officer. You will proceed as expeditiously as you can by the shortest routes : you will take no heavy baggage with you, but leave it to follow with an officer, and a proper guard.

I am, sir, &c.,

GEORGE WASHINGTON.

COL. MORGAN.

In less than an hour after the above order was received, Morgan and his corps were on the march to Philadelphia. On arriving at Trenton, he halted for a few days at that place, in obedience to orders* to that effect. The mind of the commander-in-chief was not yet altogether clear of doubt as to the real object of the enemy. But, another day seemed to render this unmistakable. The fleet had appeared off the capes of Delaware, standing in. Morgan was advised of this fact by a note† from Col. Naylor, and, in anticipation of orders, he crossed the Delaware, and pushed on without delay towards Philadelphia. The several divisions of the army were now rapidly approaching the neighborhood of Philadelphia. The militia of Pennsylvania, and of the adjoining States, immediately took the field. The approach of the enemy was rendered seemingly certain, and every preparation was made to meet them. But, once again the commander-in-chief was involved in a state of uncertainty. The fleet, after hovering about the mouth of Delaware bay for a

---

* CONNELL'S FERRY, *July* 28, 1777.

SIR : Should this reach you before you arrive at Trenton, it is his Excellency's desire that you make a halt there until further orders. Should you have passed it, you are to stop at Bristol, there to remain until you hear from him.

I am, your most humble servant,

R. R. MEADE, A.D.C.

COLONEL MORGAN.

† TRENTON, *July* 31, 1777.

SIR : A letter from Mr. Hancock informs that the enemy's fleet were yesterday in the offing, and desires that all the troops here should advance immediately. I think you had best get over your regiment as soon as you possibly can.

I am, sir, your humble servant,

STEPHEN NAYLOR, Colonel G. D.

COLONEL MORGAN.

day or two, stood out to sea in an easterly direction. Apprehending that the enemy's extraordinary movements might tend,
after all, towards the Highlands, he at once took measures to
strengthen the force in that quarter, by bodies of militia from
New York and Connecticut.*

To add to his perplexities, the intelligence of the fall of Ticonderoga, and of Burgoyne's advance, reached him about this time,
accompanied by clamorous demands for large detachments from
his army to reinforce that in the north. Feeling certain that
General Howe's designs had reference to the section of country
occupied by his army ; reflecting, besides, that the defence of this
section against the main army of the enemy was an object, superior in importance to any other existing, he felt reluctant to
weaken his force in aid of the northern army, until these designs
should be fully developed.

In the belief that the fleet had gone eastward, the army was
put in motion towards the Hudson. A day or two previous
to this movement, Morgan received orders to advance with his
corps to Maidenhead.† He had accordingly marched, and was
about crossing the Delaware, in the neighborhood of Trenton,
when counter orders‡ were sent to him. The army had not

* Sparks's Writings of Washington, vol. iv., p. 476.

† CAMP NEAR GERMANTOWN, *Aug.* 9, 1777.
SIR: You will march, to-morrow morning, the corps under your command, for
Maidenhead, in the State of Jersey, and there halt till you receive further orders. In
your march, as during your stay at that place, you will take every possible care in your
power to restrain every species of licentiousness in the soldiery, and to prevent them
doing the least injury to the inhabitants or their property ; as nothing can be more disser-
viceable to our cause, or more unworthy of the character we profess, to say nothing of the
injustice of the measure.

I am, sir, your most obedient servant,

GEORGE WASHINGTON.
COLONEL MORGAN.

‡ CAMP AT THE CROSS ROADS, *Bucks Co.*,
Sunday, 10th *Aug.*, 1777, 10 o'clock, *P.M.*
I have just received an express from Philadelphia, informing me that a large fleet was
seen off Sinepuxent Inlet on the 7th inst. You are, therefore, directed to halt wherever
this finds you, and wait till we hear further of the matter. Let me know, by return of the

¹een in motion more than a day, when intelligence was received that the fleet had again appeared on the 7th, off Sinepuxent Inlet, a place about fifty miles south of the Capes of Delaware. An immediate halt was hereupon ordered, with the determination to await the development of the enemy's plans.

The rapid advance of Burgoyne, now attracted the serious attention of Washington towards the north, whither the scene of of our narrative is about to change. Two regiments had been already ordered from Peekskill in aid of the northern army ; and more were speedily to follow. Among others, it was determined that Morgan's corps should be sent to that quarter. The terror which Burgoyne's Indian auxiliaries had spread among the people, by the murder and rapine which marked their path, required counteraction ; and it was, not without reason, believed by the commander-in-chief, that in Morgan and his corps, such a counteraction would be found. He felt assured that they would prove more than a match for the Indians, and soon reassure the affrighted people. Still, the valuable services which they had performed, made him extremely reluctant to part with them. Nothing but the appeal to his benevolent impulses, which was coupled with the desire for the aid of this corps—that an inhuman and merciless system of warfare might meet with merited chastisement—induced him to detach them on this service. Orders were accordingly issued, as follows :—

NESHAMINI CAMP, *August* 16, 1777.

SIR: After you receive this, you will march, as soon as possible, with the corps under your command, to Peekskill, taking with you all the baggage belonging to it. When you arrive there, you will take directions express, where you are, that I may know how to direct for you when I have occasion to send you orders.

I am, sir, your most humble servant,

GEORGE WASHINGTON.

P.S.—By ordering you to halt where this shall find you, I mean upon the most convenient ground near the place.

COLONEL MORGAN.

from General Putnam, who, I expect, will have vessels provided to carry you to Albany. The approach of the enemy in that quarter has made a further reinforcement necessary, and I know of no corps so likely to check their progress, in proportion to its number, as that under your command. I have great dependence on you, your officers and men, and I am persuaded you will do honor to yourselves, and essential services to your country.

I expect that your corps has been paid to the last of June; but, as you are going on this command, and they may have occasion for more money, you will make out an estimate, as well as you can, for the sum due them for the month of July, and send an officer with it, to whom the amount shall be paid. I do not mean to exclude the corps from their pay in June. If that has not been paid, include it in the estimate.

I have nothing more to add, than my wishes for your success.

> I am, sir, your most obedient servant,
> GEORGE WASHINGTON.

COLONEL MORGAN.

In obedience to these orders, Morgan put his corps in motion for the North, where he was destined to add so greatly to the laurels he had already won. The corps was in high spirits at the prospect of being speedily in a quarter where their fighting propensities might find full exercise.

While on the march, they were overtaken by further orders,* not on this occasion countermanding those preceding, but supplementary to them. In obedience to these orders the march was hastened in the direction of Peekskill.

About a week after Morgan's departure for the North, and when

---

* HEAD-QUARTERS, *Aug.* 18, 1777.

DEAR SIR: In addition to the orders already sent to you by his Excellency, I have it in orders from him to request, that you will march your corps with all possible dispatch to join the army under command of Major General Gates, and when there, you will take orders from him and act accordingly.

> I am, for his Excellency,
> Your most obed't serv't,
> JOHN FITZGERALD,
> *Aide-de-Camp.*

COLONEL MORGAN,
Colonel of rifle corps on the march for Albany.

he had proceeded too far to be recalled, intelligence was received that the British fleet had arrived in Chesapeake Bay, and that Howe, with sixteen thousand men, had landed, and was marching towards Philadelphia.*

Washington, in the meantime, had advised General Gates of Morgan's advance to join him. "From various representations made to me," he observes, "of the disadvantages the army lay under, particularly the militia, from an apprehension of the Indian mode of fighting, I have dispatched Colonel Morgan, with his corps of riflemen, to your assistance, and expect that they will be with you in eight or ten days from this date. This corps I have great dependence on, and have no doubt but they will be exceedingly useful to you; as a check given to the savages, and keeping them within proper bounds, will prevent General Burgoyne from getting intelligence as formerly, and animate your other troops, from a sense of their being more on an equality with the enemy."†

On the same subject, the commander-in-chief wrote to General Putnam on the 16th:

"The people in the Northern army seem so intimidated by the Indians, that I have determined to send up Colonel Morgan's corps of riflemen, who will fight them in their own way. They will march from Trenton to-morrow morning, and reach Peekskill with all expedition. You will please to have sloops ready to transport them, and provisions laid in, that they may not wait a moment. The corps consists of five hundred men."‡

To Governor Clinton, in a letter of the same date, he observes :—

"In addition to the two regiments which are gone from Peekskill, I am forwarding as fast as possible, to join the Northern army, Colonel Morgan's corps of riflemen, amounting to about five hundred. These are all chosen men, selected from the army at large

* Marshall's Washington, vol. i., p. 153.
† Sparks's Writings of Washington, vol. v., p. 87.   ‡ Ibid., p. 88.

well acquainted with the use of rifles, and with that mode of fighting, which is necessary to make them a good counterpoise to the
Indians; and they have distinguished themselves on a variety of
occasions, since the formation of the corps, in skirmishes with the
enemy. I expect the most eminent services from them, and I
shall be mistaken if their presence does not go far towards producing a general desertion among the savages."*

Morgan, at the head of his corps, proceeded without delay to
Peekskill. Here, having embarked his troops in the vessels which
had been prepared for their reception, he started by a more expeditious method of travelling to Albany, leaving Lieutenant Colonel
Butler to command during the passage.

Until a short time previous to this date, the operations in this
quarter had resulted in a succession of disasters to the American
cause. The reconquest of Canada was followed by the fall of
Ticonderoga, and all the other American posts on that frontier.
Burgoyne, at the head of a powerful army and an auxiliary force
of Indians and Canadians, had penetrated deep into the country,
spreading death and desolation among its inhabitants, and was
now encamped near the Hudson. Here his career was destined
to terminate. Those severe reverses which he experienced at
Bennington and in Tryon county, must have warned him of the
fate which awaited him, even before the arrival of Gates and a
large reinforcement. This officer succeeded General Schuyler in
the command of the Northern army on the 19th of August. In
reply to the letter of the commander-in-chief, Gates took in
review the state of affairs in the North at that time. He likewise expressed his thanks for being permitted to obtain the
valuable aid of Morgan and his corps. From the important
relation which Morgan bore to these affairs, a cursory glance at
them is called for. As this will be best performed by the letter
itself, its introduction here may be pardoned the more readily,

* Sparks's Writings of Washington, vol. v., p. 80.

inasmuch as its remarks regarding Morgan and his corps bring it within the scope of our legitimate labors.

HEAD-QUARTERS, *Aug.* 22, 1777.

SIR: Upon my arrival in this department, I found the main body of the army encamped upon Van Schaick's Island, which is made by the sprouts of the Mohawk river joining with Hudson's river, nine miles north of Albany. A brigade under General Poor encamped at Loudon's Ferry, on the south bank of the Mohawk river, five miles from hence; a brigade under General Lincoln had joined General Stark at Bennington, and a brigade under General Arnold, marched the 15th inst., to join the militia of Tryon County, to raise the siege of Fort Stanwix. Upon leaving Philadelphia, the prospect this way appeared very gloomy; but the severe checks the enemy have met with at Bennington and Tryon County, has given a more pleasing view to public affairs. Particular accounts of the signal victory gained by General Stark, and the severe blow General Herkimer gave Sir John Johnston and the scalpers under his command, have been transmitted to your Excellency by General Schuyler. I anxiously expect the arrival of an express from General Arnold, with an account of the total defeat of the enemy in that quarter. By my calculation he reached Fort Stanwix the day before yesterday. Colonel Livingston and Courtland's regiments arrived yesterday, and immediately joined General Poor's division. I shall also order General Arnold, upon his return, to march to that fort.

I cannot sufficiently thank your Excellency for sending Colonel Morgan's corps to this army; they will be of the greatest service to it, for until the late successes this way, I am told the army were quite panic-struck by their Indians, and their Tory and Canadian assassins in Indian dresses. Horrible, indeed, have been the cruelties they have wantonly committed upon many of the miserable inhabitants; insomuch, that all is now fair for General Burgoyne, even if the bloody hatchet he has so barbarously used should find its way into his own head.

Governor Clinton will be here to-day. Upon his arrival, I shall consult with him and General Lincoln, upon the best plan to distress, and I hope, finally defeat the enemy.

I am sorry to be necessitated to acquaint your Excellency how neglectfully your orders have been executed at Springfield. Few of the militia demanded are yet arrived, but I hear of great numbers upon the march.

Your Excellency's advice in regard to Morgan's corps, &c., &c., shall be carefully observed.

My scouts and spies inform me, that the enemy's head-quarters and main body are at Saratoga, and that they have lately been repairing the bridges between that place and Stillwater.*

As soon as time and circumstances will admit, I will send your Excellency a general return of this army.

I am, sir,
Your Excellency's most
Obedient humble servant,
HORATIO GATES.
His Excellency, GENERAL WASHINGTON.

Morgan, upon his arrival at Albany, found that preparations had already been made for the reception of his troops, and the transportation of their baggage to the scene of action. As may be inferred from the annexed letter which awaited his arrival, General Gates was anxious to avail himself of his services at as early an hour as possible :—

HEAD-QUARTERS, *Aug.* 29, 1777.

DEAR SIR : I had much satisfaction in being acquainted by General Washington of your marching for this department. I have by this conveyance ordered Colonel Lewis, D. Q. M. General at Albany, to provide you, immediately upon your landing, with carriages for your baggage, and whatever may be necessary; tents, and a camp equipage, I conclude you have brought with you. I could wish you to march as soon as possible to Loudon's Ferry, where the ground is marked for your present encampment. I have draughted one subaltern, one sergeant, one corporal, and fifteen picked men from each regiment of this army to serve with your corps and to be under your command. When you have seen your regiment to their ground, I desire you will come to head-quarters.

I am, sir,
Your affectionate,
Humble servant,
HORATIO GATES.
COLONEL MORGAN,
Commanding rifle corps, Albany.

* Wilkinson's Memoirs.

GENERAL DANIEL MORGAN. 139

Jpon arriving at head-quarters, Morgan met with a cordial
ceting from General Gates. Among other tokens of the regard
a which he was held, his corps was designated as the advance of
the army, and he was directed to receive orders only from the
general-in-chief. So flattering a reception could not fail to make
a due impression on Morgan, who now longed for a speedy opportunity of justifying the general in his favorable opinions.

In a few days his men arrived, and soon afterwards took post at
the position assigned them. They were joined at that place by
the promised reinforcement of their numbers, which was organ-
nized into a battalion of light infantry under Major (afterwards
General) Dearborn. The men of this battalion numbering two hundred and fifty, were selected from the line of the army, with careful
reference to their bodily vigor and their acquaintance with bush-
fighting. Their commander was as gallant a soldier as ever wore
a sword.* He was doubly acceptable to Morgan, inasmuch as
they had together shared in the toils, misfortunes, and glories of
Arnold's expedition against Quebec, during which a warm friendship had been cemented between them.

* Wilkinson's Memoirs, p. 280.

CHAPTER VIII.

The American army encamp on Behmus Heights—Morgan thrown forward to cbserve the enemy—He engages a German regiment, and forces it to retire—The British take a position nearer to the American camp—The events preliminary to, and attendant upon, the battle of Behmus Heights—Reflections on this battle—The letters of the opposing generals concerning it—The projected assault—Burgoyne resolves to await the expected junction with Sir Henry Clinton—Difficulty between Gates and Arnold respecting Morgan and his command—Arnold resigns his command in the army—Gates refuses to be reconciled to Arnold, or to restore him to his command—Remarks on these circumstances.

MORGAN was not destined to remain long inactive. The events of the preceding month had produced a great change in the prospects of the contending armies. The confidence which animated the British during the early stages of the campaign, had been transferred to the Americans, and the terror and despondency which the latter had experienced, had taken possession of the enemy. The withdrawal of Schuyler from the command, and the appointment thereto of Gates, had produced a favorable influence upon the militia, who now turned out with alacrity. The large reinforcements which had been sent forward were on the ground, ready for action. The time had at length arrived, when the American arms in this quarter might safely count on a triumph.

On the 8th of September, the army under General Gates, numbering at that time about six thousand men, struck their tents at the encampment at Sunset, and advanced towards Stillwater.* The day previous, Morgan was advised of the intended movement,†

* Wilkinson's, vol. i., p. 232.

† HEAD QUARTERS, *sunset, Sept.* 7, 1777.
SIR: You are to assemble the corps under your command upon the heights above

and received the instructions by which his conduct was to be guided. It was thought, at the time, that the enemy had crossed the Hudson, and that the advance of the army would certainly produce an action. The rifle corps was in high spirits at the prospect. But, these expectations were, however, disappointed, as nothing of moment occured during the march to Behmus Heights, which place, having been selected for an encampment, was occupied by the American army on the 12th.

Measures were at once taken to ascertain the position, strength, and objects of the enemy. Spies and reconnoitering parties were sent forward to gain the desired information. The rifle corps was ordered to take a position some distance in front of the American left, the quarter most likely to be assailed. Morgan was directed to observe the enemy closely, and to give early notice should they attempt a forward movement.

In a few days it was ascertained, that Burgoyne, having assembled his whole force at Saratoga, and collected thirty days' provisions, had determined to push forward to Albany, and was then marching towards the American camp.†

General Gates determined to oppose the enemy's advance. The American army had been actively employed in erecting field-works, and otherwise strengthening the camp. Their exertions were now redoubled. Expresses were sent in every direction, spreading the intelligence, and calling out the militia. Morgan

Half Moon, to-morrow morning, at gun-firing; you will direct the officer of your rear-guard to be attentive to the march of the columns upon the right and left of your corps; and you will dispatch intelligence to me and to General Arnold, of all extraordinary motions of the enemy; and everything you think it is necessary we should be informed of. You cannot be too careful in reconnoitering your front, and gaining every possible knowledge of the ground, and the surrounding country.

Reposing especial trust and confidence in your experience and capacity, I rest satisfied you will exert all your endeavors for the good of the public service. You will hear from me frequently in the course of the day's operations, which makes it unnecessary t ɪ add more at present, than that I am, with affection and esteem,

Dear sir, your most obedient humble servant,

HORATIO GATES.

COLONEL MORGAN.

* Wilkinson's Memoirs, vol. i., p. 232.   † Ibid. p. 233.

was kept far in advance, watching the movements of the enemy,
with the privilege of attacking them whenever an opportunity
offered. The terror inspired by his name among the Canadians
and Indians, had induced a general desertion of these branches
of the British force, while their regulars could not make a movement beyond the precincts of their camp, without receiving a volley of rifle balls. Thus, the American army now enjoyed, in
Morgan's corps, all the advantages which the enemy had derived
at the opening of the campaign, from a legion of Canadians and
savages.

On the 13th and 14th of September, the British army crossed
the Hudson. This step was a bold, but not a judicious one. It
proved a Rubi on of gloomy omen to Burgoyne. Advancing with
caution, however, his army arrived within three miles of the
American camp on the morning of the 18th. A detachment of
one thousand five hundred men, composed of Morgan's corps and
a part of General Poor's brigade, under General Arnold, was hereupon thrown forward. The enemy were in motion when this
detachment came within view of them. They marched in such
compact bodies, however, and with so much circumspection, as to
render it hazardous to attempt anything decisive against them.
But, Morgan fell in with and engaged a German regiment; and,
after a short encounter, in which a few men were killed and
wounded on both sides, and about a dozen Germans made prisoners, the enemy retired, and the detachment returned to camp.

The British advanced in the afternoon to a position on the
banks of the Hudson, about two miles from that occupied by the
American army on Behmus Heights, and formed their encampment. The intermediate space between the adverse armies was
partly cleared and partly woodland. The land along the margin
of the river was under cultivation; while that higher up was
covered with its native forest, with the exception of three or four
small, newly opened, and deserted farms, separated at intervals by
woodland, and interposing between the flanks of the opposing

armies most remote from the river. The ground intervening between the centre of both armies was very rugged, and covered with an impenetrable thicket.* Morgan's corps was stationed in advance of the American left wing, among these alternations of woods and clearing, having the impassable ground occupying the centre on its right. It was, consequently, in a position where, if the enemy approached, it could fight to the best advantage. The occasion was not long wanting.

On the morning of the 19th, a body of the British army was discovered moving from the bank of the river, and ascending the high ground opposite to the American left wing. General Gates immediately sent orders to Morgan to advance with his corps, directing him, should the enemy be found approaching, to hang on their front and flanks, retard their march, and cripple them as much as possible. The corps accordingly formed into two lines. The first was composed of two companies of the riflemen, headed by Major Morris, followed by Major Dearborn's light infantry, the whole commanded by Lieutenant-Colonel Butler. The second, formed of the main body of the corps, was directed by Morgan himself. The front line advanced for about half an hour, when it suddenly came upon a strong picket of the enemy, about three hundred in number, drawn up on one of the deserted clearings before mentioned, and occupying a log-house erected on the ground. A general and deadly volley was the first intimation the picket had of the proximity of such unpleasant neighbors; and this was so quickly followed by a vigorous charge by the light infantry, that the British fled in the greatest disorder. Our troops pushed on with ardor after the fugitives. They had passed the clearing and entered some distance into the woods beyond, when they suddenly and unexpectedly found themselves within a few paces of a large body of the enemy. The next instant, a heavy fire from the latter killed and wounded a number of the light infantry and riflemen, and admonished the remainder of the

* Wilkinson's Memoirs, vol. i., p. 236.

necessity of an immediate retreat. This was not effected without the additional loss of Captain Swearingen, Lieutenant Moore, and a number of men who were taken prisoners.* Lieutenant-Colonel Butler and Major Dearborn were enabled to. avoid a similar fate without much difficulty. But Major Morris, with characteristic impetuosity, was foremost in the pursuit, and the first intimation he had of the neighborhood of the enemy in such strength was to find himself in their midst. Nevertheless he gallantly dashed his horse through their ranks, riding over half a dozen men, and succeeded amid a shower of balls in effecting his escape and rejoining his command. The remainder of the corps was scattered in every direction, soon to be reunited, however, for to collect, disperse, flee and pursue, were parts of the tactics of this celebrated corps; and although few were slower in retiring before the enemy, none were more active in their pursuit. The frequent encounters which they had had with the enemy's pickets and scouting parties, generally resulted in a capture of a number of the latter. The heavily encumbered English or German soldier was no match for the lightly equipped and active backwoodsman in a trial of speed.

On hearing the fire in front, Morgan pressed forward in all haste with the second line to take part in the engagement, when he was met by a number of the fugitives. If Morgan was distinguished for any quality more than that of courage, it was for prudence and circumspection when in the neighborhood of an enemy, with the strength and disposition of whose force he was unacquainted. But once having ascertained what he had to contend against, and believing that he could overcome it, nothing could exceed the impetuosity of his assault. Indignation and alarm now by turns took possession of his feelings, under the impression that by the recklessness of his officers in rushing forward the first divison had been destroyed. Colonel Wilkinson relates in his memoirs,* that, "tempted by the firing, he found a pretext to visit the scene of strife, although forbidden by General

* Wilkinson, vol. i., p. 246.   † Ibid., vol. i., 137-138.

Gates to leave head-quarters." He arrived soon after the occur-rence of the event just described.

"The first officer I fell in with," he says, "was Major Dearborn, who, with great animation and not a little warmth, was forming thirty or forty file of his infantry. I exchanged a few words with him, passed on, and met Major Morris, who was never so sprightly as under a hot fire."

After receiving a description of the events of the action from the major, and being cautioned against exposing himself to the enemies' sharpshooters, Wilkinson proceeds:

"I crossed the angle of the field, leaped the fence, and just before me on a ridge, discovered Lieutenant-Colonel Butler with three men, all *treed*. From him I learned that they had 'caught a Scotch prize:' that having forced the picket, they had closed with the British line, had been instantly routed, and from the suddenness of the shock and the nature of the ground, were broken and scattered in all directions. Returning to the camp to report to the general," Wilkinson continues, "my ears were saluted by an uncommon noise, when I approached, and perceived Colonel Morgan, attended by two men only, and who, with a *turkey-call* (an instrument made from a turkey-bone for decoying the wild turkey), was collecting his dispersed troops. The moment I came up to him, he burst into tears, and exclaimed, 'I am ruined, by God! Major Morris ran on so rapidly with his front, that they were beaten before I could get up with the rear, and my men are scattered God knows where.'"

Remarking upon Morgan's almost invariable rule when march-ing to action, of bringing up the rear of his corps, Wilkinson observes in a note to a passage in the foregoing extract :—

"I took occasion to inquire into his motives, and he answered me briefly, 'that they were to see that every man did his duty, and that cowards did not lag behind while brave men were fight-ing.'"

Partly from discipline, and partly from the directing sounds of

7

the turkey call, a brief time sufficed to bring the dispersed division
of the corps together again. This being effected, the whole regiment
advanced in a body towards the scene of the recent conflict.—
Approaching the clearing, a large body of the enemy were found
occupying the ground. The attack which immediately ensued was
pushed with such vigor, as speedily to force the British to retire,
until they reached an eminence fronting an open piece of ground
called "Freeman's Fields." Here, through the vigorous exertibns
of their officers, and the encouragement afforded them by a reinforcement, they made a stand. A fierce and deadly struggle ensued.
But the advantages which the enemy held in a superiority of numbers and in artillery, at length yielded them a temporary triumph,
and Morgan was compelled to retire under cover of the woods.
This movement was the more necessary, as a large body of the enemy was perceived advancing to attack him in flank. At this moment two regiments of New Hampshire troops, commanded by Cols.
Scammel and Cilley, appeared and formed on the left of the Rifle
corps, and engaged the advancing body of the enemy. Thus secure
on both flanks, that on the right being covered by impenetrable
thickets and a marshy ravine, Morgan renewed the action with
those in his front with redoubled vigor. The severe loss which his
corps had sustained, served only to inspire officers and men with
greater ardor, and a keener desire for revenge. The well directed
fire of six hundred marksmen soon forced the enemy once more to
seek safety on the woody eminence, not, however, before the ground
was covered with their killed and wounded. In retiring, they were
compelled to abandon their artillery; but they took the precaution
to carry away with them their linstocks.* In consequence, the
guns could not be immediately used by their captors; it was determined however, to carry them off. The nature of the ground did
not admit of their speedy removal; and the enemy, under cover of the
woods on the hill, rallied in their defence. The attempt to bear
off the valuable prize was met by a destructive fire; and it was not

* Wilkinson, vol. i., p. 241.

until a great many valuable lives had been sacrificed in the effort, that it was relinquished. The positions respectively occupied at this time by Morgan and his opponents gave the latter an advantage which had once already forced him to retire. His troops were exposed to the fire of an enemy, for the most part, under cover. Could the guns have been made use of, the scale would have turned in his favor. But under existing circumstances, there was no alternative but to retreat to his late position. This step was not taken, however, until repeated efforts had been made to drive the enemy from their stronghold—efforts which were attended with much bloodshed on both sides.

At this period of the action, the strength of the adverse forces engaged had been greatly augmented. Soon after the arrival of Scammel's and Cilley's regiments, they were followed by those of Hale, Van Courtlandt, Livingston, Cook, and Latimer, composing the whole of Gen. Poor's brigade. As these regiments successively arrived, they formed to the left, extending the line in that direction. The enemy, in the mean time, had sent forward reinforcements to an equal, if not a greater extent, and forming on the right of their troops engaged, took position in front of the regiments just named. The American force now in the field amounted to about 2,500 men, while that of the enemy was considerably more. The latter were aided by several pieces of artillery; but the former had none.

About 3 o'clock, the action became general from right to left. At the centre, and particularly at the right, where Morgan was posted, it was warm and sanguinary; and along the whole line the firing did not cease till darkness closed upon the combatants. Again and again had Morgan driven the British troops opposed to him back on the eminence beyond Freeman's clearing. Their cannon had become almost useless from the want of men to serve them. Freed from the advantage which this powerful arm of war afforded his opponents, he made the most desperate efforts to drive them over the hill, and thus turn the left flank of the enemy. But as often was he forced to retire before the great odds which were brought to bear upon him whenever his advance threatened the accomplishment of his object.

The battle raged for upwards of five hours, with an obstinacy never before witnessed in America. Victory seemed hovering over the contending armies, undecided, as it were, in whose favor she would declare herself. At one moment, the enemy seemed on the point of achieving a complete triumph; but the next evinced a change in the tide of battle, which rendered their discomfiture apparently inevitable. While one body of Americans, too hardly pressed, might be seen retiring before their immediate adversaries, another might be noticed gallantly driving their opponents before them. The triumphant shouts of friends and enemies were often heard at the same moment, coming from different parts of the field, and blending together in a strange and terrible dissonance. The unceasing rattle of musketry, accompanied by the roar of artillery, and the rapid alternations of forward and retrograde movements, left no respite for excitement to subside, or courage to cool; while the protraction of the conflict familiarized the men with death, blunted their sense of danger, and rendered them anxious to encounter every peril which promised to lead to a victorious result.

The sun was about setting when the American ranks were further reinforced by Gen. Learned and his entire brigade, and one regiment from Gen. Patterson's brigade. A body of German and British troops had been sent from their camp, and were then occupying the right of the British line, in a position to outflank the American left. The fresh reinforcement brought these troops to action; but the fire was feeble on both sides, and soon ceased altogether.

While there was light to perceive objects, there seemed to be no abatement of the fire. Darkness at length put an end to the obstinate conflict. The opposing armies retired from the field together. The Americans returned to their camp but the

British, apprehensive of a renewal of the contest before the next morning, slept on their arms in front of their camp, a short distance from the field.

The loss of the Americans in this action, as appears by the official returns, was eighty killed, two hundred and eighteen wounded, and twenty-three missing. Among the killed, were Lieut.-Col. Adams, of Hale's regiment, and Lieut.-Col. Colburn, of Scammel's regiment. The killed and wounded of the enemy amounted to nearly six hundred men, to which may be added the loss of a large body of Indians, Canadians, and Tories, who, on the termination of the action, immediately deserted the British camp. Morgan's corps bore the brunt of the day's perils, and reaped the greater share of its glories. As may be supposed, it suffered severely, having had fifty men killed, sixty-two wounded, and six missing. The sixty-second regiment of Hamilton's brigade, against which Morgan's regiment contended, lost one hundred and fifty of its men; the troops sent to its assistance on one or two critical occasions, suffered to the extent of twenty or thirty more; and of the forty-eight men who composed the artillery corps when the action commenced, and who were likewise arrayed against Morgan, but twelve left the field uninjured.*

The force of the Americans engaged was nearly three thousand men. About one thousand more arrived on the field at an hour too late to take a part in the action. That of the British was at all times during the day superior in number, and when the action closed, must have amounted to nearly four thousand men.

The reflections to which this memorable battle give rise, have too often engaged the pen of history to call for their repetition here, excepting so far as they relate to the subject of our labors.

In this connection, a few remarks are necessary. The motives or causes to which this engagement is ascribed, are differently interpreted by various authors. There is one point, however, on which all American, and a number of foreign writers agree, that the result gave our arms an indisputable claim to victory. From

* Wilkinson, vol. i., p. 289.

the preceding 14th of the month, the British had been advancing; and the battle of the 18th was unquestionably the effect of their attempt to advance still further. It was the business of the Americans to check the progress of the British towards Albany, the point aimed at by the latter; and the effort with this end in view, was attended with complete success. It may be true, as has been asserted, that during the early part of the day, neither of the opposing Generals anticipated such important events as those which attended its close. But whatever may have been the original intentions of General Burgoyne, in making a demonstration on the American left, whether important or trivial, they must have been subservient to any and every opportunity which might be afforded him for injuring his opponents and carrying out his plans; or he did not deserve the high reputation for resolution and tact which was generally accorded to him. That General Gates did not regard the affair in a serious light at its commencement, admits of a very strong presumption, notwithstanding all that has been said to the contrary. But if he did, it was the tendency of the attack, more than the attack itself, regarding which he was solicitous. He was so absorbed in apprehensions for his right, which covered the road to Albany, and the command of which especially devolved on himself, that he could not believe anything of consequence was meditated or occurring elsewhere. This will be taken for granted when the fact is made known, that during one of the most obstinately-contested actions of the war, in which nearly seven thousand men were engaged, not a single officer above the rank of a colonel appeared upon the ground until night began to close upon the combatants, when General Learned arrived with his brigade. Although the whole of Gen. Arnold's division took an active part in the strife, that officer never appeared in the action. Gen. Wilkinson informs us that Arnold was forbidden by Gates to visit the field, and direct the operations of his command.* Our object in stating these well authenticated facts, is to show, that the credit of this glorious

* Wilkinson, vol. i., pp. 245, 246.

action, so generally accorded either to Arnold or to Gates, or to
both, properly belongs to neither. It should go to enrich the
memory of those gallant men, who, unassisted by the directing
hand of either of their commanders, but coöperating in purpose
from the impulses of a courage common to all, fought the battle
and won the day. Historic truth requires this explanation, and
public justice will give the laurels to those who won them.

And among this glorious band of heroes—it is no injustice
to the memory of any one of them to assert—Morgan was
pre-eminently distinguished. His regiment was the first in the
field, and the last out of it. Where it was engaged, the strife
was more deadly and less interrupted, than in any other
position. Its loss was greater in proportion to its numbers,
than that of any other regiment engaged, while the number
of the enemy which fell by its hands, was nearly one-half of that
admitted by General Burgoyne to have fallen in the battle.
Though Morgan was denied the merited mention in Gates' communications to Congress regarding this battle, justice claims for
him the foremost position among those who had a share in
the glories of the day. Posterity will freely accord him this, and
hail him—as did his friends and neighbors on his return home a
few months after—as " the hero of Stillwater."

The news of this victory was received throughout the country with demonstrations of joy. It was correctly regarded
as the precursor of those more important events which were
speedily to follow, and Gates and Arnold reaped a rich harvest
of undeserved honors and applause. The militia came flocking
into the camp, and evinced a commendable disposition to be
brought into action. A large number of Indians, also, joined the
army. Everything bid fair for the speedy capture of Burgoyne,
although it was some time after the battle of the 7th of December, before Gates contemplated anything beyond driving him
back to Canada.

The letters from the respective commanders, which follow, will show the light in which the result of this battle was regarded by each. They likewise aptly illustrate the danger of receiving with too much confidence the *ex parte* statements of parties regarding events, in which their interest or their honor is concerned :—

*General Burgoyne to Brigadier-General Powell.**

CAMP NEAR STILLWATER, *September* 20, 1777.

DEAR SIR : I take the first opportunity to inform you, that we have had a very smart and honorable action, and are now encamped in front of the field, which must demonstrate our victory beyond the power of even an American news writer to explain away.

The loss on each side cannot be particularly ascertained.

Be so good as to give Sir Guy Carleton an account of this event, with my respects to him, till I can have an opportunity of sending him the particulars by a safe conveyance. I am, dear sir, with great esteem,

Your most obedient servant,

J. BURGOYNE.†

‡ *Extract of a letter from Major-General Gates to the Hon. J. Hancock, President of Congress, dated,*

CAMP, HEIGHTS ABOVE BEHMAN'S, *September* 22, 1777.

Friday morning I was informed by my reconnoitering parties, that the enemy had struck their camp, and were removing towards our left. I immediately detached Colonel Morgan's corps, consisting of the rifle regiment and the light infantry of the army, to observe their direction and harass their advance. This party, at half-past twelve, fell in with a picket of the enemy, which they immediately drove ; but, the enemy being rein-

---

* Wilkinson, vol. i., p. 242.

† The above letter was found in the shot-pouch of an Indian, who was killed by Lieutenant John Hardin, of Morgan's regiment, two or three days after the action to which it refers. Hardin had been detached with a party of riflemen to the rear of the British army, to gain intelligence. On his return, near Saratoga, he suddenly met the Indian at the summit of a sharp ridge. Both presented and fired at the same instant. The Indian fell; Hardin escaped with a slight wound on his left side. The letter, with others, was delivered at head-quarters. After the war, Hardin removed to Kentucky, where he rose to the rank of a general. Having encountered numberless dangers in the service of his country, he was murdered near Sandusky, in 1791, by a party of Indians, while bearing a flag of truce, and a talk from General Washington.— *Wilkinson's Mem., vol. i., p.* 288.

‡ Wilkinson, vol. i., p. 243.

forced, after a brisk conflict they were in turn obliged to retire. This skirmish drew the main body of the enemy, and a brigade from my left, to support the action, which, after a short cessation, was renewed with great warmth and violence. At this instant, hearing from prisoners that the whole British force and a division of foreigners had engaged our party, I reinforced with four more regiments. This continued the action till the close of the day, when both armies retired from the field. Enclosed is a return of our loss; and I am well assured, by the concurrent testimony of prisoners and deserters of various characters, that General Burgoyne, who commanded in person, received a wound in his left shoulder, that the sixty-second regiment was cut to pieces, and that the enemy suffered extremely in every quarter where they were engaged. The general good behavior of the troops on this important occasion, cannot be surpassed by the most veteran army; to discriminate in praise of the officers would be injustice, as they all deserved the honor and applause of Congress. Lieutenant-Colonel Colburn, and Lieutenant-Colonel Adams, with the rest of the unfortunate brave who fell in their country's cause, leave a lasting memorial to their glory. The armies remain encamped within two miles of each other.

On the morning after the action, a deserter from the British army arrived in camp, and communicated the information, that their whole force was under arms, and that in a few minutes more they would advance, and under cover of the heavy fog which prevailed at the time, assault the American entrenchments from right to left. The lines were immediately manned, and for more than an hour the army waited the threatened attack. It never came, however; although subsequent developments proved that the information received was strictly correct. Under the circumstances of the case, had the design been carried into execution, it was the opinion of those well qualified to judge, that the result might have been disastrous to the Americans. The ammunition of a large portion of the army, particularly that now chiefly menaced, had been exhausted in the action of the preceding day; and, owing to the fatigue of men and officers, a fresh supply had not been obtained. The prevailing fog was remarkably dense, so much so as to render objects undistinguishable at the distance of

7*

thirty yards. The chief reliance in such a case would be the bayonet; yet, but about one-third of the American force were furnished with that weapon. Remarking upon this thrilling occasion, Wilkinson observes: " We passed an awful hour of expectation and suspense, during which, hope, fear, and anxiety, played upon the imagination. Many could hear the movement of the enemy, and others could discern through the floating mist the advance of their column. But, between eight and nine o'clock the sun dispersed the vapor, and we had no enemy in view. The report of the deserter was discredited, and the troops dismissed."

It afterwards appeared that General Burgoyne had made every preparation for attacking, with his whole force, the American left on that morning. But, it being represented to him that the grenadiers and light infantry, who were to lead the attack, appeared fatigued, he deferred the prosecution of the design till the day following. During the same day, a letter from Sir Henry Clinton reached Burgoyne. By this, the latter was informed that the troops from New York were already far in advance northward, that Fort Montgomery would be attacked about the 20th September, and that thereafter he should receive speedy assistance. Burgoyne replied, that he was placed in a situation of extreme difficulty; but that he could wait for the promised aid till the 12th of October. Having now determined to assume a defensive attitude until the arrival of Sir Henry Clinton, he abandoned the meditated assault upon the American camp, and commenced strengthening the defences of his camp, fortifying his right, and extending his left to the river.*

A few days after these events, Morgan and his corps became the subject of a serious difference between General Gates and General Arnold. It will be recollected that upon the establishment of this corps, the commander-in-chief, in consideration of the arduous duties it would be constantly called upon to perform, exempted it from the common duties of the line. The letters

* Wilkinson, vol. l., p. 250-252.

which passed between the commander-in-chief and Morgan, up to the time when the corps left Peekskill for the northern army, show, besides, that it received its orders from, and was held responsible only to, the former. Upon the arrival of Morgan and his corps at General Gates's camp, they were not only granted the privileges which they had hitherto enjoyed, but their numbers were augmented by Major Dearborn's battalion of light infantry, and they were the recipients, besides, of other distinguishing marks of favor. Arnold, under the impression that they were included in his command, occasionally exercised a control over their movements, which at length attracting the notice of General Gates, elicited the following general order :

" Colonel Morgan's corps, not being attached to any brigade or division of the army, he is to make returns and reports to head-quarters only, from whence alone he is to receive orders."

A violent altercation immediately ensued between Gates and Arnold. This was followed by a long and acrimonious correspondence, in which Arnold tendered the resignation of his command in the army, and asked permission to go to Philadelphia. Much to his surprise and chagrin, Gates immediately accepted the resignation, and granted the required leave. Arnold, fearing the consequences to his reputation which might follow his desertion of the army at so critical a period of the campaign, soon after made some advances towards reconciling the difficulty, in the hope of being reinstated in his command. It was, however, all in vain. The command of the left wing was assumed by Gates himself, and that of the right conferred upon General Lincoln, who arrived in camp with a body of militia from the eastern States, while the quarrel was pending.*

The services which Arnold had performed, and the courage and military talents which he had displayed, had spread his name throughout the country, as one of its ablest defenders. His removal from command was, therefore, a subject of general regret, but

* Wilkinson, vol. i., p. 253-261.

particularly so with the army, by whom he was greatly admired for his genius, boldness, and activity. This was especially the case as regarded the rifle corps, with many of the members of which, including its commander and a number of its officers, he had shared in the sufferings and dangers of the Canadian expedition. It was, perhaps, to these high characteristics of a soldier, that he was indebted for the ungenerous course which Gates persevered in pursuing towards him. The certainty of a glorious issue to the campaign, rendered Gates avaricious of its honors, while envy of an officer, at that time much more distinguished than himself, may have contributed its share. How far the refusal to restore Arnold to his command may have controlled his subsequent career down to its infamous termination, is known only to the great Director of human affairs. Yet it is easy to perceive, that but for this circumstance, such a direction might have been given to his energies, as to have led him to the acquisition of additional honors; and thus, in spite of a heart dead to every honorable impulse but courage, he might have won for himself a name proud among the proudest. The severe wound, received a few days after, which disabled him for active service—his transfer to Philadelphia—the connexions he formed, and the excesses he fell into, at that place, with the embarrassments and mortifications which they brought upon him—his appointment to West Point—and his treason—may all be traced to this source without straining a probability.

CHAPTER IX.

Letter from Washington to Gen. Gates, and an extract from the latter's reply —Critical situation of Burgoyne—His advance leads to the second battle of Stillwater- Morgan's corps routs the British light infantry—Death of Gen. Frazer—Assault on the enemy's camp—Anecdote—Cornwallis abandons his camp, and takes a new position—Morgan advances to impede the enemy's retreat—Skirmishes with their pickets—American army return to their entrenched camp, when Burgoyne retreats to the north bank of Saratoga creek, and encamps—He is overtaken by the Americans—Burgoyne meditates a retreat to Fort Edward—His advanced detachments driven back—He resolves to abandon his baggage, &c., and endeavor to escape by a night march—The hopelessness of his situation by the frustration of his scheme—Contemplated assault upon the enemy's camp—Fortunate discovery of mistake—Position of the American army—Correspondence regarding a capitulation—Termination of the campaign—General reflections—Unfriendly conduct of Gen. Gates to Morgan—The cause of this change—Anecdot -Remarks on the propriety of employing marksmen.

I⋅T is believed that Washington did not anticipate the difficulties with which, shortly after the rifle corps had been detached to the North, he was called on to contend, or he never would have parted with it. The important services it had rendered, had taught him its value; and sorely pressed as he was, by an overwhelming force at this time, he keenly felt its absence, and ardently wished for its return. To this end, he addressed the following letter* to Gates, which was received three days before the action of the 7th of October.

CAMP NEAR POTTSGROVE, *Sept. 24th*, 1777.

SIR,
This army has not been able to oppose General Howe with the success that I wished, and needs a reinforcement. I therefore request, if you have been so fortunate as to oblige Gen. Burgoyne to retreat to Ticonderoga, or

* Wilkinson, vol. i., page 265. Sparks's Writings of Washington, vol. v., p. 74.

158 THE LIFE OF

if you have not, and circumstances will admit, that you will order Col. Morgan to join me again with his corps. I sent him up when I thought you materially wanted him; and if his services can be dispensed with now, you will direct him to return immediately. You will perceive I do not mention this by way of command, but leave you to determine upon it according to your situation. If they come, they should proceed by water from Albany as low down as Peekskill; in such case you will give Col. Morgan the necessary orders to join me with dispatch.

I am, sir,

Your most obedient servant,

GEO. WASHINGTON.

MAJOR GEN. GATES.

To this Gates replied immediately. The extract which follows is all of the letter* relating to Col. Morgan and his command. The anxiety of the commander-in-chief for their return was fully equalled by that of General Gates to retain them.

CAMP, BEHMUS HEIGHTS, *Oct. 5th,* 1777.

SIR,

Since the action of the 19th ult., the enemy have kept the ground they occupied the morning of that day, and fortified their camp. The advanced sentries of my picket are posted within shot of and opposite to the enemy's; neither side have given ground an inch. In this situation, your Excellency would not wish me to part with the corps *the army of General Burgoyne are most afraid of.* From the best intelligence, he has not more than three weeks' provisions in store; it will take him at least eight days to get back to Ticonderoga; so that in a fortnight at, furthest, he must decide whether he will really risk, at infinite disadvantage, to force my camp or retreat to his den; in either case, I must have the fairest prospect of being able to reinforce your Excellency in a more considerable manner than by a single regiment.

*   *   *   *   *   *   *   *   *   *   *   *

I have the honor so be, &c.,

HORATIO GATES.

HIS EXCELLENCY, GEN. WASHINGTON.

Another battle was now approaching, the results of which rendered it the closing struggle of this eventful campaign. General Burgoyne

* Wilkinson, vol. 1., p. 266.

was anxiously awaiting the arrival of Sir Henry Clinton; yet up to the memorable 7th of October, he had received no tidings of that officer, and fearful misgivings now began to gather round his heart. His force had sensibly diminished by sickness and desertion, as well as by battle, while that of his opponent had greatly increased. Provisions were rapidly failing in his camp, and without a fortunate turn in his affairs in the course of four or five days, his supply would be entirely exhausted. Critical as was his situation, his pride and his judgment united in rejecting the idea of a retreat. He correctly believed that such a step, under the circumstances then existing, with enemies on all sides, and being far from the reach of supplies, would be attended with as many difficulties as advancing. The time for the adoption of decisive measures had arrived, however; and regarding a vigorous forward movement as the only course left him, he took his measures accordingly.

About 3 o'clock on the afternoon of the 7th, the advanced guard of Col. Morgan's regiment, posted some distance in front of the line, discovered a large body of the enemy in motion. The alarm was immediately given, the drums beat to arms, and the troops quickly formed and took their ground. This body, being the advance of the intended general movement of the enemy, was commanded by Gen. Burgoyne in person, assisted by Generals Frazer, Phillips and Reidesel.* It was accompanied by ten pieces of artillery. A body of tories and Indians, under Captain Frazer, had been pushed forward in advance, with directions to penetrate to the rear of the American left, and threaten that flank. Information was soon after received, that the enemy had entered a wheat field, about one mile and a half from the American lines, fronting the left wing; that they had formed in battle array; and that, while a party was cutting the forage which the field afforded, the officers were making a reconnoissance of the American camp from the top of the house on the ground.† The light infantry, commanded by the Earl of Balcarras, occupied the right; the

* Marshall's Washington, vol. i., p. 208.　　　　†Wilkinson, vol i., p. 267.

grenadiers, under Major Ackland, formed the left; and several battalions of English and German infantry, led by Major Breyman, formed the centre. The artillery, under the direction of Major Williams, were placed between the divisions, and at other positions along the line. The enemy's right rested on a worm fence, beyond which the ground, thickly covered with wood, abruptly ascended, forming a hill. Their left was covered, in flank by woodland, and in front by a ravine, through which ran a small stream. The centre occupied the clearing.*

Gen. Gates, having learned these particulars, made instant preparations for battle. Morgan received orders to "begin the game," by pushing forward his corps and commencing a skirmish. But having previously made himself acquainted with the ground, occupied by the enemy, and learning the disposition they had made of their force, he thought his corps could act much more advantageously, if sent, under cover of the woods, to the hill flanking their right. From that point, he said, he could effectually co-operate with the troops sent against them in front, and at all events, be enabled to render better service than could possibly be effected by the mode directed. These views were communicated to General Gates, who at once adopted them; and to this circumstance may, with perfect propriety, be attributed much of the decisive result which the day produced. The rifle corps, having received instructions to reserve fire until the action commenced in front, was put in motion, and passing beyond the American left, pushed forward through the woods, in the direction of the hill. General Poor's brigade was now ordered to advance against the enemy's centre and left, with directions to commence the action, immediately after they arrived on the ground. Other dispositions were made to add, if necessary, to the forces sent forward. Precautions were also taken against any movement which might be contemplated against the right of the American camp. Gen. Lincoln's division, posted in this quarter, was kept

* Wilkinson, vol. i., p. 267.

under arms, and held ready for any emergency; and a strong body of New York militia, which had recently assembled, was ordered forward from its position in the rear, to cover the left of the lines.

Morgan speedily arrived at the hill which overlooked the British detachment. A glance at its disposition confirmed the correctness of the previous description, and gave him the assurance of a speedy triumph. He quickly arranged his men in order of battle, and gave the necessary directions. Dearborn's light infantry, supported by a body of riflemen, were ordered to incline to the right, with the object of assailing the enemy's right in front. The main body of the corps was to attack them at the same time in flank and rear. These divisions had barely reached the positions assigned them for action, when the fire of Gen. Poor's brigade was opened upon the British left. This being the signal for commencing the attack on the right, the British light infantry were instantly assailed in flank by the riflemen, who, rushing forward at the word from Morgan, poured into their ranks a heavy and destructive fire. They were evidently taken by surprise, and for a minute or so, in contemplation of the number of dead and wounded already around them, seemed shaken. This was but momentary, however, for with soldier-like precision, they had already commenced a manœuvre generally resorted to in meeting a flank attack, when Morgan promptly ordered the light infantry under Dearborn to seize the advantage afforded by the movement, and charge. This body advanced to within sixty paces of the enemy; delivered its fire with fearful precision; and then, crossing the fence, with loud cheers, gave them the bayonet. The riflemen on their flank had in the mean time been actively and effectively engaged. The British, forced to give way, were pushed with redoubled ardor by both of Morgan's divisions, and at length obliged to flee in the greatest disorder. By the exertions of their officers, they were rallied about four hundred yards in the rear of their first position, and, for a short time, renewed the contest. So vigorously, however, were they assailed, that they were again obliged to give ground. They were retiring, in the greatest confusion, when Gen. Frazer, at the head of a body of infantry, advanced to their relief. Burgoyne, upon noticing the danger which threatened his right, had dispatched this officer with a strong body of troops to reinforce that wing, or cover its retreat, as circumstances might direct. Frazer met the whole wing flying in the utmost disorder, fiercely followed by Morgan and his men. Throwing his troops between the victors and the vanquished, Frazer attempted to stem the tide of battle. His efforts, though heroic, were vain. After an obstinate and bloody conflict, in which a free use of the bayonet alternated with discharges of musketry and rifles, at thirty yards' distance, this body of the enemy also fled, bearing with them their general, mortally wounded.

The circumstances of General Frazer's death demand especial notice here, from the direct agency which Morgan had in that event. On many occasions during the conflict, Morgan's attention was attracted towards a noble-looking officer of the enemy, who, mounted upon a splendid black charger, dashed from one end of the line to the other, appearing wherever the danger was greatest, and by his courage, judgment and activity, frequently restoring to his troops the fortunes of the day, when all seemed on the point of being lost. He recollected having seen this officer in the battle of the 19th of September, and having on that occasion admired him for the skill and bravery which he displayed. While he lived, Morgan considered the issue of the contest a doubtful one; he therefore, sternly resolved to seek for victory in his death. Selecting twelve of his best marksmen, he led them to a suitable position, when, having pointed out to them the doomed officer, he told them to kill him when next he came within reach of their rifles. "He is a brave man; but he must die"—the only observation which fell from Morgan's lips besides his directions to his men—betrayed the struggle of generosity with duty

in his breast. He afterwards said, that he attentively and somewhat anxiously observed his marksmen, when, a few minutes having
elapsed, and Frazer re-appearing within gun-shot of them, he
saw them all raise their rifles and, taking deliberate aim, fire.
Thus fell General Frazer ; and a more efficient and accomplished
officer than he, the British had not in their army.

The defeat and dispersion of the British right was soon followed
by the precipitate retreat of their centre and left, leaving behind
them eight pieces of cannon. The battle had been hotly contested
by these divisions, and although they had a much larger force to
contend against, than that which overthrew the right, they did
not yield their ground until some time after the latter had fled.
Generals Phillips and Reidesel, at the head of a reserve force, had
endeavored to cover the retreat in this quarter ; but they were
also obliged to give way.

The whole of the British forces which had been engaged were
now fleeing to the protection of their fortified camp, and thither
they were closely followed by the victors. Morgan had pursued
the defeated right division, until they reached their entrenchments,
when his advance was checked for a time by a furious discharge of
cannon and musketry. Fortunately, the woodland was within
one hundred and fifty yards of the British defences. Sheltered
by the trees, the riflemen returned the enemy's fire with effect,
letting few of those escape who exposed themselves while serving
the artillery. The remainder of the fugitives had no sooner
reached their camp, than their pursuers appeared. The battle,
now transferred to a new field, recommenced with great vigor
along the whole line of the British encampment. For an hour or
more, the discharge of cannon and musketry was uninterrupted,
during which the encampment was fiercely assaulted at several
points, in the face of a severe fire of grape-shot and small arms.
At length, the ardor of the rifle corps no longer brooking restraint,
and impatient for something decisive. they rushed tumultuously
forward, headed by Morgan, and charged upon the entrenchments

of Balcarris's light infantry. A desperate hand-to-hand struggle hereupon ensued within the enemy's works. The light infantry were about giving way, when a large body of the enemy advanced to their aid with fixed bayonets. Morgan was consequently forced to retire or meet certain destruction. Here General Arnold, who, although without command, had rendered himself very conspicuous during the day, plunging recklessly into every danger, as if courting death, received a severe wound in the leg, and had his horse shot under him.

The efforts of the American troops were more successful in other quarters. Colonel Brooks's regiment, having gained the rear of the enemy early in the action, had advanced, and assaulted the defences of the German corps, under Colonel Breyman. At the same moment, General Learned led his brigade against the Canadians, posted at the left of the Germans. Success crowned the effort of both these officers. The Canadians, after a slight resistance, broke and fled ; and the Germans, now attacked on all sides, were soon obliged to abandon their works, leaving behind them, besides a large number of killed and wounded, their tents, baggage, and artillery, and the body of their commander, who was killed in the contest. General Burgoyne, finding that the Germans had abandoned their position, ordered the works to be recovered ; but either from the approach of night, or the discouragement of his troops, the order was not obeyed. Colonel Brooks and General Learned established themselves within the enemy's camp.*

Darkness at length put an end to the struggle. But the American army had won a glorious victory; one, besides, that yielded solid advantages. Among these, was the possession of a portion of the enemy's camp, affording an opening to their right and rear.

During the night, the Americans lay upon the ground, about half a mile from the British camp, in readiness to renew the contest on the return of day.

* Wilkinson, vol. i., p. 122.

The loss in this action was great on both sides; but especially so on the part of the British, whose killed, wounded and captured, amounted to upwards of four hundred men. General Frazer, Sir Francis Clark, and Colonel Breyman were killed, and Majors Ackland and Williams, and Quarter-master-general Money were wounded and taken prisoners. The killed and wounded of the Americans amounted to about two hundred and fifty in all. Of the former, none were of a higher rank than a subaltern, and of the latter, a few only of the officers, among the rest, General Arnold. Besides the spoils of the German camp, and the artillery, a large quantity of ammunition had been obtained, the want of which had been seriously felt in the American camp for some time previously.

Morgan, upon his return to head-quarters the same night, was met by Gates, who immediately embraced him, saying,

"Morgan, you have done wonders this day. You have immortalized yourself, and honored your country; if you are not promoted immediately, I will not serve another day!"

Feeling at the moment a preference for pudding over praise, Morgan merely replied,

"For God's sake, general, forbear this stuff, and give me something to eat and drink, for I am ready to die with hunger, fatigue and exhaustion."*

The expectations entertained by the American army of completing the ruin of their opponents on the next morning, were disappointed. The British had silently abandoned their camps during the night, and removed to a position running parallel with the river, their wings being displayed on commanding eminences. For some distance in front of this position, the ground was low and very uneven, and intersected by a number of small streams, the banks of which were covered with a thick undergrowth. Advancing towards the lines, the land ascended, became clear of underbrush, and was thinly covered with trees. The position was

* MSS. of Dr. Hill.

judiciously chosen, and well calculated to resist an attack, even of the whole American force. Burgoyne saw the impossibility of maintaining his old camp, a portion of which was already in the hands of his assailants.* He hoped, besides, by a change of front, to force the Americans to dispositions of their forces less advantageous than those already made. Conjecturing that they would continue to press him closely, the strength of the new position might safely promise him successful defence, if not a victory, in case of an assault. General Gates partook of the general disappointment; but he was too cautious to realize the expectations of his opponent. He declined the battle proffered him; but he took more certain, if not more speedy measures, to bring about the overthrow of the enemy.

The next morning the American army took possession of the deserted British camp. In anticipation of the enemy's retreat, Gen. Fellowes's brigade had been thrown across the river the day previously, with orders to proceed to Saratoga, and to take such a position in the vicinity of that place, as would check such a movement if attempted. Morgan was now ordered to advance with his corps, in the same direction, on the west side of the river, fronting the enemy's lines, and endeavor to turn their right. In the execution of this order, his flanking parties fell in with a body of British provincials, who had been thrown forward to make a reconnoissance. These, after a short encounter, were put to flight, and driven under the protection of the cannon in their camp.†

No provisions had been served out to the American forces for two days, and it became necessary that they should return to their entrenched camp, to obtain a fresh supply. They accordingly marched in that direction on the evening of the 8th. Burgoyne, in the mean time, had determined upon a retreat, and at about the same hour that the Americans returned to their camp, he put his troops in motion for Saratoga. He left behind him a number

---

* Wilkinson, vol. i., p. 279.   † Ibid., vol. i., pp. 279—281.

of bateaux, laden with military stores, besides his hospital, containing 300 sick, who were recommended to Gates's care and protection.* He reached Dove-Cote the next morning, and halting at this point for a short time, proceeded on, and arrived at Saratoga on the evening of the 9th. Upon reaching this place, he found Gen. Fellowes's brigade on the opposite side of the river, strongly entrenched, and ready to dispute his passage; while, hovering upon his left, was the rifle regiment and its redoubtable leader, observing his movements, and ready to seize any advantage which might be afforded them. Remaining at Saratoga during the night, the next morning he crossed Saratoga Creek, a small stream emptying into the Hudson, and commenced the formation of an entrenched camp on the heights above the village. In this camp the English infantry were placed; the grenadiers and the Germans occupying a line of entrenchments upon the heights running parallel with the river.†

The main part of the American army having recovered from their fatigues, and prepared themselves for fresh encounters, advanced from their camp on Behmus Heights for Saratoga on the 10th, and reached the vicinity of that place the same afternoon. A party of the enemy was busily engaged at this time in unloading the bateaux which were lying at the mouth of Saratoga Creek, and transporting their contents into the camp. A couple of pieces of artillery were brought to bear on this party, the fire of which, seconded by that of a body of militia, forced it to retire, and a number of bateaux were captured. These measures drew a heavy fire from the British camp, which compelled the assailants to relinquish their prizes, and return to the main body.

The American army took post along the south bank of Saratoga Creek, Lincoln's command on the right, and Gates's on the left Morgan's corps was thrown forward in observation ‡

* Wilkinson, p. 282.
† Ibid, vol. i., p. 283.   Marshall's Wash., vol. i., p. 205.
Wilkinson, vol. i., p. 285.

Burgoyne at length meditated a general retreat. He sent a body of artificers forward, under a strong guard, to repair the bridges and open the road to Fort Edward, on the west side of the river. No sooner had this body left the camp, than it was menaced by Morgan with an attack; and it was ultimately forced to return without effecting anything. This and other circumstances convinced Burgoyne, that to effect a retreat with his baggage and stores, in the face of the American army, was impossible. Hereupon he resolved on a night march to Fort Edward, leaving everything behind but his arms and provisions. Could he succeed in crossing the ford near the fort, or that a few miles above, he thought he might yet extricate himself from the perils which environed him, and reach Fort George. A council of officers approved of this scheme, and the necessary preparations were made for putting it into execution, when it became known that the Americans had gathered in force at these fords and entrenched themselves, and that they, moreover, possessed a strong camp on the high ground, between Fort George and Fort Edward, with several pieces of cannon.*

The condition of the British army was now hopeless beyond expression. All thoughts of effecting a retreat were henceforward abandoned; and most unwillingly, Burgoyne was forced to look capture in the face.

On the morning of the 11th, a movement was made against the British entrenchments, which might have been followed by disastrous consequences to the Americans, had not the mistake in which it originated, been discovered in time. General Gates, believing either that the scheme of retreat, which had come to his ears, was about being carried into effect, or that the small British detachments which had been sent forward to reconnoitre, were really the main body of the British army, determined to storm their camp, and then push rapidly forward early the next day. With this intention, the left and centre of the army were ordered

* Marshall's Wash., vol. i., p. 206.

to cross the creek, and advance on the Albany road, while Morgan's regiment, followed by the brigades of Learned and Patterson, received directions to keep to the left along the heights. The riflemen had advanced some distance in the direction of the British camp, groping through a thick fog, when they were discovered by one of the enemy's pickets, which fired upon them, and immediately retired out of view. By this discharge, Lieut. Harrison and two men were killed, and three more wounded. Uncertain as to his position, and doubting the supposed retreat of the British, Morgan determined to await the arrival of the brigades in his rear, before he advanced any further. The desired junction had already been effected, when a heavy firing was heard in the direction of the Albany road. One of the standing orders of the army being to fall on the enemy at all points, in the event of their making a demonstration in any quarter, Morgan, Learned and Patterson, immediately advanced with their respective commands, towards the enemy's fortified camp. They had approached within two hundred yards of this point, when Col. Wilkinson galloped up, and declaring that the enemy's movements had been mistaken, begged them to halt. While hesitating as to the steps to be taken, the fog suddenly rose, and disclosed the enemy in battle array, waiting to receive them. They instantly retired to the protection of the woods, before reaching which, the enemy opened a heavy fire, killing and wounding several officers and men.

The contest on the right revealed Gates's error. The troops were in the act of crossing the creek, when they were received by the enemy with such firmness and in such numbers, as, taken with other circumstances, to leave no doubt that the latter still held their ground.

The American army resumed its position on the south bank of Saratoga Creek, all excepting Patterson's and Learned's brigades, and Morgan's corps. Patterson and Learned took strong positions on the the north bank of the Creek, in the rear of the

8

British entrenched camp, threatening at the same time the Germans and grenadiers. Morgan was posted on the left of these brigades, menacing the enemy's retreat, and observing the Albany road.*

We are now rapidly approaching the denouement of this memorable campaign. The few days which preceded the capitulation, passed without the occurrence of any thing remarkable. The fire on the British was unceasing, however. The roar of cannon followed their appearance in every quarter, and musket balls were continually showered into all parts of their camp.

On the 13th, General Burgoyne opened a correspondence with General Gates, with the object of settling the terms of a capitulation. It was proposed, in reply, that the British army should surrender as prisoners of war, and that they should ground their arms in their encampment. Burgoyne refused to comply with these demands, and intimated to Gates that if they were persisted in, the treaty was to end, and hostilities to recommence immediately. It was at length agreed, among other less important stipulations, that the British army, after marching out of their encampment with all the honors of war, should lay down their arms; that they should not serve against the United States until exchanged; and that they were to be permitted to return to England as soon as the necessary preparations to convey them thither were made.

Matters had progressed thus far, when Burgoyne received such favorable accounts of Sir Henry Clinton's operations on the Hudson, as to revive hope in his breast, and to tempt him to delay the ratification of the convention, or to recede from it altogether. But General Gates promptly met the emergency. On the morning of the 17th, the army was placed under arms, and General Burgoyne was notified, that as the time had arrived when he must either ratify or dissolve the agreement, an immediate and decisive answer was required. The articles were at

* Wilkinson, vol. i., pp. 285-289.

length returned to Gates, bearing the signature of the British commander.*

On the day of the capitulation, the effective force of the American army amounted to about twelve thousand men. The number of the British who surrendered, was five thousand seven hundred and ninety-one. Thirty-five pieces of brass artillery, five thousand stand of arms, and a large quantity of ammunition and military stores were hereby acquired.

On the next morning, the prisoners, accompanied by a guard, took up their march for Boston.†

Thus terminated a campaign, from which the British government anticipated the most decisive results. Thus fell an army, which, confident even to recklessness in its strength, overthrew or disregarded the impediments of its early career, spread death and desolation in its path, and impressed the minds of all patriots with fearful misgivings of the result. But a brighter destiny was reserved for the country, then struggling to defend itself against what must have been ever after a degrading vassalage; and to purchase with the blood of its bravest a place among the nations of earth. A better recompense was in store for the noble band who survived the fearful struggle, when a free and grateful people would honor the graves and perpetuate the memory of those who fell in their defence. It was not until this period in the history of the American war, that the British government or people could be brought to believe that the Americans possessed any warlike qualities. It never entered into their minds that their best and bravest could find themselves overmatched by these despised colonists; and that whether in the woods or on the plain, all claims to superiority must be relinquished, from the evidence of stern, and to them, humiliating results. This severe lesson was taught them at length, and by one, too, whose competency to judge, few would be willing to dispute. Gen. Burgoyne, in his " Review of the evidence taken before the House of Commons," in relation to

* Wilkinson, vol. i., pp. 298-317.   † Ibidem.

his surrender at Saratoga, and referring to the fact that Morgan's
regiment drove the British light infantry from the field, and subsequently attacked them in their entrenchments, observes, "If
there can be any person who, after considering that circumstance;
and the positive proof of the subsequent obstinacy in the attack
on the post of Lord Balcarras, and various other actions of the
day, continue to doubt that the Americans possess the *quality*
and *faculty* of fighting (call it by whatever term they please)
they are of a prejudice, that it would be very absurd longer to
contend with."

When it is considered that the glory of this campaign was
largely shared in, by a number of gallant leaders and their commands, most of whom found frequent opportunities during the
struggle to distinguish themselves; so honorable a testimony as
this from Gen. Burgoyne, in reference to Col. Morgan and his
corps, speaks volumes in their praise, and is significant of the
superiority which he assigned them. But we are not left to
inferences regarding his opinion of this corps. On his introduction to Morgan, after the capitulation, he took him warmly by
the hand, with the observation, "Sir, you command the finest
regiment in the world."

Yet, notwithstanding the important services which Col. Morgan rendered in this campaign—services which won him the
praises of the army, and made his name familiar with friends and
foes, throughout the country—they were not deemed worthy of
more than a cursory notice in the general's dispatches. His
name was not even mentioned in the official account of the
surrender, to the accomplishment of which he had contributed so
largely. This was the more extraordinary, from the fact that the
General's conduct towards Col. Morgan, from his first arrival at
camp, to the surrender, evinced a high degree of confidence in his
military character, and a friendly regard for him personally.
Before a week elapsed, after the closing scene of the campaign,
however, this conduct had undergone a total change. Gates not

only denied Morgan common justice in his communications to Congress, but in their official and personal intercourse, treated him with marked reserve.

The clue to this otherwise inexplicable circumstance is probably furnished in the following anecdote, related by Morgan himself. Immediately after the surrender, Morgan visited Gates on business, when he was taken aside by the general, and confidentially told that the main army was extremely dissatisfied with the conduct of the war by the commander-in-chief, and that several of the best officers threatened to resign, unless a change took place. Morgan perfectly understood the views of Gates, in this conference, although he was then a stranger to the correspondence which he had held with Conway and others, and sternly replied, " I have one favor to ask of you, sir, which is, never to mention that detestable subject to me again ; for under no other man than Washington, as commander-in-chief, would I ever serve."*

Gates, at this time, entertained strong hopes of being enabled to supplant General Washington in the chief command of the American armies. The combination among a number of members of Congress, and a few officers of the army, known as the "Conway Cabal," from the active part which Gen. Conway took in its machinations, had made considerable progress towards the accomplishment of their designs. But Washington was beloved by the whole army ; and who so well acquainted with his worth, and with the worthlessness of his calumniators ? The approaches of the conspirators in this quarter met with as prompt and indignant a repulse, as that which Gates experienced from Morgan.

From this time, until the spring of 1781, all intimacy between Gates and Morgan ceased. A day or two after the foregoing interchange of views, General Gates gave a dinner to the principal officers of the British army. A large number of American officers were also invited ; but Morgan was not among the number. So signal a mark of Gates's unfriendliness to Morgan, could

* Dr. Hill. Lee's Memoirs, 428..

not pass unobserved, either by himself, or by his brother officers. The cause was buried in the bosoms of the parties themselves, and conjecture, though wide spread, was at a loss to account for it. Before the entertainment was over, however, the petty indignity recoiled with severity upon its author. Morgan had occasion during the evening to seek an interview with General Gates, on business connected with his command. He was ushered into the dining-room, and having arranged the matter in hand, was permitted by the general to withdraw, without even the empty ceremony of an introduction to the British officers present. A number of the latter, struck by the commanding figure and noble mien of the colonel, and noticing that he was a field officer, inquired his name, as soon as he had retired. On learning that it was Colonel Morgan, they instantly rose to a man from the table, overtook him in the road, and severally taking him by the hand, made themselves known to him, frankly declaring, at the same time, that they had felt him severely in the field.*

British officers had good reason to know him. He frequently told his men, whom he familiarly called his boys, to shoot at those who wore epaulettes, rather than the poor fellows who fought for sixpence a day, and the sequel proved that he was obeyed to the letter. At the first glance, many would condemn a practice of this kind, as adding unnecessarily to the sanguinary features of war. But this constitutes one of the principal arguments in its defence. Every additional horror which war acquires, lessens in a corresponding degree the likelihood of a resort to it, and thus tends to perpetuate the blessings of peace. The primary object of battles being the defeat of an opponent, few means necessary to its accomplishment are considered illegitimate. Among these, is certainly not included that whereby an adversary is struck in the most vital part, else why employ marksmen, whose business it is to exercise their skill against particular objects? Even veteran soldiers have been thrown into confusion,

* Lee's Memoirs, p. 430. Major Neville. Dr. Hill.

and become little more efficient than an undisciplined mob, by
the loss of their officers. Past and daily experience shows, that
when the way to victory lies over the dead bodies of those who
give unity and efficiency to opposition, there are few commanders
who decline the opportunity of pursuing it.

General Burgoyne, in the review already quoted, noticed this
practice, and acknowledged its effects; and the absence of all
asperity in his remarks thereupon, justifies the presumption that
he regarded it as comprehended among the legitimate usages of
war. Indeed, he employed marksmen himself, to a very considerable extent, during the campaign. " The enemy," he remarks,
" had with their army great numbers of marksmen, armed with
rifle-barrelled pieces. These, during an engagement, hovered
upon the flanks in small detachments, and were very expert in
securing themselves, and in shifting their ground. In this action
(that of the 19th September), many placed themselves in high
trees, in the rear of their own line; and there was seldom a
minute's interval of smoke in any part of our line, without officers
being taken off by single shot." Indeed, the general himself
escaped being shot by one of those riflemen, only from being mistaken for another, who received the ball. Capt. Green, an aide
to Gen. Phillips, was in the act of handing a letter to Gen.
Burgoyne, when he fell from his horse, having at the moment
received a severe wound in the arm. The rich furniture of the
aide's saddle, led the rifleman to believe that the rider was
the general. In connection with this anecdote, it is worthy
of remark, that as the officer was seen to fall from his horse, it
was, for some time, believed in the American camp, that Burgoyne had been killed.

CHAPTER X.

Morgan marches from Saratoga, southward—Gates's unwillingness to supply the commander-in-chief with reinforcements—The latter's anxiety for the return of Morgan—
The opinion of the army regarding the rifle corps and its commander—Military events
—Morgan arrives at Whitemarsh—Expedition under Cornwallis—Lafayette, with a
portion of the rifle corps, engages and defeats a body of the enemy—The British
advance to Chestnut Hill—Routs the Pennsylvania militia—Engaged by Morgan and
General Gist, with Maryland militia—The latter obliged to yield—The riflemen, after a
sanguinary conflict, retire in good order—The loss severe on both sides—Death of
Major Morris—Lafayette—His generosity towards the widow and orphans of Morris—
The American army goes into winter quarters—Disposition of troops—Foraging expedition of the enemy—Morgan in observation, has repeated skirmishes with them—
Hardships he encountered from hunger, cold and want of rest—The enemy return to
Philadelphia—The distressing situation of the American army—Morgan leaves his com-
mand on a short visit home—His reception.

On the 1st of November, Colonel Morgan received orders to
march with his regiment southward, and to lose no time in joining the commander-in-chief, in compliance with the express
directions of the latter. As the rifle corps had been in readiness
to move for some days previously, it started immediately. It was
soon after followed by the brigades of Generals Poor, Warner,
Patterson and Learned, and the regiment of Colonel Van Schaick.
These forces amounted to about five thousand five hundred men,
which, when added to those already, or about, operating on
the Hudson, and in New Jersey and Pennsylvania, would make
the army under the commander-in-chief about ten thousand
strong.

Although, by the capture of Burgoyne, the war had terminated
in the north, General Gates evinced a great disinclination to com-

ply with the urgent demands of the commander-in-chief, for reinforcements. The army under Gates's command, at the time of
the surrender, was three times greater than that with which
Washington was contending against a superior force in Pennsylvania and New Jersey. It was vitally important that a portion,
at least, of this large force, now no longer employed, should be
brought to the aid of the commander-in-chief, that he might be
enabled to make head against the enemy, and to carry out the
plan of operations which had been determined on. Col. Hamilton was accordingly sent from head-quarters to Gen. Gates, with
directions to explain to that officer the nature of this plan, and to
facilitate the forwarding of the required reinforcements. The
troops already mentioned had started southward some days before
the arrival of Col. Hamilton. But the force they composed was
much below that which the commander-in-chief had a right to
expect; and even of this, the term of service of a large proportion
would soon expire. It was not until Hamilton invoked the high
authority with which he was invested, that Gates consented to
augment the reinforcements already sent forward, with the brigade
of Gen. Glover, which thereupon received orders to march southward.[*]

Washington, in his letter of instructions to Col. Hamilton on
this occasion, exhibits much anxiety for the return of his favorite
rifle regiment. "I expect," he says, "you will meet Col. Morgan
and his corps upon the way down. If you do, let them know
how essential their services are to us, and desire the Colonel, or
commanding officer, to hasten his march as much as is consistent
with the health of his men, after their late fatigues."[†]

In nearly all the letters which Morgan received while at the
North, from his friends in the main army, congratulations on his
successes were coupled with regrets for his absence. In a letter
from Captain (afterwards Colonel) Heth, dated 30th September,

1777, the writer observes: "You have been greatly wished for since the enemy's landing at the head of the Elk." In another letter, from Col. Febriger, written shortly after, occurs the following passage: "It is generally believed that some of the severest reverses we have lately experienced might have been obviated, could we have had the co-operation of yourself and your gallant corps."

Short as was the lapse of time since Morgan departed for the North, it had given birth to a number of events, amid the scenes of his previous operations, most of them disastrous, and all of them important. The battle of Brandywine had been fought; Wayne suffered a surprise from the "no flint General" Gray, and lost three hundred men. The battle of Germantown succeeded, the enemy having previously entered Philadelphia. The attempt which was made to take the fort at Red Bank, was nobly repulsed by Col. Green, Morgan's old companion in arms, with a loss to the assailants, of four hundred men and their commander, Count Donop. This fort, however, as well as the one erected on Mud Island, was subsequently evacuated; and thus, a free communication by the Delaware was at length established between the British army and navy.

Sir Henry Clinton, with between three thousand and four thousand men, had commenced operations on the Hudson, with the intention of reducing the posts on its banks, and of forming a junction with Burgoyne. He out-generaled the brave old Putnam, and captured forts Montgomery and Clinton. Forts Independence and Constitution were thereupon evacuated by the Americans. Esopus and Continental Village were wantonly burned by the British. Sir Henry, was still moving forward, when on the 26th October, he received intelligence of Burgoyne's surrender. He immediately beat a retreat. The same day, forts Montgomery and Clinton were evacuated, and the British army soon after embarked, and proceeded down the river towards New York.

The withdrawal of the enemy from the fortifications on the

Hudson was followed by a distribution of the American forces which had concentrated at Peekskill. A large body moved down the west bank of the river, and took post at Haverstraw; one thousand men were stationed in the Highlands, to guard the country and repair the works; and the remainder marched down on the east side of the river towards Kingsbridge. The object proposed by these dispositions was to hold in check the enemy in New York, and prevent a reinforcement from being sent to Gen. Howe. It was also an ulterior purpose to attack that city, should a favorable opportunity present itself.*

Morgan, in the meantime, was advancing with his corps in all haste towards the head-quarters of the commander-in-chief, then at Whitemarsh. He had marched to Albany, where, having embarked his men, their baggage, &c., in a number of sloops, he arrived in a few days at Peekskill. From this point he advanced without delay, and arrived at Whitemarsh about the 18th of November.

The fatigues of the preceding campaign, when added to those of the long-forced march which had just been performed, had caused much sickness in the regiment, and rendered most of its members unable immediately to perform duty. The men were generally without the clothing, shoes, blankets, and other essentials to their taking the field on the opening of a northern winter. But the rifle corps was composed of no common materials.

A few days were passed by the troops in recruiting their strength, and in having their want of clothing as far as possible supplied, when they evinced a readiness to take a part in the momentous operations then going forward.

On the morning of the 17th of November, Cornwallis, at the head of two thousand men, left Philadelphia, with the object, after forming a junction with a body of troops from New York, then at Chester, of reducing Fort Mercer. Upon receiving intelligence of this movement, the commander-in-chief communicated it

* Sparks's Writings of Washington, vol. v., p. 124.

to Gen. Varnum, who commanded the fort, with orders to that officer, to hold out to the last extremity. Gen. Huntington's brigade was immediately detached to reinforce Gen. Varnum; an express was sent to Gen. Glover, then marching with his brigade through New Jersey from the north, to file off to the left for the same purpose; and Gen. Green, upon whom the command of the expedition devolved, crossed the Delaware at the head of his division.

The Marquis de Lafayette accompanied this expedition, at the head of a force composed of a body of militia, and about 170 of Morgan's riflemen, being all of the corps who were fit for service at this time; the rest being unavailable from the want of shoes.*

It was hoped, by this movement, not only that the fort would be defended, but that Cornwallis would be forced to fight a superior force, under disadvantageous circumstances. Before a junction of these different bodies of troops was effected, however, Cornwallis, at the head of a force much larger than that which had been reckoned upon, advanced against the fort, which was thereupon evacuated. He then took post at Gloucester Point, and under cover of the guns of the men-of-war, transported his baggage, and the provisions he had collected, up the Delaware for Philadelphia, previously to embarking his army for the same point.

Before the departure of the British, however, Morgan's riflemen had an opportunity of adding to their enviable reputation, which was fully improved. Lafayette had obtained permission from General Green, to advance with his command, to reconnoitre Cornwallis's position. He was likewise left at liberty to make an attack, if circumstances seemed to warrant it. Cornwallis was at this time transporting his troops across the river from the Point. The marquis, accompanied by two or three officers and a guide, rode down to a point which projected some distance into the river, and commenced his observations. Being discovered by

* Sparks's Writings of Washington, vol. v., p. 167.

the enemy, a party of dragoons were sent to intercept him on his return. By good fortune, but not without some risk, he succeeded in rejoining his command. Thirsting for opportunities to distinguish himself, and as was remarked of him by Washington, " determined to be in the way of danger," he resolved to have a brush with the enemy before he returned to camp. A scouting party was accordingly pushed forward towards the British camp on the Point, to make observations. This party speedily returned with the information, that a picket guard of three hundred and fifty Hessians, with three field pieces, was posted at a position a short distance in front, and about two miles and a half from the British camp. The marquis immediately led his men against the picket, which after a few minutes' hard fighting, was forced to fly. He followed the enemy closely, and, as remarked by himself in his account of the affair to the commander-in-chief, " made them run very fast." " British reinforcements came twice to their aid," he added, " but very far from recovering their ground, they always retreated." In this engagement the enemy lost from twenty to thirty killed, and had about forty wounded. The pursuit did not cease till they had gained their camp, one or two of their men having fallen within its precincts. The loss of the Americans was but one man killed, and six wounded. The marquis represented the conduct of the riflemen as above all praise. " I never saw men," he declared, " so merry, so spirited, and so desirous to go on to the enemy, whatever force they might have, as that small party in this little fight." *

A few days elapsed, when it became known that General Howe meditated an attack upon the American camp. On the night of the 5th of December, this officer moved from Philadelphia with all his forces, excepting a very inconsiderable portion, which was left in his lines and redoubts. Capt. McLane, who had been sent forward with one hundred chosen men to watch the enemy, dis

* Sparks's Writings of Washington, vol. v., pp. 171, 172.

covered them on the advance, at a place called Three Mile Run,
and compelled their front division to change their line of march.
They passed forward, however, and appeared the next morning on
Chestnut Hill, in front of, and about three miles distant from, the
right wing of the American army. As soon as the position of
the enemy was ascertained, the Pennsylvania militia, posted on
the right of the American lines, were ordered to move forward
and skirmish with the enemy's light parties. The militia
advanced as directed; but after a slight engagement, they fled
the field in disorder, leaving behind them, wounded and a
prisoner, their commander, Gen. Irvine. The enemy changed
their ground during the night, appearing on the next morning,
advantageously posted, upon the left and within a mile of the
American lines. They remained in this position during the
whole of the 7th. The next day they inclined further to the left,
and in doing so, approached still closer to the American left.*

Appearances favored the belief that the enemy were determined
upon an action. The commander-in-chief, being equally ready to
meet them, if his inferiority in strength could be made up by
advantage of position, took his measures accordingly. Morgan
was ordered to move forward with his regiment, and attack the
advanced and flanking parties of the enemy. Similar orders were
given to Colonel Gist, who commanded the Maryland militia. A
few minutes elapsed, after Morgan had disposed his troops for
action, and put them in motion, when a considerable body of the
enemy were discovered marching down the side of a gentle slope.
At the same moment a fire was heard a short distance to the right,
which indicated that the Maryland militia were engaged. The
riflemen needed no stimulus, of words or example, to urge them
on to the attack. Never yet had they failed in driving before
them an opponent who was not vastly their superior in numbers.
They rushed on with their accustomed impetuosity and disregard
of peril. Delivering a general and well-directed fire, which spread

* Marshall's Washington. vol. i., p. 183

death broadcast in the ranks of the British column, they rapidly advanced to a closer encounter. Before the enemy could recover from the surprise, occasioned by an exhibition of such extraordinary vigor, another volley, which fell with crushing effect upon their ranks, filled them with dismay, when, after an ineffectual discharge or two, they broke into disorder and fled. Regardless of consequences, and wild with the excitement of battle, Morgan and his men fiercely pursued the fugitives. The latter had crossed the slope, when they were met by a column of British infantry, which was hastily advancing in the direction of the fire. The discomfited British immediately rallied, and the contest was now renewed with great spirit. The riflemen, nothing daunted by the presence of twice their numbers, returned the heavy fire of the enemy with the utmost resolution. Taking cover from the trees which occupied the ground rather thickly, they were screened from the enemy's shot which was showered upon them like rain; while, on the other hand, the unerring rifle seldom failed to speed a messenger of death. But the militia under Colonel Gist, who had fallen in with, and engaged a body of, the enemy, at about the same moment when the action commenced in this quarter, had been obliged to fly. Their victorious opponent, now advancing, threatened Morgan's flank and rear. Thus at the moment when victory was about to declare itself in his favor, Morgan was forced to order a retreat. The troops were drawn off in perfect order, and without experiencing any additional loss. So severely had the enemy suffered, that they did not advance a single step in pursuit.

The severe reception which the British received in this affair, probably admonished their commander of the danger of too far tempting a general engagement, and he returned to Philadelphia the next day. If the American army had exhibited a degree of resolution, at all comparable to that which was displayed by the rifle corps, it would have enabled the commander-in-chief to place General Howe in quarters far less agreeable than those to which that officer retired.

In this engagement, the slaughter of the enemy was unparalleled, considering the strength of the respective forces engaged. The precise amount of their loss has never been ascertained, however. One account from Philadelphia, soon after received, stated the number of wounded who were brought to that city, at five hundred ; and another represented that eighty-two wagons had arrived there, filled with dying and disabled men.* Although these accounts may have been somewhat exaggerated, it is nevertheless susceptible of proof, that during the period between the appearance of the enemy at three Mile Run, and their return to Philadelphia, they incurred a loss of three hundred and fifty killed and wounded. As the encounter just described was the only one, during this incursion of the enemy, in which the loss on either side was considerable, it is fair to presume, that, at least, two hundred of their numbers fell on this occasion, by the rifles of Morgan's regiment.

But, on the other hand, the rifle corps had suffered severely. Twenty-seven of their number were either killed or wounded ; and among the latter, but beyond all hope of recovery, was the noble-hearted and intrepid Major Morris. This officer, from the soldier-like qualities displayed by him on a variety of occasions, had attracted the attention and favor of the commander-in-chief; and upon the organization of the rifle corps, he was appointed its major. He possessed a disposition the most kind and generous, and a courage which no danger could shake, no misfortune could diminish. He enjoyed the confidence and regard of all who knew him ; and by the officers and men of the corps, with whom he had so often shared in the dangers and the glories of the war, he was deeply beloved. His death, which occurred a short time after this encounter, excited universal sorrow throughout the camp, and was the occasion of an act of generosity on the part of Lafayette, which is well worthy of being recorded here.

Upon the return of the rifle corps, from the North, Lafayette, brave himself, and admiring bravery in others, sought the

* Sparks's Writings of Washington, vol. v., pp. 182–182.

acquaintance of its officers. They met his advances with cordiality, and he was soon regarded by them all with warm affection. Between Morgan and Lafayette, the intimacy rapidly ripened into friendship, which existed during their lives, and even survived the grave, for it was cherished by their descendants with an ardor little abated by time or distance. A feeling equally generous had sprung up between the marquis and Major Morris ; and the death of the major, when considered in connection with the distresses which his bereaved wife and children must now encounter, thrown on the world, unprotected and penniless, gave Lafayette extreme pain. It soon occurred to him, that the most acceptable offering which could be made to the memory of his departed friend, would be to mitigate the sorrows of the unfortunate widow and orphans. Filled with this idea, he addressed the following letter to Morgan, every sentence of which was dictated by the generous and elevated impulses which habitually swelled his truly noble heart.

* * * 1777.

DEAR SIR: I just now received your favor concerning our late friend Major Morris, and I need not repeat to you how much I am concerned in the interests of his family. I spoke the other day to his Excellency on the subject, and I shall write to Congress a very particular letter, where you will be mentioned. I intend to speak as in your name, and that of all your corps, and as being myself honored with their confidence. It is my opinion that a decent estate might be given to the family, as a mark of gratefulness from their country, and that his son must be promoted as soon as possible. But, my dear sir, you know how long Congress waive any matter whatsoever before a decision ; and, as Mrs. Morris may be in some want before that time, I am going to trouble you with a commission, which I beg you will execute with the greatest secrecy. If she wanted to borrow any sum of money in expecting the arrangements of Congress, it would not become a stranger, unknown to her, to offer himself for that purpose. But you could (as from yourself) tell her that you had friends, who, being in the army, don't know what to do with their money, and as they are not in the mercantile or husbandry way, would willingly let her have one or many thousand dollars, which she might give again in three or four years, &c., &c.,

One other way could be to let her believe that you have got or borrowed the money from any town or body you will be pleased to mention ; or it would be needless to mention where it comes from.

In a word, my dear sir, if with the greatest secrecy, and the most minute regard for that lady's delicacy, you may find a manner of being useful to her, I beg you would communicate to me immediately.

I shall, as soon as possible, let you know the answer of Congress, whenever an answer will be got, and in expecting the pleasure to hear from you, I have the honor to be, very sincerely,

Your most obedient servant,
MARQUIS DE LAFAYETTE.

COL. MORGAN, *of the Rifle Corps.*

It will, doubtless, please the readers to be informed that Lafayette's benevolent intentions were fully carried into effect. The sorrows of the widow were relieved from the superaddition of want, and the orphans felt less sensibly their bereavement, from the munificence of their father's friend.

The vacancy in the regiment created by the death of Major Morris, was filled by Captain Posey, who was promoted to a majority.

A few days after the action at Chestnut Hill, the American army moved from their camp at Whitemarsh, and went into winter quarters at Valley Forge. The position of the new camp was admirably calculated to keep the enemy in check, and to afford the garrison the utmost security against danger. It greatly obstructed the intercourse between the city and the country, threatened the British army with the want of subsistence, and rendered their foragings to supply their necessities, extremely hazardous. Lastly, it guarded the country against the incursions of a ruthless enemy, and stayed the hand of the despoiler.

The more effectually to carry out these objects, several bodies of troops were detached from the camp to distant points in various directions. General Smallwood marched with his division and took post at Wilmington ; and General Armstrong, with the

Pennsylvania militia, was stationed near the old camp at White-marsh. Major Jameson, with two troops of cavalry, and the infantry under Captain McLane, guarded the east; and Captain Lee with his corps of horse, the west side of the Schuylkill. Morgan and his corps were placed in advance on the lines, on the west side of the Schuylkill, with the directions to intercept all supplies going to the city, and to keep a close eye on the movements of the enemy.*

A week had scarcely elapsed, after these arrangements had been made, when a strong body of the enemy left Philadelphia, and advanced towards Derby ; with the intention, as it afterwards appeared, of removing a large quantity of forage which had been collected on the island, above the mouth of Derby Creek. Intelligence of this movement first reached Colonel Morgan, then posted with the main body of his regiment in the neighborhood of Derby. Having sent an express to Head Quarters with the information,† Morgan advanced with his regiment to observe the enemy, and, if circumstances warranted an attack, to make it. But they were found to be so strong, and to conduct their march with so much circumspection, as to render it hazardous to assault them with an inferior force. These facts having been communicated to head-quarters, Morgan was soon after joined by Captain Lee's cavalry, a troop of Count Pulaski's horse, and a number of small detachments from the main army. He now determined to approach the enemy, and, if possible, to strike them a blow. Having appointed Radnor Meeting, as a place of rendezvous, in case of a repulse, he sent out a number of small parties to scout around the detachment of the enemy. But the severe losses which the latter had recently sustained, in petty encounters, had

* Marshall's Washington, vol i., p. 213.

† In a letter from Col. Morgan to General Washington, dated 23d December, 1777, the Col. observes :—

"An honest looking Quaker just now came to me and informed me that he was up and saw the number of the enemy that is now out. He thinks of the light infantry there was about a thousand, with four field pieces. He thinks there is more of the battalions out than has been before. They were going out from four o'clock yesterday morning, till eleven."

taught them caution, and convinced them that any indiscretion on their part would not pass unobserved, or unimproved, by Morgan. The troops which covered the foraging parties were in such numbers and so compactly arrayed—aided, besides, by several pieces of artillery—as to afford little or no opportunity for an attack, except at a great disadvantage.

But although the main body of the enemy kept him at bay, his scouting parties encountered similar bodies of the enemy in the woods, posted in observation, which in every instance were either driven in or captured, with more or less loss in killed and wounded. Lieut. Col. Butler, who commanded one of these parties, fell in with a troop of the enemy's horse. He succeeded, after a short encounter, in taking ten men and twelve horses, besides retaking a man belonging to Capt. Lee's company, who had been made prisoner, an hour or two before. Two of the enemy were killed; the rest, among whom several were wounded, narrowly escaped.*

The British, having effected their object, returned to Philadelphia. They were followed some distance by our troops; but the same degree of caution which marked their movements, at first, continued to be observed, until they reached the city; consequently nothing of moment was attempted against them during the march.

During the few days which were spent in the events just detailed, the riflemen and the other troops, sent to observe the enemy, suffered severely from exposure and the want of food and rest. The weather was intensely cold. Yet the troops, posted here and there in the immediate vicinity of the enemy, did not dare to have fires at night, lest they might thereby be subjected to surprise. In consequence of this, and their distance from every place furnishing at once shelter and security, they could not sleep; and they saved themselves from perishing with cold only by keeping in constant motion.†

* Letter, 23d December, 1777.
† MSS. Life of Gen. Hull, pp. 119, 120.

It was the intention of the commander-in-chief, on being apprised of this incursion of the enemy, to advance on them in force, and if circumstances were favorable, to bring on a general engagement. The necessary directions with this end in view were given ; when it appeared that the army was unable to leave the encampment for the want of provisions, and that from this cause, the seeds of a dangerous mutiny had been sown among the soldiery. This alarming state of affairs was made the subject of a letter to the President of Congress, wherein the commander-in-chief declared, "I am now convinced beyond a doubt, that unless some great and capital change takes place in that [the commissary] line, this army must be inevitably reduced to one or the other of these three things—starve, dissolve, or disperse, in order to obtain subsistence in the best manner they can.*

A short time after this event, Morgan turned his steps homeward, with the intention of spending a few weeks of the winter in the society of his family. Lieut. Col. Butler had recently been promoted to the command of a regiment in the Pennsylvania line. The command of the riflemen, therefore, devolved upon Major Posey. Morgan's absence was partly owing to ill health. The fatigues and sufferings experienced by him in the Canadian campaign, had seriously impaired a constitution, naturally very robust. He now, for the first time, felt their effects in those ailments which eventually compelled him to retire from the service of his country, and which, having embittered his after existence, ultimately brought him to a premature grave.

He remained at home during the winter, recruiting his health, and arranging his private affairs. Both had suffered from his devotedness to the public good ; yet he cheerfully made, not only this sacrifice, but that involved in the separation from wife, children, friends, and all the endearing associations of home. But he found a recompense, among other things, in the general respect and admiration with which his neighbors regarded him.

* Sparks's Writings of Washington, vol. v., p. 197.

The words of the venerable Isaac Lane, expressed in a letter to Morgan, just before he returned to the scene of warlike operations, gave language to the prevailing sentiment with which, at this period, he was regarded by the people of Western Virginia: "A man that has so often left all that is dear to him, as thou hast, to serve thy country, must create a sympathetic feeling in every patriotic heart."

CHAPTER XI.

Morgan returns to the army—Opening of the new campaign—Abortive attempt to surprise Lafayette at Barren Hill—Morgan, with 400 volunteers, pursues the enemy—Preparations of the latter for some important movement—Consequent precautions of the commander-in-chief—Morgan's activity—His system of commanding—His aversion to flogging — Anecdotes — The enemy evacuate Philadelphia — The movements of the American army which followed—Morgan detached in aid of Gen. Maxwell—The British march to Monmouth C.H.—Morgan gains their right flank—Captures their straggling parties—Plan to ensnare him recoils on its authors—Morgan and Dickinson meditate an attack on the enemy's baggage—Change of dispositions in the British line of march—Battle of Monmouth Court-house—Morgan's disappointment at not having had a share in the conflict—Enemy retreat to Middletown, followed by Morgan—Battle between his regiment and the British rear guard—The enemy embark for New-York, and Morgan marches for New Brunswick.

EARLY in the spring, Col. Morgan left home and rejoined his regiment. The winter had furnished few occasions for a brush with the enemy. The activity of his command, and that of the other troops stationed on the lines, effectually cut off all communication between the city and the country, and the enemy were at times greatly distressed for the want of fuel, provisions, and other necessaries.*

But a new and stirring epoch in the war was about opening, wherein Morgan was destined to gather fresh laurels. Already, indications of the opening of a new campaign were observable. The enemy, early in May, were very active in making arrangements for what afterwards proved to be the evacuation of Philadelphia, while the American army, blessed at length with a supply of everything necessary to their comfort and efficiency,

* Marshall's Washington, vol. i., p. 227.

forgot their past sufferings in the joyous anticipations of a glorious future.

At the opening of the campaign of 1778, the strength of the opposing armies was nearly equal. The enemy's force was estimated at somewhat more than 16,000 men, besides cavalry and artillery. Of these, about 10,000 men were in Philadelphia, 4,000 in New-York, and 2,000 in Rhode Island. The American force amounted to about 15,000 men, besides horse and artillery Of these, 11,800 were at Valley Forge, and at points in the vicinity of that place, 1,400 at Wilmington, and 1,800 on the North river. When the recruits and reinforcements, then on the way to join the army, arrived, its strength was about 20,000 men.*

For some time after Morgan's arrival at Radnor, where his regiment was posted, the enemy remained quiet within the city, and nothing of moment transpired to disturb the repose of either army until the 20th of May, when an unsuccessful attempt was made to surprise Lafayette, and disperse the force under his command at Barren Hill. Two days previous to this affair, the marquis was appointed to the command of a considerable force, with orders to march to the enemy's lines, between the Delaware and the Schuylkill. The objects of this movement were to furnish additional security to the American camp, to interrupt the com munications with Philadelphia, to obstruct the incursions of parties of the enemy, and to obtain intelligence of their movements and designs. The detachment was composed of choice troops, and numbered upwards of two thousand men.†

In obedience to directions ‡ from head-quarters, Morgan

---

* Sparks's Writings of Washington, vol. v., p. 360.   † Ibid., p. 368.

‡ HEAD-QUARTERS, *Valley Forge, May* 17, 1778.

SIR: His excellency is sending a considerable detachment towards the enemy's lines, which will march to-morrow morning. He desires you to select fifty men of your corps, under good officers, and send them to join that detachment. It will be at Whitemarsh to-morrow afternoon, when your party will be expected. A party of Indians will join the party to be sent from your corps, at Whitemarsh, and act with them.

I am, sir, your most ob't servant,

ALEX. HAMILTON.

Col. MORGAN, *Radnor.*

detached Capt. Parr and fifty chosen men from his regiment to
join the marquis's command at Whitemarsh. He was likewise
instructed * to redouble his vigilance in guarding against a movement of the enemy, and to keep in communication with the other
detachments stationed along the lines. It soon after appeared
that there was good reason for these extraordinary precautions.

The marquis advanced without delay, and on the 18th, took
post on Barren Hill, a commanding eminence near the west bank
of the Schuylkill, and midway between Matson's ford and another
ford of the Schuylkill, some four miles below. On the night following, General Grant, at the head of five thousand men, and
Gen. Grey, with about fifteen hundred, moved in different directions from Philadelphia and advanced on the marquis's position, with the intention of intercepting his retreat to the American camp, and, through their great superiority in numbers, of
either capturing or destroying his command.† This design was
happily frustrated by the vigilance of a party of observation, composed of Captain McLane's company, Captain Parr's detachment
of the rifle corps, and a body of Indians, the whole commanded
by Captain McLane. This force was posted in advance of
Lafayette's position about one mile. At night, however, it usually
advanced towards the enemy's lines. On the morning of the
19th, Captain McLane fell in with two British soldiers, who, after
representing themselves to be deserters, informed him that Gens.
Grant and Grey had marched the evening previous, from Phila-

---

* HEAD QUARTERS, *May* 18, 1778.

SIR: I am commanded by his excellency to desire that you will now keep the most
vigilant watch over the motions of the enemy, with both foot and horse. It is particularly
requisite at this time, as a considerable detachment marched this day towards the lines,
on the other side of the river, which may, perhaps, induce the enemy to make a move
out on this side.

I am, sir, your most ob't servant,

R. R. MEADE, A.D.C.

Col. MORGAN, *Radnor.*

P.S.—You will please to consult with Col. Jackson at the Gulf, that your parties may
not fall in with each other.

† Marshall's Washington, vol. i., p. 246.

194 THE LIFE OF

delphia; the first, with the grenadiers and light infantry, on the old York road, and the last, with a body of Germans, on the Ridge road, along the Schuylkill. These combined movements, and their direction, left no doubt on the mind of Captain McLane, that the marquis was their object.* He accordingly hastened back to Barren Hill, to communicate the intelligence. In the meantime, Captain Parr, at the head of his command of riflemen, and the Indians, advanced towards the enemy. When McLane arrived at Barren Hill, the marquis had just been apprised of the dangerous proximity of Grant, and was taking measures to meet the emergency.

Although the enemy's attempt was skillfully planned, and boldly executed, the address which Lafayette displayed in extricating himself was far more praiseworthy, and won for him the commendations of the whole army. Promptly availing himself of the only avenue of escape which remained open to him, he ordered a rapid retreat to Matron's ford, and happily succeeded in crossing the river, with all his baggage and artillery, before the enemy arrived. In the performance of this movement, General Grant was betrayed into a delay, which proved fatal to the object of his expedition. As the rear of Lafayette's force filed off in haste towards the ford, the front made demonstrations as if about giving battle to the enemy. Grant hereupon halted his forces, and made preparations to meet the expected attack. In a short time, he discovered the *ruse* which had been practised on him, and hastened towards the ford. On arriving there, however, he found the marquis so advantageously posted on the opposite bank, as to render an attack too hazardous to be attempted.†

In the meantime, a very animated contest had been maintained between Captain Parr's riflemen and Indians, and the British detachment under Gen. Grey. Advancing down the Ridge road, upon the news of the enemy's approach being made known, Parr

* Wilkinson's Memoirs, vol. i., p. 831.
† Sparks's Writings of Washington, vol. v., pp. 545-547

soon after encountered their advanced guard, which he immediately attacked. The enemy, promptly deploying into line, returned the fire of Parr's party; and for some minutes, the conflict was warm and bloody, several being killed and wounded on both sides. At length, hearing a fire at some distance in his rear, and perceiving the main body of Grey's troops coming up to the support of its advance guard, Parr and his command commenced a rapid retreat, and reached Matron's ford in time to take part in the encounter which occurred there between the rear of the Americans and the van of the British. Morgan had been early advised of this incursion of the enemy,* and in the expectation of falling in with one of their parties, had marched with the main body of his corps from Radnor, for some distance down the east side of the Schuylkill. Failing to meet an opponent, he retraced his steps, and was approaching Radnor, when he was informed of the object of the movement, and of its defeat. Before the subjoined order reached him, he had marched with all haste in the direction of the marquis, whom he found encamped a few miles from Matron's ford, on the road to Valley Forge.

Here he received a note† from head-quarters, directing him to

* HEAD QUARTERS, *May 20th*, 1778.

DEAR SIR:

The enemy are out in considerable force on the other side of the Schuylkill. Their intentions are not known. His Excellency, therefore, desires that you would send out patrols towards the bridge, to see whether there is any movement that way, and march the main body of your detachment towards camp.

I am, Sir,

Your most obedient servant,

TENCH TILGHMAN, *Aid-de-Camp*.

COLONEL MORGAN, *Radnor*

† *May 20th*, 1778.

DEAR SIR:

It appears that the enemy came out with an intention to surprise the marquis; but he has crossed the river, and will be between this and the gulf this evening. His Excellency desires you will march your party and join his, and then concert a plan to cross the Schuylkill this evening, with a party of active volunteers, from two hundred to five hundred, as they may turn out, of which you are to take command. The enemy marched all the last night, and must be much fatigued, and therefore, will probably halt. If they

raise a body of from two to five hundred volunteers, and at their head to pursue the enemy. The latter, foiled in their attempt on the marquis, had commenced an immediate retreat towards Philadelphia. It was believed, however, that from the fatigues which they had undergone in their march to Barren Hill, they would probably halt or loiter on their return, and in this event, an active party might be enabled to overtake, and seriously injure them. Accordingly, Morgan's demand for volunteers having been immediately responded to by all of his regiment then on the ground, and by about one hundred more, which included some forty Indians, a body of nearly four hundred men started with him in pursuit of the retreating foe. But after an absence of two days, they returned without having been able to effect anything, the enemy, contrary to all expectations, having used the utmost expedition in returning to Philadelphia.

The active preparations of the enemy, for some object as yet unknown, now engaged the attention of the commander-in-chief; and no exertions, calculated to lead to the discovery of their intentions, were spared by him. From the first, he correctly divined this object to be the evacuation of Philadelphia; but while a doubt remained, regarding their designs, he wisely confined his action to such measures as would increase the security of his forces, and guard them against a misfortune.* The utmost vigilance was accordingly required of the officers commanding detachments in advance and on the lines, illustrations of which are furnished in the case of Col. Morgan by the number of letters to this effect, which were addressed to him

do, you may perhaps plague them, and pick up some stragglers. If any of the Indians will go over, they may be of some service.

I am your most obedient servant,

TENCH TILGHMAN, *Aid-de-Camp.*

COLONEL MORGAN, *at Radnor.*

* Sparks's Writings of Washington, vol. v., pp. 366, 377.

from head-quarters about this time.* These officers and their commands were therefore kept constantly on the alert, in the hourly expectation of some important development.

* The following are selected from a number of letters, written with the object above stated, during the exciting period just preceding the evacuation of Philadelphia.

HEAD QUARTERS, 23d *May*, 1778.

SIR: His Excellency has this instant received intelligence that the enemy means very shortly to move your way. You are therefore desired to keep the most vigilant watch, and that as near their bridge and other places as you possibly can. Should you make discoveries opposite the Fort, you will give the very earliest notice of it. This you will please to communicate to Colonel Smith, at the Gulf, and also to Col. Van Schaick.

I am, sir,

Your most obedient servant,

R. R. MEADE, A.D.C.

COL. MORGAN, *at Radnor*.

———

HEAD QUARTERS, 29th *May*, 1778. }
3 o'clock, P. M. }

DEAR SIR: We have fresh reason to believe that the enemy are prepared to move, perhaps this night. If they come out in force, General Smallwood will expect to have the intelligence from you. You are therefore to keep two of your best horse ready mounted, and dispatch them to him, one a little while after the other, for fear of accident.

I am your most obedient servant,

TENCH TILGHMAN.

COL. MORGAN, *at Radnor*.

———

COL. JAMES MC HENRY TO COLONEL MORGAN.

HEAD QUARTERS, *Valley Forge*, 17th *May*, 1778.

DEAR SIR : His Excellency is much obliged to you for your information. There is little room, from a concurrence of circumstances, all coming different ways, to doubt of their intentions to evacuate the city.

The Indians (about forty) will be either immediately put under your command, or employed on the other side of the Schuylkill.

I am sir, with much respect,

Your very humble servant.

JAMES MCHENRY.

COLONEL MORGAN, *at Radnor.*

Morgan's regiment observed the country east of Radnor, between the Schuylkill and Derby Creek to the Delaware. While the intermediate space was covered by his numerous patrolling parties of horse and foot, the main body moved from point to point, as circumstances required; and the party was fortunate indeed who passed unobserved through the line occupied by him to or from Philadelphia.

It is to be regretted that the numerous instances of his vigilance and activity during the three months preceding the evacuation of that city by the British, should remain unrecorded. Their value may be attested by the frequent and flattering acknowledgments which they elicited from the commander-in-chief—one who, be it remarked, was never prodigal of his praise. Suffice it to say, that he performed well the duty which devolved upon him, proving, besides, that, whether in the field of battle, where courage and judgment are chiefly required, or in the discharge of those military duties which call for the exercise

HEAD QUARTERS, 29th *May*, 1778.

DEAR SIR: His Excellency commands me to inform you that, as soon as ever you shall have received certain intelligence of the enemy's having evacuated Philadelphia, you are to return with the whole of your command to camp, and not to suffer a single soldier to enter the city.

I am, with great respect, Dear Sir,

Your most obedient servant,

JOHN LAURENS, A.D.C.

COL. MORGAN, *at Radnor*.

———

HEAD QUARTERS, 30th *May*, 1778.

DEAR SIR : Colonel Meade being under the necessity of going out, I have to inform you that your letter respecting Sir Henry Clinton, is received. His Excellency is highly pleased with your conduct upon this occasion. I expect you will hear, by the time this reaches you, that the troops are evacuating Philadelphia.

I am, Dear Sir,

Your most obedient servant,

JOHN FITZGERALD, A.D.C.

COLONEL MORGAN.

of vigilance, prudence, and perseverance, his claims to the character of an accomplished soldier were alike indisputable.

The high estimation in which the rifle regiment was regarded by the commander-in-chief and the army, has been sufficiently instanced. Throughout the country it was considered the *élite* of the American forces, a reputation which it had earned, not merely from its prowess in the field, but from its patience and fortitude under privations; its prompt obedience to every order, however disagreeable; its discipline; and the general good character and patriotism of its members.

Much of this was owing to the great capacity for commanding, which Morgan undoubtedly possessed; to the example which his own conduct presented for the imitation of his men; and to the great, the almost fatherly, regard with which he inspired them. In the government of his regiment, the stern and severe system invariably followed in the management of the other regiments in the continental establishment, was unknown. He appealed to the pride, rather than to the fears of his men, in obtaining from them a prompt performance of all the requirements of duty; and thus a system of government for soldiery which had so often failed in other hands, became preëminently successful in his.

He held himself accessible to his men on all suitable occasions, and encouraged them to come to him whenever they had any just cause of complaint. He knew what every soldier was entitled to, and would never suffer them to be wronged or imposed on. He took great pains to have them provided, at all times, with a sufficiency of provisions, clothing, and everything necessary to their comfort; and the wounded and sick experienced his constant attention and care. One of the effects of this policy was, that the officers and men, from the influence and example of their commander, regarded themselves as one great family, or as a band of brothers, among whom none of the austerities of the strict disciplinarian were observed. The affection with which Morgan was regarded by his men, is instanced by the fact that almost every one of those who marched under his command to Quebec, and who survived that disastrous expedition, was now to be found in the ranks of his regiment.*

He never permitted any of them to be brought before a court martial, or to be punished by whipping. When one of them was charged with an offence which called for punishment, the accused, if guilty, was taken by Morgan to some secluded place, where no one could witness what might occur, and there, after a lecture on the impropriety of his conduct, would receive a thumping, more or less severe, according to the nature of his offence.

It once happened, when Morgan was away from his camp, that one of his favorite riflemen, who had committed some misdemeanor, was brought before a court martial, condemned, and whipped in the face of the whole regiment. When Morgan returned, and was informed of what had taken place, he was so chagrined, that it is said he shed tears, and declared that he would not have had the offender whipped on any consideration whatever—that the man belonged to one of the most respectable families in his neighborhood, and was, withal, a high spirited and efficient soldier—but that he must now be so lowered in his own esteem, as to be unable ever to recover his former self-respect and pride of feeling.†

Another instance of his manner of governing may be given. There was a rough piece of road which it was necessary to have repaired ; a party of his men were accordingly sent, under the command of an ensign, to execute the work. While they were thus engaged, Morgan rode up, and saw two of them heaving at a large rock, the removal of which was evidently beyond their strength, the ensign at the same time looking on, without giving them his assistance. " Why don't you lay hold and help these men ?" inquired Morgan, addressing the ensign. "Sir," replied the latter, " I am an officer !" " I beg your pardon," responded

* MSS. Dr. Hill.   † MSS. Dr Hill.

Morgan, "I did not think of that!" Instantly alighting from his horse, he approached the rock, seizing hold of which, he exclaimed to the men whom he was assisting, "Now! heave hard my boys!" The rock was soon removed, when Morgan, without another word, mounted his horse, and rode off.*

Such was the affection with which, by these means, Morgan inspired his men for himself, and such was the confidence which they had in his judgment and bravery, that they never hesitated to engage in any enterprise, however hazardous, when he gave the order. To resume, however, our narrative.

It became apparent about the beginning of June, that the enemy intended to evacuate Philadelphia. Sir Henry Clinton had succeeded General Howe in the command of the British army in that city, when it soon became known that an early movement was determined on. Indeed, the expected arrival of D'Estaing, with a large land and naval force, rendered Sir Henry's sojourn much longer in that quarter exceedingly hazardous. It afterwards appeared that orders for the evacuation of Philadelphia had been previously issued from the British government. It likewise became known that the destination of Sir Henry Clinton's forces was New York; but whether they would proceed thither by land or sea, was still a matter of uncertainty. The British fleet, still lying in the Delaware, could, it was believed, readily take the troops and their artillery, baggage, &c., on board. But Washington, reckoning upon the fears which the British general must naturally entertain of encountering a superior French fleet on his passage, inclined to the belief that the movement would be effected across New Jersey. The correctness of this belief was subsequently confirmed by the movements of the British army.

On the morning of the 18th June, Sir Henry Clinton broke up his quarters at Philadelphia, and crossing the Delaware, advanced with his forces slowly up its northern bank. As soon

* MSS. Dr. Hill.

9*

as the intelligence of this event * was confirmed, the commander-in-chief called in all his advanced detachments, including Morgan's regiment, and made instant preparations for a rapid forward movement of his whole force into Jersey. Anticipating that Sir Henry Clinton would cross New Jersey, Washington had previously sent General Dickinson into that State, to raise the militia, and to break down the bridges, fell trees, and adopt every other expedient calculated to retard the enemy's march. General Maxwell, with the New Jersey brigade, was soon after directed to join General Dickinson. General Lee was now ordered to advance towards the Delaware, and, crossing at Corryell's Ferry, to halt upon the first strong ground he met, until further orders. Gen. Wayne, with the first and second Pennsylvania regiments, and the brigade lately commanded by General Conway, moved in the same direction. The commander-in-chief, with the main body of the army, followed. In his train marched Morgan and his corps.†

On the 22d, the army crossed the Delaware at Corryell's ferry, when measures were taken to increase the enemy's embarrassment. Col. Morgan, with his regiment and a body of volunteers, in all 600 men, were detached in aid of Gen. Maxwell.

The main body advanced towards Princetown. On the 24th June, it lay in Hopewell township. From this point, Gen. Scott, with 1,500 men, and a detachment of Col. White's cavalry, and Gen. Cadwallader, with a body of continental troops and Pennsylvania volunteers, were sent to co-operate with Gens. Maxwell and Dickinson, against the enemy's left flank and rear.‡

* HEAD QUARTERS, *Valley Forge*, 18*th June*, 1778.

SIR :—I am informed this morning, that the enemy's rear are evacuating the city. You will immediately send down a small party of horse under a good officer, on this side, in order to ascertain the matter, or to gain intelligence. The result of his inquiry you will transmit as soon as possible, and hold yourself in readiness to join this army on the first orders.   I am, sir, your very humble servant,

COLONEL MORGAN, *at Radnor*.   GEORGE WASHINGTON.

† Marshall's Washington, vol. i., pp. 248–251.

‡ Sparks's Writings of Washington, vol. v., p. 417.

The British, since their departure from Philadelphia, had progressed slowly up the right bank of the Delaware, the heat of the weather, their immense baggage train, and the impediments thrown in their path by Dickinson and Maxwell, having greatly retarded their progress. They encamped on the 24th of June in the neighborhood of Allentown.

But they had now reached a point, once beyond which, their course would be divested of all uncertainty, when it was the determination of the American chief to take vigorous measures against them. Of the three routes to New York which here presented themselves to Sir Henry Clinton, those by way of New Brunswick and South Amboy to Staten Island, and that leading to Sandy Hook, across the strong ground about Middletown, he wisely, and to the American army, very unexpectedly, chose the latter. The slowness with which he had advanced, favored the belief that he wished for battle, and that to bring a conflict on, he would run some hazard in taking the usual, but more dangerous, route towards New Brunswick. He would then be advancing on, instead of filing off, from his antagonist, as was the nature of his movement after leaving Allentown. Another effect of this manœuvre was, relatively to change the advanced and command-ing position which the American army previously occupied on Sir Henry Clinton's left, into one at some distance in his rear. His decision created much disappointment among the Americans, and no doubt greatly marred the plans which had been formed against him. Had he determined otherwise, they felt assured of conse-quences which comprehended even the capture or dispersion of his forces.

On receiving this intelligence, the commander-in-chief imme-diately dispatched one thousand select men under Gen. Wayne, to reinforce the detachments in advance, and sent Gen. Lafayette forward to take the command of all the advanced parties, with orders to seize the first fair opportunity of attacking the enemy's rear. In the evening of the same day, the main body of the army, after leaving their baggage behind, marched from Kingston, and arrived at Cranberry the next morning.

On the day previous, duplicates of the following note were sent to Morgan through Gens. Dickinson and Maxwell :

HEAD QUARTERS, *Hopewell Township, June* 24, 1778.

SIR: You are, upon the receipt of this, to take the most effectual means for gaining the enemy's right flank, and giving them as much annoyance as possible in that quarter. Among the militia annexed to your corps, Gen. Dickinson will take care that there are persons perfectly acquainted with the country and roads, so as to prevent every delay and danger which might arise from a want of intelligent guides.

I am, sir, your most ob't servant,

GEORGE WASHINGTON.

Col. MORGAN.

Before receiving these instructions, Morgan and his command had succeeded, by forced marches, in gaining a position on the enemy's right flank. On the 26th, while the British were advancing towards Monmouth, he was encamped at Squaw Swamp.* The caution with which the enemy advanced, rendered

* SQUAW SWAMP, *June* 27, 1778, 2 *o'clock.*

SIR: I arrived at this place yesterday — encamped on the woods — sent out small parties. Capt. Lowry fell in with fifteen grenadiers, and made them prisoners; deserters are continually coming in. I have several parties out, whom I expect something from. I shall continue on the enemy's right till I have orders to the contrary. They keep in so compact a body, that it is impossible to do them much damage. However, I will annoy them as much as possible.

I have the honor to be your ob't servant,

DANIEL MORGAN.

To his excellency, GEN. WASHINGTON, *Head Quarters.*

GEN. WASHINGTON TO COL. MORGAN.

HEAD QUARTERS, *Sunday*, 12½ *o'clock.*

SIR: I have just received your letter by the dragoon. As your corps is out of supporting distance, I would have you confine yourself to observing the motions of the enemy, unless an opportunity offers of intercepting some small parties, and by no means to come to an engagement with your whole body, unless you are tempted by some very evident advantage. Gen. Greene's aid-de-camp has already written you to this effect, but the orders are repeated to guard against accident.

I am, sir, your most humble servant,

GEORGE WASHINGTON.

COL. MORGAN.

an attack on his part not only hopeless of success, but, from his want of cavalry, highly dangerous. He sent out a number of small parties, however, which succeeded in bringing in a large number of stragglers and deserters. Capt. Lowry, who commanded one of these parties, fell in with a body of fifteen grenadiers, whom he made prisoners and brought into camp. To encourage desertion from the enemy's ranks, his detachments showed themselves as often as they safely could. In consequence, large numbers of British soldiers deserted, and passed through the ranks of his corps towards the interior.

On the same day, a plan was laid by the British to draw Morgan into a snare, which led to the following circumstances : During the succeeding night, a spy of the enemy, who called himself Smith, went to Morgan's camp, and pretending to be a zealous friend of independence, told him that he had a piece of information of great importance to communicate. Upon being invited to proceed, he told Morgan that a valuable portion of the enemy's baggage was collected together in a certain place on the right of their camp, protected by a very weak guard, and that he might very easily capture or destroy the whole of it during the night. Morgan at once suspected his informant to be a spy. After a moment's reflection, he said to the man, " Look at me, sir !" and then, regarding him steadily and sternly in the face, for a minute or more, he at length observed, " Now are you sure you are telling me the truth ?" Watching the effect which this inquiry might produce, he saw the man's eye fall and his countenance change. Morgan was now convinced that the man was an emissary of the enemy, and that he had been sent to draw him into a snare or ambuscade, or to work him some injury of the kind. Carefully concealing his suspicions, however, and pretending to believe all that had been communicated to him, he clapped the spy on the shoulder with an air of well assumed confidence and regard, and observed : " Well, my good friend, I am a thousand times obliged to you for your valuable information. I have to request, however, that you will be my guide to the enemy's baggage." The uneasiness which the man betrayed at the prospect of being detained as a guide, gave further grounds for the belief that he was playing a treacherous part. He was speedily re-assured, however, upon being informed by Morgan, that as he was a good friend to his country, he would be placed under no restraint, but might go where he pleased. Before he left the camp, it was agreed that he should return the next morning at four o'clock, to conduct Morgan to the enemy's baggage.

Smith started directly to the British camp, where, having communicated the information that the riflemen were to attack their baggage train at four o'clock the next morning, formidable preparations were made to receive them. This was in perfect accordance with Morgan's conjectures and wishes. There was a considerable body of the enemy, which, he had been informed by his scouts, had taken possession of a mill, situated about a mile from the place where he was expected to appear the next morning. This body he determined to attack, while the enemy's attention was engaged in a different quarter. A short time before the appointed hour, Morgan drew up his men and marched towards the mill. Just at the time when the troops lying in ambush for him were looking for his arrival, they heard the crack of his rifles in the distance. He soon silenced the troops at the mill, took them all prisoners, and marched them off without loss or difficulty.

So cleverly had Morgan availed himself of the treachery which the enemy had employed against him, that they now believed that it had been directed against themselves. Nothing could convince them that Smith was not a spy in Morgan's employ. Without ceremony they strung him up by the neck to the limb of a tree, and marched off, leaving him hanging there.*

Everything at this time indicated that a struggle was

* MSS. of Гr Hill.

approaching. As the enemy advanced towards Monmouth, Morgan hung on their right flank, and Dickinson on their left, while pressing on their rear were the other advanced detachments, which had been reinforced the day before by two brigades, the whole being under the command of General Lee. In the meantime, the commander-in-chief, with the main body of the army, pressed forward, to be within supporting distance of the advance, should it need assistance.

Sir Henry Clinton, apprehensive for the safety of his baggage, had reversed the previous disposition of his line, placing his best troops in the rear, and his baggage train in front. In this order he arrived at, and encamped on, a piece of ground of great natural strength, in the neighborhood of Monmouth Court House, on the evening of the 27th.

It had been concerted between General Dickinson and Colonel Morgan to avail themselves of the first favorable occasion for attacking, and if possible, destroying, the enemy's baggage train. In pursuance of this object, they had been constantly on the alert, awaiting only the diversion created by a battle between the American advance and the British rear, to make the attack. Up to the evening of the 27th, no such opportunity had been afforded them. Knowing as they did, however, that another day would not pass without a conflict, they felt assured that the moment was at hand when they could carry their scheme into execution.

About five o'clock on the morning of the 28th, the enemy's baggage train, guarded by a strong force under Gen. Knyphausen, commenced moving from Monmouth towards Middletown. This fact having been communicated to head-quarters, Dickinson and Morgan put their respective forces in motion, the one on the left, and the other on the right of the British line of march. An hour or two elapsed, and some miles had been traversed, when it became known to Morgan and Dickinson that Sir Henry Clinton was still at Monmouth Court House with the main body of his forces, and that appearances indicated that he would remain there for some time longer. His object, it afterwards appeared, was to enable Knyphausen to get well in advance with the baggage, before he put the rear in motion.

This arrangement disconcerted Morgan and Dickinson in their designs on the enemy's baggage; for to continue following it under these circumstances would endanger their communications with head-quarters, and this would be a great risk as well as a violation of orders. On the other hand, to return would be equivalent to an abandonment of their scheme, for Knyphausen would reach the neighborhood of Middletown before night, in which event he would be beyond the reach of danger. While in this dilemma, however, they were apprised of the advance of the rear division of the British, and directed to halt and make preparations for an attack.

Washington had determined to seize the moment when the enemy should move from Monmouth to assail them in force. As soon as he was informed that their front was in motion, he sent orders to General Lee to attack them, "unless there should be very powerful reasons to the contrary ;" and marched with the main body to the support of the advanced division. Accordingly, when Sir Henry Clinton moved from Monmouth, he was followed into the plain by Lee. A party of about fifteen hundred men covered the rear of the enemy. Wayne was pushed forward to engage this party, while Lee, marching by a circuitous route, attempted to intercept its advance to the main body, and to cut it off before it could receive assistance.*

This manœuvre was in progress while the British were marching past the defiles in which Morgan on one side, and Dickinson on the other, had stationed their respective commands. Dickinson's men, being posted nearer to Monmouth, were the first to commence the attack. After a short encounter, they were forced to retire. Morgan and his command were eager for the

* Marshall's Washington, vol. i., pp. 251-253.

conflict in which they thought they were about engaging, when it became known that the entire body of the enemy were coun-termarching towards Monmouth.

The British general, observing the hostile demonstrations of such large numbers upon his flanks and rear, and apprehensive for his baggage, determined upon a rapid retrograde movement of his entire division, with the twofold object of dispersing the American forces in his rear, and of compelling the recall of those on his flanks. Lee was advancing to coöperate with Wayne, in the projected capture of the British covering party, when he unexpectedly discovered the whole of the enemy's rear in full march on his command. Surprised, but not disconcerted, Gen. Lee prepared for battle. But as the ground on which he found himself was unfavorable, and as a portion of his command had already commenced retreating, he ordered the remainder to retire to a better position in his rear. While performing this manœuvre, the British commenced the attack. Their dragoons charged a portion of Lafayette's command, and obliged it to give way. Advancing with impetuosity, they threw a momentary disorder into the ranks of some of the retreating regiments, which hastily retired. Matters were in this posture when Washington arrived with the main body of the army. Vexed and disap-pointed at the unexpected turn which the tide of battle had taken, he proceeded to the rear of the retreating troops, and meeting General Lee, expressed his disapproval of that officer's conduct in terms of severity.* Finding the enemy pressing closely forward, he succeeded in forming and bringing into action a part of the retreating troops. These, with the aid of some well served pieces of artillery, succeeded in checking the enemy, and gave time for a disposition upon an eminence of the left wing and second line of the main army. Lord Sterling, who commanded the American left, opened upon the approaching enemy so destructive a fire of cannon and musketry, as to put a stop to

* Marshall's Washington, vol. i., p. 254.

their advance in that direction. They next attempted to turn the American left flank; but were repulsed and driven back by detached parties of infantry. They now made a movement against the American right under Gen. Greene. This officer had been marching with his command to gain the enemy's right flank, when, hearing the fire on his left, he turned in that direction, and without waiting for orders, took a very advantageous position on the right. He met the enemy with such a heavy fire, that they were not only repulsed, but shaken. Before they could recover from the effect of these successive discomfitures, General Wayne advanced with a body of infantry, and threw into their ranks so heavy and well directed a fire, as to cause them to yield their ground, and to retire to the spot where the action began.*

Although the position which the enemy now took was very strong, their flanks being secured by woods and morasses, and their front accessible only by a narrow pass, the commander-in-chief determined, nevertheless, to attack them. Accordingly, Gen. Poor, with his own and the Carolina brigades, was ordered to move upon their right; General Woodford was directed to take a position on their left; and the artillery was commanded to open on them in front. Before these dispositions were perfected, however, night came on, and prevented a renewal of the battle.

The loss of the Americans in this action was eight officers and sixty-one privates killed, and about one hundred and sixty wounded. That of the British was much more considerable, amounting to about 300 killed, a much greater number wounded, and about 100 prisoners.†

The chief object of Sir Henry Clinton in turning on his pursuers, was that of extricating his baggage from the danger with which he clearly perceived it was menaced, by the American flanking parties, commanded by Morgan and Dickinson. These

* Sparks's Writings of Washington, vol. v., p. 426.
† Marshall's Washington, vol. 1., pp. 255, 256.

officers, on hearing the firing in the early stages of the action, felt confident of being enabled to achieve something honorable to themselves, if not disastrous to their opponents, before the day closed. They had already partially engaged the enemy, when the latter were observed retracing their steps towards Monmouth. Soon after, and while the din of the conflict that ensued was heard in the distance, Morgan received orders to join the army. Unfortunately, he took a route on his return which diverged somewhat from that leading to the field of battle; and from this cause, with the late hour of the day at which he commenced a march of some miles through a broken country, he did not reach the American army till night.

Excessive was his mortification, and that of his corps, upon being informed of the events of the day, and of the opportunities which, from want of information, they had lost, of attacking the enemy in rear during the engagement. In a letter to the commander-in-chief, written two days afterwards, at his camp near Nut Swamp, Morgan says: "I congratulate your Excellency on the victory gained over the British army. They have, from every account, had a severe flogging. If I had had notice of their situation, to have fallen upon them, we could have taken most of them, I think. We are all very unhappy that we did not share in the glory."*

Washington had resolved to renew the action upon the appearance of day on the 29th. With this object, the detachments posted on the enemy's flanks and front, were directed to

---

* TO THE ABOVE THE FOLLOWING REPLY WAS WRITTEN.

ENGLISH TOWN, 30th June, 1778.

SIR: His Excellency received your favor of this date, and thanks you for your congratulations on the victory of the 28th. It was a happy event, and will do honor to him and to the American arms. The particulars you must patiently wait to hear until you join us. You were written to by the general, this morning, for your government, and to that I refer you.

I am, Sir,
Your most ob't serv't,
RICHARD R. MEADE, A. D. C.

COL. MORGAN.

maintain their respective positions, while to support them, the
main body of the army lay upon their arms in the field of battle.
But about 12 o'clock at night, the British marched off in such
silence that although General Poor's brigade lay extremely near
them, they effected their object without being discovered. Hopeless
of being able to overtake them before they reached the high ground
about Middletown, the commander-in-chief relinquished a further
pursuit with the main body of the army. But Maxwell's brigade,
Morgan's regiment, and a few light parties under Colonel Gist,
were sent after the enemy, with orders * to press on their rear, to
countenance desertions, and as far as possible, to prevent depredations on the inhabitants.†

Before Sir Henry Clinton's forces reached Middletown, Morgan
was hovering about their rear. No opportunity was afforded him
for an attack, however, except at great hazard. But he picked
up a large number of stragglers and deserters ; and to encourage
desertion, frequently appeared within sight of the retreating
column. More than two hundred deserters passed through his
ranks between Monmouth and Middletown.‡

* HEAD QUARTERS, *English Town, 30th June*, 1778.

DEAR SIR: His Excellency desires you to remain as near the enemy as you possibly
can until they have all embarked. Gen. Maxwell will remain somewhere in the neighborhood of Monmouth Court House, to support you. You are to consider yourself left
for two purposes—to cover the country from incursions of the enemy, and to afford a
shelter for deserters to repair to ; for which purpose you are to show yourself as often
and as near as possible. The spirit of desertion that prevailed so much in the British
army will undoubtedly be heightened by their late ill fortune. Be pleased to keep an
exact account of the deserters that come to you, that we may be able to form some
judgment of the numbers that have come from them since they left Philadelphia.

I am, Dear Sir, Your most ob't serv't,

TENCH TILGHMAN.

P. S.—The commissary will leave provision to the 8th inst. for you, at Penolopy, three
miles from this place. When that is exhausted, your commissary must look out in the
country.

COLONEL DANIEL MORGAN.

To the care of Gen. Dickinson, who will be pleased to forward it.

† Sparks's Writings of Washington, vol. v., pp. 428, 429.

‡ The following is one of a number of notes which were addressed to Colonel Morgan,
from head-quarters, on the 29th June :

HEAD QUARTERS, *near Monmouth Court House, 29th June*, 1778.

SIR . As it is probable that the enemy are exceedingly harassed with the heat of the

The British having remained at Middletown for a short time to recruit their men, advanced on the 30th, and encamped, the main body about three miles, and the rear guard about one mile, from the town. Early the next morning, the place was occupied by Morgan and his corps. During the day, he threw forward a strong body of his riflemen, who attacked the advanced parties of the enemy's rear guard, and compelled them, after a sharp fire of a few minutes' duration, to fall back upon their supporters. Being soon after strongly reinforced with infantry as well as cavalry, the British made a stand. The contest was renewed with much spirit on both sides; but the enemy having sent a column on each flank of the riflemen, the latter were forced to retire to the main body of the regiment, then posted on a hill in the rear. The position afforded by this hill was one in which the riflemen could fight to the greatest advantage; it secured them, besides, from what they most dreaded, an attack from cavalry. The offer of battle which Morgan hereupon made to the enemy, was declined. They retreated to their camp, taking with them several killed and wounded. One man only of the riflemen was hurt on this occasion, and he but slightly.*

Morgan, in furnishing the commander-in-chief with a brief account of this affair, laments the embarrassment which he had experienced during the pursuit of Sir Henry Clinton, for the want of a body of cavalry. Had such a body been attached to his command, on the preceding 28th, he could have kept himself informed of the operations of that eventful day, and would doubtless have shared in the battle, if indeed, he had not rendered the victory which the Americans eventually achieved, much more

weather, and the fatigue of the engagement yesterday, his Excellency desires that you will press upon their rear, and pick up all that you possibly can. You will follow them as far as you can, consistently, with the safety of your party.

I am, Dear Sir,
Your most ob't serv't,
TENCH TILGHMAN, A.D.C.

COL. MORGAN.

* Letter, July 2, 1778.

214 THE LIFE OF

decisive in its character. In the letter alluded to, which is dated at "Middletown, 2nd July, '78, 9 o'clock," he observes: "I am, and have been, ever since I came out, at a great loss for light horse, having none annexed to me. General Scott sent me a sergeant and six, whose horses were tired, and were rather an encumbrance, as they could scarcely raise a gallop. Major Jameson was here yesterday. I applied to him for a few. He sent Captain Hanson, who stayed with me about two hours, when Col. Moylan sent for him and his party. Col. Moylan has, certainly, reasons for so doing; but, sir, you know *that cavalry are the eyes of the infantry;* and without any, my situation cannot be very pleasing, being in full view of the enemy's whole army."

Morgan continued at Middletown in observation of the enemy, who, having rested for a day or two, proceeded to Sandy Hook, and thence embarked for New York. No further opportunity having been afforded him for assailing them, he at length broke up his quarters, and in obedience to the orders * previously received, took up his line of march for New Brunswick.

* HEAD QUARTERS, *Brunswick, July 3d,* 1778.
SIR: His Excellency received your favor, dated yesterday, and desires me to request that you will join this army immediately on your finding that you can no longer do them (the enemy) injury. Should they be on the Hook, it is taken for granted that there is no annoying them; in which case you will march this way. You will be pleased to desire Col. Gist to conduct himself in the same manner.
I am, sir, &c.,
R. R. MEADE, A.D.C.
COLONEL MORGAN, *at Middletown.*

CHAPTER XII.

Morgan commands Woodford's brigade—The rifle corps—Operations of the army—
Letters from Lord Stirling—Correspondence in relation to recruiting service—Letter
from Lafayette—Movements of the enemy—American army goes into winter quarters—
Morgan appointed colonel of the 7th Virginia regiment—Operations of the enemy on
the Hudson—Gen. Woodford resumes his command—Causes operating on Morgan's
mind, determining him to retire from the service—Letter from Washington—Morgan at
home—Regret of the army at his retirement—Operations in the South—Gen. Gates
appointed to the command of the Southern army—His letter to Morgan—Their reconciliation—Morgan refuses to comply with the demand for his services without an
increase of rank—Takes the field on hearing the result of the battle of Camden.

ALTHOUGH the twelve months which succeeded the battle of
Monmouth were fruitful of most important events, all tending to
the final triumph of the American cause, they furnished Morgan
with no opportunity of adding to the laurels which he had previously gathered. But the zeal and efficiency which he displayed
during this time, in a higher sphere of action, contributed largelv
to his reputation as a commander, and proved that he possessed
capacities superior to those usually required by the partisan.

A few days after he had effected a junction of his regiment
with the main body of the army then encamped at Paramus, he
was assigned to the command of Woodford's brigade, the general
having obtained leave of absence on account of ill health. With
this event terminated Morgan's connection with his gallant rifle
corps. The occasion of their separation was productive of feelings
of mutual regret, and displayed in a striking manner the warm
attachment which existed between them. The career of this
noble regiment was now drawing to a close. Its loss in battle

and by sickness had greatly diminished its numbers, and at the expiration of the term of service of the survivors, some of them enlisted in other regiments, and the remainder returned to their homes. From the activity and boldness which it had invariably displayed on every occasion, it was much esteemed by Washington, and was not only retained under his immediate command, but was also favored with many privileges not enjoyed by the troops of the line. In the severe round of duty which it was called on to perform, its valuable services frequently received the public acknowledgments and thanks of the commander-in-chief; and by the country it was regarded as the *élite* of the army. No regiment of the revolutionary war contributed as largely to the success of the cause or to the glory of our arms, as Morgan's Rangers.

Morgan was also held in high regard by the commander-in chief, not so much for the warm attachment which that officer had invariably displayed towards himself, as for the deep devotedness to the cause of his country which his conduct had invariably evinced. These circumstances, considered in connection with the address and valor which he had never failed to exhibit in the field, and the many important services which he had rendered his country during the war, all entitled him to the enviable position which the friendship and confidence of his general assigned him.

On the 11th July, the long expected French fleet arrived at Sandy Hook. This event becoming known to Washington, he put himself in communication with the French commander, and commenced making such a disposition of his forces as would forward his intended combined operations by land and sea against New York. Leaving a respectable force, in conjunction with the militia, to occupy and guard the various posts along the west branch of the Hudson and in New Jersey, he crossed to the eastern side of that river with the main body of the army, and encamped at White Plains. Among the troops left behind, were the riflemen. Morgan, with Woodford's brigade, crossed the river with the main body.

Here he remained until the latter part of September. During this period, the operations of the enemy at Rhode Island, and on the Hudson, as well as the hostilities of the Indians to the north, called for large detachments from the main army, and gave the campaign an active and exciting character. Major Posey, with the riflemen, had been sent with the troops under Col. William Butler, against the Indians. Two large detachments of the enemy had advanced and taken positions some distance above New York, on the Hudson. That on the western side, commanded by Cornwallis, was five thousand strong. A detachment from this force surprised and cut to pieces Col. Baylor's regiment of dragoons, under circumstances of extreme barbarity. Soon after this event, Morgan and his brigade were sent across the river to reinforce the troops opposed to the enemy on that side, and Lord Stirling was appointed to the command of the whole of the forces there.

About the first of October, the enemy on the Hudson retired to New York. This was followed by a general movement of Stirling's command to positions in advance of those previously occupied by it, and in close proximity to the enemy. Morgan's brigade advanced from the neighborhood of Paramus, and took post, a detachment at Hackensack, and the main body at Newark

For some time previously, the enemy at New York had been very active in making preparations, the object of which had baffled inquiry, and still continued a mystery. As it was certain that something important was meditated, the commander-in-chief took such precautions as would equally guard against danger, whether it tended towards the west, the east, or the north.* In that part of the theatre of war occupied by Stirling's command, numerous and large parties of the troops were employed in improving the roads along the different lines of communication, in constructing new fortifications, and improving old ones. At the same time, detachments were constantly kept in advance, to

* Sparks's Writings of Washington, vol. vi., p. 64.

10

gain intelligence of the enemy's movements, while the several corps composing the division were so disposed as to be enabled to meet any exigency which might arise.

In the letter of instructions from Lord Stirling to Col. Morgan, which follows, we are furnished with a striking illustration of the activity which these anticipations of danger induced.

ELIZABETHTOWN, *Oct.* 28*th*, 1778.

DEAR SIR:

In pursuance of the orders I have received from his excellency General Washington, you are to march the brigade which you command to some situation between the Clove at Saverens, and Pompton; you will take your situation in such a place on or near the present communication from Morristown to King's Ferry, as will enable you to guard the Clove; and in case of any invasion of the enemy, to possess and defend it. You will send proper parties towards the Hudson river to gain intelligence of any movements of the enemy, and keep up a correspondence with Col. Spencer, who is at Hackensack. You will detach a captain and forty men to Morristown, for the purpose of guarding the stores and provisions at that place, which are very considerable and of great consequence. You will keep two hundred men employed in repairing and improving the roads between King's Ferry and Morristown, and dispose of them for that purpose as you think to most advantage. The Qr. M. General, Mr. Abeel, will furnish you with all necessary tools, and, I hope, with some carpenters.

Yours,

STIRLING.

COL. DANIEL MORGAN, *Newark.*

On the 20th of October, the British fleet left New York, and sailed for Boston. Soon after arriving in the vicinity of Boston Bay, a furious storm drove it to sea again. Having suffered very severely, it put into Rhode Island for repairs. D'Estaing seizing the moment which favored his escape, left Boston with his fleet, and steered for the West Indies. Thus terminated the first essay of French co-operation in our struggle for independence.*

About the first of November, great preparations were made in

* Marshall's Washington, vol. i., p. 271.

the neighborhood of the Highlands, in consequence of a rumor which reached Lord Stirling, that the British were about commencing their long threatened attack in that quarter. Morgan had removed his command to a position in the neighborhood of Pompton, a strong detachment having been thrown forward to guard the important pass called the Clove. He was apprised of this expected incursion of the enemy, for which he made due preparation.

In relation to this rumor, the following, among other letters from General Lord Stirling, was sent to Morgan for his information:

ELIZABETHTOWN, *Nov.* 8, 1778.

DEAR SIR: I have the highest reason to believe that the enemy have projected a secret expedition, which they mean to carry into execution very soon, I believe within three or four days; and as it is not improbable, it may be designed for this State, I must request you will put the brigade under your command in the best order you can. I have desired Col. Spencer to give you the most early intelligence of any of their motions which may come within his knowledge. I am told Gen. Grey, the *no flint* general, is to command. He will endeavor to act by surprise; but if we can get notice of him, we may make him repent such tricks in his way. It will be our plan to attack him as soon as possible, and give him a few fires before he gets his flints in again.

I am, sir, your most ob't servant,

STIRLING.

COL. MORGAN, *Pompton.*

If such a design as that indicated by the above letter was entertained at this time by the enemy, it was not carried into execution, nor did any military event of importance occur, during the remainder of the campaign.

The never-ending, still-beginning business of enlistments now engaged the serious attention of Congress, the State governments, and the commander-in-chief. As regarded the Virginia troops, the government of that State had offered liberal inducements to

220   THE LIFE OF

recruit their ranks; but the result did not realize the expectations
which had been formed in relation to it. The general desire of
the men to revisit their homes, furnished an insurmountable
obstacle to their re-enlistment. A considerable number, however,
professed a willingness to re-engage in the service, after they
had spent the winter at home, among their friends. In this
emergency, a plan was suggested by Morgan, which was adopted
by the commander-in-chief, and which originated an order,
granting furloughs to all those having a short time to serve, who
agreed to re-enlist and return to camp the following April.
The correspondence in relation to this matter follows :—

GEN. WASHINGTON TO COL. MORGAN.

HEAD QUARTERS, FREDERICKSBURG, *Nov.* 12, 1778.

SIR : The enclosed extract of an act of the State of Virginia for
recruiting the Continental army, was transmitted to me a few days ago by
his excellency, the governor.

The bounties and other encouragements offered by this act are so
liberal, that I hope, if proper exertions are made use of, a number of the
old soldiers and drafts may be enlisted. You will therefore be pleased to
have the terms of the act communicated to the officers of your brigade,
and by them to the men. I have some money, belonging to the State of
Virginia, in my hands. If any of the men incline to enlist, you may
assure them of the bounty at a certain day, and send up to me for the
amount. I have never been made acquainted, notwithstanding the
directions in the recuiting instructions, whether any progress has been
made in re-enlisting the drafts upon the bounty of twenty dollars.

Col. Febiger informs me that the State has sent up a number of waistcoats, breeches, shirts, and blankets, to their agents, to be sold out to the
troops at moderate prices. It will be well to deliver out the two latter
articles immediately, as the troops are in great want of them. But as
they have just drawn a full supply of waistcoats and breeches from the
Continent, I would recommend it to you, not to permit those belonging to
the State to be sold to the men till they are really wanted, or, if they have
already drawn those belonging to the State, that the bounty clothes be

reserved till wanted, as they are too apt to dispose of anything more than what they have in wear, for liquor, or for some trifling consideration.

I am, sir, your most ob't servant,

GEORGE WASHINGTON.

COL. MORGAN, *commanding Gen. Woodford's brigade, near Pompton.*

POMPTON, *Nov.* 24, 1778.

SIR: I send you a return of the men enlisted in Gen. Woodford's brigade since the recruiting orders came out. I expect Gen. Woodford forgot to leave orders with me to make returns of this kind, or I should have paid particular attention to it. You'll see the number very small; the men are exceedingly backward. For my part, I have used every method in my power, and I thought I had a peculiar turn that way. I made use of active sergeants, but to no purpose. Numbers would engage if they could get furloughs to go home. And nevertheless the high bounty offered, few I fear will enlist without that indulgence. A number of them are waiting an answer to this.

I received your excellency's instructions respecting the clothing brought on by Col. Febiger, have accordingly divided the shirts, blankets, and linen, among the three brigades, that is, proportioned them. The jackets and breeches, I purpose sending to Philadelphia, as the rest of the Virginia stores are at that place.

Col. Davis wrote to me to send some of them on to West Point, for the draughts, who, he said, were almost naked, but that I could not comply with without particular orders.

We are exceedingly distressed in this place for provender, although the place abounds with it. The people are in general disaffected, and are well acquainted with an act of this State, that nothing is to be taken from them without their consent.

Sixty-four wagons, with military stores, passed through this place yesterday; they could not get anything for their horses; they applied to me, but I could get nothing for them.

I have the honor, &c.,

DANIEL MORGAN.

TO GEN. WASHINGTON.

At this period, the American army was about moving into winter quarters. Some time previously, a resolution of Congress directed that the British prisoners, taken at Saratoga, should be removed from Boston to Charlottesville. The prisoners were now on the march to the latter place. The subjoined note from Washington to Morgan, in reference to these events, adverts, as will be seen, to the suggestion of the latter, in the foregoing letter:

HEAD QUARTERS, FREDERICKSBURG, *Nov.* 25, 1778.

DEAR SIR: You are to remain at Pompton until the rear division of the Convention troops has passed Chester, on their route to Sussex Court House. You are then to march to Middlebrook, and receive directions from the quarter-master general for the position of the brigade under your command, in the line of encampment. The regiment sent to Hackensack is to remain there, until ordered off or relieved.

I am, dear sir, your most obedient servant,

GEORGE WASHINGTON.

P.S.—I have received yours of the 24th. When the Virginia brigade are all assembled at Middlebrook, I will consider the expediency of granting furloughs to those who will re-enlist.

In due time the following circular was sent, through Colonel Morgan, from head-quarters, to the officers commanding the regiments composing his brigade:

HEAD QUARTERS, MIDDLEBROOK, *Dec.* 14, 1778.

SIR: As it seems to be the general opinion of the officers in the Virginia line, that those men who have but a short time to serve would *enlist* on being indulged with leave of absence until the middle of April next, I would have you proceed on that business immediately; and the better to accommodate the matter, it would be well that it should commence throughout the line at the same time, and when a sufficient number of men are enlisted, to form a body of men worth marching off under proper officers. The commanding officer of each regiment will appoint one to take charge of such men as he may have enlisted, with instructions to march them in good order to the most convenient place, where they may be dispersed, and proceed to their respective homes, with positive orders to rendezvous at some fixed spot at so early a season as will ensure their arrival in camp by the middle of April next. As you are acquainted with the terms of enlistment, it will be unnecessary to repeat them. I shall, therefore, only request that every exertion may be used to accomplish so desirable an end, and wish your efforts may prove successful.

I am, sir, your most obedient servant.

GEORGE WASHINGTON.

A few words, in the introduction of a letter from Lafayette to Colonel Morgan, written about this time, will not be regarded as unnecessary here. The disinterested zeal which "the marquis" had displayed in the cause of American independence, had won him the universal respect and esteem of its assertors. The courage and address which he had invariably shown in the field, invested him with an interest in the eyes of his commander and brother officers, much greater than that enjoyed by any other officer of foreign birth in the service. Having served two campaigns, with infinite credit to himself and advantage to the cause, he considered the prospect of an European war, which had now become apparent, as calling on him to offer his services to his king. But, entertaining hopes of being able speedily to return, and proud of a service in which he had acquired so exalted a reputation, he expressed a desire to be permitted to retain his commission, and to obtain an unlimited leave of absence. Congress granted his request, and accompanied the permission with an expression of the favorable sentiments which that body held regarding him. He had made every preparation for his journey, and was on the road for Boston, whence he purposed sailing, when he was suddenly seized with a fever, which was near putting an end to his brilliant career. Upon his recovery, he wrote the following letter in answer to one from Morgan* :

* A correspondence between the marquis and Colonel Morgan, was maintained from 1778 until 1782. Although most of the marquis's letters have been preserved, those from Morgan were destroyed, with the rest of the Lafayette papers, when their owner was proscribed and forced to fly from France, during the early stages of the Revolution in that country. This is to be regretted, inasmuch as it is believed that these letters would have shed much additional light on Morgan's revolutionary career, and proved an important addition to the materials in the possession of the writer.—*See letter of Mons. G. W. Lafayette, E, Appendix.*

224 THE LIFE OF

FISHKILL, *Nov.* 28, 1778

DEAR SIR: Your most kind and obliging letter arrived safe into my hands; but I was then too ill for thinking of answering to it. However, though it was at that time out of my power to express anything, I did feel all the sentiments of gratitude for the friendship and the good idea you are pleased to entertain for me. Both are extremely dear to my heart; and I do assure you, my dear sir, that the true regard and esteem, and the sincere affection you have inspired to me, will last for ever.

The strength of youth, and that of a strong constitution, have brought me again to health, and to the enjoyments of this world. Dying in a shameful bed, after having essayed some more honorable occasions in the field, would have been for me, the most cruel disappointment.

I am just setting out for France, and hope to be there in a short time. My country is at war, and I think it my duty to go myself, for offering my services to her. However, I am very far from leaving the American service, and I have merely a furlough from Congress. I am much inclined to think that the king will have no objections to my returning here: so that I am almost convinced that I'll have the pleasure to see you next spring.

I most earnestly beg you to present my best compliments to the gentlemen officers in my division. I shall for all my life feel pleased and proud in the idea that I have had the honor of being intrusted with such a division. I anticipate the happiness of finding them next campaign; and I dare flatter myself that these gentlemen will not forget a friend and fellow soldier who entertains for them all the sentiments of affection and esteem.

Farewell, my dear sir, don't forget your friend on the other side of the great water, and believe me ever,

Your affectionate

LAFAYETTE.

COL. MORGAN.

On the 3rd of December, the last division of the Convention prisoners passed through Chester, on their way to Virginia. About the same time, Sir Henry Clinton left New York with a considerable land and naval force, and proceeded up the Hudson. Intelligence of this movement reached Washington at Elizabethtown, when the general, surprised, if not alarmed, at an expedition so unexpected and unreasonable, sent expresses to the different commanders of divisions and brigades, communicating the information and giving the necessary directions. On this occasion, the following note was addressed to Colonel Morgan :

ELIZABETHTOWN. *Dec. 4th*, 1778. }
10 *o'clock*, *P. M.* }

COLONEL MORGAN—*Dear Sir* : I have just received intelligence that the enemy have several ships moving up the North river with troops and flat-bottomed boats. I don't know what their object is ; but you will hold your men collected and well supplied with ammunition and provisions, to act on the earliest order. Your heavy baggage you will send on to the camp at Middlebrook.

I am, Dear Sir,
Your most obedient servant,
GEO. WASHINGTON.

There were three objects which might have prompted Sir Henry Clinton to such a movement, viz.: a rescue of the Convention troops ; a demonstration against the rear of the army ; or a surprise of the posts in the Highlands. Circumstances justified the belief that the last was his aim, if, indeed, he had any aim of consequence.*

The brigade under Morgan's command was on the march for Middlebrook, when the intelligence and orders contained in the foregoing note were received by him. The whole army became speedily apprised of the movement of the enemy, and the long deferred expectations of decisive measures which had been indulged in, revived with double force, again however, to be disappointed.

Although the posts in the Highlands had been left in a state of security, and in the hands of a good officer, General Mc-Donald, the commander-in-chief was nevertheless uneasy, lest a disaster might happen in that quarter. He accordingly left Elizabethtown at 4 o'clock on the morning of the 5th, in the direction of the Highlands, and had approached within twelve or fifteen miles of King's Ferry, when he was met by an express, who

* Sparks's Writings of Washington, vol. vi., p. 131.

10*

informed him that the enemy had landed at that place ; and that, after having burned two or three log houses, with nine barrels of spoiled herrings, they reëmbarked and returned to New York ! In the letter of the commander-in-chief, from which the foregoing facts are taken, he indulges in some pleasantries at the expense of Sir Henry Clinton. Following the announcement that the log houses and the spoiled herrings had been destroyed, he remarks : "Thus ended this notable expedition, which was conducted in the preparation with so much secrecy, that all the flag boats to and from the city were stopped, and not a mouse permitted to creep within their lines." *

Th only effect which this " extra manœuvre " had upon the American army, was to cause a delay of four days in the arrival, at Middlebrook, of the Virginia, Maryland, and Pennsylvania troops; and in the construction of the huts, &c., necessary for their accommodation during the winter. In the meantime, the ground had been covered with snow. The troops were consequently forced to work under disadvantages, and amidst inconveniences, which, but for this abortive expedition, would have been anticipated.†

The winter of 1778-9, was one of the most stirring periods of the revolutionary war. During this time, the East, the West, the North and the South, were each the scene of active operations; while the French and English naval and military forces in the West Indies, fiercely contended with varying success for the mastery. In the neighborhood of the American camp at Middlebrook, however, it passed without the occurrence of anything remarkable. The British at New York had remained in their quarters, and save in the fitting out of several expeditions for distant points, and in one or two forays into New Jersey, they evinced no signs of activity. The chief business of the commander-in-chief being to watch the movements of the enemy at this point, and to act against them, should they take the field in

* Sparks's Writings of Washington, vol. vi., p. 181.   † Ibid, vol. vi., p. 181.

his vicinity, he remained quiet in his camp; ready at any moment, however, to put his forces in motion, should occasion call for action.

Morgan remained with his brigade at Middlebrook during the winter. In the month of March, he was commissioned by Congress as colonel of the 7th Virginia regiment.* About the 25th of May, appearances indicated that the enemy were preparing for another expedition against the posts in the Highlands. The army soon after advanced from Middlebrook in the direction of the quarter threatened. Lord Sterling's division, which included Morgan's brigade, left that place on the 2nd of June, and passing through Pompton, advanced towards Smith's Clove. The other divisions which had wintered at Middlebrook, moved in the same direction.

In the meantime, Sir Henry Clinton, with a formidable fleet, and an army of over six thousand men, moved up the Hudson. His first object was to take the posts at Stoney Point and Verplanck's Point, situate on opposite sides of the Hudson, where the Americans had thrown up works to protect King's

* THE UNITED STATES OF AMERICA, IN CONGRESS ASSEMBLED :

To Daniel Morgan Esquire, Greeting :

We, reposing especial trust and confidence in your patriotism, valor, conduct, and fidelity, do by these presents constitute and appoint you to be Colonel of the 7th Virginia regiment in the army of the United States, to take rank as such from the 12th day of November, A. D. 1776. You are therefore carefully and diligently to discharge the duty of colonel, by doing and performing all manner of things thereunto belonging: And we do strictly charge and require all officers and soldiers under your command to be obedient to your orders as colonel, and you are to observe and follow such orders and directions from time to time as you shall receive from this or a future Congress of the United States, or committee of Congress for that purpose appointed, a committee of the States, or commander-in-chief, for the time being, of the army of the United States, or any other your superior officer, according to the rules and discipline of war. In pursuance of the trust reposed in you, this commission is to continue in force until revoked by this or a future Congress before mentioned, or a committee of the States.

Witness, His Excellency, John Jay, Esq., President of the Congress of the United States of America, at Philadelphia, the 20th day of March, 1779, and in the third year of our independence.   JOHN JAY.

Entered in the War Office, and examined by the Board.

                    Attest: P. LOVELL,

                                        Secretary of the Board of War

228   THE LIFE OF

Ferry, the main channel of communication between the Middle and Eastern States.* This was effected. The garrison at Stoney Point retired on his approach; and that at Verplanck's Point was forced to surrender. He intended next to endeavor to force his way into the Highlands, make himself master of its fortifications and strong passes, and thus secure the command of the Hudson. But the precautions which the commander-in-chief had taken, in concentrating the bulk of his forces in the quarter threatened, prevented Sir Henry from putting this part of his scheme into execution.†

Leaving a strong garrison in each of the forts which he had taken, Sir Henry returned to New York about the 1st of June. Washington soon after removed his head-quarters to New Windsor, and distributed his army chiefly in and near the Highlands. To guard against any sudden incursion of the enemy, he stationed a force on each side of the river, below West Point.

About the middle of June, General Woodford returned to the camp, and soon after, resumed the command of his brigade.

For some time previously to that at which we have arrived, many circumstances had combined to lead Morgan's thoughts towards home. The considerations which now brought him to the resolution of retiring from the army, are worthy of a passing notice.

The very severe service which he experienced in the expedition to Quebec, had induced a violent rheumatic affection; and the fatigues and constant exposure to which he had been subjected as commander of the rifle corps, had so aggravated his malady, as seriously to impair his health. Being of a disposition remarkably domestic and affectionate, his long continued separations from his family were now becoming more and more the sources of disquietude to him. His reflections upon this subject were embittered by the fact, that his pay, so far from enabling

him to add to the means upon which his wife and children sub-
sisted, was entirely inadequate to the discharge of his personal
expenses. To meet these expenses, he was constantly drawing on
his own private resources, which, in consequence, were gradually
wasting away. He participated, too, in the dissatisfaction with
the conduct of Congress, which existed so generally among the
officers of the army at this time. This feeling originated in the
belief, that that body was not disposed to make any provision for
their future wants, and that it would yield nothing to their
present necessities, beyond what appeared to be indispensable to
their continuance in the service or to the preservation of the
army. They felt indignant, besides, at the injustice and partiality
which it had exhibited in promotions, and particularly at the
facilities which it had afforded to military adventurers from other
countries, of stepping over their heads to stations of honor and
consequence. It too frequently appeared, besides, that the qualifications of a politician or a place hunter, and the possession of
local influence, presented claims to advancement in the army,
which proved superior to those furnished by soldierlike qualities
and important military services. An idea prevailed for some time
with Congress, that the boasted military skill and experience of
the foreign officers who applied to it for employment, gave them
a claim to consideration over those who were identified with the
country, and the struggle in which it was engaged—whose services were a constant sacrifice to patriotism, and who more than
compensated for their lack of science by their bravery and
devotedness. Some of these foreign officers undoubtedly deserved
all the honors which they received; but by far the greater
number of them had little but assurance wherewith to supply the
want of merit. To add to the evils with which the delicate business of appointments and promotions was beset at this time, the
representatives of several States in Congress asserted a claim to
an equal division of the patronage of this nature which the army
afforded.*

* Writings of Washington, vol. iii., p. 68, vol. iv., pp. 263, 423-446, vol. vii., pp. 338, 382.

Other circumstances, more particularly referable to Colonel Morgan, conspired to create an impression in his mind, that he had not experienced that advancement to which he thought his services, considered with reference to those of others who had been more fortunate, entitled him. From the opening of the great struggle, he had been an active participator in its stirring events. On many important occasions, he had contributed largely to the success of the cause and to the glory of our arms, and had won for his name a foremost place in the list of his country's defenders. His achievements during the Canadian campaign were without a parallel in the whole course of the war. He encountered more perils, privations, and fatigues, while in command of the rifle corps, than any other colonel in the service. Numberless were the engagements which he had had with pickets, advanced parties, and detachments of the enemy; most of which, though now forgotten, and lost to history, called for the exercise of much judgment and caution, and involved greater personal hazards than those which attend a general engagement. In all of these, the enemy could seldom boast of a triumph, and when such an occasion occurred, it was purchased dearly. His numerous exploits won for him the notice and love of his countrymen, and excited the fear of their enemies ; besides which, they elicited from his commanding officers frequent and emphatic expressions of approbation.

Yet, notwithstanding these strong claims upon the favorable regard of Congress, his just expectations of promotion were not only disappointed, but he was compelled to witness the advancement over his head, of men who possessed few, if any, of the requisites of a soldier, and who, moreover, owed their good fortune to considerations foreign to those which should have governed Congress in exercising the appointing power.

But weighty as were these causes of dissatisfaction upon the fiery and impulsive mind of Morgan, he would nevertheless have continued in the service, had it not been for his broken health and impaired fortunes. His organization, moral as well as physical, eminently fitted him for war, and habit united with inclination, in making him fond of its toils, privations and dangers. He accordingly communicated his intentions to Washington, and begged permission to wait on Congress with his resignation. Within a short period, a large number of officers had left the army, and a growing distaste for the service was manifested daily by many of those who remained. Washington was fully aware of the causes of this; and while withholding his countenance from the consequences, could not deny their justice. His numerous letters to Congress on this head will show how strongly he urged upon that body the justice as well as the policy of removing all grounds of complaint on the part of the army. But in the mean time he beheld with deep regret the departure, day after day, of numbers of his best officers. He received Morgan's announcement of an intention to resign with much concern, and for a time endeavored to dissuade him from his purpose. But as it was difficult, if not impossible, successfully to resist the principal motives which impelled Morgan to this step, a reluctant consent was at length obtained, as will be seen by the annexed letter from the commander-in-chief to the president of Congress :

HEAD QUARTERS, *June* 30, 1779.

To THE PRESIDENT OF CONGRESS :

SIR : Col. Morgan, of the Virginia line, who waits on Congress with his resignation, will have the honor of delivering you this. I cannot, in justice, avoid mentioning him as a very valuable officer, who has rendered a series of important services, and distinguished himself on several occasions.

I am, sir, very respectfully, your ob't servant,

GEORGE WASHINGTON.

In a few days after the receipt of the above letter, Col. Morgan reached Philadelphia, and, waiting upon Congress, presented his resignation, which was accepted. Without delaying longer in this city than was necessary to an adjustment of his accounts, he turned his footsteps homeward, and in about a week afterwards was once more in the bosom of his family.

Thus terminated, for a time, Morgan's military career. He was destined, however, speedily to reappear upon a wider field of action, and to be the directing genius of an event which was unquestionably the most brilliant of the war.

The succeeding fifteen months were spent by Morgan at his residence in Frederick county, and in the pursuits of private life. The change from the hardships of the camp to the comforts of home, speedily effected a great improvement in his health; and his active mind and industrious habits soon found ample occupation in removing from his house and farm the evidences of years of neglect.

Although no longer an active participant in the operations of the war, few, if any, took a greater interest in its progress. He maintained a correspondence with his old companions in arms, the letters of many of which, written during this period, are still in existence. Besides the warm friendship for Morgan, which these letters invariably display, they inform us, besides, how deeply their authors regretted his retirement, how much they sympathized in its causes, and how ardently they wished for his return. One illustration of this will suffice. Gen. John Neville, then an officer of one of the regiments composing Woodford's brigade, closes a long letter, dated at "Haverstraw, Nov. 9, 1779," with a few sentences, indicative of the feelings with which the officers of the brigade regarded Morgan: "Then, say they, for old Morgan a brigadier, and we would kick the world before us. I am not fond of flattery; but I assure you, on my word, that no man's ever leaving the army was more regretted than yours, nor no man was ever wished for more to return. We saw a letter the other day from his excellency to you, to be forwarded with speed, which gave the officers great hope that you were to return agreeable to your satisfaction. God send it may be the case."

About the time that Morgan retired from the service, the attention of the enemy was seriously turned towards the South. This
section of the Union had hitherto been nearly exempt from the
calamities of war. The desperate state of the enemy's affairs in
the North required a speedy termination of the struggle, or its
transfer to a new field of action. From the feebleness of the
Northern States in population and resources, their conquest was
considered a matter of easy accomplishment. Such a result
being regarded as one highly advantageous in itself, and calculated to exercise an important influence upon the final issue of the
war, extensive preparations were made to carry it into effect.
Although this change of policy must have been extremely humiliating to the British, indicative as it was of an abandonment of
general for partial results, yet the prize was well worth the
severe and protracted struggle which was subsequently made to
obtain it.

Charleston fell on the 12th of May, 1780. Upon receiving
intelligence of this unfortunate event, Congress entered at once
into the consideration of measures, having for their object the
vigorous prosecution of the war in the South. Gen. Gates was
appointed to the command of the southern department. It was
likewise determined to call out a number of other distinguished
officers, and among the rest, Col. Morgan. Since the time when
Gen. Gates relinquished the command at Rhode Island, he had
not been actively engaged, and the intelligence of his appointment reached him at his residence in Virginia. This circumstance
was the subject of a number of letters to Morgan, the first of
which is subjoined.

TRAVELLERS' REST, *June 21st*, 1781.

DEAR SIR: I have just received an express from the Board of War,
enclosing the unanimous resolve of Congress, appointing me to the command of the Southern Department. I am also informed that Congress
had it in contemplation to call Gen. Weedon and yourself into service, and
to employ you immediately to the southward. I shall set out on Monday

morning perhaps I may receive another express before then. I am too much employed to return your visit; but if you can come to me before I leave home, I shall be glad to inform you of all particulars.

I am, dear Sir, &c.,

HORATIO GATES.

COL. MORGAN.

A short time previously to the receipt of this letter, the long standing difference between Gates and Morgan had been adjusted. Upon this occasion, Morgan proudly referred to the important services he had rendered during the campaign against Burgoyne, and dwelt with warmth upon the undeserved treatment he had experienced. Reminding General Gates of the unkindness and injustice of which he had been guilty, Morgan nevertheless exhibited a willingness to forgive and forget past injuries; and the overtures of his old friend and general for a reconciliation, were met in a generous spirit.

He had now somewhat recovered his health and strength; and the scent of war in his neighborhood had revived old instincts, and excited in him a strong desire once more to take the field. But to the proposition, made to him in the resolution of Congress, calling him into the service as a colonel, he refused to listen. After what had already occurred, he was led to believe that a call of this kind on him would certainly be accompanied by an increase of his rank. Independently of the claims which he considered he had already earned, touching his promotion to a brigadier generalship, there were some peculiarities about the service in which he was now called on to engage, which presented strong objections to his acceptance of a lower grade. The country which was then and thereafter the principal scene of warlike operations, had been divided by the State authorities into military districts, to each of which, officers had been appointed. Such of these officers as ranked Morgan as a colonel, would, in the event of his taking the field, subject him to their orders whenever he entered their districts.* In ordinary cases, it would be

---

* Gov. Rutledge, 1780. Johnson's Greene, vol. i., p. 412.

expedient to avoid such an awkward contingency. But in that in question, where military merit of the highest order might be counteracted and controlled by inexperienced mediocrity, to withhold a remedy which at once disembarrassed the public service and rewarded individual merit, would be extremely impolitic. Yet such was the course pursued by Congress; and in consequence, Morgan determined to remain at home. There seemed, besides, to be no very pressing need of his services. Gen. Gates, whose prospects were bright and unclouded at this time, was surrounded by a host of experienced and able officers. Before three months elapsed, however, the justice of pretensions which Congress neglected or undervalued, found advocates in its apprehensions and its necessities.

Morgan was still at home when the issue of the conflict on the bloody and hapless field of Camden became known to him. This disastrous intelligence brought better feelings to the surface. He recognized the occasion which had now arisen, as one, demanding the sacrifice to the public good of every private consideration; and he did not resist the silent appeal of his bleeding country. Indifferent now, regarding the issue of the numerous and influential representations which had been made to Congress, in reference to his promotion, and anxious only for an opportunity again to serve his country in any capacity, he made the necessary preparations, bade adieu to his family, and left his home early in September, in the direction of Gen. Gates's head-quarters, then at Hillsborough.

CHAPTER XIII.

The dispositions and operations of the opposing forces—Morgan joins Gates at Hills-borough—The enemy advances towards North Carolina—Morgan offered a command in the North Carolina militia—Appointed by Gates to command a legionary corps—Battle of King's Mountain—Cornwallis retreats to Winnsborough—Morgan appointed a brigadier general—Letter from Gen. Gates—Morgan advances to vicinity of the enemy—Letter from Col. O. H. Williams—Destitution of the army—Repulse of Major Wemys—Battle of Blackstock House—Capture of Col. Rugely and his command—Congress determines to supersede Gen. Gates—Gen. Greene—His arrangements, pre-liminary to taking the command of the Southern army—The general prospect—Gen. Greene's plan of action—Morgan appointed to a separate command—He marches to the west of Broad river—Greene, with the main body, moves to the Pedee—Morgan's instructions.

BEFORE introducing Gen. Morgan once more on the field in the South, a glance at the operations then going forward in that quarter is called for, from their connection with those which succeeded them, and with which he was identified.

Although by the battle of Camden, the spirit of resistance was fearfully disabled, it was not destroyed. While Cornwallis was awaiting the arrival of supplies from Charleston, to commence his long-contemplated invasion of North Carolina and Virginia, the elements of opposition were rapidly re-combining against him. The small remains of a regular army which escaped destruction at Camden, had assembled at Hillsborough. The militia of North Carolina were out in considerable force. Marion, at the head of a small body, was moving in the neighborhood of the Santee. Sumter had again assembled a respectable force, and was operating west of that river. Col. Davie, with a body of volunteer

GENERAL DANIEL MORGAN.   237

dragoons and mounted riflemen, took post in the Waxhaw settlement, and employed himself in watching the movements of the enemy. Col. Clark was at the head of a large body of Georgia and South Carolina exiles, at this time in the neighborhood of Augusta. A body of mountaineers, more formidable in numbers than any opposed to the enemy in this quarter, and composed of the united commands of Cols. Campbell, Cleaveland, Williams, Sevier, Shelby, McDowell, and others, was rapidly gathering, preparatory to a descent upon the British ports in South Carolina and Georgia.

After the American forces had been driven from South Carolina, the British army took post in three divisions near its northern boundary, the main body, under Cornwallis, at Camden ; Col. Tarleton's legion at Winnsborough ; and Col. Ferguson's brigade of Provincial troops, at Ninety-six.

The required supplies having been at length obtained, these divisions simultaneously moved from their respective posts early in September, with the object of uniting at Charlotte, and thence proceeding to the interior of North Carolina.

This movement was in progress, when Morgan, accompanied only by two or three young gentlemen who were anxious to serve with him, arrived at Hillsborough. He was warmly received by Gen. Gates, who promised, at their first interview, to take immediate measures to give him employment.

The regular forces at this point had recently undergone a new organization. The infantry had been formed into two battalions, constituting one regiment, the command of which devolved upon Col. O. H. Williams and Lieut. Col. Howard ; Majors Hardman and Anderson commanding the battalions. The artillery corps was nearly annihilated at Camden ; the remaining companies of the regiment having recently reached Hillsborough, were placed under the command of Capt. Singleton. Two brass pieces, saved from the general wreck at Camden, and four or five iron ones, found at Hillsborough, formed a respectable little park of artillery.

There were, besides, the remnants of Buford's and Porterfield's corps, and a body of raw recruits, the whole numbering about 350 men, and constituting all of the Virginia line in the field in this quarter. The whole of these forces amounted to about 1,400 men.*

The advance of Cornwallis towards North Carolina had stimulated the authorities of that State in taking measures to repel the threatened invasion; while the militia were collecting in large numbers at Hillsborough, provision was made, not only to equip this force for the field, but also to meet in a partial degree some of the most pressing needs of the regular army, the chief of which was clothing. The command of the militia had recently been conferred on Gen. Smallwood. Morgan was invited,† soon after his arrival, to take a command in the same force. Flattering as was this mark of the esteem in which he was held by the people of North Carolina, he was compelled to decline the proffered honor. Gen. Gates had already formed the plan of a legionary corps, to be raised out of the ranks of the army, the command of which he intended to bestow on Morgan. The opportune arrival of the clothing already adverted to, enabled Gen. Gates to carry this design at once into effect. From the two battalions, four companies of picked men were selected. These were formed into a light infantry battalion, the command of which was given to Lieut. Col. Howard. To these was added a company of riflemen, under Capt. Rose. The remains of Cols.

* Col. O. H. Williams' Narrative.

† The letter in relation to this, is subjoined :

HILLSBOROUGH, *Sept* 30, 1780.

Sir: At the request of the assembly, Gen. Smallwood has consented to take the command of the militia of this State, and will set off in a day or two for the back country. It would give me great pleasure for you to accompany the general.

Col. Morgan's character as a soldier is well known in America. I am persuaded your presence will give spirits to my countrymen. Gen. Smallwood, I expect, will have an opportunity of finding employment suitable to a man of your rank and gallantry.

I am, very respectfully, &c.,

J. PENN.

COL. MORGAN.

White's and Washington's regiments of cavalry, about 70 in number, were expected in camp in a few days; and it was arranged, that on their arrival, they should be embodied into one corps, under the command of Lieut. Col. Washington, and united to the commands of Howard and Rose. Morgan assumed the command of this corps about the 1st of October.

The divisions of the enemy commanded by Cornwallis and Tarleton entered Charlotte after a spirited action between their advance, composed of Tarleton's legion, and Col. Davie's corps. They remained in the neighborhood of this place for some days, waiting for the junction of Col. Ferguson. But the career of this officer had, in the meantime, met with a fearful termination at King's Mountain. A sketch of the memorable battle which was fought on this mountain, may be introduced here.

Col. Clark had been endeavoring to reduce Augusta. The effort, although conducted with courage and perseverance, was unsuccessful. The post, commanded by Col. Brown, had been defended with great vigor; and upon the approach of reinforcements to his aid from Ninety-six, Clark raised the siege, and retired towards the mountains. While the latter was retreating, Ferguson, then on the march for Charlotte, attempted to intercept him. The line of march now taken by the Provincials, indicated a design to invade the mountainous districts. This region of country, and that north and west of it, were inhabited by a race equally distinguished for courage and patriotism. It was, moreover, the asylum for the distressed and persecuted exiles from Georgia and South Carolina. Imbued with a deep hatred of the oppressors of their country, a large proportion of these people were at this time preparing, as has been already observed, to take the field. But maddened at the prospect of invasion, they universally flew to arms; and when Ferguson approached Gilbert-town, he found a force in his front, of not less than three thousand mounted riflemen.[*]

[*] Johnson's Greene, vol. i., pp. 308-4. Lee's Memoirs, pp. 103-105.

Ferguson, astonished, if not dismayed, at the unexpected appearance of an opponent every way so formidable, sent to Cornwallis for aid, and at once commenced a retreat. He was immediately followed by sixteen hundred men, all well mounted, and commanded by Col. Campbell, assisted by Cols. Cleaveland, Sevier, Shelby, Williams, and Major Chronicle. The remainder followed with their utmost speed. Ferguson was overtaken on the 7th of October, at King's Mountain. Hopeless of effecting his retreat without fighting, he posted his troops on the summit of King's Mountain, trusting to be able to make good his position until the expected reinforcements should reach him. Campbell, divining the object of his opponent, at once commenced the attack. He divided his forces into three bodies; one he led himself; the next was headed by Col. Shelby, and the other by Col. Cleaveland. After a severe conflict of an hour, during which the enemy, assailed on every side, found the bayonet ineffectual against the rifle, Ferguson fell, and all that remained of his command at once surrendered. The loss of the British was one hundred and fifty killed, and a like number wounded; while that of the Americans did not exceed ten killed and forty wounded. Including the British wounded, eleven hundred and ten men fell into the hands of the victors, besides fifteen hundred stand of arms. The American loss was rendered peculiarly distressing by the death of Col. Williams, an officer who had greatly distinguished himself in opposing the re-establishment of British authority in the South. Major Chronicle, another distinguished officer and patriot, also fell. Immediately after the action, ten of the prisoners were hung, partly in retaliation for the recent execution of a number of Americans by the British, and partly because the men who suffered had been guilty of murders and other heinous crimes, punishable by the laws with death.*

This was the first decisive blow which the enemy had experienced during their operations in the South.

* Lee's Memoirs, pp. 108–105. Johnson's Greene, vol. i., pp. 805–807.

The news of the battle of King's Mountain reached Cornwallis while on his march from Charlotte to Salisbury. This event, at once so unexpected and disastrous, effected a complete change in his views. The force thus destroyed constituted more than one-third of his active army, while the death of Ferguson greatly diminished his hopes of recruiting his ranks from the loyalists in that quarter, among whom that officer had exercised great influence. The accounts which accompanied these doleful tidings, greatly magnified the very large force of mountaineers that really were in arms, and aroused his fears, not only for the safety of the posts in his rear, constantly menaced by Marion, Sumter, Davie, and other partisan officers, but even for the security of his army, now apparently threatened by such superior numbers. These considerations determined him to defer his movement into North Carolina, until his army could be reinforced.

At this time, Gen. Leslie, with three thousand men, was at Portsmouth. Having sent directions to this officer to embark his troops and sail for Charleston without delay, Cornwallis commenced a retrograde movement on the 14th, and crossing the Catawba, took post at Winnsborough on the 29th of October.*

The success which, until very recently, had uniformly attended the efforts of the British, in the Southern States, encouraged Sir Henry Clinton with hopes that he would be eventually enabled to separate these States from the Confederacy, and re-unite them to the British realm. Regarding this as an object of the very highest importance, he spared no exertions and even ran some hazards to strengthen his forces in that quarter. On the 6th of October, Leslie, with three thousand men, was dispatched southward. Believing that Cornwallis was advancing without opposition through North Carolina, Sir Henry Clinton directed Leslie to land in the lower part of Virginia, at some point favorable to a co-operation with the former, whose orders he was directed to obey. Entering James river, Leslie landed his troops, and took

* Tarleton's Campaign, pp. 166–170.

11

possession of the country on the south side, as high as Suffolk.
After a short time, he drew in his outposts, and began to fortify
Portsmouth. He was at this place when the orders already men-
tioned, for his embarkation for Charleston, reached him.*

Winnsborough, the point selected by Cornwallis for his encampment, was nearly midway between Camden and Ninety-six, his
two principal posts in the northern part of the State, and was
moreover, the centre of a populous and fruitful district. Here he
desired to remain, until the arrival of Leslie could enable him to
resume his operations against North Carolina and Virginia.
Although the postponement of these operations was, it is certain,
mainly owing to the large American force in the field, this circumstance seems to have given him no fears for the possession of
South Carolina. A considerable proportion of his army, which
amounted in all to more than four thousand men, was distributed
in such a manner as to observe the whole frontier of the State,
and to guard the interior against revolt. The main body at
Winnsborough was in a favorable position for guarding his principal posts and checking his opponents, as well as for prosecuting
his plans of future conquest, when he should have received the
coming reinforcements.

The news of the battle, and of the subsequent retreat of Cornwallis, had a most cheering effect upon the Americans. Their
forces immediately pressed forward. The militia under Gen.
Smallwood, Morgan and his command, and Col. Davie's corps soon
after concentrated at New Providence. The main body of the
Continental troops left Hillsborough about the same time, and
marched towards Salisbury.

A few days before the army left Hillsborough, General Gates
was advised of the promotion of Gen. Morgan. The representations with this object had been so numerous and influential, and
the reasons in its favor so cogent, that at length, Congress acted
in the premises, and on the 13th of October, appointed him to

* Tarleton's Campaign, pp. 166–170.

the rank of a brigadier general.* The commission, with the
resolution of Congress, and the letter of President Huntington,
were forwarded to Gen. Gates, who, upon receiving them, addressed
Morgan the following letter:

HILLSBOROUGH, *Oct.* 27, 1780.

DEAR GENERAL:

Enclosed, I send you the resolve of Congress, appointing you a brigadier general, in the army of the United States, of which I sincerely wish
you joy. Your commission is in my hands, which I reserve to send by
the first troops that march, as this conveyance may not be altogether so
safe. The disappointments and delays by the Board of War, in supplying
the wagons necessary for our march, have been amazing; but I think they
cannot now defer it beyond to-morrow.

I am, dear general,
Yours, affectionately,
HORATIO GATES.

GEN. MORGAN.

The gratification which this announcement created in Morgan's
breast, must have been greatly increased by the consciousness

*IN CONGRESS.
October 13th, 1780.

Congress took into consideration the report of the Board of War, respecting the promotion of Col. Morgan, and it appearing from the letters of Governors Jefferson and Rutledge, and of Major General Gates, that Col. Morgan's promotion to the rank of a
Brigadier General will remove several embarrassments which impede the public service in
the Southern Department, and that it will otherwise greatly advance the said service,

Resolved, Therefore, that Colonel Daniel Morgan be, and hereby is, appointed to the
rank of Brigadier General, in the army of the United States.

Extract from the Minutes, CHARLES THOMSON, *Sec.*

PHILADELPHIA, *Oct.* 14th, 1780.

SIR: Congress have been pleased to appoint you a Brigadier General, in the army of
the United States of America,

I have now the pleasure and satisfaction herewith to enclose your commission, conform-
able to that appointment.

I have the honor to be,
With esteem and respect,
Your obedient servant,
SAMUEL HUNTINGTON.

BR. GEN. MORGAN. *Pres,*

that the honor was earned by services past, and by the expectation of services to be performed. He felt a laudable pride in the
conviction, that he was indebted for his promotion to none of
those sinister influences, which but too frequently, during these
times, misdirected the appointing power, and enabled the undeserving to obtain high rank in the army. Among the congratulations which poured in on him from all sides, those from
his brother officers, and they were numerous, were particularly
grateful to his feelings. They were the best qualified to estimate
his merits, and they would be the last to compliment him on an
undeserved honor.

In pursuance of directions from Gen. Smallwood, Morgan, now
brigadier general, advanced to the vicinity of Clermont. Having
been joined some days before, by Lieut. Col. Howard and the
cavalry, the corps was now in readiness for any enterprise which
fortune, or the incautiousness of the enemy, might afford them.

While in this quarter, Morgan received a number of letters
from his brother officers in the main army. The occasional introduction of a few of these will serve to diversify the narrative, and
at the same time furnish important links to the chain of events
which marked the times. The annexed was written by Col. O.
H. Williams, at the time adjutant general of the Southern army.

CAMP HILLSBOROUGH, *31st Oct.*, 1780.

DEAR SIR: We have been under marching orders ten days. I believe
we shall actually move to-morrow. The reports of the enemy's landing in
Virginia have detained us two days. The general has been in some
suspense ; however, I believe he is now determined to move westward.
The enemy are actually in possession of Portsmouth, and the reports say
they are from three thousand to five thousand in number—but this we are
not clear in.

What do you think of the damnable doings of that diabolical dog
Arnold ? I have not an idea of a punishment adequate to the enormity
of his crime. André suffered like a hero, and was really an object of
admiration. In the full career of glory, twenty-eight years of age, major
in the British army, adjutant-general in America, heir to a large estate, of

a good family, master of a fine education, and endowed with superior abilities. His address only failed him in an enterprise in which few excel, but many cut a distinguished figure. If he deserved hanging, Arnold will be damned, according to the opinions I have of degrees of punishment.

Perusing your obliging letter about the third time, I accidentally turned the first leaf, on which you had signed "Daniel Morgan," and I found your N. B. just in time. The committee had closed their proceedings, and almost the blue ells were gone. No such stuff was left in store. I have secured eight yards of the lining for you, and have two pairs of socks of my own—you shall go halves.

I thank Col. Howard for his letter of the 23d of October—the deserters he mentions have not joined us. My best compliments to him and all the gentlemen of the light infantry. If you are with Gen. Smallwood, present me to him and family. To-morrow we leave this dirty, disagreeable hole, Hillsborough. Adieu.

Yours, sincerely,

O. H. WILLIAMS.

P. S.—Pardon me—I must be permitted to congratulate you on the justice Congress have been pleased to do you in your appointment. Pardon me, I say, for making my best compliments by way of P. S.

OTHO.

BRIG. GEN. MORGAN.

An amusing instance of the straits to which even officers high in rank were put, at this time, is furnished in the foregoing. There is no room for any feelings but sorrow and pity, in contemplating the sufferings then experienced by the army, in consequence of its general destitution. Winter had set in with constant and drenching rains; yet the greater part of the men were without anything worthy the name of clothing; and tents, and many other things usually considered among the necessaries of an army, they had not. Although Morgan's command had received a tolerable supply of clothing—an indispensable preliminary to its taking the field—it was yet to be furnished with tents, wagons, and other articles of field equipage. It was thrown upon its own resources entirely for support; and seldom enjoyed the much valued ration of rum. For some time after this corps took the field, it had no shelter from the storm, no covering in repose, beyond those afforded by the branches of a tree, or the leeward side of a hill.

The tranquillity of Cornwallis was greatly disturbed by the operations of Marion and Sumter. He accordingly took measures which aimed at their destruction. Marion beat up the country between the Pedee and Santee rivers, and besides intimidating the loyalists and encouraging the whigs, seriously threatened the communications between Charleston and Camden. Sumter ranged through the district west of the Santee; and being now at the head of a large force, menaced Ninety-six and Augusta. Col. Tarleton and his legion were sent against Marion; while Major Wemys, with a regiment of infantry and a troop of cavalry, was dispatched after Sumter.

Marion, on the approach of danger, retired to the swamps in his neighborhood. From an unavailing pursuit of this officer, Tarleton was hastily recalled, to make amends for the discomfiture which Sumter had in the meantime inflicted on Wemys. This officer left Winnsborough in the evening, and reached the outskirts of Sumter's camp before daylight the next morning, Sumter had profited by the severe lesson he received in the previous August; and reckoning upon an attempt at surprise, was fully prepared to meet it. A strong advanced guard, commanded by Col. Taylor, met the enemy; and after an animated contest, the British were driven from the field, leaving behind them thirty killed and wounded. Among the latter was Major Wemys, who was found on the ground the next morning, severely wounded, having received a ball through both thighs.*

After this affair, Sumter, in concert with Colonels Clark and Banner, made preparations for a descent on Ninety-six, when he was apprised by a deserter, of the approach of Tarleton, with a powerful force. Sumter immediately retraced his steps; but in a short time his adversary was close upon him. Crossing the

* Johnson's Greene, vol. i., pp. 316, 317.

Ennoree, Sumter pushed on towards the Tyger river. On his arrival at Black Stock House, on the banks of that stream, he prepared for battle. Tarleton, apprehending that Sumter would exert himself to escape, pressed forward with about four hundred cavalry and mounted infantry, leaving three hundred more, including his artillery, to follow as fast as they could. On coming in sight of the American forces, he posted his men on an eminence opposite to their position, with the intention of awaiting the arrival of the remainder of his command, before he took any further steps. But Sumter, aware of the divided state of the enemy, promptly seized the moment most favorable for attacking them. A warm action ensued; but the British at length fled the field, leaving behind them no less than ninety-two killed and one hundred wounded.*

In this action, Sumter received a severe wound in the breast, which perhaps prevented him from realizing still more decided advantages from the victory he had gained. It certainly deprived his country of his valuable services for some months after. Having buried the dead, and ministered to the necessities of the wounded, including those of the enemy, who were all left on the field, the victors crossed the Tyger, and retreated towards the mountains. Dispersing a few days after, to re-unite again when a favorable opportunity for action offered, these gallant spirits retired to their homes—all but a small party, who escorted their wounded commander to a place of security, in the interior of North Carolina.†

A short time prior to these cheering events, another, equally gratifying, occurred, in which the cavalry of Morgan's command was engaged. This was the affair of Rugely's farm, in which the redoubtable colonel " of that ilk " was so cruelly circumvented. The movement which led to the capture of this officer and his command, originated in objects of more importance. The loyal-

---

* Lee's Memoirs, pp. 112–114; Johnson's Greene, vol. i., pp. 318–321.
† Ibidem.

ists in the neighborhood of Lynch's Creek and the Waxhaw settlements, were meditating a general removal of their families and
property, to Camden. To prevent this, Col. Davie had been
dispatched to that quarter. But, under the protection of a body
of four hundred British and loyalists, sent from Camden, for the
purpose, the tory inhabitants began to remove, and to carry with
them, not only their own effects, but those of the whigs in their
neighborhood. Davie's force being too weak to perform the duty
upon which it was sent, in the face of the British covering party,
Morgan was dispatched with his corps, towards Hanging Rock,
the place where the British were posted, with directions to attack
them, and to intercept the removal of property to Camden.

Morgan accordingly advanced with his whole command, to the
neighborhood of Hanging Rock. But the British detachment
had been apprised of its danger, and made a timely retreat to
Camden. During the march, the cavalry scoured the country to
the right and the left, and in advance of the infantry; but saving
a few inconsiderable captures, and the collection of forage,
nothing was effected. Morgan was about retracing his steps,
when he was informed that a considerable body of loyalists and
some British troops were then assembled at a farm called
Clermont, the property of a tory named Rugely. He likewise
learned that the object of this collection was to facilitate
recruiting among the disaffected in the neighborhood, that
something more than nominal effect might be given to Colonel
Rugely's new commission. Morgan felt a strong desire to uproot
this nest of tories; but as it was within ten miles of Camden,
and still nearer to a strong outpost of the British army, to
approach it with his infantry was deemed too hazardous. Col.
Washington was, however, sent with his cavalry to reconnoitre
the enemy, and received permission to avail himself of a fair
opportunity of capturing or dispersing them.

Col. Rugely, learning that an enemy was approaching, took
post with his men in a large log building, around which had

been constructed an entrenchment and a line of abatis. Confident in his ability to defend himself against a troop or two of horse, or any other description of force unaccompanied by artillery, he calmly prepared himself for the expected attack. On coming in sight of the place, Washington immediately discovered that nothing could be effected against it by surprise, and moreover, that it was easily defended against a force such as that he commanded. But reckoning on the inexperience of his adversary, he hit upon an expedient for arousing Rugely's fears, which was crowned with success. Having prepared the trunk of a small pine tree into some sort of resemblance to a cannon, and mounted it upon the wheels of a wagon, he made a disposition of his forces, as if preparing for a cannonade, and then sent a corporal of dragoons with a flag, to the fort, to summon its commanding officer to an immediate surrender. The gravity with which the farce was enacted, from the levelling of the pine cannon to the solemn summons of the corporal, confirmed the imposition on the mind of Col. Rugely, who instantly complied with the summons. In a few minutes after, himself and his garrison of about one hundred men, marched out of the barn, prisoners of war.

The extent to which Col. Rugely was *outgeneralled* in this affair, may be comprehended from the fact, that on the ludicrous circumstances of his capture being communicated to Cornwallis, the latter introduced a letter on the subject, with the declaration: "Rugely will not be made a brigadier!" *

* Rugely was subsequently paroled to Charleston. His application to this end was made the subject of the following letter from Morgan to Greene, by which it would appear that he was held in as little respect as a military man, by his enemies, as he was by his friends.

NEW PROVIDENCE, 5th Nov., 1780.

SIR : Colonel Rugely will apply for a parole to go to Charleston. I believe he may be depended on, but when they get him there I fear they won't be anxious to exchange him, as they won't, after this, look upon him as a great military character. Col. Isaacs, who has been a very active man in the State of North Carolina, is now a prisoner, and is sent up to St. Augustine. If a partial exchange could be effected, Rugely for Isaacs

11*

After burning the log house, and collecting a quantity of provisions and forage found at the place, Washington returned with his prisoners to rejoin Morgan. The latter soon after took up his line of march for the neighborhood of New Providence. Here he was informed that Gen. Gates had given orders for the different detachments to march to Charlotte ; and that General Greene had recently arrived at that place, and had assumed the command of the army.

The introduction of this distinguished officer to the reader as the future general of the Southern army, calls for a brief review of the circumstances which led to his appointment to this command.

The high hopes entertained by Congress and the nation, at the opening of this campaign, that the conquerer of the North would gather fresh laurels in the South, were crushed by the disastrous issue of the battle near Camden. With this event, the confidence so generally reposed in his abilities was succeeded by distrust; and although the prudence and perseverance which he subsequently displayed contrasted favorably with his previous course, and gave promise of better results for the future, it soon became apparent that his reputation had suffered an incurable wound.

A belief that his fame was unsupported by any distinguishing marks of soldiership, and that it was indebted for its existence to a fortunate combination of circumstances, had long prevailed to a great extent among the officers of the army. This belief, when considered in connection with his known participation in the intrigues of Conway and others against the commander-in-chief, needed not the confirmation afforded by his recent misfortunes, to render him exceedingly unpopular with this patriotic and influential class.

it would give a great deal of happiness in relieving a friend of mine, and a sincere friend to his country. Col. Martin, of the Board of War, can give you his character.
I have the honor to be your obedient servant,
DANIEL MORGAN,
MAJOR GENERAL GREENE.

Exhausted as were the resources of the country, the utmost exertions of Congress were yet unproductive of means adequate to the fearful emergency which had arisen; and its hopes of success depended almost entirely upon the zealous coöperation of the militia. In ordinary cases, the citizen soldier was slow to join the standard of an unworthy or an unpopular officer. But when, as in the present case, the impulses of patriotism were barely able to overcome the suggestions of prudence, and when despair of the cause was spreading far and wide, to look for his appearance under a leader whom he regarded as having forfeited all claims upon his confidence, was to indulge in expectations at war with all experience.

The destruction of a fine army, and the subjugation of two States of the confederacy, under circumstances as yet unexplained, should not, it was thought, be permitted to pass without inquiry. A proper regard for the interests of the confederacy, a decent respect for public sentiment, and justice to the unfortunate general himself—all concurred in demanding an investigation.

An examination of the circumstances which preceded the defeat of the army under General Gates, unavoidably led to conclusions unfavorable to his judgment and prudence, and suggested, among other measures necessary to be taken in the creation of a new army, his removal from command in the South. Fearful consequences were expected to ensue, unless the feeble means of resistance about being put forth were confided to a successor, whose past services gave him an undoubted claim to public confidence, and who was capable of reassuring the people, and of terminating, at their head, the enemy's career of triumph.

Although these and other considerations called imperatively for the supersedure of General Gates, Congress, entertaining a high respect for his private worth, and a grateful recollection of his former services, deferred a compliance. It was hoped that time might yet enable the aged warrior to retrieve his character, and by a fortunate stroke, reëstablish himself in public favor. But although three months had nearly elapsed, no such opportunity occurred ; and the period for action being at hand, further delay was attended with too much danger to be permitted. A resolution was accordingly adopted by Congress, on the 5th of November, ordering a court of inquiry to be held on the conduct of Gen. Gates as commander of the Southern department, and moreover, directing the commander-in-chief to appoint some other officer to command that department during the inquiry. Thus at length the blow was struck. Though justice might have hesitated in pronouncing this sentence, policy demanded the sacrifice.

Gen. Gates, although unapprised of the intention to supersede him until late in November, seems to have anticipated such a step with indifference, if not with pleasure. In a letter to Morgan, dated the 13th of that month, he observes : " I hear by report that I am to be recalled, and that General Greene is to succeed to the command of the Southern department. But of this I have not the smallest intimation from Congress, which, I conceive, would have been the case, had the business been finally settled. I think exactly as you do in regard to the command, and am impatient for the arrival of General Greene."

A few days after this letter was written, the resolution of Congress already referred to, reached him at Salisbury. The unpleasant intelligence conveyed by this communication, served, to all appearances, only to stimulate his exertions in the public service. His efforts to establish magazines and collect supplies, as well as to organize his forces, regular and militia, were indefatigable, and in some degree successful. The movements of the enemy were watched with sleepless vigilance, and his precautionary measures against them were indicative of intelligence and zeal. Upon learning that Cornwallis was collecting his forces in the neighborhood of Camden, he broke up his camp at Salisbury, and marching to Charlotte, sent directions to his advanced detachments to concentrate at that place, with the determination of opposing the enemy, should they advance upon him.

These operations were going forward, when General Greene

arrived in the American camp. This officer, who had served with great distinction from the commencement of the war, and had won for himself an enviable position in the estimation of Congress and the country, was selected by the commander-in-chief to succeed Gen. Gates. Reluctantly accepting the honorable, but responsible command, he received his instructions, and on the 23d of November, accompanied by General the Baron Steuben and his aids, Major Burnett, and Colonel Morris, commenced his journey for the South.*

The route which General Greene had marked out for himself, ran through Philadelphia and the seats of government of Delaware, Maryland, Virginia, and North Carolina. At each of these places he stopped a short time to make his requisitions, and to ascertain the extent to which it was probable they would be complied with. To arouse the authorities to a just sense of their danger, and to convince them of the necessity of providing means for the increase and support of his army, he addressed them respectively with a force and earnestness, well calculated to produce the desired results. These letters, besides exhibiting that vigor of thought and felicity of expression which characterize all Gen. Greene's epistolary remains, were marked by a judicious application of their subject to the peculiar circumstances of each State. In all of them, however, the main features of his subject stood prominently forth, and were considered in terms substantially the same. Referring to the great strength and known objects of the enemy, and picturing in vivid colors the consequences which would follow their success, he frankly declared his inability to resist them, unless the assistance demanded was promptly given. These letters, which reflect no little credit on their author's mental resources, were followed by good results; and perhaps the subsequent successes of his sword are attributable, in some degree, to the previous achievements of his pen.

All that Gen. Greene obtained at Philadelphia, beyond promi-

* Johnson's Greene, vol. i., p. 332.

ses, was the annexation of Maryland and Delaware, with the troops belonging to those States, to the Southern department, and a small supply of cash, to defray his personal expenses. Leaving Col. Febriger at this place to take charge of the promised supplies, he pushed on to Delaware, and thence to Maryland. Having made his requisitions on these States, and appointed Generals Gist and Smallwood to superintend the organization and forwarding of the troops to be raised, he proceeded to the capital of Virginia. This State, being the first in population, wealth, and resources, among her sisters in the South, and being second to none in the confederacy in her zeal for independence, and in the amount of sacrifices she had made for its maintenance, was that on which the intention of the enemy centered, and against which, all their efforts had ultimate reference. The liberality with which this State had contributed to carry on the war, when united to the losses she had incurred from unsalable products, the suspension of trade, and the ravaging hand of invasion, had exhausted her resources; and at this time, so far from being able to contribute her quota to the ranks of the Southern army, she was unable to repel the enemy, who were even at the moment establishing themselves on the soil. But although her means were gone, her spirit of resistance had experienced no diminution; and while almost all her remaining energies were combining to confine Leslie to the seaboard, General Greene's arrangements indicated a determination to make a grand rally on her southern frontier, should the enemy so far prevail against him. He established a number of magazines and laboratories at different points, judiciously chosen, and made extensive arrangements for the speedy deposit therein of a large supply of stores and provisions. He set on foot a quartermaster's department, placing at its head Colonel Carrington, who at once entered zealously into the business of obtaining a supply of wagons, tents, and other necessaries. Measures were taken for a thorough examination of the Dan, Yadkin, Catawba, and

other rivers of North and South Carolina, with an eye to future
military operations ; and orders were given for the construction
of a number of boats to be placed on these rivers for the
transportation of troops and stores, as occasion might require.
Conferring the command in this State on Baron Steuben, who
was directed to facilitate the raising and forwarding of supplies
and reinforcements, General Greene resumed his journey, and in
a few days reached Hillsborough. More apprehensive of Leslie
than of Cornwallis, the authorities of North Carolina had
recently left Hillsborough and reassembled at Halifax. But the
imminent danger which threatened the State on all sides, had
thoroughly aroused its government and people ; vigorous efforts
had therefore been made to increase the means of resistance.
The same causes which produced a removal of the authorities of
this State, had directed a large proportion of its militia towards
the eastern frontier. Having informed the governor that ample
provision had been made in Virginia, for the employment of the
enemy in that quarter, and urged the assemblage of the militia in
the quarter threatened by Cornwallis, General Greene resumed
his journey, now rapidly drawing to a close. On the 2nd of
December, he arrived at the American camp at Charlotte, and on
the 4th, assumed the command of the army.*

A manly resignation marked the conduct of General Gates,
upon the arrival of his successor, whom he received at head-
quarters with that liberal and gentlemanly air which was so
habitual to him. General Greene observed a plain, but respectful
demeanor, neither betraying compassion nor the want of it. He
was announced to the army as its future commander, on the
morning of the 4th, by General Gates. On the same day, General Greene paid his predecessor the compliment of confirming
all his standing orders.†

To the intimation that a court of inquiry had been ordered to
convene and take into consideration his conduct as commander of

* Johnson's Greene, pp. 882–883.   † Col. O. H. Williams.

the Southern army, Gen. Gates responded by expressing his
willingness to proceed to an immediate investigation. But the
principles on which the court was to be constituted, rendered this
impracticable. It would have been, besides, unjust and cruel,
under existing circumstances. Gen. Gates had yet to learn the
recent death of a much-loved son, his grief for whom would, for
a time, naturally absorb all other considerations, and render him
incapable of an efficient defence. The inquiry was therefore
necessarily deferred; and Gen. Gates, after a few days spent in
familiarizing Gen. Greene with the details of his command, bade
adieu to the camp, and returned to his residence in Virginia.

This part of our subject will close with the remark, that Gen.
Gates was spared the mortification of an inquiry. The resolution
with this object was subsequently rescinded by Congress, and the
general restored to his rank in the army.*

The situation of affairs in the South when Gen. Greene took the
command, was lamentable in the extreme. A mind less determined, less fertile in resources, than that possessed by this
commander, would have shrunk from the fearful task he assumed.
The States of South Carolina and Georgia were in the possession
of the enemy. Virginia and North Carolina were invaded, and
threatened with a similar fate. The State governments of Georgia
and South Carolina had only a titular existence. The large
bodies of militia which North Carolina had injudiciously kept in
the field, served only to impoverish the country and exhaust the
resources of the government, without yielding any benefit in
return. From this cause, and the divisions of public sentiment,
it at length became difficult to assemble even militia, and quite
impossible to raise the State's quota of 500 men to the continental
line. The condition of affairs in Virginia has already been
noticed. Bereft of almost every resource but the firm hearts and
stout arms of her sons, this State was unprepared to resist the
danger which stood on her threshold, and could add but little to
the strength of the Southern army.

* Col. O. H. Williams.

The aspect of the country around Gen. Greene was not more encouraging. The predatory war which had hitherto been prosecuted in the Carolinas, had banished industry as well as the hopes which nerve the arm of labor. The fields not visited by the despoiler, of one party or the other, were those only from which nothing was to be gleaned. The general demoralization which naturally followed, was incalculably increased by the rancor of party feeling. A large proportion of the people were attached to the British rule ; but much the greater number were the friends of independence. Many of these two parties, which were known by the names of whig and tory, took an active part in the war ; and their animosity to each other constantly displayed itself with little less than savage fury. As one act of cruelty generally originates another, in the frequent encounters of these partisans, the claims of mercy were seldom regarded ; while murders, robberies, and burnings were daily committed, under the sanction which war so commonly affords to crime. The whigs, actuated by a love of country, and a desire of independence from European control, stimulated, perhaps, by personal losses and wrongs, were only sustained in their efforts by the hopes of an ultimate triumph ; and, in pursuit of this, they endured every privation, and made every sacrifice. The tories, encouraged and protected by the British, and sharing largely in the money so lavishly expended by the latter, took the field in numbers, and fought with a constancy and a courage that would have done honor to a better cause. Up to this period, some three thousand of these loyalists had been raised and brought to a state of efficiency little inferior to that of the British regulars.

The army under Cornwallis, strong in numbers, and complete in all its equipments, was awaiting only the arrival of Gen. Leslie's reinforcement to prosecute to a completion the threatened subjugation of the South. The strength of this army has never been accurately ascertained. But there is abundant evidence to show that it was not less than 4,000 men. These, rendered confident from the success which had hitherto attended them, were eager for the opening of the campaign.

To meet an emergency attended by such discouraging circumstances, Gen. Greene was placed at the head of an army, not exceeding 2,000 men in all, of which but 800 were regular troops. Small as was this force, it was almost naked, badly armed, short of ammunition and supplies, and destitute of tents and wagons—in short, deficient in every requisite of an army. For some time previously to Gen. Greene's assumption of the command, it had literally lived from hand to mouth; there were now but three days' provision in store, and no certain prospect of a fresh supply before that was exhausted. The country for some miles around the American camp had been completely stripped of provisions, while the want of wagons rendered it impossible to obtain the supplies which were abundant at a greater distance. If anything were wanting, in addition, to merge discouragement into despair, it existed in the belief that the army was more likely to diminish, from the limitations of service, and desertion, than to increase from the promised reinforcements. The intelligence received by the general from Congress and the State governments in the Southern department, did not encourage his hopes of being able to take the field against the enemy before the succeeding spring. Yet it became evident that the latter would commence operations before that time, and carry into effect the threatened invasion of North Carolina.*

The policy adopted by Gen. Greene under these circumstances was indicative of sound judgment; its correctness was subsequently confirmed by the success which attended it. He determined to divide his forces into two bodies, and to take post on the right and left of the enemy. The main body, under his own direction, was to occupy a position on the waters of the Pedee; while a strong detachment, the command of which was confided to Gen. Morgan, was to operate in the country between the Broad and Pacolet rivers. The reasons for this disposition may be briefly stated.

* Correspondence; Johnson's Greene, vol. i., pp. 340–346.

The scarcity of provisions in the neighborhood of Charlotte required a change of situation; and the quarters to which the troops were about moving would, it was believed, furnish an abundance. The people in these districts were mostly zealous whigs, and under the protection afforded them by a regular force, it was expected that they would take the field in large numbers. Although the road was thus left open for Cornwallis to advance into North Carolina, he could not take this step without exposing his flanks and the posts in his rear to the assaults of Greene and Morgan, leaving out of account the opposition he might possibly meet with in front, from the patriotic inhabitants, particularly those of Mecklenburg and Rowan, and the mountain warriors who destroyed Ferguson. Camden and Ninety-six, the principal of these posts, kept the whole country below them in subjection; they were, besides, the main depositories of stores and provisions for the British army. The capture of these places would be followed by a general uprising of the whigs throughout South Carolina, and perhaps prove fatal to the objects of the enemy in the South. But notwithstanding all these risks, should the British persevere in advancing towards Virginia, they would yet be much further from Hillsborough, a point intersecting the usual route thither, than the main body of the Americans. This division, retreating to that place, would be enabled to throw themselves before the enemy, and preserve their communications with the North, from whence they expected their supplies and reinforcements. The division under Morgan could in the meantime retreat before the enemy and impede their advance; or fall upon and harass their rear. It was at liberty, besides, to descend into South Carolina, and re-exciting by its presence the spirit of revolt, gather around it a militia force sufficiently strong to enable it to capture successively the British posts, and perhaps to effect the re-conquest of the country north and west of Charleston.

But Gen. Greene's main object was to alarm Cornwallis for the safety of his posts to such a degree, as to induce him to defer the prosecution of his designs on North Carolina and Virginia, and to detain him in South Carolina, until an army could be raised sufficiently strong to fight him with a prospect of success. In this Greene to some extent succeeded.*

On the 20th of December, the divisions of the American army moved in opposite directions from Charlotte. The main body, under the command of Gen. Huger, took up its line of march towards the Pedee, and crossing to the eastern bank of that river, moved down a few miles, and on the 26th, encamped at Hick's Creek, nearly opposite the Cheraw Hills. The detachment commanded by Morgan, consisting of three hundred and twenty light infantry, two hundred Virginia militia, and about eighty cavalry, in all five hundred and eighty men, was put in motion for the country watered by the Broad and Pacolet rivers.

A few days previous to this movement, Morgan received a letter from Gen. Greene, announcing his appointment to the command of this corps, and containing his instructions, the nature of which will be best understood by the letter itself.

INSTRUCTIONS.

Sir: You are appointed to the command of a corps of light infantry, a detachment of militia, and Lieut.-Col. Washington's regiment of light dragoons. With these troops you will proceed to the west side of the Catawba river, where you will be joined by a body of volunteer militia, under the command of Brig. Gen. Davidson, of this State, and by the militia lately under the command of Brig. Gen. Sumter. This force, and such others as may join you from Georgia, you will employ against the enemy on the west side of the river, either offensively or defensively, as your own prudence and discretion may direct, acting with caution and avoiding surprises by every possible precaution. For the present, I give you the entire command in that quarter, and do hereby require all officers and soldiers engaged in the American camp to be subject to your orders and command.

The object of this detachment is to give protection to that part of the

* Johnson's Greene, vol. i., pp. 348–351.

GENERAL DANIEL M)RGAN. 261

country and spirit up the people, to annoy the enemy in that quarter, collect the provisions and forage out of the way of the enemy, which you will
have formed into a number of small magazines in the rear of the position
you may think proper to take. You will prevent plundering as much as
possible, and be as careful of your provisions and forage as may be,
giving receipts for whatever you take to all such as are friends to the
independence of America.

Should the enemy move in force towards the Pedee, where this army
will take a position, you will move in such direction as will enable you to
join me if necessary, or to fall back upon the flank or into the rear of the
enemy, as occasion may require. You will spare no pains to get good
intelligence of the enemy's situation, and keep me constantly advertised
of both your and their movements. You will appoint, for the time being,
a commissary, quarter-master, and forage-master, who will follow your
instructions in their several lines.

Confiding in your abilities and activity, I entrust you with this command,
being persuaded you will do everything in your power to distress the enemy,
and afford protection to the country.

Given under my hand at Charlotte, this 16th December, 1780.

NATH. GREENE.

To BRIG. GEN. MORGAN.

CHAPTER XIV.

Morgan marches towards the Catawba river—His expectations of being joined by the militia disappointed—Causes of their non-appearance—Letter from Gen. Davidson—Morgan's arrangements—Detaches Col. Washington against a body of Tories—The latter cut to pieces—Washington destroys Fort Williams—Morgan sends another detachment to cover Washington's retreat—Letters: from Morgan to Greene; from Gov. Rutledge to Morgan; from Greene to Morgan; from Col. O. H. Williams to Morgan; from Greene to Morgan; from Morgan to Greene; from Greene to Morgan—Cornwallis directs Tarleton to advance against Morgan—Cornwallis puts his army in motion.

PURSUING his march, Morgan crossed the Catawba at Biggin's Ferry, a short distance below the mouth of the Little Catawba, on the evening of the 20th of December; and crossing Broad river, above the mouth of the Pacolet, encamped at Grindall's Fort, on the north bank of the latter river, on the 25th.

Upon starting from Charlotte, he felt assured of being joined on his route by a considerable body of the large militia force, which it was expected would now be on foot, to coöperate with both divisions of the army. The hopes of the people, now recovered from the shock which they received at Camden in the preceding August, burst forth anew with a more ardent zeal ; and the representations which poured in upon the American commanders, justified them in believing that the host which gathered at Gilbertown upon the approach of Ferguson, were ready at the word of command, to descend from their native hills and reënact the tragedy of King's Mountain. To produce such a result, letters had previously been addressed to Generals Marion, Sumter, and Davidson, Colonels Pickens, Campbell, Clark, Twiggs, Cleaveland, and other zealous and influential commanders, apprising them of the contemplated movement, and invoking their aid at the head of the militia. But a recent incursion of the Indians had given the militia employment in another direction; and the disappointment which Morgan experienced from this circumstance, was coupled with the intimation it afforded him of an early movement of the British army. Hitherto the commencement of general operations on the part of the British, had always been heralded by the advance of their savage allies into those districts from whence the militia were to be drawn. The latter were thus compelled to remain in their own section of country, to guard their families and homes against the chances of murder and devastation. Two or three days elapsed after Morgan reached the banks of the Pacolet, before he received any aid of this description, when about two hundred and sixty mounted Corolinians, under Col. Pickins and Major McCall, arrived. In lieu of General Davidson, who, it was confidently expected, would immediately join him at the head of from six hundred to one thousand men, the following letter from that officer, explaining the causes of his non-appearance, overtook Morgan on the march.

CAMP RAMSON'S BATTLE GROUND, *Dec. 14th,* 1780.

SIR: My orders from General Greene were to join you as soon as possible after you crossed the river, which I should have effected before this time, had the troops joined, agreeable to my expectations. But the expedition against the Cherokee Downs, and the murders committed in Rutherford and Burke counties, have entirely drawn off the attention of the people who were to compose my command. I suspect it to be a stratagem, as Davis was undoubtedly concerned in the murders. I have not ninety men; but have some hopes from Shelby and Cleaveland, on which I shall wait until Tuesday, when I shall move to join you, be my force what it may. Do remedy as much as possible the present disappointment. I have dispatched orders to all the colonels in the district of Salisbury, to make their drafts immediately, and forward them to Charlotte against the 10th day of next month. The whole will amount to one thousand. I consider it of the utmost importance to support the western settle-

ments of South Carolina and Georgia. I should be happy to know
where to find you.

I have the honor to be, &c.,

WM. DAVIDSON.

GEN. DANIEL MORGAN.

On the 28th or 29th of December, Gen. Davidson arrived at
Morgan's camp, bringing with him only one hundred and twenty
men. But he returned immediately for the drafts alluded to
above, who, to the number of five hundred or more, were then
embodied at Salisbury.

Reckoning on the coöperation of a large body of the finest
militia in the country, General Morgan had previously concerted
a plan of offensive operations, within the scope of which, an attack
upon Cornwallis in his camp was even included. Had his expectations of reinforcements been but partially realized, he intended
attacking and taking successively the posts of Ninety-six and
Augusta. Hereupon being joined by Marion (who at this time
was operating against Georgetown), with their combined forces,
such additional advantages over the enemy might be obtained, as
the courage and strength of their forces, and the fortune of war,
might afford them. It was therefore a source of bitter mortification to Morgan to be compelled, from the feebleness of his force,
to' relinquish designs which promised results equally important
and glorious, and to confine himself to a line of duty, which,
while it subjected him to the most imminent peril, was secondary
in its nature and objects. But the circumstances of the case
admitted of no alternative, and in conformity with his instructions, he immediately commenced measures, having for their
objects, the injury and annoyance of the enemy, the augmenta-
tion of his forces, the collection of provisions and forage, and the
establishment of magazines of supplies in the rear of his position. His first step was to organize the means of obtaining
speedy, correct, and frequent information of the enemy's
movements. To this end, a number of active and intelligent

men were sent forward into the neighborhood of the British camp, with directions to note everything that transpired there, and to report to him at least twice in twenty-four hours. He opened a correspondence with a number of the most influential militia officers in the district under his command, explaining the important objects which might be effected with the aid of a large body of militia, and entreating them to join him with their commands, at the earliest practicable moment. Captain Chitty, the commissary of provisions, in conjunction with the forage-master, was dispatched from camp, with directions to collect all provisions and forage to be found in the country between the Broad and Catawba rivers, and to deposit them in magazines to be established for the purpose. These matters having been arranged, his attention was now directed towards the enemy, in the hope that some opening might speedily offer, through which he could annoy them. Such an opening soon after presented itself, and was promptly seized. The consequences which followed are well worthy of recital, less from their intrinsic importance, than from the material influence which they undoubtedly exercised on the subsequent operations of the British army.

Two or three days after Morgan had taken post on the Pacolet, one of his spies returned to camp with the information that a body of loyalists from the Savannah river, about two hundred and fifty in number, and led by Col. Waters, were laying waste the settlements on Fair Forest Creek, distant about twenty miles from the American camp. The inhabitants in the neighborhood of this creek were all staunch whigs, and the pretext of a design on their part to take up arms was framed for the purpose of giving something like a legal sanction to the outrage and robbery of which they were made the victims. Against this body of tories, Morgan dispatched Lieut. Col. Washington with his cavalry and about two hundred mounted militia under Major M'Call, with directions to surprise them if possible, but at all events, to disperse them.

12

Arriving at Fair Forest Creek, Washington was informed that the tories, having been apprised of his approach, had decamped the day previously. He subsequently learned that they had retreated to Hammond's Store, a place about twenty miles further South, where, deeming themselves secure from danger, Winnsborough being on their right, and Ninety-six on their left, they intended reposing for a few days. In the hope of surprising them in their camp, Washington resumed the pursuit, and after an unceasing march of nearly forty miles, at length came up with them.

The result was fearful and bloody, and furnished a lesson of retribution that forever after influenced the conduct of the disaffected in South Carolina. The rapine and cruelty which marked the footsteps of the tories in the settlements at Fair Forest Creek, inspired the American troops with such feelings of high-wrought indignation, and such a keen desire for revenge, as to render them impatient and reckless in the pursuit, as well as merciless and uncontrollable in the work of death. Instantly charging in front and flank the panic-stricken foe, whose efforts from the onset were directed rather towards flight than defence, a rout immediately followed; and notwithstanding the strenuous efforts of Washington and McCall to restrain the fury of their men, the slaughter ceased not while an object of vengeance remained within reach. Of the two hundred and fifty men whom Waters commanded previous to the action, one hundred and fifty were killed and wounded; only forty were taken prisoners; the remaining sixty, with their commander, succeeded in escaping.

The detachment was now so far advanced within the British lines, as to admonish Washington of the prudence of an immediate and speedy return. But another opportunity of dealing the enemy a blow presented itself; and although the attempt would greatly increase his danger, he could not resist the temptation to make it. The object of this fresh enterprise was a British post, which had recently been established at a point some fifteen miles northeast of Ninety-six, and on the line of communication between that place, Winnsborough and Camden. At this post, in a strongly stockaded log house, called Fort William, was a small garrison of about one hundred and fifty men, under Gen. Cunningham. The place was reducible only by artillery or surprise. In the hope of being able to surprise the garrison, a party of forty mounted militia, under Col. Hays, and ten dragoons, under Cornet Simons, were sent forward to make the attempt. But Cunningham, having received intelligence of Waters's defeat, and of Washington's approach, made preparations for decamping; and he had just evacuated the fort when the small party sent against him appeared. The superior numbers of Cunningham's command, added to the firm countenance it displayed, prevented Col. Hays from reaping any advantage over it. But he took possession of the abandoned fort, which, having destroyed, he rejoined Washington. The latter now rapidly retraced his steps towards the neighborhood of the Pacolet.

In the mean time, the lengthened and unaccountable absence of Washington's detachment filled Morgan with anxiety. Being at length informed of its success, and of the great distance to which it had penetrated within the enemy's lines, he became seriously alarmed for its safety, and at once determined to run some hazard in order to secure its retreat. More than one half of his remaining force accordingly crossed the Pacolet, and advanced southward some twenty miles. Being soon after joined by Washington and his command, the troops in advance returned, and the whole detachment re-assembled on the north bank of the Pacolet, on the 6th of January.

This affair, with an account of the reinforcements he had received, a glance at the difficulties and dangers which surrounded him, and the suggestion of an expedition to Georgia, was made the subject of the following letter to Gen. Greene.

CAMP ON PACOLET CREEK, *Dec.* 31*st,* 1781.

DEAR GENERAL: After an uninteresting march, I arrived at this place on the 25th of December. On the 27th, I received intelligence that a body of

Georgia tories, about two hundred and fifty in number, had advanced as far
as Fair Forest, and were insulting and plundering the good people in this
neighborhood.   On the 29th, I dispatched Lieut.-Col. Washington, with his
own regiment and two hundred militia horse, who had just joined me, to
attack them.   Before the colonel could overtake them, they had retreated
upwards of twenty miles.   He came up with them next day, about twelve
o'clock, at Hammond's store-house, forty miles from our camp.   They were
alarmed and flew to their horses.   Lieut.-Col. Washington extended his
mounted riflemen on the wings, and charged them in front with his own
regiment.   They fled with the greatest precipitation, without making any
resistance.   One hundred and fifty were killed and wounded, and about
forty taken prisoners.   What makes this success more valuable, it was
attained without the loss of a man.   This intelligence I have just received
by the Baron de Glaubec, who served in the expedition as a volunteer.   To
guard against any misfortune, I have detached two hundred men to cover
the retreat of the fortunate party.   When I obtain a more particular account,
I shall transmit it to head-quarters, and recommend to your particular attention those men who have distinguished themselves on this occasion.

The militia are increasing fast, so that we cannot be supplied in this
neighborhood more than two or three days at farthest.   Were we to
advance, and be constrained to retreat, the consequence would be very
disagreeable; and this must be the case should we lay near the enemy,
and Cornwallis reinforce, which he can do with the greatest facility.

General Davidson has brought in one hundred and twenty men, and has
returned to bring forward a draft of five hundred more.   Col. Pickens has
joined me with sixty.   Thirty or forty of the men who came out with him
have gone into North Carolina to secure their effects, and will immediately
repair to my camp.

When I shall have collected my expected force, I shall be at a loss how
to act.   Could a diversion be made in my favor by the main army, I
should wish to march into Georgia.   To me it appears an advisable
scheme, but should be happy to receive your directions on this point, as
they must be the guide of my actions.   I have consulted with Gen.
Davidson and Col. Pickens, whether we could secure a safe retreat, should
we be pushed by a superior force.   They tell me it can be easily effected
by passing up the Savannah and crossing over the heads of the rivers along
the Indian line.

To expedite this movement, should it meet with your approbation, I
have sent for one hundred swords, which I intend to put into the hands
of expert riflemen, to be mounted and incorporated with Lieut. Col.

Washington's corps. I have also written to the quarter-master to have me one hundred packsaddles made immediately—should be glad if you would direct him to be expeditious. Packsaddles ought to be procured, let our movements be what they may, for our wagons will be an impediment, whether we attempt to annoy the enemy or provide for our own safety. It is incompatible with the nature of light troops to be encumbered with baggage.

I would wish to receive an answer to this proposition as soon as possible. This country has been so exhausted, that the supplies for my detachment have been precarious and scant ever since my arrival, and in a few days will be unattainable; so that a movement is unavoidable. At my particular request, Col. Malmady has been so obliging as to undertake the delivery of these dispatches. He will be able to give you a just idea of our situation and prospects.

I have the honor to be, &c.,

DANIEL MORGAN.

N. B.—Should this expedition be thought advisable, a profound secrecy will be essentially necessary, as you know it is the soul of enterprise. Col. Lee's corps would ensure its success. D. M.

HON. MAJ. GEN. GREENE.

After the affair at Hammond's store, and until a fortnight had elapsed, nothing occurred to cause Morgan any uneasiness, or to give intimation of the thrilling events which were so soon to follow. The interim may therefore be advantageously employed in the consideration of such portions of his correspondence as will serve to illustrate the narrative, display the private feelings of some of the writers, and afford a correct insight of the views and objects of others.

Governor Rutledge, the writer of the following letter, was one of the most distinguished men of the period. His talents and patriotism have won for his memory a bright page in the history of his country. He was earnestly in favor of a descent on the British posts on the Saluda and Savannah rivers, and concurred with Morgan in the belief, that such an attempt, if successful, would seriously interfere with the designs then entertained by

Cornwallis against North Carolina and Virginia.* But the absence of a sufficient force of regular troops or militia rendered the enterprise too hazardous to be attempted. The Indians of Georgia and South Carolina, to whom this letter chiefly relates, took an active part in the struggle, and generally on the side of the British, who took care to conciliate their friendship by the profuse distribution of presents among them. As has been already noticed, they were generally sent forward in advance of a movement of the British army, to harass the inhabitants of the whig districts, and by arousing the fears of the latter for the safety of their families, to prevent their assembling in arms when their aid was most needed. To check an evil attended with such mischievous consequences, was of the utmost importance, and his efforts were at length crowned with success.

CHARLOTTE, *Dec. 22d*, 1780.

DEAR SIR: The bearer can give you some account of the enemy's works (two forts, one of them a stockade, and two redoubts) at Ninety-six. I think their stockade may appears formidable to the country people ; but that regular troops would find the taking of it no very difficult matter, if it has neither ditch nor abattis, and if Mr. Brown's other accounts of it are true. However, I refer you to him for particulars on this head, which may be somewhat satisfactory.

He tells me that Galphin (who I heard was dead) is alive, at home. He is certainly our staunch friend, and his influence among the Indians, especially the Creeks, is still great. I wish you could send a confidential person to him, with this message from me, viz.: To use his utmost influence and interest with the Creeks, to keep them quiet—to inform them that a large fleet and a number of troops sailed from Havana, in October, against St. Augustine or Pensacola, and that more were preparing to go against these places—that the Spaniards will certainly soon have the Floridas—and that the other States and the French will soon get back South Carolina and Georgia ; therefore advising the Indians to get all the goods they can from the British, but by no means to take up the hatchet, or kill any of our people ; for if they do, as soon as the English are beaten, we shall fall upon them, the Indians. This may have a good

* Letter, Rutledge, Jan. 12, 1781.

effect, and in a measure may be absolutely necessary, as the bearer says
he hears that Brown has a good many Creeks at Augusta, and that he
expects more there, to act against our people. Indeed, if we can regain
Ninety-six, we must not suffer the enemy to possess Augusta, for they
will hold their influence over the Indians while they hold that place. Col.
Polk tells me that he heard, yesterday, from Gen. Davidson, that volunteers were flocking in to him briskly. I hope he will soon join you with a
respectable force. Success attend you.

I am, &c.,

J. RUTLEDGE.

GEN. MORGAN.

The arrival at the Cheraws of the main body of the American
army, the landing of Gen. Leslie at Charleston, and other
matters, form the subject of the following letter from General
Greene :

CAMP ON THE CHERAWS, on the east side of Pedee, }
Dec. 29th, 1780. {

DEAR SIR : We arrived here the 26th inst., after a very tedious and disagreeable march, owing to the badness of the roads and the poor and
weak state of our teams. Our prospects with regard to provisions are
mended, but this is no Egypt.

I have this moment received intelligence that Gen. Leslie has landed at
Charleston, and is on his way to Camden. His force is about two thous-
and, perhaps something less. I also am informed that Lord Cornwallis
has collected his troops at Camden. You will watch their motions very
narrowly, and take care and guard against a surprise. Should they move
in force this way, you will endeavor to cross the river and join us. Do
not be sparing of your expresses, but let me know as often as possible, of
your situation. I wish to be fully informed of your prospect respecting
provisions, and also the number of militia that has joined you.

A large number of tents and hatchets are on the road. As soon as
they arrive you shall be supplied. Many other articles necessary for this
army, particularly shoes, are coming on.

I am sir, your most obedient servant,

NATHANIEL GREENE.

GEN. MORGAN.

A warm friendship existed between the writer of the annexed

letter and Morgan. He was one of the most accomplished and gallant officers that took a part in the great drama of the revolution.

CAMP HICKS'S CREEK, *on Pedee, Dec.* 30*th*, 1780.

DEAR GENERAL: I enclose you a number of letters, by a sergeant of Lieut. Col. Washington's regiment, which I hope will arrive safe. We are at present in a camp of repose, and the general is exerting himself, and everybody else, to put his little army in a better condition. Tents in sufficient numbers for a larger army than ours, are coming from Philadelphia; they are expected to arrive early in January. We also expect a number of shoes, shirts, and some other articles essentially necessary.

Col. Marion writes the general, that General Leslie landed at Charleston, with his command, on the 20th inst., and that he had advanced as far as Monks's Corner. You know Lord Cornwallis has collected his force at Camden—probably they mean to form a junction, and attempt to give a blow to a part of our force while we are divided, and most probably that blow will be aimed at you, as our position in the centre of a wilderness is less accessible than your camp. I know your discretion renders all caution from me unnecessary; but my friendship will plead an excuse for the impertinence of wishing you to run no risk of a defeat. May your laurels flourish when your locks fade, and an age of peace reward your toils in war. My love to every fellow soldier, and adieu.

Yours, most truly,

O. H. WILLIAMS.

The reader will have noticed in the two preceding letters, that the objects of the enemy's movements were differently interpreted by the writers. Greene always suspected that these movements had reference to himself; Williams believed that they had ultimate designs against Morgan; and in this opinion he was joined by the latter.

The following, from Gen. Greene, was in reply to Morgan's letter of the 31st:

CAMP SOUTH CAROLINA, AT KURSHADT'S FERRY, *east side of Pedee,*
Jan. 8*th*, 1781.

DEAR SIR: Col. Malmady arrived here yesterday, with your letter of the 31st December. Nothing could have afforded more pleasure than the successful attack of Lieut. Col. Washington upon the tories. I hope it will be attended with a happy influence upon both whig and tory, to the reclaiming of the one, and the encouragement of the other. I wish you to forward me an official report as soon as possible, that I may send it to the northward.

I have maturely considered your proposition of an expedition into Georgia, and cannot think it warrantable in the critical situation our army is in. I have no small reason to think, by intelligence from different quarters, that the enemy have a movement in contemplation, and that in all probability it will be this way, from the impudence of the tories, who are collecting in different quarters, in the most inaccessible swamps and morasses. Should you go into Georgia, and the enemy push this way, your whole force will be useless. The enemy having no object there but what is secure in their fortifications, will take no notice of your movement, but serve you as General Prevost did General Lincoln, oblige you to return by making a forward movement themselves; and you will be so far in the rear that you can do them no injury. But if you continue in the neighborhood of the place you now are at, and they attempt to push forward, you may interrupt their communications with Charleston, or harass their rear, both of which will alarm the enemy not a little.

If you employ detachments to interrupt supplies going to Ninety-six, and Augusta, it will perplex the enemy much. If you think Ninety-six, Augusta, or even Savannah can be surprised, and your force will admit of a detachment for the purpose, and leave you a sufficiency to keep up a good countenance, you may attempt it. But don't think of attempting either, unless by surprise, for you will only beat your heads against the wall without success. Small parties are better to effect a surprise than large bodies, and the success will not greatly depend upon the numbers, but on the secrecy and spirit of the attack.

I must repeat my caution to you to guard against a surprise. The enemy and the tories both will try to bring you into disgrace, if possible, to prevent your influence upon the militia, especially the weak and wavering.

I cannot pretend to give you any particular instructions respecting a position. But somewhere between the Saluda and the north branch of Broad river appears to be the most favorable for annoying the enemy, interrupting their supplies, and harassing their rear, if they should make a movement this way.

If you could detach a small party to kill the enemy's draft horses and recruiting cavalry, upon the Congaree, it would give them almost as deadly

12*

a blow as a defeat. But this matter must be conducted with great secrecy and dispatch.

Lieut. Col. Lee has just arrived with his legion, and Col. Green is within a few days' march of this, with a reinforcement.

> I am, dear sir, truly yours,
>
> NATHANIEL GREENE.

GEN. MORGAN.

The difficulties and dangers of Morgan's position are the chief topic of the following letter to Gen. Greene :

CAMP ON PACOLET, *Jan.* 4, 1781.

DEAR SIR : As soon as I could form a just judgment of your situation and prospects, I dispatched Col. Malmady to give you the necessary information, and I flatter myself he has done it to your satisfaction. The account he brings you of Lieut. Col. Washington's success at Hammond's store is as authentic as any I have been able to collect. It was followed by some small advantages. Gen. Cunningham, on hearing of Waters's defeat, prepared to evacuate Fort Williams, and had just marched out with the last of his garrison, as a party, consisting of about forty militia horsemen under Col. Hays, and ten dragoons under Mr. Simmonds, arrived with an intention of demanding a surrender. The enemy's force was so superior to theirs, that they could effect nothing more than the demolition of the fort.

Sensible of the importance of guarding against surprise, I have used every precaution on this head. I have had men who were recommended as every way calculated for the business, continually watching the motions of the enemy; so that unless they deceive me, I am in no danger of being surprised.

I have received no acquisition of force since I wrote you; but I expect in a few days to be joined by Cols. Clark's and Twiggs's regiments. Their numbers I cannot ascertain. The men on the north side of Broad river I have not yet ordered to join me; but have directed their officers to keep them in compact bodies, that they may be ready to march at the shortest notice. I intend these as a check on the enemy, should they attempt anything against my detachment.

My situation is far from being agreeable to my wishes or expectations. Forage and provisions are not to be had. Here we cannot subsist, so that we have but one alternative, either to retreat or move into Georgia. A retreat will be attended with the most fatal consequences. The spirit which now begins to pervade the people, and call them into the field, will be destroyed. The militia who have already joined will desert us, and it is not improbable but that a regard for their own safety will induce them to join the enemy.

I shall wait with impatience for your directions on the subject of my letter to Col. Malmady, as till then my operations must be suspended.

I am, dear sir, truly yours,

DANIEL MORGAN.

MAJ. GEN. GREENE.

The annexed letter is in reply to the foregoing:

CAMP ON THE PEDEE, *Jan.* 18, 1781.

DEAR SIR: I am this moment favored with your letter of the 4th inst. Col. Malmady also delivered me your dispatches of the 31st of December, which I answered the 8th inst., wherein I informed you that I cannot think an expedition into Georgia eligible at this time. Since I wrote you I have received letters from Virginia, informing me of the arrival of Gen. Phillips, with a detachment of 2,500 men from New York. This circumstance renders it still more improper for you to move far to the southward. It is my wish also that you should hold your ground if possible; for I foresee the disagreeable consequences that will result from a retreat. If moving as far as Ninety-six, or anywhere in the neighborhood of it, will contribute to the obtaining more ample supplies, you have my consent. Col. Tarleton is said to be on his way to pay you a visit. I doubt not but he will have a decent reception and a proper dismission. And I am happy to find you have taken every proper precaution to avoid a surprise.

I wish you to be more particular respecting your plan and object in paying a visit to Georgia.

Virginia is raising 3,000 men to recruit this army.

I am, &c.,

NATHANIEL GREENE

GEN. MORGAN.

Before this letter was received, the anticipated meeting had taken place, and a blow had been struck, which gave a new and decisive character to the subsequent operations of the contending armies.

The recent advance of Lieut. Col. Washington to the vicinity of Ninety-six, confirmed Cornwallis in the belief that Morgan meditated serious designs against that important British post. The fortifications of this place were not sufficiently strong to resist the attack of regular troops, particularly when aided by cannon. This Cornwallis well knew ; but regarding the strength of Morgan's force, or whether it was accompanied by cannon, he was not so certain. Even could the post be successfully defended against an assault, little advantage would result to the British, unless the adjacent country, which furnished subsistence to the garrison and the tories in the district, could also be protected. This, to Cornwallis's mind, was in imminent danger, and called for prompt precautionary measures.*

Other causes of anxiety to the British had arisen from Morgan's movements. Previous to the tragedy of Hammond's store, Cornwallis reckoned, not without reason, upon the co-operation in considerable numbers of the tories in that quarter. But so dispiriting were the effects of the severe blow which they received on that occasion, that nothing thereafter could induce them to take the field, and Cornwallis was obliged to relinquish all hopes of aid from them.

These considerations were engaging the attention of the British commander, when he received information that Morgan was in full march for Ninety-six.†

Under feelings, partaking partly of alarm and partly of vexation, he determined to take immediate and vigorous measures against Morgan, even though their prosecution should derange the main operations, the commencement of which he had intended deferring until the arrival of the reinforcement under Leslie.

Accordingly, on the first of January, an aid was dispatched to Lieut. Col. Tarleton, then lying with his command at Brierly's Ferry, with directions to cross Broad river and counteract Morgan's supposed designs. The day following, Cornwallis communicated further instructions to Tarleton in the annexed note :

* Tarleton's Campaign, p. 210.   † Ibid

WINNSBOROUGH, *Jan.* 2, 1781.

DEAR TARLETON: I sent Haldane to you last night, to desire you would pass Broad river with the legion and the first battalion of the 71st as soon as possible. If Morgan is still at Williams's, or any where within your reach, I should wish you to push him to the utmost. I have not heard, except from McArthur, of his having cannon, nor would I believe it, unless he has it from very good authority. It is, however, possible, and Ninety-six is of so much consequence, that no time is to be lost.*

Yours sincerely,

CORNWALLIS.

On receiving these orders, Tarleton put his troops in motion. These, according to his own accounts, consisted of the legion cavalry and infantry, of five hundred and fifty men ; the first battalion of the seventy-first regiment, of two hundred ; and two three-pounders, with a detachment of the royal artillery in sufficient numbers to serve the pieces.†

Proceeding in a westerly direction for about twenty miles, Tarleton received such information as satisfied him that Ninety-six was in no immediate danger, and that Morgan was far from its vicinity. He thereupon halted his troops, as well to allow time for the arrival of their baggage, which had been left behind, as to furnish Cornwallis with correct information, and to propose for his lordship's sanction, a plan of operations against Morgan, which struck him as promising great advantages. Informing Cornwallis that Morgan, with his command, was on the west side of Broad river, and that he threatened Ninety-six, Tarleton proposed a simultaneous movement of the troops on both sides of Broad river towards the Americans. He suggested, that while the detachment under his command, after being reinforced, should advance, and either destroy Morgan or push him before it over Broad river towards King's Mountain, the main body should move forward to the same point, and in case Morgan's forces succeeded in crossing the river, intercept their further retreat,

* Tarleton's Campaign, p. 244. † Tarleton's Campaign, p. 211.

and compel them either to fight, disperse across the mountains, or surrender.

Cornwallis gave the proposed joint operations his approval, and sending with the legion's baggage two hundred men of the seventh regiment (designed as a reinforcement to the garrison at Ninety-six), and fifty dragoons of the seventeenth regiment, informed Tarleton that he would put the main body in motion on the 7th. On the arrival of the baggage and troops, Tarleton resumed his march. Two days were spent in crossing Indian and Dunken creeks. Learning here that Morgan's force was rapidly increasing, he was deterred from advancing farther on unknown dangers. He accordingly made a halt, to gain information, and to wait for the permission, solicited of Cornwallis, to retain under his command the detachment of the seventh regiment, until the operations in hand were completed. The main army had in the mean time advanced from Winnsborough to a place called McAllister's. His request having been granted, Tarleton resumed his march on the 12th. He proceeded in a westerly direction, in order to avail himself of the most practicable fords of the Ennoree and the Tyger, and at the same time to lessen the probabilities of Morgan's retreat, by a rapid movement in his front towards Georgia. On the 14th, he crossed the Ennoree and Tyger rivers, above the Cherokee road. On the same day he learned that Cornwallis had reached Bull's Run; that Leslie, having surmounted the obstacles which had so greatly retarded his march, was advancing, more rapidly, to effect a junction with the main body ; and that Morgan, posted on the north bank of the Pacolet, was guarding all the fords of that river. Apprising Cornwallis of his intention to force a passage of the Pacolet, and compel Morgan either to fight or retreat, and requesting his lordship to proceed up the eastern bank of Broad river, and act in co-operation should it be necessary, Tarleton advanced towards the Pacolet, the neighborhood of which he reached on the 15th.*

* Tarleton's Campaign, pp. 211–213.

The day following, Cornwallis reached Turkey Creek. Although eight days had elapsed since this officer broke up his camp at Winnsborough, he had advanced only forty miles. He was now some twenty-five miles in the rear of the ground, about being the scene of conflict, instead of being that distance in advance of it. It is true, recent heavy rains, and the consequent swelling of all the water courses, presented serious obstacles to a rapid progress, with such an immense baggage train as accompanied his army. But other considerations had made their way to his mind during his march, admonishing him of the danger of precipitancy, if not causing him to regret the premature movement into which he had been drawn by Tarleton. His active forces were divided into three bodies, each separated from the others by a distance of from thirty to forty miles, and by two large rivers, now greatly swollen, and impassable, save at points widely apart. The American army being divided into two bodies only, one on his right, and the other on his left, the numerical superiority of his forces was thus practically diminished, if not entirely neutralized. Under the belief that the militia were gathering in very large numbers around Greene and Morgan, his fears were aroused lest one of his divisions should be overwhelmed, and that his entire force would thus be destroyed in detail. An attack upon Leslie by Greene, struck him as an enterprise no less feasible than one by Morgan upon himself, now that his cavalry, light infantry, and other troops detached under Tarleton, composing a force quite as effective as that remaining with him, were absent. For Tarleton he seems to have entertained no apprehensions. The activity and courage of this officer, and the almost uniform success which had attended him in his numerous enterprises, inspired his commander with the confident belief that he would fulfill his promise, either to destroy Morgan's corps or drive it over Broad river. Convinced that in the latter event it was not in the power of his much incumbered army to cut off the retreat of a corps so active and bold, and even if it were, that the danger thus incurred would more than counterbalance the utmost advantage to be gained, Cornwallis ordered Leslie to join him with all convenient speed, and in the mean time delayed his march until the desired junction could be effected.

But precautions came too late to shield him from the consequences of a premature movement. While congratulating himself on having repaired his error, and thus avoided the consequences which it involved, misfortune overtook him from a quarter least of all expected.

CHAPTER XV.

Morgan determines to take a position nearer to the fords of Broad river—Tarleton approaches—Morgan retires to Burr's Mills—Tarleton crosses the Pacolet—Morgan marches to the Cowpens, where he announces his intention of awaiting the enemy—Letter from Morgan to Greene, and reply thereto—Tarleton follows Morgan—A comparison of these officers—The motives which actuated them respectively in risking a battle—Morgan's preparations for the expected conflict — Anecdote — Tarleton approaches—Skirmish between the enemy's advance and the American patrol—The Cowpens—Description of the field—Morgan's disposition of his forces—His directions and exhortations to the men—The enemy's cavalry drive in the American front—Tarleton's dispositions—His advance to the attack—The battle—The enemy routed—Conflict between Washington and Tarleton—The latter escapes capture only by a mistake of his pursuers—The results—Official account of the battle, with a list of the officers engaged therein.

MORGAN had been a watchful observer of the movements just described. Up to the 14th, his determination had been to resist a passage of the Pacolet by Tarleton. But the advance of Cornwallis on his left and towards his rear, while Tarleton menaced him in front, admonished him of the danger of persevering in this design. A successful defence of the fords of the Pacolet, would be attended by no other important result, than to give Cornwallis time to gain his rear; while a defeat, under such circumstances, must have been followed by the ruin of his command. The instructions of General Greene, without revealing any determinate plan of operations, required him to hold his ground as long as possible, and consented to a retreat only when no other means were left of securing his corps from a misfortune. To continue longer in his present advanced position, was but courting destruction. The country in the neighborhood of the Pacolet had thus far afforded him a scanty supply of provisions and forage ; but so bare had it become, that a change to some other was now demanded by the wants of his force, independently of the additional reasons furnished by the proximity of the enemy. Yet to retreat from the district, would have a most dispiriting effect upon its patriotic inhabitants, would subject them to persecution, and cause the militia to abandon him. His accurate knowledge of Cornwallis's position, assured him of the practicability of retiring across Broad river, in spite of his lordship, if the attempt were promptly made. But the loss of two or three days more in the desire of engaging Tarleton at the Pacolet, might leave him no other alternative than a retreat towards the mountains. Such a step, under existing circumstances, would be little less disastrous than a defeat. As will be seen, his efforts to prepare for such a necessity, by establishing magazines of supplies in that quarter, were rendered nugatory by the opposition of Col. Sumter ; and without such supplies, a retreat in that direction was impracticable. Before the advance of Leslie to the aid of Cornwallis, and the subsequent development of their designs, a descent into Georgia had been seriously considered by Morgan. Although the scheme did not meet the approval of Gen. Greene, a modification of it was suggested by that officer, which, contemplating assaults upon the British posts of Ninety-six and Augusta, embraced the contingency of an attack upon the enemy's flank and rear, should they advance. In the present posture of affairs, however, it was regarded by both Greene and Morgan as of the utmost importance to preserve their communications with one another, and to be enabled to effect a junction of their forces, should the enemy evince a design to prosecute a winter campaign. Had Morgan been at liberty to move into Georgia, however, he could not have done so without subjecting himself to an attack from Tarleton, who, anticipating such a movement, had advanced in such a direction as to place himself between that State and his adversary. Morgan was, therefore, denied this resort even in an extremity. The guarded and deliberate manner in which

Tarleton advanced upon him—so unlike that officer's usual mode of approaching an opponent—had, besides, aroused his suspicions of a design—such as that which had really been concerted between Cornwallis and Tarleton—to entrap him.

Under these circumstances, Morgan determined upon taking ground nearer to the upper fords of Broad river, where the dangers of his present position would be greatly diminished, and where he could safely defer a retreat for a few days longer. If forced to fight, he would be nearer to the reinforcements of militia, then on the march to join him, and to those on the north side of Broad river, which he had ordered to be held in readiness to take the field in such an event. Should Cornwallis remain stationary, or keep so far in the rear as to leave the way open for his retreat, and should the reinforcements arrive in sufficient numbers to render his forces something like a match for those of Tarleton, he determined to hold his ground in defiance of that officer, and to risk a battle in its defence. If compelled by the movements of Cornwallis to retreat, however, he could cross without much difficulty, to the country watered by the Catawba. He could thus gain a position better calculated to furnish him with supplies, to yield him the coöperation of the militia, to increase his means of obstructing the progress of the enemy, and, at the same time, facilitate a junction of his forces with the main body under Greene.

These considerations occupied Morgan's attention, when the approach of Tarleton was announced. Being now convinced that the movements of Cornwallis and Tarleton had direct reference to himself, he broke up his encampment at Grindall's ford, and having sent a number of small detachments, with directions to observe the different fords of the Pacolet, and to retire and report when the enemy effected a passage of the river, he put his troops in motion, and in the afternoon of the 15th, encamped at Burr's Mills, on Thicketty creek.

On the evening of the same day, Tarleton reached the Pacolet,

284 THE LIFE OF

which he proposed crossing without delay. Here, however, he found the detachments which Morgan had left in observation on the opposite bank. Supposing that officer to be there in strength, and sensible of the danger of attempting to force a passage in the face of an adversary so wily and resolute, he resorted to stratagem to effect his purpose. With the feigned object of gaining the ford at the iron works, at some distance up the river, and of crossing before sufficient assistance could be given to the guard at that point to repel him, Tarleton moved in that direction on the same night. After marching about three hours, he suddenly ordered a halt. Having given his men a short period of repose, he retraced his steps, and before daylight the next morning, crossed the river without interruption at Easterwood shoals.*

On the appearance of the enemy on the Pacolet, and their advance up its southern bank, Morgan's detachments collected and marched up the opposite shore, their movements corresponding with those of the enemy. When the latter encamped, apparently for the night, the detachments also encamped. Learning the next morning, however, that Tarleton had crossed the river about an hour before, at Easterwood shoals, a few miles below their camp, they retreated without delay in the direction of the main body.

Morgan, having been apprised of Tarleton's passage of the Pacolet, a few hours after its occurrence, immediately put his troops in motion. Pushing forward on the mountain road leading to Hancocksville, he passed that place; then turning into a by-road, he proceeded towards the head of Thicketty creek. Arriving at the Cowpens about sundown, he ordered a halt; and having ascertained that he would be joined at that place in a few hours by a considerable reinforcement of militia, he communicated to his troops his intention of awaiting the enemy there.†

During the march from the Pacolet to the Cowpens, Morgan

* Tarleton's Campaign, p. 213.　　　　　　　　† Orion, vol. iii., p. 88.

wrote to Gen. Greene. This letter, and the reply thereto, are invested with no common interest, inasmuch as they are the last which passed between the writers, while as yet the views of neither were influenced by the action of the 17th. They are likewise of some historical importance, as they serve to display the motives and objects which governed the actions of both Greene and Morgan, previously to that memorable event—points, particularly as regards the latter, that have been the subject of much misrepresentation. They are accordingly inserted.

CAMP AT BURR'S MILLS, THICKETTY CREEK,
 Jan. 15th, 1781.

DEAR GENERAL: Your letters of the 3rd and 8th instant came to hand yesterday, just as I was preparing to change my position; was therefore obliged to detain the express until this evening.

The accounts I have transmitted you of Lieut. Col. Washington's success, accords with his opinion. The number killed and wounded on the part of the tories must depend on conjecture, as they broke on the first charge, scattered through the woods, and were pursued in every direction. The consequences attending this defeat will be fatal to the disaffected. They have not been able to embody.

Sensible of the importance of having magazines of forage and provisions established in this country, I have left no means in my power unessayed to effect this business. I dispatched Captain Chitty (whom I have appointed as commissary of purchases for my command), with orders to collect and store all the provisions that could be obtained between the Catawba and Broad rivers. I gave him directions to call on Col. Hill, who commands a regiment of militia in that quarter, to furnish him with a proper number of men to assist him in the execution of this commission; but he, to my great surprise, has just returned without effecting anything. He tells me that his failure proceeded from the want of the countenance and assistance of Col. Hill, who assured him that General Sumter directed him to obey no orders from me, unless they came through him.

I find it impracticable to procure more provisions in this quarter than are absolutely necessary for our own immediate consumption: indeed it has been with the greatest difficulty that we have been able to effect this. We have to feed such a number of horses, that the most plentiful country must soon be exhausted. Nor am I a little apprehensive that no part of this State accessible to us can support us long. Could the militia be persuaded to change their fatal mode of going to war, much provision might be saved; but the custom has taken such deep root that it cannot be abolished.

Upon a full and mature deliberation, I am confirmed in the opinion that nothing can be effected by my detachment in this country, which will balance the risks I will be subjected to by remaining here. The enemy's great superiority in numbers, and our distance from the main army, will enable Lord Cornwallis to detach so superior a force against me, as to render it essential to our safety to avoid coming to action. Nor will this be always in my power. No attempt to surprise me will be left untried by them; and situated as we must be, every possible precaution may not be sufficient to secure us. The scarcity of forage renders it impossible for us always to be in a compact body; and were this not the case, it is beyond the art of man to keep the militia from straggling. These reasons induce me to request that I may be recalled with my detachment, and that Gen. Davidson and Col. Pickens may be left with the militia of North and South Carolina and Georgia. They will not be so much the object of the enemy's attention, and will be capable of being a check on the disaffected, which is all I can effect.

Col. Pickens is a valuable, discreet and attentive officer, and has the confidence of the militia.

My force is inadequate to the attempts you have hinted at. I have now with me only two hundred South Carolina and Georgia, and one hundred and forty North Carolina, volunteers. Nor do I expect to have more than two-thirds of these to assist me, should I be attacked, for it is impossible to keep them collected.

Though I am convinced that were you on the spot, the propriety of my proposition would strike you forcibly; should you think it unadvisable to recall me, you may depend on my attempting everything to annoy the enemy, and to provide for the safety of the detachment. I shall cheerfully acquiesce in your determinations.

Col. Tarleton has crossed the Tyger at Musgrove's Mill; his force we cannot learn. It is more than probable we are his object. Cornwallis, by last accounts, was at the cross-roads near Lee's old place.

We have just learned that Tarleton's force is from eleven to twelve hundred British.   I am, dear general,

Truly yours,

DANIEL MORGAN.

MAJOR GEN. GREENE.

DEAR SIR : Your favor of the 15th was delivered to me last night about 12 o'clock. I am surprised that Gen. Sumter should give such an order as that you mention to Col. Hill, nor can I persuade myself but that there must be some mistake in the matter ; for though it is the most military to convey orders through the principal to the dependents, as well from propriety as respect, yet this may not always be convenient, or even practicable ; and therefore to give a positive order not to obey, was repugnant to reason and common sense. As the head was subject to your orders, consequently the dependents also. I will write Gen. Sumter on the subject ; but as it is better to conciliate than aggravate matters, where everything depends so much upon voluntary principles, I wish you to take no notice of the matter, but endeavor to influence his conduct to give you all the aid in his power. Write to him frequently, and consult with him freely. He is a man of great pride and considerable merit, and should not be neglected. If he has given such orders, I am persuaded he will see the impropriety of the matter and correct it in future, unless personal glory is more the object than public good, which I cannot suppose is the case with him, or any other man who fights in the cause of liberty.

I was informed of Lord Cornwallis's movements before the arrival of your letter, and agree with you in opinion that you are the object ; and from his making so general a movement it convinces me that he feels a great inconvenience from your force and situation. Gen. Leslie has crossed the Catawba to join him. He would never harass his troops to remove you, if he did not think it an object of some importance ; nor would he put his collective force in motion if he had not some respect for your numbers. I am sensible your situation is critical, and requires the most watchful atention to guard against a surprise. But I think it is of great importance to keep up a force in that quarter, nor can I persuade myself that the militia alone will answer the same valuable purposes as when joined by the continental troops.

It is not my wish you should come to action unless you have a manifest superiority, and a moral certainty of succeeding. Put nothing to the hazard : a retreat may be disagreeable, but not disgraceful. Regard not the opinions of the day. It is not our business to risk too much. Our affairs are in too critical a situation, and require time and nursing to give them a better tone.

If Gen. Sumter and you would fix upon a plan for him to hold the post which you now occupy, to be joined by the militia under Gen. Davison, and you with your force, and the Georgia and Virginia militia, to move towards Augusta or into that quarter, I should have no objection to such a movement, provided you think it will answer any valuable purpose, and can be attended with a degree of safety. I am unwilling to recall you if it can be avoided ; but I had rather recall you by far, than expose you to the hazard of a surprise.

Before this can possibly reach you, I imagine, the movements of Lord Cornwallis and Col. Tarleton will be sufficiently explained, and you be obliged to take some decisive measures. I shall be perfectly satisfied if you keep clear of a misfortune ; for though I wish you laurels, I am unwilling to expose the common cause, to give you an opportunity to acquire them.

As the rivers are subject to sudden and great swells, you must be careful that the enemy do not take a position to gain your rear, when you can neither retreat by your flanks or your front. The Pedee rose twenty-five feet last week in thirty hours. I am preparing boats to move always with the army ; would one or two be of use to you ? They will be put on four wheels, and made to move with little more difficulty than a loaded wagon.

Gen Davidson is desired to receive orders, and in conjunction with Gen. Sumter, to consult with you a plan for a combined attack upon one of the divisions of Lord Cornwallis's army, and also respecting your movements into Georgia.

I am, with great esteem, &c.,

NATHANIEL GREENE.

GEN. MORGAN.

These, and the preceding letters from Greene to Morgan, will enable the reader to arrive without difficulty at the real causes which led to the battle of the Cowpens.

On crossing the Pacolet, Tarleton had taken possession of some log houses which stood near the ford, and which were constructed some months before with a view to defence by Major Ferguson. Still supposing that Morgan was in his neighborhood in force, and believing that he would be attacked as soon as his passage of the river became known, he made active preparations for a defence. He was busied in availing himself of the advantages which the log houses would afford his troops in case of an assault, when he was informed that Morgan had decamped some time previously, and was then in full march towards Broad river. Hereupon he ordered his light troops to occupy the deserted encampment; parties of patrols and spies, under the protection of a large detachment of dragoons, were directed to follow and observe the Americans; the main body in the meanwhile enjoyed a few hours of repose, preparatory to a rapid forward movement, to be made in the path of the fugitives.*

The manifold successes of Tarleton during the revolutionary war, while they fully established his claims to courage, also displayed its distinctive character. This seems to have borne a stronger affinity to the ferocity of the bloodhound than to the bravery of the bull-dog, and to have been more thoroughly aroused by the flight of an enemy than by his opposition. And herein, it may be remarked, will be found a striking point of contrast between Morgan and Tarleton. While Morgan presented, or appeared to present, a menacing aspect, Tarleton was as circumspect in his movements as the most prudent officer could desire. But the moment Morgan appeared to fly from him, he forgot his caution as well as his coöperative arrangements with Cornwallis, and dazzled with the *éclat* of an anticipated triumph over the war-worn hero of Saratoga, rushed hotly forward in pursuit.

The determination taken by Morgan, upon learning that he was pursued, was equally characteristic. As his retreat filled his adversary with the desire to overtake and grapple with him, in like manner the pursuit rendered him the more eager to meet the struggle. But thoughts more worthy of a commander coincided with the impulses of his invincible spirit to bring him to the resolution of giving Tarleton battle. It was now quite apparent that the latter would oppose his passage of Broad river; † and should the movements of Cornwallis render this step necessary, to attempt it in the face of an officer so active and enterprising, would inevitably be attended by the most disastrous consequences.

* Tarleton's Campaign, p. 214.　　　　† Ibid. 214.

13

It was equally apparent that he could not much longer hold his ground ; and when a retreat was forced upon him, the safety of his corps and the public good alike required that he should aim at a junction with the main body. Should he attempt to seek safety in immediate flight, the militia, many of whom fought under the certainty of execution in case of capture, would desert him in hundreds, while his regular troops, thus left without support, harassed by forced marches, and dispirited by pursuit and the apprehension of capture, would fall an easy prey upon being overtaken.

The obligation to fight had become imperative; safety was only to be found in a battle. And in truth, the circumstances by which he was more immediately surrounded, all tended to encour- age him to incur the risk. On the night following his arrival at the Cowpens, he was joined by Col. Pickens, who, after a short absence, returned with a body of about one hundred and fifty militia, from the north side of Broad river. Others, he was informed, were on the march from various points, in considerable numbers, to join him, many of whom were expected to arrive before morning. During the night, small parties, altogether to the number of about fifty more, reached the camp. The troops under his command were worthy of his utmost confidence, and they enjoyed it. His infantry was the flower of the gallant brigade of Marylanders, who, in the disastrous battle of Camden, drove the British left wing before them at the point of the bayonet. A more effective corps of cavalry, considering its numbers, than that commanded by Colonel Washington, was not to be found in the country. Those of the Virginia militia who were not practised marksmen, skilled in the warfare of the woods, were experienced soldiers, who, having served one or more terms in the continental army, were now the substitutes of those who had been drafted in Virginia for militia duty. His officers were equally worthy of the trust reposed in them. Such men as Howard, Washington, Brooks, Giles, Triplett, Pickens, Jackson,

Cunningham, and McDowell, are seldom met together on the same field. Officers and men were alike full of confidence in their ability to cope with any body of the enemy, not too greatly their superior in numbers; and their late success over the tories had put them in high spirits, and rendered them eager for an encounter with a nobler adversary.

The nature and strength of Tarleton's force had been accurately made known to Morgan. Its great numerical superiority, which embraced twice his number of infantry, and three times his strength in cavalry, with the important addition of artillery, were fearful odds to contend against. But great as were these advantages, they might, he confidently believed, be counterbalanced by those secured to him in the choice of position, his defensive attitude, and the efficiency and spirit of his forces. He had set against the enemy's great superiority in bayonets and sabres, the deadly rifles of his militia, who, full of zeal in the cause, and rendered desperate by personal wrongs, were for the most part in that state of feeling when militia becomes truly formidable.

Among the other presages of success which presented themselves to his mind, were those springing from the errors into which, he anticipated, Tarleton would be betrayed, by a blind confidence in himself, and a contempt for what he now supposed was a flying adversary.

Finally, he learned that Cornwallis was still at Turkey creek, awaiting Leslie's arrival.

The announcement of Morgan's intention to meet the enemy took the army by surprise, and was received with lively demonstrations of joy. The necessary preparations were accordingly made. The first measure taken by Morgan had for its object the strengthening of his cavalry corps. The powerful array of horse which Tarleton was about bringing against him rendered an increase of his cavalry force a matter of the greatest importance. Volunteers for this description of service were consequently demanded. Forty-five men immediately stepped forward. These having been equipped, were organized into a cavalry corps of two companies; the one commanded by Major McCall, the other by Major Jolly; the whole under the command of McCall*, and subject to the direction of Col. Washington. A number of patrolling parties were sent in different directions on the flanks and in the front, to watch the movements of the enemy, and guard against stratagem or surprise. The baggage was directed to proceed at daylight a few miles in the direction of Broad river, and then to halt for further orders. Expresses were sent towards the different bodies of militia which were on the way to join the army, with orders to hasten their march. The troops were dismissed to seek rest and refreshment in repose, before they were called to battle, on the dispositions for which Morgan now deliberated in a council of his principal officers.

Although Morgan had no very exalted opinion of militia, few officers were more popular with this description of troops, or could obtain more efficient service from them. Irreconcilable as these facts may appear, a multitude of instances could be cited, proving that such was the case. He was indebted to this influence to a number of causes, among which may be included his large martial figure, his established reputation for judgment and courage, his almost unvarying success, and his easy familiar manners. The officer who possesses all these qualifications, seldom fails of subjecting to his will the minds and hearts of his soldiery. An anecdote is told by Major Thomas Young, a volunteer at the battle of the Cowpens, which illustrates one of the methods by which Morgan inspired his men with a portion of his own courage and confidence. "The evening previous to the battle," the Major goes on to say, "he went among the volunteers, helped them to fix their swords, joked with them about their sweethearts, and told them to keep in good spirits, and the day would be ours. Long after I laid down, he was going about among the soldiers, encouraging them, and telling them that the 'Old Wagoner

* Major Thomas Young.

would crack his whip over Ben (Tarleton) in the morning, as sure as he lived. 'Just hold up your heads, boys,' he would say, 'three fires, and you are free! And then, when you return to your homes, how the old folks will bless you, and the girls kiss you, for your gallant conduct.' I don't think that he slept a wink that night."*

The next morning, at three o'clock, Tarleton, having called in his pickets, and directed his baggage to remain on the ground till daybreak, put his troops in motion towards Morgan's position. Three companies of light infantry, supported by the legion infantry, formed the advance; the 7th regiment, the artillery and the first battalion of the 71st, composed the centre; and the cavalry and mounted infantry brought up the rear. The morning being exceedingly dark, and the road much broken and frequently intersected by creeks and ravines, the progress of the troops was very slow. Before dawn, Thicketty creek was passed, an advanced guard of the cavalry was ordered to the front. A few minutes after, one of Morgan's patrolling parties discovered the advancing foe. The party immediately returned to report; but it was pursued by the British cavalry, and after a short running fight, a few on both sides were wounded, and one of the Americans made prisoner. Two troops of the legion cavalry were then ordered to reinforce the British advanced guard, and to push forward and harass the rear of the Americans, who, up to this moment, were supposed to be on the retreat. This order had hardly been issued, when it was reported to Tarleton that the Americans were discovered in front, and moreover, that they were evidently preparing for battle.†

Some time before daylight, Morgan had been apprised of the enemy's approach, and in a few minutes afterwards, the American camp was in motion. The troops having breakfasted, were promptly formed, and led to the position which had been determined upon. This was a piece of ground about six miles from Broad river, and known by the name of the Cowpens. This

* Orion, vol. iii., p. 88.   † Tarleton's Campaign, pp. 214, 215.

name has since given place to another; but the spot is associated with events too important, recollections too glorious, to countenance a fear that its identity will ever be lost. In the early settlement of this part of the country was a place of considerable notoriety, from a trading path with the Cherokees which passed by it. In the early grants of land in that neighborhood, it was called Hannah's Cowpens, it being part of the grazing establishment of a person named Hannah.* In time it became known as the Cowpens, and is now occupied by the iron works of Messrs. Hampton and Elmore, in Spartansburg District, South Carolina. The position extended from front to rear about five hundred yards, and was crossed by two eminences, the first of which, gently ascending and stretching to the right and left, attained its highest point about three hundred yards from the front. The ground then descended for about eighty yards, when it gradually rose into the second eminence. The position was far from the neighborhood of swamps, and in a country free from underbrush and covered with an ordinary growth of pine trees.

The disposition of the troops was going forward, when the near approach of the enemy was announced by Capt. Inman, of the Georgia militia, who, at the head of the patrolling party already alluded to, had just returned from the running fight with a body of Tarleton's cavalry.† This intelligence lent additional fire to the happy spirit which evidently animated the troops, and with joy Morgan plainly saw victory foreshadowed in their assured looks and confident bearing.

Many that have written in relation to this battle, have greatly overrated the numbers of the Americans who were engaged on this occasion. Tarleton puts them down at something in the neighborhood of two thousand; and other authors, whose motives for exaggeration are less impeachable, state them at about one thousand men. Both of these estimates are beyond the mark.

* Johnson's Greene, vol. i., p. 377.
† Gen. Jas. Jackson's letter, Jan. 20, 1795. See appendix, D.

Besides that furnished in the letters of Morgan himself, there is abundant evidence to show, that the whole number of his forces engaged did not much exceed eight hundred. It is true, his entire command, including all the militia that arrived previous to the battle, would appear to be about nine hundred and eighty men, if army returns and muster rolls were alone consulted. But every one acquainted with military affairs knows that such evidences of strength always exceed the reality. A number of his regulars were sick at the time, and many of the militia were absent. One detachment had been sent off with the baggage, another had gone to Salisbury in charge of prisoners, and a third guarded the horses of the militia. Besides, after the retreat of the militia from the front line, several of them never again appeared in the field, and a few mounted their horses and fled from the ground. Such men should not be permitted to lesson the glory of the achievement, by sharing in the honors of the victors as well as diminishing the mortification of the vanquished. The forces engaged in the battle under Morgan did not exceed eight hundred and fifty men.

Near the brow of the main eminence, Morgan placed his best troops. Howard's battalion of light infantry, numbering two hundred and eighty men, took position in the centre of the line. The Virginia militia, under Major Triplett and Captain Gilmore, formed on the left of the light infantry ; and the Augusta riflemen, commanded by Captains Tate and Buchanan, took post on their right flank. The nominal battalion which these four companies composed, numbered about one hundred and twenty men, and was commanded by Major Triplett. The line thus formed, was placed under the direction of Lieut. Col. Howard, and consisted of about four hundred men. Upon it Morgan chiefly relied in the approaching conflict.

Upon the second eminence, being about one hundred and fifty yards in the rear of the main body, Colonel Washington was posted with his cavalry. The corps under this officer's immedi ate command numbered about eighty men. The addition of Major McCall's corps of volunteers, gave, however, a very effective cavalry force of one hundred and twenty men.

One hundred and fifty yards in advance of the regular force, the militia, in all about three hundred and fifty strong, were formed in open order, their line extending from right to left, about 300 yards. Fronting the main body were posted the Georgians and North Carolinians; the first, commanded by Major Cunningham, aided by Col. James Jackson, to the left; and the second, under Major McDowell, to the right. On the right of Major McDowell, Colonels Brannen and Thomas, of the South Carolina militia, took post; and on the left of Major Cunningham, Colonels Hays and McCall, also at the head of the South Carolinians, were stationed.

These dispositions having been made, Major McDowell, with about 60 picked men of his command, and Major Cunningham, with a like number of Georgians, all having been selected with reference to their courage and their skill as marksmen, were advanced about one hundred yards. Here they were extended in loose order along the front, Cunningham on the left, and McDowell on the right.

In the rear of the cavalry, the horses of the militia were secured by the boughs of a grove of young pines, saddled and bridled, and ready for immediate use, as the issue of the conflict might determine.

These arrangements had hardly been completed, when the advance of the British appeared some distance in front; and a few minutes afterwards, it became evident that they contemplated an immediate attack.

With this departed the last vestige of anxiety from Morgan's mind. Delay was the policy which Tarleton should have adopted, but which Morgan deprecated above all things, save defeat. It might have led to those consequences which were aimed at by the joint movements of Cornwallis and Tarleton, in spite of all the efforts which Morgan would have made to avoid them. It certainly would have had a most unfavorable effect upon the spirits of his troops, who were now wrought up to a pitch of enthusiasm which rendered them formidable adversaries. It relieved Morgan from the apprehension of being compelled, either to fight at every disadvantage, or to retreat in a direction which threatened him with the starvation or dispersion of his troops.

While the enemy were forming their line of battle, he availed himself of the short but awful period which preceded the strife to give to the respective lines of his army the necessary directions, and to make a final appeal to their courage and patriotism.

Riding up to the marksmen in the front line, he directed them to take the cover of the trees, and upon the advance of the enemy's line within good shooting distance, to show whether they were entitled to the reputation of brave men and good shots. They were directed to retire as the enemy advanced, seeking shelter from the trees, as opportunity might offer, loading and firing until they reached the main body of the militia, with whom they were then to act. The disposition of this line, the right being composed of Georgians, and the left of Carolinians, was adopted by Morgan with the view of exciting a spirit of rivalry, which might add to the effectiveness and spirit of the whole. "Let me see," said Morgan, as he turned from this line, " which are most entitled to the credit of brave men, the boys of Carolina or those of Georgia."

To the main body of the militia he now addressed himself. He ordered them to reserve their fire until the enemy approached within fifty yards, when, after delivering two well-directed rounds, they were to retire in good order, and take position on the left of the line in the rear, firing by regiments as they fell back. These and other directions for the regulation of their conduct having been given, he addressed them with a few observations well calculated to increase their confidence and courage. He complimented them upon the spirit which they had so frequently

13*

displayed, under all the disadvantages which attend militia when contending alone against regular troops, and expressed his fervent hopes that upon this occasion they would add to the reputation they already enjoyed. Although required to contend against cavalry and infantry, he reminded them that they were also supported by similar troops, but of a quality far superior, who would afford them ample protection. He asked but an ordinary display of manhood on their part to render victory certain; frankly declaring, at the same time, that flight would but ensure their destruction, while safety as well as advantage and honor were to be found only in a determined resistance. For himself, he said, he had not a doubt of the result, if they performed their simple duty. He glanced at a few of those brilliant engagements, in which, at the head of his glorious rifle regiment, he told them, he had humbled foes far more formidable than the one now before him, and expressed the mortification he had experienced at having been compelled, in obedience to orders, to avoid grappling with an opponent whom he felt satisfied he could crush whenever he chose. Closing his remarks to this line with a repetition of his orders, and an exhortation to obey them with firmness, he proceeded to the line formed by his regular troops.

His remarks to the Continentals and militia which composed this line were very brief, and chiefly consisted in giving his orders and explaining those already issued. This body needed not the stimulus of spirit-stirring speeches to fit them for the performance of any achievement within the reach of well-disciplined courage, regulated and directed by judgment and experience. He prepared them for the retreat of the militia, by repeating the orders he had given to that portion of his force; and explained the objects he sought to accomplish by the manœuvre. He directed them to fire low and deliberately, not to break on any account, and if forced to retire, to rally on the eminence in their rear, where, supported by the cavalry and militia, defeat he regarded as impossible. He reminded them of their former achievements, and of the confidence he had always evinced in their well tried valor and discipline, and concluded by declaring that upon them the fortune of the day and his hopes of glory depended.

Orders were dispatched to Colonel Washington, whose corps of cavalry was held in reserve upon the eminence in the rear, to assist in rallying the militia should they fly, and to protect them should they be pursued. He was likewise directed to protect the horses of the militia, and to hold himself in readiness to act as the emergencies of the day might require. The position occupied by the cavalry was admirably chosen. The eminence in their front, and the gradual descent beyond it, secured them from the enemy's fire, without withholding from them a horseback view of the field of battle, for some distance in front of the main line. It furnished, besides, a secure rallying point for the militia, as the events of the day proved.

Every preparation having been made, Morgan took post in the rear of the main line, and composedly awaited the approach of of the enemy.

The British, in the meanwhile, having advanced within four hundred yards of the American lines, halted and commenced the preparations for an attack. Tarleton moved forward with a small party to ascertain the strength and disposition of his opponents; but a few shots from the front line convinced him that the service was attended with too much danger to be persevered in. A body of cavalry was accordingly directed to charge the line, and drive it in upon its supporters under Pickens.* Cunningham and McDowell strictly obeyed the orders they had received. Their men retired slowly, keeping up a desultory but effective fire, and at length fell into the second line, after having unhorsed fifteen of their assailants.

On the return of the British cavalry, it was intended that McDowell and Cunningham should resume their position in the front. Before this could be effected, however, Tarleton's artillery

*Tarleton, p. 215.

had opened a warm fire, under cover of which his right wing had formed, and was advancing. It was therefore determined that the militia should remain together, and meet the enemy in a body.

The light and legion infantry of Tarleton's troops, having disencumbered themselves of everything except their arms and ammunition, formed on the right; and under the fire of a three-pounder, which was placed on their left, advanced to within three hundred yards of the line of the militia. The seventh regiment, led by Major Newmarsh, formed on the left of the light infantry, and the other three-pounder was placed between its right and left divisions. A captain with fifty dragoons was stationed on each flank. This completed the dispositions of the line. The first battalion of the seventy-first infantry, under the command of Major McArthur, and two hundred of the legion cavalry, were posted about one hundred and fifty yards in the rear of the left wing, and composed the reserve.*

These dispositions were no sooner completed, than Tarleton, taking his post in the rear, ordered the line to move forward.

Under the fire of their guns, the British steadily advanced until within about one hundred yards of the American front, when the militia opened a close and deadly fire upon them. The effect of this and the succeeding discharges told heavily upon their ranks, but particularly so upon their officers, not one of whom made himself conspicuous, that was not brought to the ground. This was immediately seen in the disorder which pervaded their line, and the slackened pace of their advance. The militia behaved nobly; they did more than was required of them, and for a time, manifested a disposition to dispute the farther progress of their opponents. But the conduct of the British equally evinced courage and discipline; and although having already suffered a heavy loss, they still pressed forward in the face of the deadly fire. It was not until they had advanced to within one hundred

* Tarleton's Campaign, p. 216.

and fifty yards of the main line, that the militia, who had retired facing them and firing, at length broke, and in obedience to orders, made for the American left. Before Pickens could bring his men to order at this point, however, they were charged by the cavalry posted on the British right, and being forced to give way, sought protection from the reserve behind the hill, whither they were closely pursued.

On the flight of the militia, the British, deeming the victory already secured, set up a deafening shout, and advanced with accelerated, but uneven, pace towards the main line. The latter, as soon as the militia had passed along their front to the left, opened their fire; and now commenced the deadly struggle. For fifteen minutes the contest was maintained at this point with the greatest obstinacy, and was attended with great execution on both sides. The Americans held their ground, as if rooted to the spot, and rapidly delivered their fire. The British evidently hesitated; their advance became slower every minute, until at length, ceasing altogether, and indications of a disposition to retire making themselves manifest, Tarleton ordered the reserve infantry and cavalry into action, the first to take post on the left, while the latter was to coöperate by attacking the American right.[*]

Morgan hailed the indications, furnished by this movement, of the enemy's failing strength or spirit, as omens of approaching victory, and communicated his thoughts to his men. But the advance into line of the reserve infantry re-animated the British, who again moved forward; while their cavalry, taking a wide sweep to the left, was evidently preparing to attack the American right flank.

At this moment, that portion of the British horse, which had followed the militia in their retreat, flew past the American left, hotly pursued by Washington's cavalry; while the militia, having rallied and re-formed behind the hill, appeared, with the redoubtable Pickens at their head, moving up to the support of the American right.

* Tarleton's Campaign, p. 216.

The British line still advancing, their left, which extended some distance beyond the American right, now threatened the latter with a flank attack. At the same time their reserve cavalry was preparing to charge in the same direction. These manœuvres, unless promptly provided against, would have had an important influence on the issue of the conflict, and already they were in operation. The moment was critical, the danger imminent; but Morgan was equal to the emergency. Perceiving his cavalry returning from the pursuit of the British detachment of horse and resuming their position in the rear, he dispatched Col. Brannon with orders to Col. Washington to charge the British cavalry, before they effected their object on his right flank. He then galloped down to the militia, and exhorted them to lose no time in advancing and opening their fire upon the enemy's left.

In the meantime, Col. Howard became apprehensive for the safety of his right flank. Until the cavalry and militia could be brought to its assistance, a change of its front suggested itself to his mind as the means best calculated to hold the enemy temporarily in check. The flank company was accordingly ordered to perform the evolution, which would have placed its line at right angles with that of the main body. But from a misunderstanding of the officer's orders, the men, after coming to the right about, instead of wheeling to the right, marched strait forward. From a belief that a retreat to the hill in the rear had been ordered, the misconception quickly communicated itself to the whole line, which now followed the example of the flank company, faced about, and moved in that direction.

This movement, which at first threatened the Americans with defeat, served ultimately but to render their victory the more splendid and decisive. Howard's first impulse was to rectify the mistake. Instantly struck, however, with the superiority of a retrograde movement of the whole line, over a change of front on his right flank in warding off the embarrassments of the moment, and rendered confident by the admirable deportment of the men,

who marched as steadily as if on parade, he allowed the movement
to proceed.

The line was thus in full retreat, when Morgan returned to it
from the militia. Under feelings of astonishment and alarm, he
immediately rode up to Col. Howard, who briefly explained to
him the cause of the movement, and at the same time removed
the apprehensions he expressed for the event by pointing to the
line and observing " that men were not beaten who retreated in
that order." He was instantly re-assured, and at once determined
upon the measures which the exigency required. Directing
Howard to ride along the line and to order the officers to halt
and face about the moment the word to that effect was given,
Morgan rode forward to fix on the spot where the line should
again be brought into action.*

At this crisis in the contest, the militia having again come into
action, opened a galling fire upon McArthur's battalion, forcing
it not only to forego its attempts upon the American right, but
to retire some distance. At the same moment, Washington
made a furious onset upon the British cavalry, just as they were
in the act of charging the Americans in flank. Dashing completely through their column at the first encounter, he quickly
wheeled and charged on them again with terrible effect.† This
attack was the more successful, as it was in a measure unexpected.
It resulted in the immediate dispersion of the main body of the
enemy's cavalry, which thereafter took no part in the action.

The moment had nearly arrived when Morgan intended renewing the conflict, when he received a message from Col. Washington, who, having advanced some distance in pursuit of the enemy's
cavalry, was now on the left flank of the advancing British, and
beheld the confusion which prevailed in their ranks. " They are
coming on like a mob ; give them a fire and I will charge them,"
were the words of this message. The American line had descended
the rear of the eminence on which the action began, and com

Col. Howard.   †Major Young. Orion, vol. iii., p. 100.

304 THE LIFE OF

menced the ascent on which the cavalry had been posted, when the order to halt and turn upon the enemy flew from right to left. "Face about, boys! give them one good fire, and the victory is ours!" was reiterated by Morgan as he galloped along the line. The order was promptly obeyed.*

At this period, the enemy, confident of victory, and unapprehensive of further resistance, were rushing on in the most impetuous and disorderly manner, and had approached within thirty or forty yards of the American line. Stunned by this unexpected and terrible fire, they instantly recoiled; and before they recovered from the shock, Howard's order to "charge," which mingled with the reverberations of the musquetry, brought the American bayonets to their breasts.

A few minutes before, there was room for their escape by flight. But the defeat and dispersion of their horse left them without protection; and Washington, now in their rear, was advancing with his cavalry upon them at full speed. The greater part of the 7th regiment immediately threw down their arms, and prostrated themselves upon the ground in token of submission. The light and legion infantry also flung away their arms and fled towards the road. But they were speedily overtaken by the volunteer cavalry, and with the exception of a few, surrendered, about two hundred yards from the ground.*

At the feet of our troops, suppliants for mercy, were now the men who had seldom shown mercy to an American under similar circumstances. Furious at the recollection of their manifold cruelties, the cry of "Tarleton's quarters," resounded from one end of the American line to the other. The work of slaughter was about commencing, when Morgan, Howard, and the American officers generally, interposed in behalf of the vanquished foe. Happily for the honor of our arms, they succeeded in preventing a general massacre.†

The eagerness of the enemy's advance threw their artillery

* Major Young.　　　　　† Johnson's Greene, vol. i., pp. 881, 882.

some paces in the rear. When the fire of the American line, and its subsequent charge, forced them to recoil, the pieces were again brought into the front. One of these was captured by Captain Anderson, and the other by Captain Kirkwood. The detachment of royal artillery, which served the guns, bravely attempted to bear them off. It was, however, speedily overpowered.*

The only part of the field where the contest was still maintained, was on the American right, between the militia and Major McArthur's battalion. The latter, deserted by the cavalry, and fiercely assailed in front and on the flank by Pickens and his men, were falling back, in the vain hope of being able to extricate themselves from the fate which had already befallen their companions of the line. Up to this moment they had preserved order in their ranks, and manfully maintained the unequal contest with the entire militia force, when Howard wheeled upon them with the right wing of the American line. This movement immediately threw them into confusion, upon which the militia rushed forward, and were soon engaged in a hand-to-hand combat. Col. Jackson seized the colors of the regiment; but failing to secure them, he pushed on at the head of his Georgians, and succeeded in taking Major McArthur prisoner.† Broken and dispirited, deserted by their friends and surrounded by their enemies, the men of the battalion responded to Howard's summons to surrender by grounding their arms. Col. Pickens received their commander's sword, and the militia took charge of the prisoners.

Tarleton, in the meantime, had been endeavoring to induce the cavalry of his legion to advance and cover Mc'Arthur's retreat, and that of such of the fugitives as had escaped from the field. Failing in this, he advanced at the head of his detachment of the 17th dragoons, accompanied by fourteen officers, principally of the legion cavalry, with the object of bearing off the artillery.‡

Col. Howard.   † Letter from Gen. James Jackson. See Appendix.
‡ Tarleton's Camp., pp. 217, 218.

Approaching near the ground, and observing that he had arrived too late, he wheeled to retire. Col. Washington had just effected his brilliant charge upon the British line, and was aiding at the time in securing the prisoners, when the dragoons were noticed. Rightly conjecturing that Tarleton was to be found with this body of the enemy, and burning with the desire to crown the glory of the day by his capture, Washington commanded a pursuit. Dashing forward at full speed, he not only soon overtook the retreating foe, but placed himself far in advance of his troops who followed. Unfortunately, in the confusion of the moment, a few only of his command heard and obeyed his orders to follow him. Upon his near approach, Tarleton and two of his officers, who brought up the rear of their party, wheeled about and made a charge on him. Nothing daunted, he struck at the first that approached, being the officer on Tarleton's right; but the encounter of their swords proved the inferiority of that wielded by Washington, which broke near the hilt. The British officer now rose in his stirrups to give vigor to the blow which was intended to cut Washington down. But at this critical moment, a lad named Collin, who attended on and was much attached to Washington, rode up, and discharging the contents of one of his pistols in the officer's shoulder, the uplifted arm fell powerless. The other officer also made a cut at Washington, now rendered defenceless. But this attack was rendered as abortive as the first by the opportune arrival of Sergeant Major Perry, who parried the blow and gave one in return, which took effect in the officer's sword arm. Tarleton hereupon pushed forward and made a thrust at Washington, which the latter parried with the remains of his sword. The close approach of the American cavalry now admonishing Washington's assailants of the danger of longer delaying to rejoin their retreating troopers, they decamped at full speed, Tarleton taking a parting shot at Washington, whose horse received the ball.*

Great as were the advantages thus far obtained by the Ameri

* MSS. Johnson's Greene, vol. i., p. 382 ; Howard ; Dr. Hill.

can arms 'over the enemy, there were others yet to be reaped which were well worth the gathering. A large body of the legion cavalry, and a number of the infantry had escaped, and that portion of Tarleton's baggage as yet free from capture, was but a few miles distant on the route of the fugitives. Morgan dispatched his cavalry and a large body of mounted militia in pursuit.

Tarleton lost no time in his retreat; and to the celerity of his movements, and the error of his pursuers in taking the wrong road, he was undoubtedly indebted for his escape. After pushing forward a few miles he reached his baggage wagons. The baggage guard, having been informed that the battle had terminated in the destruction of their commander, abandoned their charge on the road, and mounting the wagon horses, fled towards Cornwallis's encampment at Turkey Creek. A body of tories, who were attached to Tarleton's command, and had been employed by him as guides and spies, were busily employed in appropriating the contents of the wagons to their own use, when he unexpectedly appeared among them. Supposing them to be whigs, he charged on them with his troop of cavalry, and killing a number, dispersed the rest.* A short time was spent in destroying what remained of the baggage, when he resumed his march. He reached Broad river at Hamilton's ford the same evening, and crossing to the opposite bank, encamped for the night.

The legion cavalry had crossed at this point some time before, and succeeded in reaching Cornwallis's encampment the same night.

The pursuit was continued for more than twenty miles, and did not cease till the day was drawing to a close. Unfortunately, it took a wrong direction, almost from the outset, one of the roads leading to the Pacolet being followed by the Americans instead of that taken by the British towards Broad river. Although every effort was made, after the discovery of the mistake, to

* Johnson's Greene., vol, i., p. 385.　　　　* Tarleton's Campaign, 218.

308 THE LIFE OF

recover the lost time, the fugitives had gained too much ground to be overtaken. But the service, although baffled in its main object, was by no means unproductive of advantages. Washington at length gave over the pursuit, and on his return, sweeping the country on each side of his route, succeeded in capturing and bringing into the American camp nearly one hundred more prisoners.

The action commenced about 7 o'clock in the morning, and continued for nearly an hour. Its glorious results may now be briefly summed up.

The American loss was astonishingly small, when compared with that of the enemy. Twelve were killed and sixty-one wounded; no officer of rank was among either. This loss was chiefly sustained by the continental troops, and particularly by the flank companies, posted on the right of the main line.

The loss of the British was admitted by their own accounts to be upwards of one hundred and fifty killed and wounded, besides four hundred taken prisoners.* This is far below the correct number, however. Morgan estimated their loss at one hundred and ten killed, two hundred wounded, and five hundred and two prisoners. But as will be seen in his account of the affair, he does not pretend to accuracy; and while it is probable that he overrated the number of killed and wounded, he is certainly under the mark as regards the prisoners. An examination of all the sources of information on this point will establish the fact, that at least eighty were killed, ten of whom were officers, and one hundred and fifty wounded, while the prisoners, including those taken by Washington's and other detached parties after the battle, amounted to full six hundred men. Twenty-seven commissioned officers were also taken, and subsequently released on parole.

The trophies of victory were two stands of colors, two three-pounders, eight hundred muskets, thirty-five wagons, with the

* Tarleton's Campaign, p. 218.

baggage of the seventh regiment, sixty negroes, one hundred cavalry horses, one travelling forge, and all the enemy's music.

The official account* of this action may here be appropriately introduced. The letter, of which the following is an abridgment, was written by Morgan to Gen. Greene, while the former was on his retreat from the field of the Cowpens.

CAMP NEAR CAIN CREEK, *Jan.* 19, 1781.

DEAR SIR : The troops I have the honor to command have gained a complete victory over a detachment from the British army commanded by Lieut. Col. Tarleton. The action happened on the 17th inst., about sunrise, at a place called the Cowpens, near Pacolet river.

On the 14th, having received certain information that the British army were in motion, and that their movements clearly indicated their inten- tions of dislodging us, I abandoned my encampment at Grindale's Ford, and on the 16th, in the evening, took possession of a post about seven miles from the Cherokee Ford on Broad river. My former position subjected me at once to the operations of Lord Cornwallis and Colonel Tarleton, and in case of a defeat, my retreat might easily have been cut off. My situation at the Cowpens enabled me to improve any advantages I might gain, and to provide better for my own security, should I be unfortunate. These reasons induced me to take this post, notwithstanding it had the appearance of a retreat. On the evening of the 16th, the enemy occupied the ground we removed from in the morning. An hour before daylight, one of my scouts informed me that they had advanced within five miles of our camp. On this information, the necessary dispo- sitions were made ; and from the alacrity of the troops, we were so prepared to receive them.

The light infantry, commanded by Lieut. Col. Howard, and the Virginia militia, under Major Triplett, were formed on a rising ground. The third regiment of dragoons, consisting of eighty men under the command of Lieut. Col. Washington, were so posted in their rear as not to be injured by the enemy's fire, and yet be able to charge the enemy, should an occasion offer. The volunteers from North Carolina, South Carolina and Georgia, under the command of Col. Pickens, were posted to guard the flanks. Major McDowell, of the North Carolina volunteers, was posted on the right flank, in front of the line one hundred and fifty yards, and Major Cunningham, of the Georgia volunteers, on the left, at the same distance

* For the original report of the action at the Cowpens, see Appendix

in front. Colonels Branner and Thomas, of the South Carolinians, on the right of Major McDowell, and Col. Hays and McCall, of the same corps, on the left of Major Cunningham. Captains Tate and Buchannan with the Augusta riflemen were to support the right of the line. The enemy drew up in one line four hundred yards in front of our advanced corps. The 1st battalion of the 71st regiment was opposed to our right; the 7th regiment to our left; the legion infantry to our centre, and two light companies, one hundred men each, on the flanks. In their front moved on two field pieces, and Lieut. Col. Tarleton with two hundred and eighty cavalry, was posted in the rear of his line. The disposition being thus made, small parties of riflemen were detached to skirmish with the enemy, on which their whole line advanced on with the greatest impetuosity, shouting as they advanced. Majors McDowell and Cunningham gave them a heavy fire and retreated to the regiments intended for their support. The whole of Col. Pickens's command then kept up a fire by regiments, retreating agreeable to their orders. When the enemy advanced to our line, they received a well directed and incessant fire; but their numbers being superior to ours, they gained our flanks, which obliged us to change our position. We retreated in good order about fifty paces, formed, advanced on the enemy and gave them a brisk fire, which threw them into disorder. Lieut. Colonel Howard observing this, gave orders for the line to charge bayonets, which was done with such address that the enemy fled with the utmost precipitation. Lieut. Colonel Washington discovering that the cavalry were cutting down our riflemen on the left, charged them with such firmness as obliged them to retire in confusion. The enemy were entirely routed, and the pursuit continued for upwards of twenty miles.

Our loss is very inconsiderable, not having more than twelve killed and sixty wounded. The enemy's loss was ten commissioned officers killed, and upwards of one hundred rank and file; two hundred wounded; twenty-nine commissioned officers and more than five hundred privates, prisoners, which fell into our hands, with two field pieces, two standards, eight hundred muskets, one travelling forge, thirty-five wagons, seventy negroes, and upwards of one hundred dragoon horses, and all their music. They destroyed most of their baggage, which was immense. Although our success was complete, we fought only eight hundred men, and were opposed by upwards of one thousand chosen British troops.

Such was the inferiority of our numbers, that our success must be attributed to the justice of our cause and the gallantry of our troops. My wishes would induce me to name every sentinel in the corps. In justice to the bravery and good conduct of the officers, I have taken the liberty to enclose you a list of their names, from a conviction that you will be pleased to introduce such characters to the world.

Major Giles, my aid-de-camp, and Captain Brookes, my brigade major, deserve and have my thanks for their assistance and behavior on this occasion. The Baron de Glaebeut, who accompanies Major Giles with these dispatches, served with me as a volunteer, and behaved so as to merit your attention.

I am, dear Sir,

Your obedient servant,

,DANIEL MORGAN.

To GEN. GREENE.

A list of the commissioned officers in the action of the 17th of January, 1781, *of the Light Infantry.*

JOHN HOWARD, Lieutenant-Colonel commandant.

BENJAMIN BROOKES, Captain and Major of brigade.

CAPT. ROBERT KIRKWOOD, Delaware.	LIEUT. BARNES.	Virginia.
CAPT. ANDERSON,	Maryland.	LIEUT. MILLER,	"
CAPT. DOBSON,	"	ENSIGN KING,	"
LIEUT. EWING,	"	ENSIGN DYER,	Maryland.
LIEUT. WATKINS,	"	ENSIGN SMITH,	"
LIEUT. HANSON,	"	LIEUT. ANDERSON,	Delaware.

Of the third Regiment of Light Dragoons.

LT.-COL. WM. WASHINGTON, Virginia.	LIEUT. BELL,	Virginia.
MAJOR RICHARD McCALL,	"	CORNET SIMMONS,	South Carolina.
CAPTAIN BARRETT.	"		

Of the Maryland State Regiment.

EDWARD GILES, Major and acting Aid-de-Camp of the Virginia militia.

MAJOR TRIPLETT,	ENSIGN COMBS,	Virginia militia.
CAPT. BUCHANNAN, Virginia militia.	ENSIGN McCOSKELL,	"
CAPT. TATE,	"	ENSIGN WILSON,	"
CAPT. GILMORE.		

The Baron de Glaubeck served as a volunteer in Gen. Morgan's family, and Mr. Andrews with Colonel Washington's regiment.

Colonel Pickens and all the officers in his corps behaved well; but from their having so lately joined the detachment, it has been impossible to collect all their names or rank, so that the general is constrained not to particularize any, least it should be doing injustice to others.

By orders B. Gen. Morgan,

(*Copy.*)   Edward Giles, A.D.C.

Jan. 19*th*, 1791.

CHAPTER XVI.

Reflections suggested by the battle of the Cowpens—Morgan's conduct on that occasion
defended—The news of the victory received with joy throughout the country—Resolutions of Congress and letter of President Huntington—Resolutions of Virginia House of
Delegates, and letter from Speaker Richard M. Lee—Congratulatory letters from Gen.
Davidson, Gov. Rutledge, Col. O. H. Williams and Gen. Sumter—After the battle, Morgan retreats across Broad river towards the Catawba—Cornwallis, deterred by the
result of the battle, awaits a junction with Leslie before marching in pursuit of Morgan
—Believing that the latter intended remaining north of Broad river, Cornwallis marches
in that direction—Discovers his mistake—His unavailing pursuit—Morgan reaches the
east bank of the Catawba—His letter to Gen. Greene—Reflections upon the military
events just detailed—Morgan resolves to defend the fords of the Catawba—His letters to
Gen. Greene from this quarter.

MAKING due allowance for the numbers engaged in the battle
of the Cowpens, and for the particular circumstances under which
it was fought, the victory was certainly the most brilliant that
had ever been achieved by the arms of America. It is even
doubtful if our subsequent military annals furnish anything of the
kind, which, under like limitations, at all approaches it in splen-
dor. The scene of this memorable engagement was in an open
wood, affording to the movements of an army all the facilities of
a plain. The ground offered none of those advantages which
swamps, thickets, and a broken surface afford to the weak against
the strong, and to those carrying on defensive operations. It was
pronounced by Tarleton himself to be as proper and convenient a
place for an action as he could desire.* The American force
engaged was not more than eight hundred and fifty men, more
than half of whom were undisciplined militia. That of the

* Tarleton, p. 221.

14

British, composed for the most part of the *élite* of their army, numbered from one thousand and fifty men to eleven hundred and fifty men, having the additional advantages of artillery and a large numerical superiority in bayonets and cavalry. The obstinate and sanguinary contest which ensued was not attended by any of those fortuitous events which occasionally turn the tide of battle against all the calculations of experience, as well as all the efforts of well directed courage. From first to last it was a deadly struggle, the termination of which, while it brought destruction on one of the combatants, gave victory, complete and decisive, to the other, as the reward of superior courage and constancy. The result will stand for all time, a proud and imperishable memorial of American prowess.

But brilliant as was this achievement, the solid advantages which it secured to the cause of independence constitute its chief claim to remembrance. As Cornwallis's first expedition into North Carolina was terminated by the destruction of Ferguson, so the second was crippled and eventually arrested by the overthrow of Tarleton. The affair of King's Mountain removed the impression which had until that event been deeply sunk in the public mind, that the British were invincible, and must ultimately succeed in their designs. That of the Cowpens re-animated the expiring hopes of the people, and after a brief period of doubt and despondency, marshalled them by thousands against the enemies of their country. It was the first link in the chain of events, which, baffling the efforts and blasting the hopes of the enemy, at length led to their expulsion from the country, and to a glorious termination of the struggle.

The numerous and valuable services which Morgan rendered during the war, had won him a conspicuous place in public estimation. But after this brilliant and important achievement, he was deservedly ranked among the most illustrious defenders of his country. Yet strange as it may appear, the unexampled success which attended him on that occasion, was subsequently made the means of inflicting a serious wound on his military reputation. Notwithstanding the many reasons which combined, forcing him to give the enemy battle, he was blamed for incurring the risk. Notwithstanding the military genius which he displayed in the selection of his position, the disposition of his forces, and the conduct of the engagement, his censurers condemned it all as indicating temerity rather than judgment. The indomitable courage, the unyielding constancy, which, through his happy adaptation of means to circumstances, were brought on that occasion into full operation, seem to have been considered as secondary elements in the military combinations of his scientific accusers, who evidently based their censures upon the hazardous assumption, that it was impossible for a body of Americans, however brave and well-disciplined, or however well conducted, to contend successfully against an equal number of the enemy under a competent commander. Morgan's determination to fight sprung from opinions totally different. His dispositions for battle were made under the conviction that his troops, rested, refreshed, and full of confidence, were more than a match for the fatigued, panting adversary approaching him, and that the hopelessness of escape by flight, involved in his position, would secure him such a hearty co-operation from the militia, as must necessarily result in a triumph. There never was a moment during the action, in which he feared or had cause to fear, for the result. The misapprehension which caused the main line to retreat, only gave new strength to his confidence, from the discipline and unshaken courage which the men displayed on that occasion. Colonel Tarleton, however, has interpreted these dispositions to the discredit of Morgan's judgment, and seems, even in the contemplation of his defeat, to be astonished at the temerity which should venture to meet him on equal terms, and rest for the issue on skill and courage alone. "The ground which Gen. Morgan had chosen for the engagement, in order to cover his retreat to Broad river," remarks Col. Tarleton, "was disadvantageous for the Amer-

icans, but convenient for the British; an open wood was cer·
tainly as proper a place for action as Lieut. Col. Tarleton could
desire. America does not produce many more suitable to the
nature of the troops under his command. The situation of the
enemy was desperate in case of misfortune; an open country and
a river in their rear, must have thrown them entirely in the
power of a superior cavalry, whilst the light troops, in case of a
repulse, had the expectation of a neighboring force to protect
them from destruction."* These opinions and reasonings, if not
adopted, were in a great measure concurred in by those who
employed themselves in detracting from the well earned fame of
Gen. Morgan. But the following brief justification of himself,
while it displays the dauntlessness of character and originality of
mind which distinguished the man, leaves Tarleton as little to
boast of from his reasoning as from his fighting. "I would not,"
Morgan once observed, in remarking upon objections similar to
the above, "have had a swamp in view of my militia on any consideration; they would have made for it, and nothing could have
detained them from it. As to covering my wings, I knew my
adversary, and was perfectly sure I should have nothing but
downright fighting. As to retreat, it was the very thing I wished
to cut off all hope of. I would have. thanked Tarleton had he
surrounded me with his cavalry. It would have been better than
placing my own men in the rear to shoot down those who broke
from the ranks. When men are forced to fight, they will sell
their lives dearly; and I knew that the dread of Tarleton's
cavalry would give due weight to the protection of my bayonets,
and keep my troops from breaking, as Buford's regiment did.
Had I crossed the river, one-half of the militia would immediately
have abandoned me."†

The reasons which brought Morgan to the determination to
fight Tarleton have already been given, and that they were the
true ones, cannot be disputed without also disputing the authen-

*Tarleton's Campaign, p. 221.   † Johnson's Greene, p. 376.

ticity of the evidence furnished in his own and General Greene's
letters; and rejecting the inferences which all the circumstances
naturally educe. Yet Col. Lee ascribes this determination to a
sudden fit of ill temper, " which," he adds, " overruled the suggestions of Morgan's sound and discriminating judgment." His
masterly retreat, after the battle, in the face of the enemy, to the
Catawba, was regarded as an escape little less than miraculous;
and although the natural result of a correct judgment of his situation, formed upon a knowledge of Cornwallis's intentions and
movements, its success was ascribed to circumstances indicating a
providential interference in behalf of the cause in which he was
engaged. But these, and other inaccuracies less pardonable, will
be noticed in their proper connection. To assaults of this nature,
Morgan never vouchsafed a formal answer. This is to be
regretted, for his injured fame may be cited in proof of the fact,
that there are few names which are rendered so impregnable in
the good opinions of the world as never to need defending. None
are above the reach of calumny or misrepresentation. Reputa-
tions are like riches;—it is not easy to determine which is the
more difficult task, to keep, or to acquire them. Satisfied in the
belief that his conduct and character were properly estimated by
the people at large, he treated with proud indifference the opinions of those whose strictures he justly considered as the suggestions of prejudice or of envy. Prejudice is blind, and envy will
not see. Genius, in whatever form it presents itself, always
arouses the antipathies of natures less richly endowed. It can
only be judged by its achievements; and after all, success furnishes its own best defence. Yet the world is too apt to adopt
the judgments of a lower order of minds, and to condemn the
bold and adventurous spirits who leave the beaten track and
follow the promptings of " the divinity which stirs within them,"
to the attainment of their ends. Much of weak argument, and
more of misrepresentation, have thus found their way into history,
and at length impressed the present age with the belief, that

Morgan was a brave, but not a judicious officer, and that he was indebted more to fortune than to ability for his laurels. Against such conclusions truth and justice alike demand that his reputation should be defended.

For some time previously to this glorious affair, the attention of the whole country had been drawn with breathless interest towards the military operations of the South. The result of the pending struggle in that quarter would, it was generally believed, exercise an important, if not a decisive, influence upon the issue of the war. The co-operation of the French, the liberty of the South, and the integrity of the confederation itself, were supposed to depend upon a fortunate turn in the events then approaching development. But the ill-fortune which had hitherto attended the efforts of Howe, Lincoln and Gates, and the feebleness of Greene's present force, when compared with the powerful array of the enemy, filled the breast of every patriot with the most gloomy presentiments. Under these circumstances, it is not difficult to imagine the burst of joy with which the cheering news of this victory was received throughout the land, and the thanks and honors which a grateful people showered upon the brave men who achieved it. Congress manifested their approbation by the passage of a preamble and resolutions expressive of their thanks to the officers and men who participated in the battle, and directing a gold medal, with suitable inscriptions, to be presented to Morgan. They likewise presented Pickens, now a brigadier general, with a sword; Lieut. Cols. Washington and Howard with a silver medal each, and Major Triplett with a sword. The House of Delegates of Virginia passed resolutions of approval and thanks; directing also, at a subsequent period, that Morgan should be presented with a horse, fully caparisoned, and a sword. The Legislatures of a number of the States marked the event with proceedings expressive of their gratification. From the most distinguished quarters poured in upon him congratulations, mingled with expressions of condolence upon the unfortunate state of his health, and of hope for his speedy recovery.

From these numerous manifestations of a nation's joy and gratitude, a few have been selected for publication, some from their historical importance, and others from their intimate connection with the narrative of events, and the honor which is deservedly associated with the names of the writers.

THE UNITED STATES IN CONGRESS ASSEMBLED.

Congress, impressed with the most lively sentiments of approbation at the conduct of Brigadier General Morgan and the officers and men under his command, on the seventeenth of January last, when, with eighty cavalry and two hundred and thirty-seven infantry of the troops of the United States, and five hundred and fifty-three militia from the States of Virginia, North Carolina, South Carolina, and Georgia, he obtained a complete and important victory over a select and well appointed detachment of more than eleven hundred British troops, commanded by Lieutenant-Colonel Tarleton, do therefore

Resolve : That the thanks of Congress be presented to Brigadier General Morgan and the officers and men under his command, for their fortitude and good conduct displayed in the action at the Cowpens, in the State of South Carolina, on the said seventeenth of January last.

That a medal of gold be presented to Brigadier General Morgan, representing on one side the action aforesaid, particularizing his numbers, the numbers of the enemy, the numbers of killed, wounded and prisoners, and his trophies; and on the other side, the figure of the general on horseback, leading on his troops in pursuit of the flying enemy, with this motto in the exergue, *Virtus unita valet.*

Passed March 9th, 1781.

Note.—Many years elapsed before General Morgan received the medal thus voted to him. In the meantime, the design directed by the resolutions was materially changed, as may be seen by the engraved representation of the medal. On the obverse side, the original directions were mainly observed; but on the reverse, Morgan is represented as receiving a crown of laurels from the Genius of America; the background is filled up with the trophies of victory; while on the top is the inscription "*Danieli Morgan duci exercitus,*" and at the bottom, "*Comitia Americana.*"

Hon. Samuel Huntington to Gen. Morgan.

PHILADELPHIA, April 11th, 1781.

SIR: Your letter of the 28th ult. hath been duly received, with the standard of the 7th British regiment which fell into your hands in the battle of the 17th of January. This will be deposited with other trophies in the War Office, to remain a lasting evidence of the victory that day obtained with so much gallantry and bravery.

I am sorry to find your health so much impaired; hope by your present retirement and relaxation from the toils of the field that it may be perfectly restored, and your country reap signal advantages from your future services.

I have the honor to be, &c.,
SAMUEL HUNTINGTON.

BRIG. GEN. MORGAN.

IN THE HOUSE OF DELEGATES.

Friday the 9th of March, 1781.

Resolved: That Brigadier General Morgan be requested to accept of a horse with furniture, and a sword, as a further testimony of the high esteem of his country for his military character and abilities, so gloriously displayed in the victory gained by him and the troops he lately commanded in South Carolina, and that the Governor be desired to direct some proper person to procure the said articles, and convey them to the said General.

Teste.

JOHN BECKLEY, C. H. D.

18<i>th March</i>, 1781.
Agreed to by the Senate.
WILL. DREW, C. S.

Governor Nelson to General Morgan.

RICHMOND, July 20th, 1781.

SIR: It will give me the greatest pleasure to comply with the resolution of the Assembly, directing that you shall be presented with a horse, sword, &c., as I shall ever be happy to contribute towards rewarding distinguished merit.

I am under some difficulty with respect to the horse, because I may procure one that may not suit you. If you know of one that you wish to have, I will immediately direct that he shall be purchased. The Assembly intended the present should be a genteel one; the horse, therefore, ought to be of the first quality.

> I am, Sir, with great esteem,
> Your ob't and very humble serv't,
> THOMAS NELSON.

BRIG. GEN. MORGAN.

Hon. Richard Henry Lee to General Morgan.

RICHMOND, *March 21st,* 17~ *1.*

SIR: It is with peculiar pleasure that I execute the order of the House of Delegates, in transmitting to you their sense, and through them the sense that your country entertains of the many signal services perfoi·ned by you in the various victories that you have obtained over the enemies of the United States, and more especially in the late well-timed total defeat given to the British troops in South Carolina. I am directed to request of you, Sir, that you will convey to the brave officers and troops under your command in the action of the 17th of January, the sense entertained by the House of Delegates of their valor and great services upon that occasion.

Having thus discharged my duty to the House of Delegates, permit me to lament that the unfortunate state of your health should deprive the public of those eminent services in the field which you are so capable of perform· ing; and let me hope that it will not be long before return of health will restore you to the army and to your country.

> I have the honor to be, &c.,
> RICHARD HENRY LEE, Son

BRIG. GEN. MORGAN.

Gen. Davidson to Gen. Morgan.

CHARLOTTE, *Jan. 21st,* 1761.

DEAR GENERAL: You will please to accept my warmest congratulations on your late glorious victory. You have, in my opinion, paved the way for the salvation of this country. I hope Major McDowell and the volun· teers answered the character I gave you of them.

The militia are coming in fast to this place. Against Wednesday or Thursday, I shall be ready to march with a considerable number of pretty good men, wherever it may be proper; and several gentlemen from the country have offered to embody the militia that are at home, to conduct the prisoners to any place that may be directed. If you think well of

14*

this, I will thank you to let me know by the bearer of this, Parson McCaully, as I have men here from every company, who can carry dispatches for the purpose immediately. I think I shall have six hundred men, at least, at the place of rendezvous.

I have the honor to be, &c.,

WM. DAVIDSON.

GEN. MORGAN.

P.S. I believe your boats are ready at Major Davidson's. Let me know if you have any flints to spare. I want about two thousand. A thousand compliments to the officers.

Gen. Davidson to Gen. Morgan.

CHARLOTTE, *Jan. 23d,* 1781.

DEAR SIR: The enclosed dispatches from head-quarters came to hand to-day, with a letter from General Greene. The General mentions to me the plan you suggested of making a diversion to the westward, and seems to depend much upon your judgment respecting that matter. In the meantime, I am directed to make you acquainted with my numbers and situation, and to hold myself in readiness to execute any order you may think proper to give. As the troops are now collecting, returns cannot be made for some time. Seventeen British soldiers, taken on the retreat, the 17th instant, were brought in here to-day. Your victory over Tarleton has gladdened every countenance in this part. We have had a *feu de joie* to-day, in consequence of it.

I have the honor to be,

Your very obedient and humble servant,

WM. DAVIDSON.

HON. BRIG. GEN. MORGAN,
Commanding on the West of the Catawba.

Gov. Rutledge to Gen. Morgan.

CHERAWS, *Jan. 25th,* 1781.

DEAR SIR: I request that you will be pleased to accept my warmest and most cordial thanks, and that you will present them to the brave officers and men under your command, for the good conduct and intrepidity manifested in the action with Lieut. Col. Tarleton, on the 17th instant. This total defeat of chosen veteran British troops, by a number far inferior to theirs, will forever distinguish the gallant men by whom the glorious victory was obtained, and endear them to their country. I

reflect on it with the greatest pleasure, as a presage of the happiest consequences. It will excite many to emulate their patriotism; and by the
undaunted courage and perseverance of freemen who are determined to
maintain the independence of America, that must (with the blessing of
God on our arms), be firmly established. Col. Pickens's behavior justified
the opinion I have always had of that gallant officer. Enclosed is a
Brigadier's commission, of which I desire his acceptance.

I am, &c.,

J. RUTLEDGE.

GEN. MORGAN.

COL. WILLIAMS TO GEN. MORGAN.

CAMP PEDEE, Jan. 25, 1781.

DEAR GEN.: I rejoice exceedingly at your success. The advantages you
have gained are important, and do great honor to your little corps. I am
peculiarly happy that so great a share of the glory is due to the officers
and men of the light infantry. Next to the happiness which a man feels
at his own good fortune, is that which attends his friend. I am much
better pleased that you have plucked the laurels from the brow of the
hitherto fortunate Tarleton, than if he had fallen by the hands of Lucifer.
Vengeance is not sweet if it is not taken as we would have it. I am
delighted that the accumulated honors of a young partisan should be
plundered by my old friend.

We have had a *feu de joie*, drunk all your healths, swore you were the
finest fellows on earth, and love you, if possible, more than ever. The
General has, I think, made his compliments in very handsome terms.
Enclosed is a copy of his orders. It was written immediately after we
received the news, and during the operation of some cherry bounce.

I have only to add a repetition of my best wishes for you. Compliments to Howard and all friends. Adieu.

Yours sincerely,

O. H. WILLIAMS.

BRIG. GEN. MORGAN.

GEN. SUMTER TO GEN. MORGAN.*

CATAWBA RIVER, 28th January, 1781.

DEAR SIR: I have every reason to believe that the enemy are not more

---

* A few remarks are suggested by this letter. It is generally believed that the opposition of Col. Sumter to the efforts of Morgan, in relation to the establishment of maga-

than 1,600 strong. I have had them repeatedly counted, and could ascer
tain their number to a man, if I knew what had escaped the defeat of Col.
Tarleton—upon which happy event I most heartily congratulate you.

                                        I am, &c.,
                                                    THOMAS SUMTER.
    GEN. MORGAN.

The battle over, Morgan made preparations for an immediate
retreat. Far from being intoxicated by his victory, or from considering it as affording him a prospect of security, he felt that it
must necessarily have the effect of greatly increasing his danger.
However strong were the reasons for a retreat before the contest,
they had now become imperative in their nature. The British
army was not more than thirty miles distant from the scene of
action. The fugitives from the field, he knew, would reach Cornwallis's camp that night. For some time previously this officer
had kept his troops under marching orders. It was taken for
granted, that upon learning his loss, he would make instant and
prodigious efforts, not only to obtain revenge, but to liberate his
captive soldiery, and to recover their arms and baggage. Morgan
accordingly resolved to make a dash for the Catawba. The fords
of that river were, however, nearer to Cornwallis than to himself;
and, however great the diligence he displayed in the effort to
reach them, he felt assured that the enemy might intercept him,
should they correctly divine his intentions, and act with promptitude. But there was a possibility that Cornwallis would lose this
advantage, from a misconception of his adversary's designs. Mor-

---

zines, already alluded to, originated in a dislike of the latter by the former, and that the
circumstance in question tended to increase the ill feeling between these distinguished men.
There is reason to believe that the judicious efforts of General Greene, to reconcile this
matter, were not unsuccessful, and that Morgan and Sumter thereafter regarded each
other with friendly eyes. Sumter was a man who scorned everything like dissimulation,
and, as occasion offered, was as free in the display of his hatreds as he was of his friend-
ships. Under this view of his character, which is undoubtedly the correct one, the letter
above would never have been written had, he entertained feelings of dislike towards
Morgan.

gan used the chance thus afforded him to the best advantage. While hurrying his preparations, justly considering that every minute lost would but add to his danger, he kept his ulterior designs a secret to all but his principal officers, and gave currency to the impression that it was his intention to hold the country north of Broad river.

Colonel Pickens, with a body of militia, was directed to remain on the ground, under the protection of a flag, for the purpose of burying the dead, and of ministering to the sufferings and wants of the wounded of both armies. The baggage of the enemy furnished tents, bedding, and other comforts, which were appropriated to the use of the wounded. The prisoners were collected, the arms, cannon, and other valuable trophies were placed in wagons, and the troops formed in marching order. The detachment under Washington being still absent in pursuit of the enemy, orders were left for it to follow the main body without delay, upon its return. These and other arrangements having been made, the line was put in motion about noon. Before the close of the day, the army crossed Broad river at the Cherokee ford, and encamped for the night on its northern bank

Long before daylight next morning, Morgan had resumed his march. Anticipating difficulty, if not disaster, he took every precaution, and prepared for the worst. Being soon after joined by Washington and the cavalry, the prisoners were placed under their charge, with directions to move higher up the country, and to cross the Catawba at the Island ford. The main body, in the mean time, struck into and advanced upon the direct road to Ramsower's Mills, situated on the Little Catawba. Morgan justly considered, that should the enemy approach and attack him, or cut off his retreat towards the Catawba, there was, by this arrangement, a change still left for the preservation of his prisoners from recapture.

While pressing his march, he expected every hour to hear that the enemy were at hand · and looked with anxiety for the return of some of his spies with information of their movements. Great was his surprise and joy upon learning that night, not only that the enemy had not moved up to a late hour of the day, but that they did not intend to move until a junction had been effected with Leslie. Cheered by this encouraging news, Morgan pushed forward with renewed vigor early the next morning.

The news of Tarleton's defeat reached Cornwallis, through the fugitives from the field, on the night of the 17th, and came upon him with the stunning effects of a thunderbolt. Uncertain as to Morgan's position and strength, and believing that the militia were out in overpowering numbers, he had hesitated in his advance, and at length determined not to rush upon unknown dangers, until his forces were strengthened by the approaching reinforcements. The intelligence he now received, while it increased his respect for Morgan's courage and address, confirmed his opinion as to that officer's force. For Tarleton, in palliation of his defeat, represented Morgan's strength at 2,000 men, a number more than double that of which it really consisted. Equally uncertain as to Morgan's future movements, Cornwallis determined to defer a pursuit until he could obtain the desired information, or be joined by the force under Leslie. He was encouraged to adopt this course, from the belief that the defeat of Tarleton would exercise a fatal influence upon Morgan—tempting him either to remain in the neighborhood of Broad river, or to advance towards Ninety-six.

The desired junction with Leslie was effected the next day. But no intelligence regarding Morgan, his strength, position, or tendency, had yet been received. On the 19th, the British army moved towards King's creek. Another day passed without yielding any information of Morgan, when Tarleton was directed to recross Broad river with the dragoons and the yagers, and endeavor to obtain the desired intelligence. This officer returned the same evening, having learned that Morgan, soon after the action, had marched from the field of battle with his corps and the prisoners, leaving the wounded under the protection of a flag and that he had crossed Broad river at the upper fords.*

The enigma involved in Morgan's movements and designs was now apparently solved. It appeared to the British commander that his adversary meditated holding his ground in the neighborhood of Broad river. Full of the hope of being able to corner Morgan, and to regain his captured troops, Cornwallis now put his army in active motion. Crossing Buffalo creek on the 21st, he reached Little Broad river the next morning. Passing this stream also, he continued to advance in the direction of King's Mountain, when he learned that he had been deceived, and that Morgan had eluded him.

The latter, fully alive to the critical nature of his situation, and conscious that he was still in the power of the enemy, if they acted with judgment and promptitude, lost not a moment in prosecuting his retreat. Yet in spite of all his efforts, and notwithstanding the active character of his troops, his progress was so slow, as to fill him with the greatest anxiety and alarm. There were many circumstances which conspired to retard his advance. A very rainy season had rendered the numerous streams difficult to ford, and the roads heavy and fatiguing to travel. His troops were harassed by the hard duty of the preceding fortnight, and were unequal to their usual exertions when rested and refreshed. But even were it otherwise, they dragged along with them a prize in the captured arms, too valuable to be relinquished while a hope of escape remained, but which greatly retarded their progress. The heavy baggage of the enemy, after supplying the wants of the wounded, Morgan had destroyed; but the muskets and ammunition were clung to as the means of arming those who were even at the moment embodied for service, but of no avail for the want of arms. To these causes of delay, was added that growing out of the necessity of collecting provisions and forage for the daily wants of the army; and taken together, prevented the advance at a pace more rapid than ten miles a day.

* Tarleton's C   200

On the 19th, Morgan crossed Little Broad river. Two days afterwards, he passed the Little Catawba at Ramsower's Mills; and on the morning of the 23d, took post at Sherrald's Ford, on the east bank of the Catawba.

No time was lost in apprising Gen. Greene of the progress of events, which would exercise so important an influence upon the measures of that officer. The following is the first of Morgan's letters which reached him from Sherrald's Ford:

SHERRALD'S FORD, CATAWBA RIVER, *Jan.* 23, 1781.

SIR: I arrived here this morning. The prisoners crossed at the Island Ford, seventeen miles higher up the river. I expect them to join me this evening; shall send them on to Salisbury in the morning, guarded by Major Triplett's militia, whose time expires this day. If they are to be sent any further, Major Triplett wishes, and thinks is right, that the militia under Gen. Stevens should have the trouble of them, as they have not underwent so much fatigue as his men.

Lord Cornwallis, whether from bad intelligence, or to make a show, moved up towards Gilbertown, to intercept me, the day after I had passed him. I am apprehensive he will (if he is not coming this way) return or send a party by the field of action, and take his wounded, which I neglected taking a receipt from the doctor for,* and perhaps some of the arms left

* A few days after the battle, the wounded of the British were removed from the field to Camden, with an understanding that they were to be regarded as prisoners of war. The wounded of the Americans were taken care of by the patriotic inhabitants of the district, who also collected and carried away the arms, accoutrements, baggage, &c., which were left behind. In relation to this subject, the following letters are among Gen. Morgan's correspondence:

COL. TARLETON TO GEN. MORGAN.

Near TURKEY CREEK, *Jan.* 19, 1781.

SIR: The action of the 17th inst., having thrown into your hands a number of British officers and soldiers,

I primarily request of you, that attention and humanity may be exhibited towards the wounded officers and men, for whose assistance I now send by a flag, Dr. Stewart, and the surgeon's mate of the 7th regiment.

I secondly desire you to inform me of the number and quality of the prisoners which the fortune of war has placed in your possession.

I have the honor, &c.,

BAN. TARLETON, *Lieut. Col. Com.*, B.L.

P.S.—I have sent some money for the use of the prisoners.

BRIG. GEN. MORGAN.

on the field, that I had not time to collect. But I left orders for that purpose with the well affected inhabitants.

I received your letters of the 13th inst., and would have endeavored to get the cloth; but being obliged to come so far out of the way with the prisoners, puts it entirely out of my power. However, I will communicate the matter to Col. Pickens; perhaps he may have some enterprising followers that would undertake it. I have engaged one of his captains to go round and kill the enemy's horses; perhaps he may do the other business.*

Jan. 18, 1781.

SIR: As the wounded must suffer much for the want of necessaries, and even medical assistance, with your permission, I should wish to inform Lord Cornwallis of their situation; that if he thinks proper, he may order something for their relief; some surgeons of the general hospital, and some hospital appointments. From your very great politeness to me, I am confident you will grant everything that is reasonable or proper.

I have the honor, &c.,

ROBERT JACKSON, *Surgeon's Mate, 1st Bat. 71st Reg't.*

HON. BRIG. GEN. MORGAN:

MR. JORDAN'S, NEAR THE COWPENS, *Jan.* 22, 1781.

DEAR GENERAL: Inclosed I send a flag which arrived yesterday from Col. Tarleton. You will see his own requisitions, in addition to which, Dr. Jackson, in conjunction with the gentlemen who came with the flag (finding it impossible to have their wounded properly provided for in this country) are desirous of having the men paroled, and to have permission to take them within the British lines. They will give a receipt for the number of wounded men they receive, and make a return of those that may recover, to our commissary of prisoners, whom they will exchange. I am of the opinion, also, that they cannot be provided for here, and think their proposals of equal advantage to us. There has been one instance of the kind, at Stoney Point. If it is not agreeable to you to have the men paroled, the surgeons will give a receipt for the men and be accountable for them. Some of them are still in the field. You will please to dispatch an answer as soon as possible, that we may know in what manner to act. I wrote you two or three days past, but have received no answer. I wish some mode could be established to remove our wounded to Salisbury. We have no salt; there is no regular supply established yet. I am entirely out of bandages and lint, and shall soon want a supply of medicines

I am, &c.,

R. PINDELL.

BRIG. GEN. MORGAN, *Commanding on the west of Catawba.*

* The closing sentence of the above paragraph is in answer to the suggestion, made by Gen. Greene in his letter to Morgan, of the 8th of January, 1780, that a party should be

I intend to stay at this place till I hear from you, in order to recruit the men and to get in a good train. We must be fitted out with pack horses, for as I wrote you before, wagons will not do for light troops. I intend to send Col. Pickens back immediately, in order to keep up a show of opposition, and to cut off small parties that may be sent out for the purpose of destroying the country, as I expect that will be their aim, to prevent us from getting supplies from that back country. I have got men that are watching the enemy's movements, and will give you the earliest accounts. But I think they will be this way, if the stroke we gave Tarleton don't check them.

I have the honor to be, &c.,

MAJ. GEN. GREENE.   DANIEL MORGAN.

Col. Washington has this moment joined me with the prisoners. Twenty-seven more were taken by our light parties—men of the legion, chiefly dragoons, and some red coats. He says he has heard of a number more being taken; so that at this time, we have six hundred prisoners at least.

Upon reaching the Catawba, Morgan's apprehensions of being overtaken departed for ever. Nothing could deprive him of the glory which he had acquired. But a correct conception of his designs, and an ordinary exercise of celerity by the enemy, might have

sent to kill the enemy's draft and cavalry horses, then collected at the Congaree. The letter referred in the same paragraph is as follows:

GEN. GREENE TO GEN. MORGAN.

HEAD QUARTERS, Jan. 18, 1781.

DEAR SIR: There are six wagon loads of cloth on the way from Charleston to the Congaree river, the property of one Wade Hampton, who, it is said, wishes it to fall into our hands. It will halt on the Congaree, at Friday's Ferry; but in that situation you cannot get at it; and the man, it is reported, is willing to move it on towards Ninety-six, as if to relieve that garrison. To satisfy yourself respecting the matter, you must send a man to Mr. Hampton and inquire respecting the report; and if true, concert with him a plan for getting possession of the cloth, as it would be of infinite importance to get it into our possession. You will readily see, from the nature of the thing, that it is not to be considered as plunder; nor must anybody but yourself know anything of the transaction, as it would inevitably ruin the man. Great caution should be taken to guard against those evils.

I am, &c.,

N. GREENE.

GEN MORGAN.

stripped him of many of the advantages which the victory had
yielded him, and have forced upon him the adoption of new
measures to extricate his troops from danger. At the time the
battle was fought, the positions of the adverse armies were nearly
equi-distant from the point where a junction was formed by the
two roads, which led from each to the fords across which Morgan
had passed. Had Cornwallis divined the intentions and movements of the Americans after the battle, and been correctly
informed as to their force, he could have easily cut off their
retreat towards Broad river. But his uncertainty on these heads
produced a delay and a misdirection of efforts highly advantageous
to Morgan. The latter founded all his hopes of effecting his
retreat on the enemy's ignorance or misconception of his intentions.
His early movements from the field were accordingly conducted
in such a manner as to encourage the belief that he designed
remaining in the neighborhood. The *ruse* was completely successful. While Morgan was pushing forward in an easterly direction towards the Catawba, Cornwallis was hurrying on in pursuit,
on a course nearly northwest to a point, which had long since
been passed by his wily adversary.

But now the attempts at interception were changed into a pursuit. Hastily recrossing Little Broad river, Cornwallis led his
army in the direction taken by Morgan. But the same obstacles
which had hitherto clogged his movements continued to render
his progress extremely slow, and it was not until the 24th that he
reached Ramsower's Mills. Here he learned that Morgan had
crossed two days previously, and that ere that time, that officer
had doubtless gained the east bank of the Catawba.

It was now that the danger which threatened not only his
operations, but his military reputation, broke upon his view.
Although he had exerted himself to the utmost to overtake the
Americans, and in part retrieve the disasters he had experienced,
by their destruction, they had evidently gained upon him. The
sanguine hopes in which he had previously indulged of recovering

his light troops, were now succeeded by misgivings that they were irrecoverably lost, unless some extraordinary measures were taken. As if these circumstances were not in themselves sufficiently vexatious, he could not shut his eyes upon the fact that they were calculated to reflect unfavorably upon his character as an officer of judgment and activity. He had led the British government to believe that he had conquered South Carolina and Georgia, and that North Carolina was but the high road to Virginia, where a junction with Phillips, it was fondly hoped, would not only insure him the conquest of that State, but open a passage northward. Yet what were the facts. His authority was resisted everywhere beyond the reach of his sword. His first attempt to invade North Carolina was abandoned in consequence of the destruction which fell upon a portion of his forces at King's Mountain, and the determined resistance which was manifested to his progress by the patriotic inhabitants of Mecklenburg, Ruhan, and the adjoining districts. His more recent disaster overshadowed the prospects of his second invasion, and should it render his efforts equally abortive with the first attempt, it was apparent even to himself that blame, if not disgrace, would come home to him. In sight, as it were, of his head-quarters, a large and valuable detachment of his army had been captured; yet he had suffered it, together with its arms, cannon, baggage, &c., to be borne off by an inconsiderable force, in a circuitous route towards a point which he ought to have known would be aimed at, and which was nearer to himself than to his opponent. He never made one well-directed, vigorous effort to make amends for his mishaps, until the time had passed when efforts might have been availing. Maddened by the combined effects of losses and disappointments, and alarmed at the ruin which threatened alike his operations and his fame, he justly contemplated his situation as desperate; and as usual with men under such circumstances, he resorted to a desperate remedy. He clung with tenacity to the hope that it was still possible to overtake the conqueror of the

GENERAL DANIEL MORGAN.   333

Cowpens, and took his measures accordingly. He came to the resolution of halting at this point until he could disencumber his infantry of everything calculated to render their movements less active than had been those of his captured light troops ; and by the destruction of all his baggage, not absolutely indispensable, to give his army a facility for marching, favorable to the accomplishment of his wishes. · If a misgiving as to the ultimate consequences of so serious a measure had lingered in his mind, it was banished upon learning that Morgan, instead of pursuing his retreat, had coolly taken post on the east bank of the Catawba, and was busily employed in preparations to oppose a passage of the river.

Nothing but the certainty of overtaking Morgan could have justified Cornwallis in resorting to a measure which necessarily involved an abandonment of the design of prosecuting the campaign. It had been too long deferred to be beneficial, was wholly unnecessary to the end proposed, and finally rendered his subsequent operations fruitful of nothing but suffering and disaster.

Two days were occupied in burning the baggage, and in collecting provisions, when on the 27th the British army advanced towards the Catawba.

Upon reaching this river, Morgan promptly took such measures as his situation and circumstances required. His attention was first directed to the preservation of his prisoners and the arms from the danger of recapture. These, as may be inferred from his letter of the 23d, were sent forward the next day towards Virginia, under escort of Triplett's militia. He next addressed the various commanders of militia in the vicinity, advising them of the probable advance of the British army that way, and urging them to lose no time in assembling their respective commands, and joining him. Scouts and patrolling parties were thrown forward to obtain intelligence, the results of which were promptly communicated to Gen. Greene.

Although laboring under severe illness, which had now become almost insupportable, Morgan spared no exertions to prepare for a vigorous defence of his position, should the enemy approach. His efforts, however, so increased his malady, as to force him to contemplate a brief retirement from service, as the only means of obtaining relief. These, and other interesting details, will be found in the following letters, which, displaying as they likewise do, the sagacity which could divine the objects of the enemy, and suggest the means best calculated to defeat them, will be read with interest:

CAMP, SHERRALD'S FORD, 24th Jan., 1781.

SIR: I just received your letter of the 19th inst., and am much obliged to you for your cautions against a surprise. Mr. Tarleton might as well have been surprised himself as been so devilishly beaten as he was. I approve much of having boats with the main army, but would not wish to have any with me; my party is too weak to guard them.

I am convinced a descent into Georgia would answer a very good purpose. It would draw the attention of the enemy that way, and much disconcert my lord's plans. I am convinced, from every circumstance, he intends to march in force through this part of the State, towards Virginia, and his making a junction with Leslie fixes me in that opinion.

I should be exceedingly glad to make a descent into Georgia, but am so emaciated that I can't undertake it. I grow worse every hour. I can't ride out of a walk. I am exceedingly sorry to leave the field at such a time as this, but it must be the case. Pickens is an enterprising man, and a very judicious one: perhaps he might answer the purpose. With regard to Gen. Sumter, I think I know the man so well that I shall take no notice of what he has done, but follow your advice in every particular.

I have not had any intelligence from Lord Cornwallis this two days. I expect to hear from him every hour. If anything interesting [transpires] I will let you know it immediately. The last account I had of him, he had retreated to Smith's ford on Broad river.

The prisoners are gone on to Salisbury. Seventeen more of their scatterers were brought into Charlotte by some of our parties.

I have the honor, &c.,
DANIEL MORGAN.

MAJ. GEN. GREENE.

N.B.—My detachment is much weakened by this fight with Tarleton. I expect we have near fifty men disabled. Returns shall be sent you of the effectives. We have nothing to drink.

CAMP, SHERRALD'S FORD, 25th, *Sunrise.*

SIR: I am this minute informed by express, that Lord Cornwallis is at Ramsay's Mill, on their march this way, destroying all before them. I shall know the truth of this in a few hours, and let you know immediately.

I am, your obedient servant,

DANIEL MORGAN.

TO THE HON. MAJ. GEN. GREENE.

CAMP AT SHERRALD'S FORD, *Jan.* 25th, 1781, 2 o'clock.

DEAR GENERAL: I receive intelligence every hour of the enemy's rapid approach, in consequence of which I am sending off my wagons. My numbers at this time are too weak to fight them. I intend to move towards Salisbury, in order to get near the main army. I know they intend to bring me to an action, which I am resolved carefully to avoid.

I expect you will move somewhere on the Yadkin to oppose their crossing. I think it would be advisable to join our forces and fight them before they join Phillips, which they certainly will do if they are not stopped. I have ordered the commanding officer at Salisbury to move off with the prisoners and stores. If you think it right you will repeat it. I cannot ascertain their (the enemy's) numbers, but suppose them odds of two thousand; that number, if they keep in a compact body—which I make no doubt they will—we cannot hurt. I have sent to Gen. Davidson to join me, which I expect he will do to-morrow. His strength I do not know, as his men were collecting yesterday.

I am, dear General, &c.,

DANIEL MORGAN.

CAMP, SHERRALD'S FORD, 25th *Jan.*, 1781, 12 o'clock.

SIR: The enemy encamped last night at Ramsower's Mills, in force; they marched near thirty miles yesterday. It is my opinion they intend to make a forced march through this part of the State, and perhaps make, or try to make, a junction with Phillips, high up in the country. If so, the position you have taken will be much out of the way. If Cornwallis and Leslie have joined their force, we are not able to contend with them. All the Southern militia have dispersed. What numbers Gen. Davidson has I am not able to inform you, as they were only collecting yesterday.

From this information, you'll be able to dispose of your army in the best manner.

I am convinced Cornwallis will push on till he is stopped by a force able to check him. I will do every thing in my power; but you may not put much dependence in me, for I can neither ride nor walk; a pain in the hip prevents me. I will continue to give you every intelligence in my power.

I have the honor to be, &c.,

DANIEL MORGAN.

MAJ. GEN. GREENE.

I this moment received intelligence that the enemy are within a few miles of this place, moving on rapidly. My party is so weak that I think I must give way.

CAMP AT SHERRALD'S FORD, *Jan.* 28, 1781.

SIR: Lord Cornwallis, on the 24th inst. encamped at Ramsower's Mills, with his main body, on his way from Broad river. His advanced corps moved eight miles farther this way in the night, and returned the next day to their main body. He still continues at that place. My reason for not writing to you these two days was to find out which way they really intended, that I might have it in my power to inform you fully.

I am trying to collect the militia, to make a stand at this place. Gen. Davidson, with five hundred militia—two hundred and fifty of which are without flints—I have ordered to Beatty's ford. We are filling all the private fords so as to make them impassable. The one that I lie at I intend to leave open. On Lord Cornwallis's approach, I thought it advisable to order all the prisoners and stores from Salisbury towards the Moravian town. I am told they are gone under a weak guard; I hope some of them don't get away. If the enemy pursued, I ordered them towards Augusta in Virginia; should be glad you'll give orders respecting them.

I shall continue to inform you of every material circumstance. I am a little apprehensive that Lord Cornwallis intends to surprise me, lying so still this day or two. But if the militia don't deceive me—whom I am obliged to trust to as guards, up and down the river—I think I will put it out of his power.

If I were able to ride and see to every thing myself, I should think myself perfectly safe; but I am obliged to lie in a house out of camp, not being able to encounter the badness of the weather. However, nothing in my power shall be left undone to secure this part of the country, and annoy the enemy as much as possible.

I have the honor to be, &c.,

DANIEL MORGAN.

MAJ. GEN. GREENE.

BEATTY'S FORD, 29th Jan. 1781.

SIR: I have just arrived at this place to view our situation. Gen. Davidson is here with eight hundred men. The enemy is within ten miles of this place, in force; their advance is in sight. It is uncertain whether they intend to cross here or not. I have detached two hundred men to the Tuckascega Ford, to fill it up and defend it.

An express has just arrived, who informs, that they have burned their wagons, and loaded their men very heavily. We have taken four prisoners, who say they (the enemy) are for Salisbury.

I am just returning to Sherrald's Fords, where our regulars lie. I expect they will attempt to cross in the morning. I will let you hear of every particular.

I have the honor to be, &c.,

DANIEL MORGAN.

MAJ. GEN. GREENE.

CHAPTER XVII.

The disappointment of Morgan's expectations of efficient aid from the militia—Joined by Gen. Davidson with eight hundred men—The British at length approach the Catawba—The river becomes suddenly impassable—Gen. Greene arrives at Sherrald's ford—The Catawba subsides, when Morgan retreats to the Yadkin—The fords of the Catawba guarded by Davidson and his militia—The enemy cross the river—Battle at McCowan's ford, and death of Davidson—Tarleton's cruelty at Tarrant's tavern—Morgan crosses the Yadkin—His rear guard attacked by the enemy, who are repulsed—Cornwallis advances to the Yadkin, now also become impassable—He marches to the shallow fords—The American divisions concentrate at Guilford, C. H.—Morgan becomes too unwell to continue in the field—His letters to Gen. Greene regarding his ill-health, and signifying his wish for leave of absence—Greene determines to retire still farther—Remarks on the condition, objects and prospects of the contending forces—Morgan offered the command of the light troops—He obtains leave to retire—He is solicited to take command of the North Carolina militia—American army retreats towards Boyd's ferry—Morgan proceeds to Virginia—Reflections on the military events subsequent to the battle of the Cowpens, and on his participation therein—The misstatements regarding these events, and Morgan, which have crept into history, exposed.

MORGAN had determined to oppose Cornwallis's passage of the Catawba, if his expectations of aid from the militia should be realized. His force which had fought the battle of the 17th, had, in the meanwhile, greatly diminished. A large proportion of the Georgia and South Carolina volunteers had left him soon after; the Virginia militia had completed their term of service, and were on their way home; and Pickens had been sent back with his command to the neighborhood of Broad river. Yet, contrary to his hopes, and to the assurances which had been previously given him, his force received no considerable accession of strength. The period had arrived when the people prepared the ground for the seed, on which the future hopes of their families for food

depended, and they were now nearly all engaged in that important occupation.   The ardor so quickly created by the success of
their brethren at the Cowpens, and which disposed them to take
the field, was as quickly cooled by the subsequent advance of
Cornwallis in the direction of their country.   It had been the
constant practice of the British to burn every house in their way
which was known to belong to a whig, if the owner was not
present to obviate the presumption that he was out with the militia.   Their march tended towards that very region on which
Morgan chiefly relied for aid; and the inhabitants, deeming the
preservation of themselves and families from ruin as involving
obligations of duty superior to those presented by their country,
felt constrained to remain at home.   Large numbers from the
mountainous districts were also expected; but their situation was
too remote, and the summons for their aid too recent, to countenance a hope for their arrival in time to aid in checking the
further advance of the enemy.   It afterwards appeared that they
had been fully employed in defending their homes from the
incursion of the savage allies of the enemy.

The consequent disappointment was felt the more keenly by
Morgan, inasmuch as it had not been foreseen.   He had tasted
of the bitterness of blasted hopes, when forced, by a similar disappointment some time previously, to forego his projected expedition against Ninety-six and Augusta.   But such representations
had been made to him of the forces collecting in the country he
now occupied, with the object of joining him, as led him to give
them some share of his confidence, and to base his future operations upon the expected aid they would render him.

There were yet a considerable number, however, whose zeal in
the cause absorbed all other considerations, and among these was
the gallant Davidson, doomed in a few days to offer up his life in
the struggle, and to add another to the long list of heroes whose
blood purchased the rich inheritance we enjoy.   While Morgan
was approaching the Catawba, Davidson was actively engaged in

assembling the militia at Salisbury. Yet after all his exertions, coupled with those of other commanders, no more than eight hundred men ever assembled. With this force, Davidson advanced to the Catawba, and joined Morgan at Sherraid's ford on the 26th January.

The intelligence that Cornwallis had halted at Ramsower's, and that he did not intend to resume his march immediately, was very acceptable to Morgan. His troops could now have time to recover from their recent fatigues, whilst their presence would encourage the militia, and perhaps induce them to assemble in force. His prisoners and baggage would be removed still farther from the danger of recapture, while his troops would no longer be embarrassed in a care for their preservation. The continued delay of the British at Ramsower's, with a knowledge of its cause, was a source of high gratification to Morgan. For the reasons already stated, every additional hour of time gained was so much of an increase to his advantages. To these was added a knowledge of the designs of the enemy, which were completely unmasked by the destruction of their baggage. It was now evident that they meditated a rapid advance towards Virginia.

The militia, in the meantime, were slow in joining him. His expectations of being able to meet the enemy at this point were therefore necessarily relinquished. He determined, nevertheless, to hold his present position until the enemy approached so close as to render his longer remaining hazardous, in which event he intended retiring towards the Yadkin. He was not without hope that by the time he reached that river, a junction of his corps with the main body of the army, and a large militia force, might be effected. An effort, he thought, might then be made to check the further progress of the enemy.

At length, on the 29th, the near approach of the enemy was announced. It was vain to attempt the defence of the numerous fords by which the Catawba was crossed, with such a handful of men, against so powerful an opponent. Morgan was therefore preparing to retire, when an event occurred, which, for a time, relieved his mind of all apprehensions of the enemy.

On the 27th, Cornwallis, having completed the destruction of his baggage, put his army in motion towards the Catawba. The weather for some time previously had been very wet; but on the 28th and 29th, it rained incessantly. On the evening of the 29th, the Catawba began to swell. This river rises with great rapidity after a heavy rain; and when much swollen, flows with an irresistible current. So high had it risen during the night, that on the morning of the 30th it was perfectly impassable.

Cornwallis was hereupon forced to pause. Another and an unexpected cause of delay was thus added to those which had already baffled his efforts, and nearly driven him to madness. Morgan, on the other hand, derived fresh encouragement and additional advantages from a circumstance which seemed, and indeed was regarded at the time, as a special interposition of Providence in behalf of his bleeding country.

On the morning of the 30th, the British approached the river in different directions, giving Morgan equal apprehensions for several fords, when the waters should subside sufficiently to render them practicable. This was an event which might speedily occur; for in common with all mountain streams, the Catawba fell with the same rapidity that it rose. In the hope that it would continue unfordable until Greene could advance towards Salisbury, and be joined by the milita in that quarter, Morgan determined to oppose its passage while a hope of success remained. He had already rendered a number of the fords impassable; and he now made such a disposition of his force as was best calculated to guard them all, and to defend those likely to be attempted. The regulars guarded the point at Sherrald's ford. Five hundred of Gen. Davidson's militia were posted at the different fords above and below the one named, embracing a distance of more than twenty miles, with directions to guard against and give notice of any attempt at surprise. The remainder of the militia, to the number of three hundred men, all mounted and armed with rifles, were held together, with their patriotic leader at their head, and directed to observe the movements of Cornwallis, and be ready to assist the guard at any point which might be attempted.

These arrangements of the adverse commanders were in progress—the one bent on crossing the river, the other on the alert to oppose the attempt—when, on the morning of the 30th, General Greene, accompanied only by one aide and a small escort of cavalry, arrived at Morgan's encampment.

As may readily be supposed, this distinguished commander had been a watchful observer of the movements west of the Catawba, which preceded the battle of the Cowpens. The advance of the British from Winnsborough and Camden was at length recognized as the resumption of Cornwallis's invasive operations. Measures were accordingly taken to prepare the army on the Pedee for an early movement. Should it appear that the desire of forming a junction with Phillips, then in Virginia, had tempted Cornwallis to prosecute a winter campaign in that direction, General Greene readily saw the necessity of moving at once higher up the country, and of throwing his army between the quarter threatened and the enemy. He could thus cover and protect his advancing supplies, and reinforcements, and await the moment when his forces would be sufficiently increased to risk a battle. Should the enemy, on the other hand, succeed in interposing between Morgan and himself, and at the same time cut off his communications with Virginia, his situation would be embarrassing in the extreme. These and other considerations—having reference to the operations of Marion and Lee in the South, and to those of Morgan in the West, to the wants and sufferings of his army, and the disappointment of his expectations of reinforcements and supplies—absorbed his attention, and wore him down with care and anxiety. His solicitude for Morgan, who, by the last accounts was completely environed by the enemy's entire force, was happily relieved on the evening of the 25th, when he received intelligence of the battle of the 17th. He learned at the same time that Morgan was retreating towards the Catawba, and that Cornwallis was marching in the same direction at the head of his whole army.

No longer in doubt regarding the enemy's intentions, instant preparations were made for an early movement. The army was immediately placed under marching orders. An express was sent to Col. Lee, with instructions to that officer to return from below with the greatest expedition, and join Morgan by the shortest route. All the detachments were called in, and the whole of the provisions which did not lie on the intended route of the army, were brought into camp. At this critical moment, Stevens's brigade of Virginia militia had completed their term of service, and were about returning home. They were instantly dispatched on their way, with orders to take charge of the prisoners then at Hillsborough, and hastening on with them so as to overtake the prisoners captured at the Cowpens, to relieve the detachment having the latter in charge, and press on with the whole of the captives to the interior counties of Virginia. The heavy baggage was also ordered immediately forward in charge of the Virginia brigade, and directed to pursue the route to Hillsborough, where, being joined by the baggage removing from that place, to pursue the march across the Dan, or until countermanded. The army was divided into two brigades, the Virginia troops composing one under the command of Gen. Huger, the Maryland and Delaware troops, the other, under Col. O. H. Williams. While these preparations were going forward, the general addressed letters to the governors of the threatened States, and to the most distinguished commanders of the militia, informing them of the danger with which they were threatened, and imploring their aid to enable him to meet the enemy.

Everything being arranged, on the 29th, the army, led by Gen. Huger, moved from Hicks's creek on the Pedee, and crossing at

Haley's ferry, proceeded towards Salisbury. The evening pre-vious, General Greene had started across the country to join Morgan.*

The position of the adverse armies on both sides of the Catawba, upon the arrival of Gen. Greene, has been already described. During the same day the river began to fall; and before night, it became evident that in the course of two or three days more the fords would be practicable. The enemy appeared determined upon crossing; and although every preparation had been made to oppose them, their success in the attempt was foreseen, and measures were taken accordingly. In this event, it was intended to retreat towards the Yadkin. In the hope of being joined in that quarter by the main body of his army, as well as by a considerable accession to his present militia force, General Greene wrote to General Huger, directing the latter to hasten his march thither as much as possible.

On the 31st, the Catawba subsided so rapidly, as to leave no doubt that it would be fordable the next day. This was a severe disappointment to the American commanders. Had the river continued high for a few days more, a force would have been collected on its banks, composed of the united divisions of the regulars and the numerous bodies of militia present and approaching, which would have been sufficient to dispute its passage, and perhaps put a period to the farther progress of the enemy. But no more militia were expected for a week, the forces under Huger had advanced but a short distance on their march, and the enemy were in motion with the object of crossing the river at the earliest practicable moment. This, it was now evident, would arrive in the course of a few hours; and their active condition, no longer embarrassed with a heavy baggage train, rendered them much more dangerous neighbors than they had hitherto been. Under these circumstances, it became advisable that Morgan and his corps should retreat. He accordingly moved off in silence on

* Johnson's Greene, vol. i., pp. 391–408.

GENERAL DANIEL MORGAN. 345

the afternoon of the 31st, and pushing forward all that night and a part of the next day, gained a full day's march ahead of the enemy.* Pursuing his journey with unabated rapidity towards the Yadkin, we leave him and his gallant command on their way thither, and return to the Catawba, now about being the scene of stirring events.

At 1 o'clock in the morning of the 1st of February, the British army approached the Catawba in two divisions, with the intention of crossing. The first division, under the command of Lieut. Col. Webster, was directed to approach Beatty's ford, where, it was supposed, the weight of opposition might be experienced, and to make a great demonstration of an intention to force a passage. The main body, consisting of the brigade of guards, the regiment of Bose, the 23rd regiment, two hundred cavalry, and two three-pounders, commanded by Cornwallis in person, approached an unfrequented ford near McCowen's ford, where it had been determined that the real attempt to cross the river should be made.

Webster, upon approaching Beatty's ford, found it abandoned. The division crossed the river without delay, and took post on the opposite bank. Cornwallis, with his division, reached the river a little before daylight, and was surprised to find, judging from the number of fires on the opposite bank, that the opposition to his crossing would be greater than he had had reason to expect.† Whether from secret intelligence or from the vigilance with which every movement of the enemy was watched and provided against, Davidson became acquainted with the nature of this one, in time to prepare for its development. At the head of four hundred riflemen, he stood ready to dispute the passage of the river against a force composed of the main body of the British army. Nor was the attempt rash in conception, nor hopeless of success. Between Davidson and his opponent interposed a stream

* Johnson's Greene, vol. i., p. 414.
† Tarleton, p. 224. Lee's Memoirs, p. 136.

15*

five hundred yards in width, from two to four feet in depth, and with a current so rapid as to require the greatest care and exertions on the part of those crossing to prevent them from being swept away. Cornwallis would have shrunk from the attempt had his judgment been uncontrolled by other considerations. But independent of those reasons which already existed, demanding his advance at all hazards, the certainty that the rain, which had recommenced falling, would again render the river impassable for a few days, and that in the interim General Greene would be enabled to concentrate his forces, and perhaps be in strength sufficient to oppose him, left him no alternative.* The guards were accordingly ordered to move forward, and they were followed by the rest of the troops. When about midway in the stream, the head of the column was discovered by the Americans, who immediately opened a fire upon it.† At this moment the British were deserted by their guide, who, alarmed at his danger, suddenly disappeared. This circumstance, which at first threatened Cornwallis with the most serious consequence, proved in the end to be one of the most fortunate for his movement that could have occurred. From the point where the guide deserted, the ford diverged widely to the right; and at the usual landing-place, some three hundred and fifty yards below, Davidson and his men were posted, ready to shower destruction upon the enemy as soon as they approached within range. The latter, struggling slowly forward through an impetuous current, and fully employed in keeping their equilibrium and preserving their arms and ammunition from the water, could have made no resistance until they reached the opposite bank. To effect this under the most favorable circumstances, would have taken from fifteen minutes to half an hour. During this time, the deliberate fire of four hundred marksmen would have produced a dreadful slaughter, and perhaps driven the enemy back. The Americans were aware of their great advantages, and were fully prepared to reap them.

*Tarleton, p. 262.   † Tarleton, p. 224.

But unfortunately for their expectations as well as for the result, the British advance, now left to its own guidance, continued to move in a straight line across the stream, and, at length, landed without much opposition at a point three hundred yards above the place where it was expected. The darkness of the morning prevented this deviation from being observed by Davidson until the head of the column was approaching the margin of the river. Persevering, nevertheless, in his determination to oppose the landing, this officer moved towards the threatened point; but before he arrived there, the light infantry of the guards had reached the shore. A sharp action immediately ensued; and although no decisive advantages could be expected from a contest so unequal, now that the enemy had effected a landing, it was continued by the militia some time with great spirit. The advance of the militia had, however, placed them between the light of their camp-fires and the enemy, giving the latter an advantage too great to be long resisted. Davidson was in the act of mounting his horse to lead off his men, when he was perceived by the enemy. A volley of musketry was immediately fired at him, and unfortunately, with deadly effect. Thus fell one of the bravest and most patriotic of the host of heroes whose names shed lustre on the page of American history. The militia, upon the fall of their commander, immediately dispersed.*

An earnest of the havoc which might have been made in the British ranks but for the remarkable event just related, is furnished in the loss which they actually sustained on this occasion. Not less than sixty of their men were killed and wounded, and among the former was Lieut. Col. Hall, the commanding officer of the regiment of guards. They acknowledge a loss of forty; but a number, never accounted for, were killed or wounded in the river, and swept away by the current. The American loss was trifling in numbers, but rendered irreparable in that of the lion-hearted Davidson.

As soon as the landing at this point was completed, Tarleton,

---

* Tarleton's Campaign, pp. 224–5. Johnson's Greene, p. 415. Stedman's American war.

with his cavalry and the 23rd regiment, was ordered to move rapidly forward towards Sherrald's and Beatty's fords, and attack the American forces, which were still supposed to be encamped at those places, Upon arriving at Beatty's ford, Tarleton was informed that Morgan had moved towards Salisbury the evening before. He also learned that the militia, having retired from the different fords, were to assemble that afternoon at Tarrant's tavern. At this place, distant about ten miles from the Catawba, the roads from the different fords converged into that leading to Salisbury. Leaving the infantry about five miles east of the river, Tarleton, accompanied by the cavalry only, pushed forward towards the place of meeting, with the intention of attacking the militia, should they be found there.*

When Morgan retreated towards Salisbury, orders had been given that the militia, stationed at the different fords, and held in observation, should retire in the same direction, if the enemy succeeded in effecting a passage of the river. To give precision to this order, a rendezvous was named at the house of Mr. Carr, on the road to Salisbury, about sixteen miles from the Catawba, where, it was expected, the militia would assemble in undiminished numbers. But the retreat of the regular force, the fall of Davidson, and the advance of the British, combined to render this expectation exceedingly illusory. A large proportion of the militia who had been in the field up to this time, now directed their steps homeward, some under the belief that a farther struggle would be unavailing, and others, from the fear that the discovery of their absence by the enemy would leave them without a home to go to. A number, however, too zealous in the cause to desert it in the hour of adversity, proceeded towards the designated place of meeting. But of the eight hundred who were in arms the day before under Davidson, not more than three hundred ever re-assembled. Nearly this number, however, met at Tarrant's tavern, about noon, and believing themselves beyond

* Tarleton, p. 225.

the reach of immediate danger, halted to take some rest and refreshment before they resumed their journey. Fortunately, the usual precautions against surprise had not been neglected, and the approach of Tarleton was announced in sufficient time to enable the militia to prepare themselves for fight or flight, as circumstances might determine. Col. Jackson, who so greatly distinguished himself at the Cowpens, assumed the direction of the militia. Owing to his exertions with a few officers and men, the loss of the Americans in the contest which ensued was trifling, compared to what it otherwise might have been; while that of the enemy was far too great to compensate for the empty triumph they obtained. As Tarleton approached, the militia, mounted and ready for flight, poured a well directed volley into his ranks, which killed and wounded seven of his men, and dismounted fifteen more. Then dashing into the woods, they eluded the charge directed against them, and were soon beyond the reach of pursuit.* A few old men and boys, some of them non-combatants, and others too badly mounted to hope for escape by flight, sought for mercy in submission. But notwithstanding their supplications, which were drowned in the enemy's cries of "remember the Cowpens" — the watchword given by Tarleton † — they were barbarously cut down. The recollections of that glorious battle should have taught this inhuman commander mercy to the vanquished above all things else. In this way was swelled the number which he claims as the sacrifice to victory on that occasion.

Morgan in the mean time was prosecuting his retreat towards the trading ford on the Yadkin with the greatest diligence. His destruction, he knew, was a darling object with the British commander, who, he felt assured, would spare no exertions, and run all hazards, to effect it. During the march, the rain fell in torrents, which he foresaw would probably render the Yadkin unfordable before he reached its banks. But this caused him no anxiety, beyond that arising from his own bodily sufferings, which

* Johnson's Greene, pp. 415-416.   † Tarleton's Campaign, p. 226.

were thus greatly increased, and from a desire for the comfort and health of his men. Some days before he left the Catawba, and in anticipation of a retreat to the Yadkin, he had taken the pre-caution to cause a number of boats to be collected at the point towards which he was now tending. Thus, if the pursuit was so hot as to compel him to cross the river, he had all the facilities for effecting the movement, even if the fords were impassable; while in this event the enemy would be compelled, from the want of boats, to make another halt until the waters subsided, before they could effect a passage.

On the morning of the 2nd of February, Morgan reached Salisbury. Proceeding thence to the trading ford on the Yadkin, he encamped on the western bank of that river the same day.

The next morning, Morgan received intelligence that the enemy were approaching Salisbury. The river also began to rise. Pru-dence therefore dictated a passage of his forces to the opposite bank. The boats were accordingly soon employed in the trans-portation of the infantry and baggage, while the cavalry and mounted militia swam or waded the stream.

During the march from the Catawba to the Yadkin, hundreds of the inhabitants of the intermediate country, apprehensive of remaining behind, and experiencing the tender mercies of the British, had collected with their families and effects in the rear of the corps, and followed its footsteps. Men who belonged to the region which was denounced as "the most rebellious in America," had good reason to fear contact with an enemy, whose cruelties extended even to the loyalist inhabitants. To protect these unhappy victims of war, and to facilitate their passage across the river, was a duty, the force of which no man could feel stronger than Morgan. While the boats were passing and repassing, bearing their families and effects across, a strong rear guard remained on the western bank of the river. About dark, information was received that a body of the enemy was approach-ing. The measures for effecting the passage of the fugitives, their wagons, &c., across the river were now expedited; but before the business was completed, the advanced guard of the British had arrived.

We left Cornwallis on the eastern side of the Catawba. Immediately after passing the river, he recommenced vigorously the pursuit of Morgan. His progress was, however, so impeded by the miserable state of the roads, as to induce him to destroy the scanty store of baggage which remained on his hands from the conflagration at Ramsower's. Learning, upon his arrival at Salisbury, on the 3d of February, that Morgan was still on the western bank of the Yadkin, Gen. O'Hara, with the guards, the regiment of Bose, and the cavalry, was sent to attack him. Owing to the rain, to the darkness, and to the bad roads, the detachment did not reach its destination till near midnight.

The country people had, in the mean time, crossed the river with all their effects, excepting a few wagons. The rear guard and a number of militia still remained behind. Notwithstanding the imposing array of the enemy, and the eager haste of their pursuit, which implied overtaking as equivalent to capturing the whole of Morgan's command, they were courageously met by this handful of men; and after a smart skirmish, repulsed with considerable loss. An attempt by the guards to seize the boats was rendered signally abortive; and the enemy, having succeeded in capturing the remaining wagons at the cost of about twenty of their men, retired from the contest, leaving their opponents undisturbed in effecting a passage of the river.*

The next day Cornwallis approached the river, which in the mean time had become impassable by fording, and opened a furious cannonade upon the American forces on the opposite bank. The latter were so posted, however, as to secure them from danger, yet near enough promptly to repel any attempt to cross the river. But this was impossible, as all the boats had been carefully withdrawn beyond the reach of the British. The cannonade seems to have been nothing more than a vent for disappointed rage, and resembled the barking of an angry dog that was precluded from biting.

Hitherto Cornwallis had endeavored to overtake Morgan before a junction of that officer's corps could be effected with the main body under Huger. He now adopted the resolution of getting between the united American forces and the upper fords of the Dan, and of forcing them to an engagement before they could be reinforced by the North Carolina and Virginia militia, then preparing to march to their assistance. Could he gain these fords before Greene, the obligation of the latter to fight, he fancied, would follow as a necessary consequence, because he knew that the lower fords of the Dan were not practicable, and he did not suppose that preparations would or could be made at these points for crossing the army in boats. Full of this idea, he put an end to his idle cannonade, withdrew from the bank of the river, and put his troops in motion for the shallow fords, some fifteen miles higher up the stream.*

In consequence of the enemy's rapid advance, the expectations of being able to concentrate the American forces on the Yadkin were necessarily abandoned. The orders which had previously been given to Gen. Huger to march towards Salisbury were accordingly countermanded. He was now directed to proceed with all expedition to Guilford court-house, at which place Gen. Greene now intended to effect a junction of his forces. Thither the troops on the Yadkin were also ordered to proceed without delay. On the morning of the 5th, Morgan's corps, under the command of Lieut. Col. Howard, took up their line of march to the point indicated.

At this time Morgan had become so much enfeebled as to disqualify him for the performance of any active duty. It was necessary, however, that arrangements should be made at Guilford court-house to provide the troops with quarters and supplies

* Johnson's Greene, vol. i., p. 419.

in advance of their arrival at that place. These arrangements were best ensured by the personal superintendence of the commanding officer. Morgan accordingly started in advance of the corps in a carriage, and reached Guilford the same evening.

On the evening of the 5th, the corps encamped in the neighborhood of Salem. Halting at this point for two days, to obtain intelligence of the enemy's movements, the march was resumed on learning that Cornwallis was in full march for the shallow fords of the Yadkin. Proceeding without further delay, the troops reached Guilford court-house on the evening of the 8th.

Morgan, although so unwell as scarcely to be able to appear abroad, had nevertheless made ample provision for their reception. Comfortable quarters, or a sufficiency of good food, to say nothing of luxuries, had long been strangers to this gallant body of men. Their commander did not rest until he had secured them the enjoyment of both upon their arrival.

This duty having been performed, Morgan's thoughts were seriously turned towards retiring from active service for a short period ; hoping that in the meantime his health might be restored. The violent malady which, in 1779, forced him to relinquish a sphere of action as serviceable to his country as it was honorable to himself, had again returned. This, when added to the fever and ague, and other complaints which had afflicted him almost from the outset of his career in the South, had worn him to the bone, and at length left him no alternative but to relinquish his command, and to seek relief in rest and tranquillity. Before the battle of the Cowpens, and subsequently, up to the time when he took post on the east bank of the Catawba, the appeals of bodily sufferings were unheeded amid the anxieties and excitements of that stirring period. But when it became apparent that the enemy had determined to prosecute a winter campaign, he felt himself quite unable to encounter the hardships and fatigues which must necessarily follow. While lying at Sherrald's Ford, he communicated the following letter to Greene.

stating his inability longer to keep the field, and soliciting a temporary leave of absence :

CAMP, SHERRALD'S FORD, CATAWBA, *Jan.* 24, 1781.

DEAR SIR : After my late success, and my sanguine expectations to do something clever this campaign, I must inform you that I shall be obliged to give over the pursuit, by reason of an old pain returning upon me, that laid me up for four months of last winter and spring. It is a sciatica pain in my hip, that renders me entirely incapable of active services. I have had it these three weeks past, but on getting wet the other day, it has seized me more violently, which gives me great pain when I ride, and at times when I am walking or standing, am obliged to sit down in the place it takes me, as quick as if I were shot. I am so well acquainted with this disorder, that I am convinced that nothing will help me but rest; and were I to attempt to go through this winter's campaign, I am satisfied it would totally disable me from further service.

I am not unacquainted with the hurt my retiring will be to the service, as the people have much dependence in me; but the love I have for my country, and the willingness I have always showed to serve it, will convince you that nothing would be wanting on my side were I able to persevere. So that I must beg leave of absence, till I find myself able to take the field again, which will, I imagine, be some time in the spring. If I can procure a chaise, I will endeavor to get home. Gen. Davidson, Col. Pickens, and Gen. Sumter (when he gets well, which, I am told, will not be long first) can manage the militia better than I can, and will well supply my place.

                              I have the honor, &c.,
                                                    DANIEL MORGAN.
MAJ. GEN. GREENE.

Perceiving at length that his illness increased, and that relief was hopeless while he essayed to perform the duties of his command ; convinced, besides that delay in seeking the necessary repose would only have the effect of protracting his recovery, the following letter on this and other matters, was written to Greene :

GUILFORD COURT HOUSE, 6*th Feb.* 1781.

SIR : I arrived here last evening, and sent a number of prisoners that were here to join the main body. About four thousand pounds of salted pork and bacon is promised me, corn meal equivalent, forage, &c.

I am much indisposed with pains, and to add to my misfortunes, am violently attacked with the piles, so that I can scarcely sit upon my horse. This is the first time that I ever experienced this disorder, and from the idea I had of it, sincerely prayed that I might never know what it was. When I set everything in as good a train as I can respecting provisions, &c., I shall move on slowly to some safe retreat, and try to recover.

Col. Buford is left upon the lower road to Hillsborough, not able to go further.

I am, sincerely, &c.,
DANIEL MORGAN.

MAJ. GEN. GREENE.

The troops under Gen. Huger, with the cavalry of Col. Lee's legion, reached Guilford court-house on the 9th of February. There were now assembled at this place a force somewhat over two thousand, of which six hundred were militia. The enemy's numbers were supposed to range between two thousand five hundred and three thousand. Gen. Greene, under the impression that the junction of his regulars would be immediately followed by a large accession to his militia force, had pre-determined to face about and meet the enemy as soon as this junction could be effected. With the aid of one thousand or one thousand five hundred additional militia, and the advantages of position, the chances would have greatly preponderated in his favor. For although the enemy outnumbered him vastly in regular troops, those of that description under his command were inferior to none in the world. It was advisable, besides, that some vigorous effort should be made, which would deter the tories from assembling, revive the drooping spirits of the whigs, and weaken the impression, now rapidly spreading abroad, that the advance of the British would be a career of successive triumphs. But so disheartened had the people in this region become by the persecutions and losses which they had experienced, and by the gloomy prospect of the cause, that their immediate co-operation was not to be expected; and with feelings of deep mortification, not unmingled with alarm, Gen. Greene contemplated a continuance of his retreat. A movement of this kind by the upper fords of the Dan, if ever seriously considered by him, was now impracticable. The enemy had reached a point nearer to these fords than that occupied by his forces, and equally near to those below. A retreat to the lower fords would necessarily be a trial of speed between the opposing armies; and unless ample preparations were previously made to transport the American troops across without delay, such an attempt, in the face of an enemy powerful and active, and aware of his adversary's object, would be exceedingly dangerous. The absence of the expected aid from the militia, however, rendered it highly imprudent to risk a battle; and the assurance which was now given Gen. Greene, that every preparation had been made for effecting a speedy passage of the Dan at Boyd's ferry, threw the weight of reasoning in favor of a retreat.*

There was one alternative left to Gen. Greene besides, and that was, to retrace his steps into South Carolina. But the objects to be gained by such a movement, however important in themselves, were yet subordinate to those which he hoped to accomplish by that now under consideration. Among these were the protection of the country as yet free from the footsteps of an invader; the people of which, he felt assured, would aid him by thousands when the danger approached their doors; the prevention of a junction between Phillips and Cornwallis, and the preservation of his communications with those quarters, whence his means of subsistence were derived, and his reinforcements were expected. Another and a powerful reason in favor of a retreat was furnished in the unprovided state of the enemy. By the destruction of their baggage, they had rendered themselves unequal to the accomplishment of any enterprise, covering a wide field of operations and requiring time for its development. The militia of the country in their rear were already on foot, with Sumter and Pickens at their head; thus all prospect of being supplied from

* Johnson's Greene, pp. 246-248.

GENERAL DANIEL MORGAN. 357

their depots in South Carolina was effectually cut off. Should
the retreat be successfully prosecuted, General Greene felt assured
that the result would yield him all the practical advantages of a
victory. The unavailing efforts of the enemy to overtake him
would but increase their difficulties, and hasten the period of their
final overthrow.

The determination to retreat was followed by the adoption of
measures the best calculated to bring it to a successful issue.
Among these was one, having for its object the formation of a
powerful and active corps of light troops, to cover the rear of the
retreating army, and to check and impede the advance of the
enemy. Howard's battalion of light infantry, Lee's legionary
corps, and Washington's cavalry, with two companies of riflemen,
numbering in all over seven hundred men, were accordingly
thrown together, and organized for this service. The command
of this splendid corps was offered to Gen. Morgan. But as may
be inferred from the tenor of his letters, already given, in relation
to his ill-health, he was forced to decline the honor; and, indeed,
the offer was made more as a tribute of respect due to his rank
and to his merits and services, than from any expectation of
his accepting it. With a heavy heart he declined the proffered
command, and repeated his desire for leave to retire until sufficiently recovered to justify his return to the army.

The occasion was one on which Gen. Greene could badly spare
the aid and counsels of a man, in whose address and judgment he
placed the most unbounded confidence. A heart as courageous,
and a head as cool, might, he thought, be often wanting in the
course of the hazardous operations on which he was about
embarking. But he well knew that the desire to remain was felt
as strongly by Morgan as it could possibly be by himself; and to
venture upon persuasion in the face of circumstances which proclaimed the impossibility of a compliance, was a course too
ungenerous to be resorted to by Gen. Greene. He accordingly
yielded the solicited leave of absence in the form and words fol
lowing:

CAMP AT GUILFORD, C. H., *Feb. 10th*, 1781.

Gen. Morgan, of the Virginia line, has leave of absence until he recovers his health, so as to be able to take the field again.

NATHANIEL GREENE.

Before Morgan departed, another offer of command was made to him, which, while it paid a high compliment to his reputation, and displayed in a manner highly flattering to his feelings, his great popularity with the people, must at the same time have added to the bitterness of his regret in being forced to decline it. As has been already stated, the advance of the British beyond the Yadkin was immediately followed by a general uprising of the whigs west of that river. But the fall of Davidson had left them without a leader, whose name and talents would exercise a controlling influence, and whose judgment and courage would inspire confidence. To provide for this deficiency, a meeting of the leading whigs was held at Charlotte, three days after the British had left that place, the result of which was an application to Gen. Greene to permit Morgan to command them. The assurance was added that a compliance would be attended by the most cheering effects, and draw hundreds to the field who would otherwise keep aloof. But to comply was impossible, and Gen. Greene, in replying, remarked, " The general is so unwell that he could not discharge the duties of the appointment if he had it."*

Although Morgan could not take the command of the light troops, he influenced the choice of his commander in the selection of an officer for that post. At his instance and recommendation, the command was conferred upon his friend Col. O. H. Williams, an officer well worthy of that or any other trust, however important, as was signally proved in his masterly conduct of the retreat.

On the 10th of February, the main body of the army left Guilford court-house, on the direct road to Boyd's Ferry; while Williams, with his detachment, advancing towards the upper fords of the Dan as if with the intention of passing across them,

* Johnson's Greene, vol. i., pp. 413–427.

placed himself in front of the enemy.   The aim of the manœuvre
was to gain time, and it was successful.   Cornwallis, uncertain as
to the force of his opponent and the object of this movement,
halted to acquire the necessary information and to guard against
an attack, by contracting his much extended line of march.
Before the British were again in motion, Greene, pushing forward
with the greatest expedition, had gained nearly a day's march on
them.*

On the same day, Morgan departed from Guilford court-house,
and crossing the Dan at Lower Saura, proceeded on the direct
route to Fredericksburg.

Here, for a time, terminated the connection of Morgan with the
important events of the revolutionary struggle.   Like him, we
reluctantly bid adieu to the campaign in the Carolinas, then
pregnant with so many glorious fields, and since associated with
such fond recollections; while with feelings of regret akin to
those he experienced, we follow his footsteps from the field.

The numerous errors into which historians generally have been
led regarding the memorable events just detailed, have unfortunately produced impressions on the public mind, in relation to
these events, which truth and justice alike demand should be
removed.   These errors have had the effect, besides, of greatly
impairing the value of the services rendered by Morgan, during
the period to which they refer, and of inflicting undeserved injury
on his fame.   A cursory examination of the facts will serve to
illustrate the truth of these assertions.

The events previous to, and attendant on, the battle of the
Cowpens, have already been sufficiently considered.   Those which
followed that memorable affair, up to the time when Morgan
reached Guilford court-house, will now engage attention.

Nearly all those authors who have made the revolutionary war
and its prominent men the themes of their pens, appear enraptured
with the conduct of Cornwallis during that stirring period.   On

* Johnson's Greene, vol. i., p. 431.

the other hand they seem to regard Morgan as the peculiar favorite of fortune, and to attribute his extrication from the grasp of his adversary, to causes reflecting little credit on his judgment or address. These erroneous ideas originated in a grave misconception of the motives and the acts of the respective commanders.

Believing that the best method of extricating truth from error is always furnished in a plain recapitulation of events, in our narration of those under consideration, we had a constant and careful reference to accuracy, particularly so as regards dates; and happily, the means of placing the whole subject in the clearest and most convincing light were at our disposal in the greatest abundance. If the reader is satisfied that the accounts we have laid before him were gathered from authentic sources—and we assure him that they were—he need not be informed at this stage of Morgan's life, that much of error regarding the period and the man defaces the page of history.

With respect to Cornwallis, it is asserted, that from the moment when intelligence reached him of the battle of Cowpens, he pursued Morgan with great rapidity, and that nothing but the sudden interposition of an impassable river prevented his efforts from being successful. The sacrifice of his baggage to the desire of overtaking Morgan is mentioned as an event preliminary to the pursuit. His conduct during this part of the campaign is commented on with peculiar marks of favor, and has earned him plaudits on both sides of the Atlantic. His failure to overtake Morgan is attributed to causes beyond human control, and the hand of Providence itself is recognized in the succession of almost miraculous circumstances, which, it is alleged, contributed to baffle the efforts of one commander, and to favor those of the other.

It has already been seen with what little justice, wisdom of decision and vigor of action have been accorded to Cornwallis, and denied to Morgan. One of the first duties of a commander is to keep himself well informed of the movements of his adversary. He thus acquires the means of penetrating the intentions of his opponent ; and this, in the opinion of one of the greatest captains of the age, is the chief element of military success. Yet, besides other proofs which might be adduced, we have the evidence of Cornwallis's official letters, to show that he was in constant ignorance of Morgan's position, strength, and movements.* Three days elapsed after the battle, before information was received on which he thought he could act decisively. Yet the defectiveness of this was such as to lead him in a direction almost the reverse of that pursued at the same moment by Morgan. Many other 'equally culpable proofs of Cornwallis's neglect, in this respect, during the campaign of 1781, might be cited. His belief that Greene would be unable to cross the lower fords of the Dan for the want of flats,† and that the latter was conseqently in his power, is a memorable instance. Morgan, on the contrary, had always paid the greatest attention to this important duty. To his care in this respect is to be attributed the fact, that notwithstanding the dangerous description of service in which he had been engaged during his long military career, he never experienced a surprise. His conduct and his letters alike prove the watchfulness with which he regarded Cornwallis, and the care which he took to provide himself with correct information regarding that officer's movements. He overrated the sagacity of his adversary when, after the battle, he expressed the liveliest apprehensions of being cut off in his retreat to the Catawba. The tardy and ill concerted attempt with this object which was really made, proved how correctly Morgan divided the objects of his opponent, and displayed the judgment which dictated a prompt and rapid retreat.

The destruction, by Cornwallis, of his baggage, was not a measure preparatory to his pursuit of Morgan. It took place eight days after that pursuit commenced. So far from deserving

* Tarleton's Campaign, pp. 242–252.
† Letter, 17th of March, 1781, to Lord George Germain.

16

the applause which certain historians have showered upon him for this act, he merited the severest condemnation. By it, he hazarded every chance of success in the attainment of an object of secondary importance, the accomplishment of which he must have seen, had his judgment been uncontrolled by passion, was forever beyond his reach. Both Morgan and Greene had the sagacity to perceive that this desperate resort, if turned to good account, would but hasten his downfall, and subsequent events confirmed the correctness of their conclusions.

Morgan's retreat and Cornwallis's pursuit to the Catawba have been described as a trial of speed between the contending generals.* So much does this idea prevail among writers on the subject, that nearly all of them unite in regarding the contest as " a military race." Yet, judging from the time employed and the distance accomplished during the movement, it doe$ not appear that either of these commanders is entitled to much credit on the score of rapid travelling. The average of Morgan's daily march from the field of the Cowpens, was not more than ten miles, and at no time did it exceed twenty miles in a day. The distance from the battle-field to Guilford court-house, is about one hundred and fifty miles; yet the time employed on the march between these points was twenty-three days. His troops seem to have enjoyed on this occasion more than the usual share of repose allotted to armies on the retreat before an enemy. The evening after the battle he halted for the night on the north bank of the Broad river. The night of the eighteenth was passed in the neighbor- hood of the Cane Creek. Upon reaching the eastern bank of the Catawba, he paused for eight days. After retreating to the Yad- k two days were spent in the neighborhod of that stream, and two days more were passed inactively near Salem before the troops reached Guilford court-house. So far from being a precip- itate flight, as has been asserted on respectable authority, it was one of the most admirably conducted retreats on record. Until

* Ramsay vol., ii., p. 207

Morgan reached the Catawba, the rapidity and direction of his movements were influenced by those of his powerful opponent. These, as has been seen, furnished no cause for extraordinary exertions. Morgan's solicitude ceased upon his learning, the evening after the battle, that Cornwallis was still in his camp at Turkey Creek. From the moment when he reached the Catawba, and had secured his prisoners and baggage from recapture, his after movements were continued invitations of pursuit. He justly thought that if a force sufficient to fight and beat the enemy could not be collected at the Yadkin, every additional step taken by the latter beyond that point, in their present unprovided state, would serve only to increase their difficulties, and to add to the number of their opponents.

The admiration which history has awarded to Cornwallis for the conduct of his army during the period in question was justly the right of Morgan. At one time timid to weakness, at another rash to desperation, now full of activity and boldness, and then relaxed and spiritless, his operations could have had no more fortunate issue than that which befell them. The judgment and vigor which Morgan displayed, crowned all his efforts with signal success ; and the result stands an imperishable memorial of his great military merit.

Other charges of a graver and more direct nature have been made against Morgan. These will now be disposed of.

It is asserted that Morgan, having crossed the Catawba, meditated crossing his army and prisoners over the mountains ; and that the remonstrances of General Greene against the prosecution of this design were productive of a serious disagreement between these officers.* A dialogue of an unpleasant nature in relation to this, is foisted upon the world as having really occurred between them. It is also asserted that Morgan's designs evinced a disregard for the safety of the main body of the army.† These are all misstatements.

* Ramsay, vol. ii., p. 206.   Moultrie, vol. ii., p. 260.
† Lee's Memoirs, p. 431.

After Morgan succeeded in passing the Catawba, there was no longer the slightest necessity for resorting to so desperate a measure as that of crossing the mountains. Thenceforward the road to Virginia lay invitingly open before him. His letter to Gen. Greene, of the 23d January, the day when he reached Sherrald's Ford, proves that he had no such designs. It proves, moreover, that he intended holding his ground until he had heard from his commander. From this letter and another written the day following, both of which have been inserted, conclusive evidence is furnished, that the prisoners were sent on to Salisbury on the 23d. Greene arrived at Morgan's camp on the 30th. Thus before it was possible for an altercation to occur between Greene and Morgan, we find the former cordially acquiescing in the only suggestion, which the latter had occasion to make regarding them. As will be noticed in the letter of the 23d, Morgan suggests that Major Triplett's command, which had been sent forward with the prisoners, should be relieved of their charge by the brigade of militia under Gen. Stevens. Gen. Greene acquiesced in this arrangement and gave orders accordingly.* No reliance is to be placed on the statement that any misunderstanding ever took place between Morgan and Greene. A large number of their letters are now before us, and the uniformly friendly tone which pervades them, gives a prompt denial to the unsupported charge.

Nor are we left in doubt as to the tendency of Morgan's designs, particularly as they affected the operations of Gen. Greene. All his measures, all his communications, before and after the battle of the Cowpens, conclusively prove, that he did not merit the imputation of having disregarded the wishes or obstructed the designs of his general. One of his letters from Sherrald's Ford, dated the 25th, expresses the expectation that Greene will move towards the Yadkin to oppose its passage by the British; and with this view, declares the intention of the writer, " to move towards Salisbury, in order to get near the main army." His

* Johnson's Greene, pp. 398, 399.

attempts to establish magazines of provisions and forage above his position on Broad river, have also been cited in proof of a design to act independently of his commander. But as may be seen by reference to the letter of instructions, written to Morgan by Greene, the idea of these magazines originated with that officer himself. Their establishment was ordered as a measure indispensable to a rapid movement towards the mountains, should the enemy leave Morgan no other means of escaping a conflict with an overwhelming force, or of effecting a junction with the main body.

But the most serious charges of all are founded upon the circumstance of Morgan's retirement from the army. It is insinuated that the illness which was assigned by him as the reason for his wish for a temporary leave of absence, was by no means serious, if not altogether simulated. It is more than hinted that he adopted this determination from an apprehension that the contest would ultimately be unfortunate for his country, or from a conviction that his reputation had been accidentally acquired, and would not survive the vicissitudes of the war. It is furthermore stated that his departure left impressions upon many in the army, not very favorable to the purity of his patriotism.*

During the dreadful campaign of 1775, in Canada, Morgan contracted a sciatical affection. From this and other ailments, he was forced, in the year 1779, to retire from the army and return to his home. Shortly after the period when he took the field under Gates, he was seized with an ague and fever. A letter now ·before us from his friend, Col. O. H. Williams, dated November 8th, 1780, contains this passage : " I hope you have become perfectly well, and feel no more of your ague and fever." But the friendly expectation was not realized; his health grew worse; and at the time when he was ordered across the Catawba, he was suffering severely from this distressing complaint. Shortly after

* General Lee.

operations commenced on Broad river, the weather became
exceedingly cold and rainy. The exposure as well as the fatigue
to which he was constantly subjected, not only aggravated his
ague and fever, but also brought on a fresh attack of his sciatica.
During his subsequent movements, up to the time when he
reached Guilford court-house, he suffered from the combined
effects of these and other complaints to the verge of human
endurance; and on his arrival at that place, he was completely
exhausted, and quite unequal to further exertions.   His ill-health
is a subject of remark and condolement in nearly all the letters
addressed to him for some weeks previously to his retirement.
In the letter granting the solicited leave of absence, and in that
replying to the offer of command by the whigs of Mecklenburg,
Gen. Greene declares that Morgan was unable to keep the field.   It
is susceptible of proof that he was obliged to pause for a fortnight
on his journey homeward, owing to the severity of his sufferings;
and that for some time after his return to his family, he was
unable to appear abroad.   The congratulatory letters which subsequently reached him from Congress, the authorities of Virginia,
and other high sources, consequent upon his victory at the Cowpens, all offered him their condolence on account of his ill-health.
He left the army with extreme reluctance, cheered only with the
belief that he would soon be sufficiently restored to rejoin it.
But for months afterwards, his illness rather increased than
diminished; and during the remainder of the war, his health was
too feeble to permit him to take more than a partial part in its
operations.   When, during the succeeding summer, Cornwallis
seriously threatened the independence of Virginia, Morgan, as
will be seen in the sequel, essayed once more to wield his sword,
and by the side of his young friend, Lafayette, to meet again his
old adversary, Cornwallis.   But he was speedily obliged to relinquish the design, and to seek relief from pain in the curative properties of the waters at Bath.

    Little need be said in vindication of Morgan's claims to be

considered a pure and zealous patriot, and an active and able
commander. His life was a succession of sacrifices to the good
of his country; and in this is to be found his best defence against
the charges referred to. From the commencement of the war to
its close, he was a fervent advocate of American independence;
and when out of the field of warlike operations, he was in the
prisons of the enemy, or on the bed of sickness. During this
period, his services, whether we regard their amount, their value
or their brilliancy, were not surpassed by those of any other
officer in the army, except the commander-in-chief. He participated in, or had the direction of, nearly fifty contests with the
enemy, eight of which were general engagements; and of the
number of those in which he commanded, in no instance did he
fail of success, except under circumstances that awarded him all
the merit due to a victory. His patriotism was proof to the
tempting offers of Sir Guy Carleton, who sought to make him
exchange the squalid and hopeless lot of a prisoner for the rank
and emoluments of a colonelcy in the British army. Its purity
was again signally displayed in his resistance of the seductions of
those who would have perilled the cause in their effort to supersede the man, then as now regarded by all well-wishers of their
country as its ablest defender. Few men in those times succeeded
in establishing a higher reputation on a broader or firmer founda-
tion; still fewer were they whose zeal in the cause was more
ardent, or whose confidence in its ultimate triumph was more
unflagging. The charges more than implied in the strictures of
his detractors, that he had ever shown a disinclination to face the
enemy, or that he had ever betrayed a lukewarmness in the
cause, are contradicted by his whole career, and cannot be sustained by a particle of proof.

Not less unfounded is the statement that his departure from the
army left impressions unfavorable to his patriotism. His illness
had been of too long standing and too much severity to escape
general notice or to leave room for a doubt as to its reality. The

motive assigned for his retirement was therefore too obvious to be
mistaken. But even had it been otherwise, the high estimation
in which he was held by the army would have secured him
against misconstruction, even where his conduct admitted of
question. The regret with which all witnessed his departure was
unmingled with any feeling incompatible with the warmest
regard, the highest respect. His subsequent correspondence with
Gen. Greene and his other friends in the army, portions of which
will be given, furnished nothing whatever, showing that the relations of regard and confidence which existed between them had
been disturbed. On the contrary, it indicates that these feelings
had acquired additional strength from his absence. It shows,
that while he is constantly deploring his inability to take a part in
those active measures which he is as constantly suggesting, his late
companions in arms are profuse in their professions of friendship
and admiration, and lament the unavoidable causes which compel
them to defer their hopes for his return to the field.

Let us, then, vindicate the truth of revolutionary history, and
expunge from its pages representations of the man and his services which are so palpably erroneous, and which seem to be based
upon a false estimate of his character and motives.

CHAPTER XVIII.

Morgan determines to go home—Compelled from weakness to stop on the way—Extracts
from a letter to Gen. Greene—His letter to Greene from Carter Harrison's—Reaches
home—Letter from Gen. Greene, giving an account of the battle of Guilford C. H.—
Morgan's reply—His health partially restored—Is solicited by the authorities of Virginia
to give his aid in resisting her invaders—Letter from Lafayette—Resolution of the
House of Delegates—Letter from Gov. Jefferson—Morgan suppresses the Claypoole
insurrection—Rumors of the advance of the enemy into the valley—Removal of the
prisoners—Martial spirit aroused—Address of the speakers of the Virginia Legislature
to Morgan, soliciting his assistance—He raises a force of horse and foot, and marches
to join Lafayette—Letters from the latter—Battle at Jamestown—Morgan joins
Lafayette the day following—Is invested with the command of the cavalry and the
light troops.

BEFORE Morgan left Guilford court-house, his illness so
increased as to leave little hope of a speedy recovery, and to
induce him to make the best of his way homeward, where, he
knew, such attentions and kindness awaited him, as could not be
expected elsewhere. While on the road thither, he became so
weak, that he was forced to stop at the house of Gen. Lawson.
A few days were spent under this gentleman's hospitable roof, in
recruiting his strength, when he resumed his journey. But,
although suffering constant and severe pains, and experiencing
great bodily weakness, his mind and heart were still unsubdued.
They appear to have been absorbed in solicitude for the fate of
his recent companions in arms; and in devising measures for
augmenting their means of resistance, superadded to which was
an impatient desire to be so far recovered as to be enabled speedily
to rejoin the army. Before leaving Gen. Lawson's, he addressed

16*

a letter to Gen. Greene, under date of the 17th of February. "As I expect," he remarks, "you are much distressed for assistance, and as the militia are collecting fast, I have advised Gen. Lawson to go to, and give you, all in his power. But the militia want guns. Gen. Stevens's men have deposited theirs at Pittsylvania court-house. Don't you think those could be put in hand?" He concludes a letter, full of suggestions, indicating zeal and judgment, by adverting to the state of his health. "I wish," he observes, "I was able to give you my aid; but I find I get worse."

A few days more were passed by Morgan on the road, when his failing strength obliged him again to stop by the way. The house of Carter Harrison, Esq., received him on this occasion, and here he was compelled to remain for several days. From this place, he addressed to Gen. Greene the letter which follows:

CARTER HARRISON'S, *Feb.* 20, 1781.

DEAR SIR : I have been doctoring these several days, thinking to be able to take the field again. But I find I get worse. My pains now are accompanied by a fever every day. I expect Lord Cornwallis will push you until you are obliged to fight him, on which much will depend. You have, from what I see, a great number of militia. If they fight, you will beat Cornwallis; if not, he will beat you, and perhaps cut your regulars to pieces, which will be losing all our hopes.

I am informed that among the militia will be found a number of old soldiers. I think it would be advisable to select them from among the militia, and put them in the ranks with the regulars; select the riflemen also, and fight them on the flanks, under enterprising officers who are acquainted with that kind of fighting; and put the militia in the centre, with some picked troops in their rear, with orders to shoot down the first man that runs. If anything will succeed, a disposition of this kind will. I hope you will not look on this as dictating, but as my opinion on a matter that I am much concerned in. I am informed there are some odds of a hundred of the garrison regiment disposed of on little guards round about Richmond. If they were collected in a body, and militia in their places, they would make a pretty little reinforcement.

I have the honor, &c.,

DANIEL MORGAN.

It may be premised, that the foregoing letter has a historical importance of no ordinary character. It is admitted by Judge Johnson, in his life of Gen. Greene, that in the dispositions of the latter, at the battle of Guilford C. H., the suggestions of this letter were implicitly adopted ;* and to this fact is to be attributed, in all human probability, the practical defeat which the British sustained on that occasion.

About the beginning of March, Morgan reached his home in a state of extreme suffering and debility. The tender ministerings of a devoted wife and family, and the enjoyment of comforts to which he had been so long a stranger, were soon followed by an improvement in his health. But for some time, he continued unable to leave his house; and it was not until April that he could appear abroad. His recovery was no doubt retarded by the impatience he manifested at being forced to remain at home, during a campaign so active and exciting. In the meantime he was in the constant receipt of the proceedings of legislative bodies, and the letters of distinguished individuals, congratulating him upon his victory at the Cowpens. A number of these flattering testimonials have been already introduced.

Soon after his return home, the news of the battle of Guilford C. H. reached him. The following letter from Gen. Greene to Gen. Morgan, is chiefly in relation to this memorable encounter.

* This advice [that contained in Morgan's letter] was obviously followed, both in the constitution of the flanking parties, and in the disposition of the second line. The regulars could not, in justice to Stevens and Lawson, be withdrawn from their brigades ; nor did it comport with other arrangements and views, to place the militia in the centre of his line. If Morgan meant the middle line, when speaking of the centre (which appears highly probable), then was his advice in this particular literally pursued. We affect not to arrogate to Gen. Greene, the originating of measures conceived by others. We think it more creditable to a commander, to rise superior to the low jealousy, which rejects the advice of an inferior, or regards with envy the well earned fame of a brave competitor. Greene respected Morgan's understanding and experience; the advice was good, and was adopted. It was an emanation from the same bold and original genius, which soared so far above ordinary views and measures, on the day of the Cowpens.—*Extract from Johnson's Life of Gen. Greene*, vol. ii., p. 7.

DEAR SIR: Since we crossed the Dan, we have made many manœuvres and had much skirmishing. I have not time to give you the particulars. Until the 11th, our force was inferior to the enemy's, which obliged us to act cautiously. But forming a junction with a body of North Carolina and Virginia militia, and Col. Campbell coming up with a detachment of eighteen months men from Virginia, I determined to give the enemy battle. It was fought a little west of Guilford C. H. We were drawn up in three lines; North Carolina militia in front; the Virginia militia formed the second line, and the Continental troops the third. Col. Washington with the dragoons of the first and third regiments, a detachment of eighty regular light infantry, and two hundred riflemen under Col. Lynch, formed a covering party for the security of our right flank. Lieut. Col. Lee and his legion, and about two hundred and fifty riflemen under the famous Col. Campbell, formed a covering party for our left. The battle begun about twelve o'clock, and lasted about two hours. The conflict was bloody and severe, and had the North Carolina militia done their duty, victory would have been certain and early. But they deserted the most advantageous post I ever saw, and without scarcely firing a gun. The Virginia militia behaved with great gallantry, and the fate of the day was long and doubtful. But finally we were obliged to give up the ground; and as all our artillery horses were killed before the retreat began, we were obliged to leave our artillery on the ground.

The enemy's loss is very great, not less than between six hundred and seven hundred men, and perhaps more. Our loss is much less, though considerable. The greater part fell upon the regular troops. We retreated in good order three miles, and there halted and collected all our stragglers; after which we retired about ten miles from the place of action, where we have remained ever since. The enemy are now retiring from us, and have left us one hundred and seventy or eighty of their wounded. They are moving towards Bell's Mill. We shall follow them immediately, with the determination for another touch. The enemy had many officers killed and wounded. Among the latter, Gen. Moira is said to be mortally wounded.

The bearer of this, one of Lee's legion, waits upon you to get the colors taken at the Cowpens, to convey them to Congress, there to be deposited as a lasting monument of your gallantry and good fortune.

Marquis de Lafayette is coming to Virginia, with a detachment of light infantry from the Northern army.   Arnold must fall.   I have not time to be more particular.   God bless you with better health.

With esteem, I am, &c.,

N. GREENE.

To GEN. MORGAN.

To this letter Morgan wrote the subjoined reply.

SARATOGA, 11th April, 1781.

DEAR SIR: I was honored with your letter of the 28th of March. I assure you, sir, it gave me very great satisfaction, both from the intelligence and the mode of conveyance.   I have been particularly happy in my connections with the army, and am happy to tell you, sir, you are among the number I esteem.   Your good conduct as an officer and a gentleman while I had the pleasure of serving with you, created that esteem, and your gallantry and good conduct since that period has confirmed it with me, and I believe with every other person.   If you get your due, which I make no doubt you will, you will have the thanks of your country: for in my opinion you have done wonders, in repelling the enemy when the whole country stood trembling at their approach, and indeed, thought it almost impossible, as matters stood, to stop their career.

Your determination to give the enemy battle was in my opinion well-timed, and the disposition well concerted.   Such conduct and bravery will seldom fail of success.   You perhaps will call this a flattering letter.   But it has always given me pleasure to give every one his due; and I think it right, or where is the grand stimulus that pushes men on to great actions? On the other hand, I am as willing to give a person his demerits, if the person be worthy of notice.

I was not at home when the express arrived, nor did he await my coming.   But I sent the standards on to Congress, and informed the President by your order.

I expect by this time you have come up with my Lord Cornwallis, and am in hopes, with an army sufficient to cope with him; but much fear it, as I know what militia can do.   But I think Cornwallis's army must be dispirited, from the manner they were handled in the last engagement. God send you success.

I am directed by our Assembly to send their thanks to the officers and men that fought with me on the 17th of January last; will be much obliged to you to put it out in orders.

The pain in my hip has left me; but I believe the same kind of pain has taken me in the head, which makes me blind as a bat two or three times a day. But the cold bath seems to help me; and I am in hopes ere long to give you some little assistance.

Please to make my compliments respectfully to the gentlemen of your family.

> I have the honor, &c.,
> DANIEL MORGAN.

HON. MAJ. GEN. GREENE.

By the beginning of May, Morgan had, to all appearances, so far recovered, as to have afforded him a prospect of gratifying his wish to take the field again. He was about following Greene into South Carolina, when the alarming operations of the enemy in Virginia, together with the solicitations of the authorities of the State and of General Lafayette, gave a new direction to his thoughts.

While Morgan was in the field in the Carolinas, Arnold, with 1,600 men, invaded Virginia, captured Richmond, and destroyed an immense amount of property, public and private. Soon after Morgan's return home, a reinforcement of 2,000 men, under General Phillips, arrived from New York. This force being joined by that under Arnold, and Phillips assuming the command, the business of devastation recommenced. The country between the James and York rivers was completely overrun. Petersburg, Chesterfield C. H., and other important places were taken. All the shipping, tobacco, corn, and other property, public or private, which could be found were destroyed. Every horse which came within reach of the invaders was seized, and used by them in strengthening their cavalry force,* and in facilitating the movements of their troops. In short, for a time Virginia seemed doomed to destruction ; and

---

* The danger of this proceeding was foreseen by Morgan as early as the preceding October, when he addressed a letter to Governor Jefferson on the subject. The governor's reply, which is dated November 26, 1780, commences with the following paragraph :

"I am much obliged by your favor of October 30th. The recommendation for removing horses from the reach of the enemy in cases of invasion, is perfect, and shall be intimated to the members of assembly, who alone can give me powers to execute it."

the alarm which her impending fate created throughout the country, was divided with astonishment at the feebleness of her resistance. Had her energies been concentrated and well directed, she could have overwhelmed the invaders. But at this crisis of her fate, Lafayette arrived with his command from the North. This untoward state of affairs in the State of Virginia called for the utmost exertions of her government and people. Prompt and strenuous as these exertions were, they were begun too late to avert the loss, if not the disgrace, which was inflicted upon them by an insolent foe. Among other measures, Morgan was called upon to embody the militia in the region of country in which he resided, and to march with them against an enemy nearer home.

First among the inducements to a compliance on his part, was a letter, received about this time, from Lafayette, which follows :

RICHMOND *May 21st*, 1781.

MY DEAR SIR : having very often heard that on your recovery, you had set out for the southern army, I made no doubt but what you had arrived in South Carolina. Every account led me to believe you were on your way to General Greene's, and the intelligence had not been hitherto contradicted. But I hear you are not yet gone; and with the freedom of an old and affectionate friend, take the liberty to request your assistance.

You know that Gen. Greene is before Camden, where he had lately an engagement with Lord Rawdon. Had the general been properly supported, this manœuvre would have re-conquered a great part of South Carolina, and obliged Cornwallis to abandon the other State. But our small army in that quarter is so weakened, so destitute, and prospects of reinforcement are so far off, that I am afraid the taking of Camden will be a difficult matter.

When I was at Baltimore with a small but excellent detachment, I heard of Gen. Phillips's preparations at Portsmouth. We left baggage and artillery, made an uncommon forced march, and reached Richmond the evening before Phillips moved up near the town, with the intention of making an immediate attack. But our arrival disappointed them. He re-embarked, and went down the river, from whence, in consequence of advices from Lord Cornwallis, he came up again, landed on the south side, and marched to Petersburg, where he was covered by the James and Appomattox rivers, on the latter of which he had broken the bridges in the first invasion.

Lord Cornwallis, whom everybody had assumed to have embarked, came without opposition to Halifax. No more than 150 men could be raised on this side of the Roanoke. We could not leave James river unless we had crossed far above Petersburg, thereby abandoning this shore of the country from which reinforcements were expected. The two armies, the smaller of which is far superior to our regular force, have formed an easy junction, at Petersburg, and will no doubt begin offensive operations.

Gen. Phillips's death having left the command to the infamous Arnold, his army consisted of two thousand three hundred regulars, rank and file, fit for duty, and has received a small reinforcement from Portsmouth. The force of Lord Cornwallis you will better know than I do, when I tell you it consists of the 23d, 71st, 33d, British, one Hessian regiment, the Light Infantry and Guards, Tarleton's Legion, and some other corps—one of them is Hamilton's. The enemy have an entire command of the waters. They have much cavalry and we have for the present forty. Our regular force is near nine thousand; our militia are not very strong upon the returns, and much weaker in the field. We have not a hundred riflemen, and are in the greatest need of arms. The Pennsylvanians were long ago to join us, and their march has been deferred from day to day, no official account of them, nor of a battalion of Maryland recruits.

Under these circumstances, my dear sir, I do very much want your assistance, and beg leave to request it, both as a lover of public welfare and as a private friend of yours. I ever had a great esteem for riflemen, and have done my best to see them much employed in our armies. But in this little corps they are particularly wanting. Your influence can do more than orders from the executive. Permit me, therefore, my dear sir, entirely to depend on your exertions.

Another very great reinforcement to our small diminutive of an army and such a one as will I am sure, produce the happiest effects, is your personal assistance in the field. I beg leave my dear sir, most warmly to entreat you to join us, if the state of your health will permit. With the assurance that nothing would give me more pleasure than to see you once more in arms, and with the hope that I shall soon have that satisfaction, I remain, my dear sir, most affectionately your friend.

LAFAYETTE

GEN. D. MORGAN.

Soon after the receipt of this letter, and when Morgan had already determined on complying with the wishes of the marquis, he received the resolution of the Virginia House of Delegates, with the accompanying letter from Gov. Jefferson which follows :

IN THE HOUSE OF DELEGATES.

SATURDAY, *2nd June*, 1781.

Resolved, That His Excellency the Governor be desired to call for the immediate assistance of Brigadier General Morgan, to take the command of such volunteers, militia, or others, as he may be able speedily to embody, and march to join the army under command of the Honorable Major General Marquis de Lafayette. That this assembly have the utmost confidence in the active exertions of General Morgan in the present emergency ; and that the Governor do transmit to the said General so many proper commissions as may be necessary for the field officers, captains, subalterns, and others, to be by him appointed.

TESTE,   JOHN BECKLEY, C. H. D.

A Copy.

JOHN BECKLEY, C. H. D.

GOV. JEFFERSON TO GEN. MORGAN.

Charlottesville, June 2, 1781.

SIR : I have the pleasure to enclose to you a resolution of the House of Delegates, assented to by so many of the Senate as were here, by which you will perceive the confidence they repose in your exertions, and the desire they entertain of your lending us your aid under our present circumstances. I sincerely wish your health may be so far re-established as to permit you to take the field, as no one would count more than myself on the effect of your interposition. I enclose you commissions for the officers of three battalions. They are of necessity dated at the time of my signing them, and it will be well if you endorse on each the date from which it is to give rank.

I am, with great respect, sir,

Your most humble servant,

THOMAS JEFFERSON.

BRIG. GEN. MORGAN, *Berkeley.*

Morgan had already taken measures with the object of raising a large militia force from among the inhabitants of Frederick and

the adjoining counties. But although his efforts were now redoubled, the result did not realize his expectations. The period
of the year was at hand when the people would be engaged in
gathering their crops. As these would be the recompense for
their previous labors, and as they were their only hope for future
support, they showed an unwillingness to take the field until they
were gathered. Volunteers came in slowly in consequence.

An event occurred about this time, however, which, presenting
hostility to the State in a new and startling form, aroused the
patriotic and warlike feelings for which the people of Northwestern Virginia were ever distinguished. A party of tories,
residing on Lost river, in the then county of Hampshire (now
Hardy) had collected together, and raised the British standard.
John Claypool, a Scotchman by birth, and his two sons, were at
the head of the insurgents.* It was reported at the time, that
Claypool's sons had some time previously seen and communicated
their designs to Cornwallis, who appointed and commissioned
them both as captains, and sent a commission as colonel to their
father. Claypool had succeeded in drawing over to his party a
considerable majority of the people on Lost river; and a number
of those on the south fork of the Wappatomica. They first
manifested symptoms of rebellion, by refusing to pay their taxes
and to furnish their quota of militia. Upon complaint of these
proceedings, and of being resisted in the discharge of his duty,
by the sheriff, the military authorities of the county ordered a
captain and thirty men to his aid. But it does not appear that
this measure had the desired effect. On the contrary, the spirit
of disaffection increased. The tories began to organize, they
appointed officers, and made John Claypool their colonel, with
the intention of marching off in a body to join Cornwallis, in the
event of his advancing into the valley, or near it.

The danger became so alarming, that at length the authorities
of Hampshire sent expresses to those of the adjoining counties,†

* Kercheval's Valley Virginia, p. 195.   † Ibid. p. 196.

communicating the intelligence and requesting the aid of ᴏᴜeir militia. Colonel Smith, of Frederick county, immediately beat up for volunteers. The people showed the utmost alacrity in obeying the summons, and in a few days, an army of four hundred men were equipped, and ready for service. At the solicitation of the entire force, Gen. Morgan assumed the command.

About the 18th or 20th June, the army marched from Winchester, and in two days reached the tory section of Hampshire county. Arriving at Claypool's house, and finding him and some of his confederates on the premises, the whole were taken prisoners. One of these, in attempting to escape across the field, was fired at by one of Morgan's men, and badly wounded. Claypool having expressed repentance for the part he had taken in the movement, and given bail for his appearance when called upon, was set at liberty.

From Claypool's the army moved up Lost river, and on the route, took a number of implicated persons prisoners.* Having proceeded some distance, the troops crossed the South Branch Mountain, on or near the summit of which, a log house was discovered. General Morgan ordered the house to be surrounded, observing, "it is probable some of the tories are now in it." As the troops approached the cabin, ten or twelve men ran out and fled. An elderly man named Mace, and two of his sons, were of the number. Among the pursuers was Capt. William Snickers, one of Morgan's aids. Being mounted on a fine horse, he soon overtook the elder Mace, who, finding himself so closely pursued, surrendered. At this instant, one of Mace's sons looking round, and seeing Snickers making demonstrations of what he thought was a design to cut his father down, drew up his rifle and fired at him. The ball passing through the crest of the horse's neck; he fell, and threw his rider over his head. Under the impression that Snickers was killed, one of Morgan's men ran up to the elder Mace with a pistol, and shot him dead on the spot. All the

* Kercheval's Valley of Virginia, p. 19

fugitives were overtaken, and added to the number of the prisoners.

The army next visited the house of a wealthy German, named John Brake. This man owned a fine farm with extensive meadows, a mill, a large distillery, and a great number of cattle and swine. He was an exception, in his political course, to his countrymen, who were, almost to a man, true whigs, and friends of their country. He had joined the tory band, and his house was their place of rendezvous, where they feasted on the best he had. All this appearing unquestionable, Morgan marched his army to the residence of Brake, there halted, and spent two days and nights with his reluctant host.* His troops lived on the very best which the farm, mill and distillery afforded, while their horses fared no less luxuriously upon the fine unmown meadows and oat fields.

On the morning of the third day, the army left Brake's house, and returned to Winchester, after a service of about ten days.

"Thus," remarks Kercheval, from whose interesting work on the valley of Virginia the foregoing account of this affair is taken, "this tory insurrection was crushed in the bud. The party themselves became ashamed of their conduct, and in some degree to atone for it, and to wipe off the stain, several of the young men volunteered their services and marched to aid in the capture of Cornwallis."

The humanity of Morgan's character was strikingly displayed, when, shortly after this affair, he exerted all his influence, and with success, in averting from Claypool† the heavy consequences which threatened to follow his crime.

---

* Kercheval's Valley of Virginia, p. 198.

† The following are among the letters which Claypool addressed to Morgan during the period after his arrest and previous to his trial. The evidences of Morgan's interposition in his behalf will be found in passages of letters from the executive of Virginia and the commander-in-chief, which will appear in their proper connection.

May 31st, 1781.

Sir: These are to inform you th at I am heartily sorry that I have been so far blinded

In the meantime, the situation of affairs in the lower part of the State had become more critical than ever. Cornwallis, having entered Virginia from the Carolinas, had formed a junction with the forces lately commanded by Phillips, and at the head of the whole, had advanced towards the interior of the State, pushing Lafayette before him; while Tarleton· and Simcoe were spreading havoc on both sides of his line of march. A day or two after the force engaged in suppressing the Claypool insurrection had been disbanded, intelligence was received

in this riotous affair, which, was it to do again, I would suffer all that I have to be taken from me before I would undertake such a thing, as I am convinced that I was out of my duty to stand against the laws of our State. And if you would be so kind as to exert your favor and ability in my behalf, I shall look upon it as a particular favor, and do hereby promise to be faithful for the time to come, to the United States of America. I would appear at the time appointed, but it is thought my life lay at stake, although I know not that I have had any ill design, only I thought our burthen seemed too heavy. But further considering the expense in supporting the war to protect our liberty, I plainly see my fault, and beg pardon from you, and not only from you, but from all in authority.

From, Sir, your very humble servant,
JOHN CLAYPOOL.

P.S. If you will please to send me an answer to the above request, you will oblige yours.

LOST RIVER, Feb. 5th, 1782.

SIR: Nothing could induce me to trouble you but an absolute necessity, which you and all my countrymen are fully acquainted with, in regard to my unhappy affair, for which I stand charged in acting so precipitately, in consequence of which I most sincerely lament. Your honor, by reading the enclosed, I doubt not will put the most favorable constructions on my address to you, in praying your sentiments on the occasion. I herewith send you a petition to approve or condemn. The death of that gentleman whose humanity induced him to do all he could for me, is most deplorable. But the deportment by which I have conducted myself the chief part of my life, added to my conduct since my resignation to trial, will extort your lenity in saving my life. I hope an act agreeable to the laws of heaven and an attribute peculiar to the great Judge himself, who knows the acute conflicts I feel, the consequence of base and dishonorable actions, for which I again request your approbation to live. My trial is to be brought on the next month, and the indisposition I now labor under calls aloud for a suspension of trial a while longer, which I presume may probably be in your power. I pray your sentiments in writing, if agreeable to your pleasure.

I am, Sir, with due respect,
Your most obedient, humble servant,
JOHN CLAYPOOL.

N.B. SIR: You have favored me once before with a letter on the occasion, which I transmitted to Mr. Hogg, but it was misplaced.   J. C.

that Tarleton was on his way to Winchester, with the object of liberating the British prisoners, who, to the number of some hundreds, were then confined at that place. About the same time, directions* were received from Lafayette, for the removal of these prisoners. Four hundred of the militia were accordingly called out and equipped, under the escort of which the prisoners were removed without delay to Fort Frederick, in Maryland.

During this momentous period, Lafayette displayed his usual ability and promptitude, and succeeded in disappointing the overconfident expectations of his adversary. Having at length effected a junction with Wayne and his Pennsylvanians, and been joined by a large body of militia, he boldly turned upon the enemy.

Matters were in this posture, when Morgan received the following letter from the speakers of the two Houses of Assembly of the State, explaining to him the necessity of his immediately taking the field with whatever force he had succeeded in raising. Perhaps no more forcible illustration of the alarming state of affairs in Virginia at this time could be found, than that which is furnished in a letter, written under such extraordinary circum-

---

* The following letter from Lafeyette contains the orders referred to, as well as a statement of the circumstances under which they originated :

GEN. LAFAYETTE TO COL. WOOD OR GEN. MORGAN.

HEAD QUARTERS, CORBYN'S BRIDGE. ⎫
June 3rd, 1781. ⎰

DEAR SIR: The want of decision in the movements of Lord Cornwallis hitherto, as they equally tend to Fredericksburg and up the country, with the inefficiency of our present force to oppose them, added to the accounts I have received of an insurrection having happened not far from Winchester, induces me to anticipate the governor's arrangement respecting the removal of the Convention troops. I herewith send you a copy of the resolve of Congress of the 23rd of May, and a letter from the Board of War to his Excellency, the governor, which I fortunately opened. I request that you will immediately use your utmost exertions to march them to the places appointed. You will endeavor to collect a sufficient guard to move with them; and as the cattle sent on by the Board of War cannot be sent on in time, you must consult with the commissary of your post on the best mode of providing provisions on your route. You will please communicate this to Gen. Morgan, and take his advice relative o your proceedings.

I have the honor to be,
Your obedient servant,
LAFAYETTE.

To COL. WOOD OR GEN. MORGAN, at Winchester.

stances as was this one. Since the 2d of June, when the House of Delegates called on Morgan by resolution to take the field, that body had been surprised during its sittings at Charlottesville, and seven of its members captured. The remainder, with the governor and the executive officers, being forced to fly, dispersed in every direction ; and for a time, the only evidences of the continued existence of a governing power in the State, were furnished in instances, of a character similar to this :

STAUNTON, *June* 14, 1781.

SIR: By Major Holmes we are this day informed you are raising a body of men, with which you design to join the army, commanded by the marquis. We had before heard of your intentions, and hoped by this time you had been able to have begun your march. The major's account gives us great concern, as he tells us it will be yet ten days before you set out.

We have to inform you that the enemy, with their whole force, are a little below the fork of James river, near, if not quite, five thousand strong ; that the marquis is on the branches of James river, at one Allegree's, twenty-five or thirty miles from Lord Cornwallis's head-quarters, and thirteen from Charlottesville, on the Three Notches road, perhaps equal in number to his lordship. About seven hundred riflemen from this and the adjacent counties have joined him ; one thousand more are ordered, and will in the course of next week get to camp. So much is at stake on the fate of a battle, that it is not only our wish, but that of every member of the assembly we have heard speak on the subject, that you march with what men you have raised as soon as you possibly can, leaving orders for others to follow you. We are truly sensible of the alacrity with which the people on this side of the mountains will join you ; they wish to be commanded by you. We therefore entreat that you lose no time in joining the marquis. Had we an executive body, qualified to act, we doubt not they would have addressed you on this subject; but we flatter ourselves, that this requisition, coming from the speakers of the two Houses of Assembly, will have the same weight as from that body.

As the situation of the two armies will probably be different from what they now are before you join, we must refer you to such intelligence as you will receive for the route you take. It is impossible to form any judgment what steps his lordship will pursue; but thus much we can inform you, that the distress of all wherever he marches, is equal to anything you have known from them during the war ; and his numerous horse puts it in his power to extend his depredations to a great distance from his main body.

We are, with much esteem,

Your very humble servants,

ARCHIBALD CARY,

BENJ. HARRISON.

BRIG. GEN. MORGAN, *Frederick.*

Morgan had been indefatigable in his exertions to raise a respectable force of cavalry and riflemen. From the causes already mentioned, however, his wishes were not realized. But the recent expedition to Lost river, taken in connection with the serious state of affairs below, and the belief that Tarleton was on the road to that part of the State, fully aroused the martial spirit of the people. A fine body of cavalry was speedily raised and mounted ; but they lacked clothing, swords, pistols, and every other requisite of a dragoon. A considerable number of riflemen were also embodied. They were, however, without arms and ammunition ; nor could their wants in these respects be supplied at any point nearer than the neighborhood of active operations. The militia who formed the escort of the prisoners to Fort Frederick had taken with them all the arms and ammunition which could be found at the time in the public magazines at and near Winchester. The force of riflemen was not so numerous as Morgan desired. But the mass of the people could not be induced to engage in a tour of duty which would prevent their return home in time to gather their crops. He was assured, however, that as soon as the harvesting was over, thousands would follow him to the field and join his standard.

There being a pressing necessity for an increase of Lafayette's cavalry, Morgan permitted no obstacle to prevent the force of that description which he had raised from proceeding to the marquis without delay. Having clothed the men at his own expense, and placed them under the command of Capt. Nelson, they were sent forward, with directions to obtain swords and the other necessary equipments from some of the magazines of stores east of the mountains, and to lose no time in reaching the head-quarters of the marquis.

He addressed the speaker of the House of Delegates, intima-ting his speedy advance at the head of a considerable force, and stating that to obtain clothing for the cavalry, he had contracted, on his own responsibility, a heavy debt, which he hoped would be assumed and paid by the State.* A few days before he put his troops in motion, he informed the marquis of the progress he had made, and of his speedy approach. To the letter on this subject the marquis wrote the following reply:

MIDSHUNK CREEK, *June* 12, 1781.

MY DEAR SIR: With the greatest satisfaction I have received your letter, mentioning the exertions you have made for our support. Your

---

* To this letter he received the subjoined reply from Gov. Nelson:

STAUNTON, *June* 22, 1781.

SIR: Your letter of the 15th inst., addressed to the speaker of the House of Delegates, is referred to the Executive.

The readiness you show to assist our invaded country gives general satisfaction, and I doubt not but this will meet you far advanced on your march to join the marquis, with such volunteers as you have been able to collect. I am sensible of the great incon-veniences arising to the people by being called out at the approach of harvest; but I have my hopes that some capital blow may be struck, time enough to enable the com-mander of the troops to dispense with their services at that time. Should this not be the case, I flatter myself the militia and volunteers above will consider the distress occasioned to the lower country, where the ravages of the enemy, unless speedily suppressed, will involve the inhabitants in total ruin.

When the accounts of the tradesmen for necessaries furnished Major Nelson's corps on your order, be laid before the Board, they will immediately take measures for their discharge. They are convinced of the propriety of the proposition contained in your letter; but our present situation demands dispatch. And so much time would elapse before the whole system could be effectuated, that the advantages to be derived from a vigorous and an immediate effort, would be lost. But as soon as the situation of the State will admit, they will, with pleasure, patronize a scheme, which they trust will be pro-ductive of the most salutary effects.

I am, sir, your ob't servant,

THOMAS NELSON.

GEN. MORGAN, *Frederick Co.*

17

assistance is very necessary to us, and your success in collecting the troops is even above my expectations. The sooner they are with us, my dear friend, the better it will be, and I shall be particularly happy in taking by the hand a friend for whom I have ever felt the highest regard and sincerest affection.

The enemy are opposite to Elk creek. We moved this day from South Anna river to this place. It appears Lord Cornwallis expected us where he did not intend to go, and part of his army moved up to a place called Byrd's Ordinary, thirteen miles below this. Our stores are again behind us; what fell into their hands is very trifling; and our junction with the Pennsylvanians enables us to some resistance. But we are still much inferior to his lordship. To-morrow or the day after decides which way he intends to move.

The young man who carried your letter is in so much of a hurry that I have not time to receive a positive answer about the lead. There is but little to be got. I have directed the commissary of military stores to send you what he can obtain. Our equipments are dispersed, and I do not know what Baron de Stüben has ordered for them. I am afraid this will not be an easy matter. We can get short swords; but you know they are not very useful to dragoons. As to saddles and bridles, it is better to impress them than to leave the State without defence.

Adieu, my dear sir; it is late, and your young man is impatient to go. I shall, therefore, only add, that with the most perfect regard and attachment, I have the honor to be, dear sir,

Your most ob't, humble servant,

LAFAYETTE.

P. S.—Whatever you think better for the good of the service, that comes within the bounds of my power, I request you will either mention to me, or have executed in my name.

By the movement referred to in the foregoing letter, Cornwallis's designs upon the military stores in Albemarle, and upon the flank of Lafayette's force, were both frustrated. The latter being soon after reinforced by six hundred mountaineers, evinced a disposition to oppose the further progress of the enemy. Cornwallis was, no doubt, impressed with the danger of persevering in his designs. He accordingly commenced a retrograde movement towards Richmond. The marquis followed him with cautious circumspection. On the way down he was joined by Steuben, with four hundred men. His force at this time numbered two thousand regulars and three thousand two hundred militia. That of Cornwallis was about the same number of veteran troops.

On the 29th of June, the enemy evacuated Richmond, and retreated towards Williamsburg. The next day, Lafayette pursued them with his entire force. When within six miles of Williamsburg, the enemy's rear guard, commanded by Col. Simcoe, was attacked and severely handled by the American advance, under Col. Butler. Cornwallis occupied the town for a day or two, during which time Lafayette took post in the neighborhood.

Cornwallis, who had determined to retire from Portsmouth, was overtaken on the 6th of July, by the marquis, at Jamestown, where a severe encounter took place. With the design of attacking the enemy's rear, when the main body should have passed the river at Jamestown, Lafayette pushed forward the Pennsylvania troops, a body of riflemen and the cavalry. Cornwallis, divining the object of his opponent, made such a disposition of his force as induced the marquis to make an attack upon disadvantageous terms. The riflemen advancing, soon drove in the British pickets. But an advanced post, which covered their encampment, was perseveringly maintained. Lafayette, at length discovering his error, hastened to call in his men. But Wayne, with characteristic ardor, had dashed at the head of his Pennsylvania troops into the contest without delay; and before he could be recalled, he was closely engaged. Although menaced by what was now discovered to be the main body of the British army, he maintained his ground; and when the order to retreat and form a line with the light infantry in the rear reached him, he was charging the British line with the bayonet. The retreat was effected without any serious sacrifice, and the whole force was soon re-united and in good order about half a mile in the rear of the field of battle. The enemy declining to pursue, Lafayette retired to a position about six miles from Greenspring, the scene of conflict, where he encamped.

The loss of the Americans in this action, was one hundred and thirty-nine men, in killed, wounded and prisoners. That of the enemy was seventy-seven killed and wounded.*

It was during the night of this eventful day that Morgan, with a portion of the forces he had succeeded in raising, reached Lafayette's camp.

Having dispatched Nelson's command of cavalry forward, he marched about the 20th of June, with the force of riflemen he had succeeded in raising, towards Albemarle, in the vicinity of which he expected to be enabled to effect a junction with Lafayette. But the latter had then been some days on the march in pursuit of Cornwallis, who was retreating to Richmond. From the neighborhood of this city, the annexed letter was received by Morgan while on the advance.

HEAD QUARTERS, 20th June, 1781.

MY DEAR SIR: I have but the time of writing you two lines. The enemy have evacuated Richmond, and seem retiring towards Williamsburg. If it is the case, the retreat from Elm creek will be upwards of one hundred miles, and their friends in this State will be not a little disappointed.

Your junction with us, my dear friend, is very important. If you bring us a large body, we may, I think, cope with their army. I am for the present following them, but agree in opinion with you, and unless a very favorable opportunity offers, will not risk a battle.

As soon as Nelson's horse are ready, I wish you would order them on with the greatest celerity. We are in great want of dragoons.

Adieu, my dear Sir,
Most affectionately yours,

LAFAYETTE.

GEN. MORGAN.

Morgan and his command pushed forward to effect the desired junction. But Lafayette, in pursuit of the retreating foe, also advanced; thus several days elapsed, when it was found that they

---

* Tarleton, in his remarks on this battle, takes occasion to pay a deserved compliment to Lafayette's military talents, declaring it to be "the only instance of this officer's committing himself during a very difficult campaign."—*Tarleton's Campaign*, p. 355.

were as far from effecting their object as at the outset. It was not until the evening of the 6th of July, when they had travelled more than two hundred miles, that they reached the head-quarters of the marquis, near Jamestown.

Morgan was received by the marquis in the most cordial manner, and immediately invested with the command of all the light troops and the cavalry.*

The morning following his arrival, Tarleton, with his cavalry and a body of mounted infantry, was dispatched by Cornwallis in quest of Lafayette. On his approach to the American camp, Tarleton encountered a patrolling party of mounted riflemen. The latter immediately fell back towards their camp. They were, however, closely followed by the British horse, and had lost several of their number, when a body of riflemen came to the rescue. These troops, during the previous night, had encamped some distance in front of the main body. Their position, consequently, not only gave them the first intimation of the attack, but enabled them to be the first to meet it. At the commencement of the alarm, they were instantly under arms, and on the approach of Tarleton, opened upon his force such a heavy and destructive fire, that he was forced to an immediate and precipitate retreat.

---

* The command of Nelson's corps, and the Maryland volunteer dragoons, was conferred upon him through the letter which follows:

RICHMOND, *July 16th*, 1781.

DEAR SIR: I have attached to your command Major Nelson's corps, and the Maryland volunteer dragoons. I beg leave to recommend the latter to your attention. Most of| them are men of fortune, who make great sacrifices to serve their country. You will not, therefore, put them upon the duties of orderlies, or the common camp duties, which can be as well performed by the Continental horse. In everything else you will find them answer your expectations. As they are only to be subject to your orders, when you have accomplished the objects mentioned in my letter of yesterday, or when it is decided that Tarleton intends southerly and is beyond the reach of being struck, you will be good enough to order their return to head-quarters. It is my wish to dismiss them the moment it is in my power.

I am, dear Sir,
Your obedient servant,
LAFAYETTE.
BRIG. GEN. MORGAN.

CHAPTER XIX.

SOON after the action at Jamestown, Lafayette, with the main body of his army, retired, first to the forks of the York river, and afterwards to Richmond. Wayne, with his Pennsylvanian troops, and Morgan with the dragoons and riflemen, were detached across James river to Goode's Bridge.

Cornwallis, having crossed to the southern side of James river, resumed his march towards Portsmouth. Arriving at Suffolk he dispatched Colonel Tarleton from this point with his cavalry, and a body of mounted infantry, to New London, in the county of Bedford, distant not less than two hundred miles. Cornwallis's objects in ordering a movement so extensive and hazardous, were the destruction of a magazine of stores, said to have been collected at that place for Green's army, and the interception of a body of American light troops, which he was informed were on their march from the south to the assistance of Lafayette.

Upon the first intimation of this movement, Wayne and Morgan, with their respective commands, were sent by Lafayette to counteract it, and if possible to intercept and cut off Tarleton upon his return. Accordingly, Wayne advanced into Amelia county, while Morgan held the ground in the neighborhood of Goode's Bridge. Their confident expectations of entrapping Tarleton were, however, disappointed. This officer having proceeded first to Prince Edward and next to Bedford, found that the stores which he sought at these places had some time previously been dispatched southward. He ascertained, besides, that the expected detachment of light troops had not been sent northward, Greene having full employment for every soldier he commanded. Upon his return, he was informed of the danger which awaited him, in time to take the necessary measures to avoid it. After destroying his wagons he struck into a lower route across the head waters of the Nodaway and Blackwater rivers, and arrived without molestation at Suffolk on the 24th.*

It is a matter of surprise that Lafayette should have allowed an opportunity so favorable for intercepting and destroying this detachment to escape him. The extreme caution which he appears to have observed on this occasion, was, perhaps, one of the consequences of his rash attack at Jamestown. It must be observed, however, that the movements of Tarleton were conducted with such rapidity, that information regarding them, at any stage of their progress, must have reached Lafayette at a time too late to be useful. Besides the object of the expedition, and the scope of its operations, were alike unknown to the Marquis. The force of which it was composed was believed by him to be much greater than it really was.† Had Wayne and Morgan been per-

---

* Tarleton, p. 357 ; Lee's Mem. p. 306.

† This expedition was the subject of the following among other letters, addressed by Lafayette to Morgan :

RICHMOND, *July 17th*, 1781.

DEAR SIR,

My former intelligences were decisive upon Tarleton's going towards Roanoke. But

mitted to move forward, as appears to have been their desire, the probability is that the force under Tarleton would have been intercepted and dispersed. Indeed, this opinion is, in substance, expressed by Tarleton himself. *

About this time, Lafayette moved his army from the neighborhood of Richmond, and encamped at Malvn Hill. Wayne and Morgan were left with their respective detachments at Goode's Bridge.

Lafayette, supposing that the next movement of the enemy would have reference either to Virginia or the Carolinas, composedly awaited the development of their plans, holding himself at the same time in readiness to act as circumstances might require. "Two or three days will determine what the enemy intend to do," he observes in a letter to Morgan, dated at Malvin Hill, on the 21st of July, "and the distribution of their forces will determine what is to become of ours." That he anticipated another attack from Cornwallis, and that he had resolved to meet it, are rendered evident by a passage in the same letter. "Should you not find any position," he remarks, "where you might fight to advantage the mounted part of the British army, or should you fear to be unacquainted with their movements, it would of course be more

I just now hear that he was last night at Walker's house, seven miles above Walker's Mill, on Nodaway river, thirty-two miles south of Petersburg. He was expected in that town this night. Gen. Wayne is over the river and has orders to be very cautious. But if Col. Tarleton could be surprised to-night at Petersburg, he is to make the attempt. I think, my dear friend, we are rather scattered, and it will be better for you to fall back towards Chesterfield Court House; so that if instead of attacking, Wayne is attacked, he may retire to you. By the last accounts, Lord Cornwallis was at Portsmouth. I hardly believe Tarleton will come to Petersburg. At all events you may take such positions in the woods as will effectually cover you from his horse. But we are so distant that I leave with you to act according to circumstances.
Yours,
LAFAYETTE.
You will please have dragoons at Budford's to give Gen. Wayne notice.
BRIG. GEN. MORGAN, *Goode's Bridge.*

* A detachment from the Marquis de Lafayette's army, might have been transported over the James river near City Point, and by posting themselves near the head of Blackwater, would have endangered the retreat of the British, by blocking up the pass at that place, and over which they must unavoidably return; because the banks of Blackwater are in other parts so marshy, that there is no approaching them, either to make use of rafts, or to cross the river by swimming.—"*Tarleton's Campaign*, p. 359.

prudent to be on this side. But in the other case, independent of
my aversion to fresh fatigues, I am glad to keep the enemy in
suspense ; and should they move up in consequence of our divided
state, it will retard their preparations for the relief of New York.'
The first of the series of movements which ended in the capture
of Cornwallis was now made. On the 30th, the detachments of
Wayne and Morgan moved from Goode's Bridge to Deep Creek
Bridge, in Amelia county. The new position afforded, among
other advantages, greater facilities for marching towards Portsmouth or the Carolinas, as events might determine.* On the
next day, Morgan received the following letter from Wayne, communicating the orders it contained from the marquis.

CAMP AT WATKIN'S MILL, *July 30th*, 1781.

DEAR SIR: I have it in command from the Marquis de Lafayette to
direct Gen. Campbell with all the riflemen to join Gen. Muhlenberg at
Bland's Mills, to the southeast of Petersburg, the soonest possible. You
will therefore be so obliging as to order him to take up his line of march
at four o'clock to-morrow morning. He may easily reach that place in
three days. You will also be so obliging as to order Capt. Reed, with
Nelson's dragoons, to join me at this place immediately.

The marquis likewise informs me that your people are coming in, and
wishes you to proceed to his quarters to arrange them.

That their numbers and appointments may be equal to your expectations,

---

* GEN. ANTHONY WAYNE TO GEN. MORGAN.

CAMP AT GOODE'S BRIDGE, *29th July*, 1781.
DEAR SIR: The ground in and about this camp begins to be so disagreeable, that it has
determined me to march to-morrow morning, at half past 5 o'clock, for Deep Creek
Bridge, in Amelia county, about eight miles from this place. This change is necessary,
not only for the health of the troops, but for the more easily procuring flour and forage.
It is also a position from which we can move with facility towards Portsmouth or Carolina, as events may determine.

I leave it with you to march the riflemen and Baltimore dragoons under Capt. Moore
to that place, or to remain where they are for the present.

You will be so obliging as to order Capt. Reed, with his corps of cavalry, to precede the
infantry in the morning, and to take post with us.
Interim, I am,
Your most obedient humble servant,
ANTHONY WAYNE.

and that life and laurels may attend you on all occasions, is the sincere
✻✻✻h of
Your most obedient servant, &c.,
ANTHONY WAYNE.
BRIG. GEN. MORGAN, at Maj. Goode's.

While the military events just detailed were in progress, Morgan became so unwell from a return of his sciatical complaint, as at length to confine him to his bed. The first night he passed in Lafayette's camp, at Greenspring, was followed by an attack of this malady. For a few days he bore up against a renewal of his sufferings, as well as the more painful presentiment that his career as a soldier was drawing to a close. But about the beginning of August, his illness so increased, that he was obliged to retire from the field, and to seek a renewal of his health in the comforts and quietude of home.

His reluctance again to leave the army under such circumstances was evinced until the last moment. A letter to Gen. Greene, written by him about ten days before his departure, admits a misgiving that he was no longer fit for service, but gives no intimation of his intention to retire. Such a design was too repugnant to his inclinations to be entertained, until it became unavoidable. The letter referred to is annexed.

CAMP, GOODE'S BRIDGE, 24th July, 1781.

DEAR SIR: As the marquis has written you, no doubt he has given you a better account of the enemy's situation than I could; shall, therefore, say nothing on that head. After making use of the cold bath for upwards of two months, I thought myself so far recovered as to be able to take the field, and intended to have joined you in Carolina. But my lord making so deep a lunge at the Old Dominion, that both houses of the Assembly requested me to raise as many volunteers as possible, and join the marquis, which I did, the day after the action at Jamestown. My lord has embarked some of his troops; what he intends, time only can discover. But if they are sent southerly, we are on our way to join you.

How are all the old heroes, Washington, Lee, Howard, &c., &c.? I have not time to write them. Will you be pleased to make my compli ments to them, also to Gen. Huger, Col. Williams, and your own family respectively.

I saw your letter to the marquis, and was very unhappy at your situation. That d——d reinforcement arrived very unluckily for us.*

I lay out the night after arriving at camp, caught cold, and have been laid up ever since. I am afraid I am broke down. I sincerely wish you every species of good luck, and all the happiness that country can afford you.

I have the honor, &c.,
DANIEL MORGAN.

MAJ. GEN. GREENE.

To the foregoing, Morgan received the subjoined reply, shortly after his return to Frederick:

HEAD QUARTERS, CAMDEN, *August 26th*, 1781.

DEAR SIR: Your letter of the 24th July arrived safe at head-quarters, and your kind compliments to Williams, Washington, Lee, and the other gentlemen you mention, have been properly distributed. Nothing would give me greater pleasure than to have you with me. The people of this country adore you. Had you been with me a few weeks past, you would have had it in your power to give the world the pleasure of reading a second Cowpens affair. Gen. Sumter had the command; but the event did not answer my expectations. If I deserve any credit for the manœuvres of this campaign, it was for that I gave the enemy a blow where they least expected it. But, alas! the execution failed. However, we got upwards of one hundred and forty prisoners, and took and destroyed a great quantity of stores. The expedition ought to have yielded us six hundred men, and the chance was more than fifty times as much in our favor as it was at Tarleton's defeat. Great generals are scarce—there are few Morgans to be found. The ladies of Charleston toast you. Don't you think we bear beating very well, and that we are something of the nature of stock-fish, the more we are beat, the better we grow? I may say with the king of Prussia, Fortune is a female, and I am no gallant. She has jilted me several times this campaign; but in spite of her teeth, I pursue her still, in hopes the old adage will be fulfilled—a coy dame may prove kind at last. I am not well pleased with her rebuffs; but I bear them with patience. I was content at the flogging at Guilford; but I lost all patience at first with that of Lord Raw-

* The arrival at Charleston of three British regiments, which event was followed by the advance of Lord Rawdon to the relief of Ninety-six, at the time invested by Gen. Greene.

don's. In the one I considered victory as doubtful: in the other, certain. Under these impressions, you may well think the disappointment was not pleasing; and to add to my vexation, that cursed reinforcement must arrive by two days too soon. But upon the whole, we are as well off as could be expected; and the less we are indebted to fortune, the greater our merit. I claim nothing—the army deserves everything.

Nurse your old bones and stick by the marquis, until the modern Hannibal unfolds his great designs. While you and Wayne are with him, 1 think he will be well supported, and I shall feel perfectly easy.

We are trying to collect a body of militia to give the enemy battle. If we succeed, perhaps you may hear of a few being sent to the shades on both sides. The Dominion has been in great jeopardy this campaign. Let it prove a warning to be better prepared in future. But under all her oppressions she rises in glory, and will soon shade all her sister States, especially as Nelson has got at the head of the government.

With much esteem, I am, &c.,

GEN. MORGAN.   NATH. GREENE.

Soon after Morgan returned to Frederick, he proceeded to Bath Springs, from the healthful properties of the waters of which, he had previously experienced relief from attacks, such as that under which he labored at this time. In a few days his pains left him, and his strength was measurably restored. But the impression had, in the meantime, fixed itself in his mind, that his constitution was no longer able to withstand the hardships and exposures incident to an active campaign—that his return to the field would be followed by a return of his malady. Yet, notwithstanding this, it is certain that he was impatient for the acquisition of sufficient strength to enable him to rejoin the marquis.

While at this place, he received the letter which follows, from Lafayette:

GEN. LAFAYETTE TO GEN. MORGAN.

MONTOK HILL, August 15, 1781.

MY DEAR FRIEND : I have been happy to hear your health was better. I hope the springs will entirely recover it; and then, my dear sir, I shall be happier than can be expressed, at seeing you with the army. You are the general and the friend I want; and both from inclination and esteem, I lose a great deal when you go from me, and will think it a great pleasure and a great reinforcement to see you again. But let me entreat you not so soon as to expose your health. Great services have been rendered by you—great services are justly expected. So that you cannot, consistent with your duty, trifle with your own life. By the time you are called to come, perhaps the scene may be interesting.

Your influence, my dear sir, may render us the greatest service. The militia ordered out are coming in very slow—so slow that I will be soon left with the Continentals. For God's sake, tell them to come on. It appears the enemy had rather expose New York and pursue their serious intentions against Virginia. I do every day expect a new campaign, and never was worse provided. We put on the best face we can; but I confess, I dread consequences. At the same time that you hurry on the militia, let them take their arms with them—rifles particularly, as riflemen are the soldiers I most wish for. If there are Continental or State arms within your reach, I request you will forward them on. Advise Col. Davies of the march of any militia.

We have many horse accoutrements at Noland's Ferry, at Fredericktown in Maryland, and perhaps some other places. I wish wagons may be impressed and those articles immediately sent. White has two hundred fine men and horses, who, for want of accoutrements, are entirely useless. The best way will be to send them by the upper road and forward them to our camp.

Could it be possible to procure a quantity of shoes? The whole army are barefoot.

These articles, my dear friend, I only mention, in case your health permits you to attend to them. I beg you will not take any trouble about them that might give you improper fatigue, or disturb for one instant the care I entreat you to pay to the recovery of your health.

Lord Cornwallis's army is divided between York and Gloucester. At York they don't fortify: but they do at Gloster. It appears Portsmouth will be evacuated, and everything brought round to York river. Accounts from New York assure us that part of the troops is certainly recalled: but nothing here that indicates it for the present.

The light infantry and militia are between the forts of York river, the first four miles, the second eight miles from West Point. Gen. Wayne is for the present at Bottom's Bridge, and should the enemy detach to York, he will go to South Carolina. I am nursing the few horse we have; boats are patrolling down the river; Mathews, with some militia, is between this and Williamsburg ; a larger corps with the volunteer horse under Col. Lane, is foraging in Gloster county. This position looks both ways, and saves transportation.

The enemy's movements I explain on two accounts. That a force had been ordered to New York is certain. But the plan had afterwards been altered. If Lord Cornwallis expects a French fleet, he will confine his defences to Glostertown, and there fight in protection of his army and shipping. He will regard it dangerous to divide his force, and would have little or nothing on the York side. If, on the contrary, his lordship means to be offensive, the fortifications at Gloster are means to protect his vessels, his magazines and hospitals, and in case of a misfortune to ensure his retreat. The latter seems the most probable. I soon expect to be hard pushed, and never was worse provided.

There is some rumor of a fleet being near the Capes ; but I do not believe it. Adieu! my dear Morgan.

Most affectionately, your friend,
LAFAYETTE.

P. S. If you hear of ammunition, send it to us.
BRIG. GEN. MORGAN.

Judging, as well from the recollections of those who were acquainted with Gen. Morgan, as from the records he has left behind him, his mortification at being unable from ill-health to sustain to the end the prominent part he had taken in the great drama of the revolution, was excessive, and doubtless, it contributed in no mean degree to aggravate his physical sufferings. The termination of the mighty struggle was plainly foreshadowed about this time. The French fleet had arrived in the Chesapeake, and blocked up the enemy's egress to the ocean: while Lafayette guarded the avenues to escape southward, and the Marquis of St. Simon those to the interior, " the modern Hannibal," was advancing with the main army from the north. Cornwallis, it was evident, had at length been caught in the toils of his adversaries.

Under the feeling to which these auspicious circumstances would naturally give rise in the breast of a patriot and soldier, kept by sickness from being present at the virtual close of a struggle in which he had participated so largely, Morgan addressed the letter which follows to Washington :

September 20th, 1781.

SIR : At a time like this, when your excellency's every moment must be devoted to the grand business of America, I know you can have but little leisure for private letters—but the feelings of my heart will not permit me to be silent : I cannot avoid congratulating your excellency on the present favorable appearance of our affairs : I cannot avoid telling your excellency how much I wish you success, and how much I wish that the state of my health would permit me to afford my small services on this great occasion. Such has been my peculiar fate, that during the whole course of the present war, I have never, on any important event, had the honor of serving particularly under your excellency. It is a misfortune I have ever sincerely lamented. There is nothing on earth would have given me more real pleasure than to have made this campaign under your excellency's eye, to have shared the danger, and let me add, the glory too, which I am almost confident will be acquired. But as my health will not admit of my rejoining the army immediately, I must beg leave to repeat to your excellency my most earnest wishes for your success, and for your personal safety.

I have the honor to be, with sentiments of the highest esteem,
Your excellency's obedient and humble servant,
To GEN. WASHINGTON.   DANIEL MORGAN.

Washington, at the head of the French and American forces, was vigorously prosecuting the siege of Yorktown to a triumphant close, when the foregoing letter reached him. The following was written in reply :

HEAD QUARTERS, BEFORE YORK, 5th Oct., 1781.

SIR : Surrounded, as I am, with a great variety of concerns, on the present occasion, I can yet find time to answer your letter of the 20th ult., which I have received with much satisfaction ; not only as it is filled with such warm expressions of desire for my success on the present expedition, but as it breathes the spirit and ardor of a veteran soldier, who, though impaired in the service of his country, yet retains the sentiments of a soldier in the primest degree.

Be assured that I most sincerely lament your present situation, and esteem it a peculiar loss to the United States, that you are, at this time, unable to render your services in the field. I most sincerely thank you for the kind expressions of your good wishes, and earnestly hope that you may be soon restored to that share of health which you may desire, and with which you may again be useful to your country in the same eminent degree as has already distinguished your conduct.

With much regard and esteem,
I am, sir, your most obedient servant,

BRIG. GEN. MORGAN.   GEO. WASHINGTON.

Morgan was still at home recruiting his shattered health, when the joyful news of the surrender of Cornwallis was spread through the country. A large proportion of the prisoners surrendered on that occasion, were marched to Winchester, and guarded by a body of militia, were confined in the barracks near that place, under the direction of Col. Wood, the commissary of prisoners in that section of country. The untoward consequences which followed the arrival of these prisoners in Frederick, were the subject of a number of letters from Morgan to Washington, Governor Harrison, Colonels Wood and Smith, and others in authority. As the subjoined letter, besides being an interesting link in the chain of correspondence between Washington and Morgan, furnishes a detail of the consequences referred to, in a manner so complete, as to render further remark thereupon unnecessary ; it possesses a double claim to notice :

SARATOGA, November 25th, 1781.

SIR: After acknowledging the honor of your very friendly and polite letter, dated " Before York, 5th Oct.," give me leave most sincerely to congratulate you on our late signal success over the British arms under Lord Cornwallis, which has afforded me unspeakable satisfaction, not only on account of the additional laurels it has gained to your excellency in particular, and the army in general, but because it has also dispersed the black clouds of adversity which hung lowering over our country, and exhibits a bright prospect of a peaceable hereafter. But while I rejoice in the occasion that subjected so many of our enemies to our power, I cannot but lament the great loss of prisoners which will, or I fear already has, taken place.   I beg leave to lay before your excellency, the situation of those sent to this country. The barracks for their reception were scarcely adequate to half their numbers, and the staff department entirely unprovided with axes or tools of any kind for the building of more ; add to this the weather growing cold, and the guards, which were militia, not being attended with sufficient discipline and law, the prisoners are so dispersed, that of those sent to Winchester, not more than eight hundred could be paraded a few days ago. On hearing this disagreeable account, I have ordered them all to be called in, but as the barracks are built in a tory settlement, five miles above Winchester, and a chain of tories extending thence along the frontiers of Maryland and Pennsylvania, who would rather assist than prevent their escape, I fear the order will not be attended to with the wished-for success, especially as many of them have been already seen passing the Potomac in hunting-shirts and other dresses of disguise. I shall visit them to-morrow, to see how many are together, and give the best orders for their future security our circumstances will permit.

The Governor of this State has sent Nelson's corps of horse to act as guards to the prisoners; but the inhabitants refuse furnishing either them or the prisoners with provisions. Under our present regulations, they are uneasy at not being paid in hard money for their property, as they conceive the people of other States are, and indeed, are arming, and threaten to oppose the laws with force. My health, though by no means perfectly re-established, is sufficiently repaired to permit me to attend to any directions you may think proper to honor me with in this quarter ; and I beg leave to assure your excellency, that I am never happier than when serving my country in the prosecution of your orders. I have just received a letter from the senior British officer, prisoner at Winchester, which I take the liberty of enclosing.

I have the honor to be your excellency's most obedient and humble servant,

DANIEL MORGAN.

N. B.—There are a number of soldiers straggling through the country who were prisoners at Charlestown and elsewhere ; some of them escaped from confinement, and others deserted, after listing into the British service—they have never been apprehended, because they were never considered as deserters. Your excellency's directions would, I think, be attended with an advantageous effect.

HIS EXCELLENCY, GEN. WASHINGTON, D. M.
    Philadelphia.

Before the subjoined reply reached him, he had contributed by his influence and personal exertions to collect the greater part of the prisoners together, to obtain for them additional quarters and the necessary subsistence, and at the same time to allay the spirit of resistance which the impressment of provisions &c., had aroused among the inhabitants.

PHILADELPHIA, 12th Dec., 1781.

DEAR SIR: I have received your favor of the 25th November, and return you my sincere thanks for your kind congratulations upon the late important success of the allied arms.

I am obliged to you for the trouble you had taken with the prisoners of war, and for the offers which you make of rendering further services in that way. But the Secretary of War, Maj. Gen. Lincoln, into whose department the charge of that business now falls, had given his directions in the matter to Col. Wood, who has long had the superintendence of prisoners upon the frontier. A very troublesome business, and not to be envied.

What you mention respecting those soldiers of ours, who, after returning from captivity, have never joined their corps, and those, who while prisoners, enlist with the enemy and then desert, deserves attention. If the terms for which they were enlisted have not expired, they are certainly liable to be called into service; and you will be pleased to look upon yourself as authorized to apprehend all such as cannot make it appear that their times have expired.

I wish you a perfect recovery of your health, and am with esteem, dear sir, your most obedient and humble servant,

GEO. WASHINGTON.

BRIG. GEN. MORGAN. ⋅

During the preceding year, Morgan, having purchased a piece of land, lying about two miles N. E. of White Post, had, in the mean time, employed a number of the British prisoners who were quartered in the vicinity, in erecting on it a handsome and spacious residence, which was very appropriately named " Saratoga." Into this building he removed his family from his former residence near Berrysville, early in the spring.

Soon after his return home from the field on this occasion, his eldest daughter, Nancy, was married to Col. Presley Neville,* son of John Neville, of Pittsburg, one of his old and much esteemed friends.

Before the winter of 1781–2 elapsed, Morgan had, to all appearances, sufficiently recovered his health and strength to enable him to take the field again. But the energies of the enemy had been palsied by the capitulation of Yorktown, and already the indications of an approaching termination of the war were apparent. In the spring of 1782 he resumed his command. But no occasion for service offered itself until the preliminaries of an eventual treaty of peace were arranged. He continued with the army, however, and was at the head of his command when the continental troops was disbanded.

It appears that Morgan was a sharer in the dissatisfaction, so greatly felt and expressed at this juncture by the army, at the alleged illiberal spirit which Congress and the State governments

---

* Col. Presley Neville (the only son of Gen. John Neville, of Pittsburgh), was born in Virginia. He took an early part in the revolutionary struggle, during the continuance of which, he was an active and prominent actor in its vicissitudes. In July or August, 1775, he was commissioned a lieutenant. In the succeeding year he was promoted to a captaincy. In October, 1778, he was advanced to the rank of lieutenant-colonel. During the years 1777 and 1778, he served as aid to the Marquis de Lafayette. He was a partaker in all the battles in which the Virginia line was engaged, up to the period when the Hessians were captured at Trenton, on which occasion he was also present. At the battle of the Short Hills, in New Jersey, he commanded the advanced corps: had a handsome skirmish with the enemy at Cocksbridge, near Christiana; and received at the head of the brigade, the thanks of the commanding general. At the battle of Brandywine, which took place a few days after, he had a horse killed under him. In the succeeding battle of Germantown, was one of the few survivors of a small detachment that attempted to set fire to Chew's house. He was at the battle of Monmouth, and immediately afterwards went to Rhode Island; passed the batteries of Newport in Count d'Estaing's ship; was in the siege from the commencement, and in the battle when Gen. Pigot made a sortie on the American army, after the departure of the fleet. He was then detached to the South, and was in the memorable siege of Charleston, where he fell into the hands of the enemy. In 1781, he was exchanged, and participated in the siege of Yorktown and the capture of Cornwallis. Soon after the peace, he received an appointment in the department of war, the duties of which he discharged for many years. In the meantime, he married, and established himself at Pittsburg. He subsequently removed to Neville, Ohio, where he passed the remainder of his days in the quietude of domestic life.

displayed towards it. He was not exempt from the embarras-
ment which a devotedness to the public cause had produced in the
private affairs of almost every officer in the service. His causes
of-complaint, his necessities, and his feelings, are well explained by
himself in the annexed letter, written in reply to one from Gen.
Greene, introducing to Morgan, Capt. Osborn, of South Carolina.

SARATOGA, 28th July, 1782.

DEAR SIR : I had the pleasure to receive your favor of the 10th June,
by Capt. Osborn. I assure you, sir, that it gave me great pleasure to find
you still in the land of the living, as knowing that in that country accident
and changes are daily waiting on the human frame. If, by his vigilance
and sagacity, he eludes every other danger, the fogs are apt to take possession of his lungs.

The recommendation you gave Capt. Osborn will give him a place in my
esteem ; and should he stand in need, I will recommend him to those of
my acquaintance that have money. For my own part, I have none, having
spent the time in the service of my country [during which] I might have
provided for myself. And that country is ungrateful enough to allow,
or at least, to pay me nothing for my services. Our Assembly gave the
officers certificates for two years' pay, which were to be paid out of the
money arising from the sales of the confiscated property. But those fellows who have deserted their country, and, by the laws, have forfeited
their estates, have left friends enough to have them remitted when condemned. Our Assembly have made an act to raise three thousand men,
and to give a bounty of forty dollars and clothe them. This would have
been sufficient to raise the men, could they have any hopes of being
clothed and paid : but they have been so eternally deceived, that they have
no longer any faith in public promises, and the officers' spirits are so much
broken, that they don't, nor won't exert themselves. Upon the whole, I
see little prospect to fill our line, or indeed, to make any progress towards
it. Our Assembly have made a law to pay themselves and those of the
Council, and others acting in the civil line, quarterly, and very liberally,
out of the public treasury. But when they talk about the army, they say
they ought to be paid ; but that the people are not able to pay a tax sufficient to pay them ; but they make no doubt they will be paid ! I was so
sure of being paid the two years' pay, and thinking I should have a respite,
undertook the building of a house, which will, in a short time, totally

exhaust my funds, and leave me without either money or house, for I shan't be able to finish it. Withal I find myself growing very rusty. My clothes are nearly worn out, and my laurels fade. It is high time to attempt some enterprise.

I am told you have had it in your power to get some clothing for the army under your command. Could I not, with propriety, be considered as a part of that army, and be equipped with a suit of clothes. It would be needless to mention particulars, for I want everything, from top to toe. If such a thing can be done, my friend, Capt. Gill, will take charge of them, and convey them to me.

I have the honor to be, &c.,

DANIEL MORGAN.

HON. MAJ. GEN. GREENE.

The feeling thus displayed, although justified by the circumstances which gave rise to it, was the result, rather of momentary irritation, than of settled conviction. When relieved from the pecuniary pressure to which he alludes, a more generous spirit was manifested, and a more liberal if not a juster interpretation was given to the motives and intentions of the governing power.

This was fully shown when the troops of the Virginia line were disbanded. His conduct on this occasion was the counterpart of that which Washington adopted under similar circumstances towards the main army, and it was equally successful.

Up to this time, the medal which Congress had voted to Morgan in token of its estimation of his services at the Cowpens, had not appeared; and he felt a pardonable anxiety to obtain it. The letter from Gen. Mercer, in reply to that from Morgan, both of which follow, besides presenting a vivid picture of the times and the critical circumstances which invested public affairs, testifies to the judicious and praiseworthy part which Morgan acted upon the disbandment of the command.

GEN. MORGAN TO MR. JOHN F. MERCER.

SARATOGA, February 6th, 1783.

DEAR SIR: I am induced to trouble you with a few lines for two reasons; the first through a reliance on your friendship, which I flatter myself would prompt you to serve me if in your power; and second, because you are the

only gentleman in office in Philadelphia, whose acquaintance would countenance such a request.

The honorable Congress, after the action of the Cowpens, thought
proper to vote me a medal for my conduct in that affair, and as such an
acknowledgment of my country's approbation, could not but be flattering
to the mind of a soldier, I have made frequent application to get it, and
have been as frequently disappointed. Gen. Lincoln once informed me
that nothing prevented its being sent to me, but the low situation of finan-
ces, and that I should have it as soon as there was money sufficient to be
had to defray the expenses. Now, sir, I not only wish you to expedite the
making of it, but that you may also pay some attention to the manner in
which it may be done, and with devices, properly emblematical of the
affair. I have so good an opinion of your taste and general knowledge, as
to wish to submit the matter entirely to your direction. The expense can
not be considerable, and I flatter myself the financier, on a proper application, would advance a sum sufficient to defray it, especially to gratify
the inclinations of a man whose principal aim it has been, to obtain his
country's appplause to his conduct.

I am, sir, very respectfully your obedient servant.

                                        DANIEL MORGAN.

JOHN MERCER ESQ., Philadelphia.

            JOHN F. MERCER TO GEN. MORGAN.

                        PHILADELPHIA, *April 24th*, 1783.

DEAR GENERAL: Col. Wood disappointed me, and left town without my
answer to the favor which you did me the honor to write me, some time
since, and the casual conveyances which chance offers to your part of the
country, have not compensated for his neglect.

The change in our circumstances which the late pacification has made,
will now permit the secretary of war to carry into immediate execution
a resolve of Congress, directing him to furnish the medals, voted to those
whose distinguished merit has drawn that mark of applause and gratitude
from their country during the late war. You may depend upon my attention to yours, and if I have any talent at design (which, by the way, I
doubt extremely), it shall be aided by the assistance of those whose
imagination I esteem as elegant as correct, and I hope will eventually
produce what ought to equal your expectation, from the hands you
have committed it to, if it does not merit your approbation.

A late communication from the Comte de Vergennes, gives us every reason to expect a speedy completion of the definitive treaty. The paper however, which I do myself the honor to enclose, contains a very interesting debate. You will observe that the supplies are voted for the ensuing year on the war establishment, and it is plainly to be discovered that no orders had been sent to Sir Guy Carleton for the evacuation of New York on the 3d March, thus corroborating suspicions which a studied ambiguity of expression, and marked reserve in the communications of that officer, had before suggested. It will become a very serious step, the compliance with the stipulations of the provisional treaty on our part, particularly that article which directs the liberation of prisoners, the performance of which Sir Guy presses with incessant ardor. The reinforcement of so formidable a force as they now hold in the heart of our country, with 6,000 or 8,000 men, would be a perilous measure in the present disordered, nay distracted, state of our political systems. If we find that they hover over us to seize the first advantage which the paroxysms of disappointment and disgust may occasion, it will then require every exertion of the real patriots to strengthen the hands of government, relaxed to a degree that borders on anarchy. The councils of the United States are devoted to the grand objects of satisfying the demands of the army, and those public creditors whose zeal and confidence, have animated them to exertions ruinous to themselves, although contributing to the preservation of America. If the are properly supported, union and harmony may spring from a perman establishment of a happy government, enjoyed in peace at home and abroad. But if the separate states will pursue measures subversive of all public credit, and thwart the united councils by municipal prejudices, our revolution will be productive of scenes of confusion, destructive of foreign and domestic quiet.

Your exertions in directing the views of the Virginia line to the proper objects, have been similar to those that the general has, with a degree of firmness alone equal to the task, pursued in the grand army; and their consequences will be not less beneficial to America, than the most splendid military exertions. With sincere wishes for your health and happiness,

I am, dear general,

Your most obedient humble servant.

JOHN F. MERCER.

P.S. I had forgot to mention that the court of Spain had at length received Mr. Carmichael in his official character as charge d'affaires, although it came but with a bad grace. He had his audience the 10th of January. Mr. Van Beckel of Rotterdam, brother of our friend Mr. Van

Beckel the pensionary of Amsterdam, the father of the American interest in the States General, is appointed minister to the United States.

GEN. MORGAN.

The disbandment of the Virginia troops commanded by Morgan, gave rise to an incident, which, though signally creditable to his goodness of heart, was, singularly enough, afterwards interpreted much to his disadvantage, and for a considerable time excited great prejudices against him. The circumstances were these: the government had no money to pay the arrearages due to the soldiers when they were disbanded. In lieu of better means, it resorted to the issue of certificates, acknowledging the amount of debt, and promising payment at some future day. This was certainly a poor recompense to men, who, having encountered unheard of privations and perils, during a long and bloody war, in winning for the country the rich prize of independence and nationality, were now, penniless, ragged, and broken down in health and spirits, dismissed, and left to find their way to their distant homes as best they could. Their situation excited the sympathy of the generous and patriotic. It also attracted the attention of a knot of spectators, who, intent upon making money, no matter how, saw in the occasion nothing but the advantageous opening which it afforded them for a profitable investment. They did not neglect the golden opportunity, and soon they obtained a number of the soldiers' certificates for the most trifling and inadequate sums of ready money. Morgan, perceiving this, and indignant at the sacrifices to which his soldiers were reduced by their necessities to submit, resolved to counteract the sharpers as far as his influence and means would permit. He advised the men not to part with their certificates, which, he assured them, would certainly be paid at some future time, and perhaps, at an early day. In this event, he said, they would realize something like an adequate recompense for the great services which they had performed. He begged them to decline the speculators' unreasonable offers, and to trust to the kind and hospitable feelings of the inhabitants on their route, for food and lodging, until they reached their homes. But, he added, there might be a few who would be obliged to make every sacrifice to obtain money. To all such, he observed, that he was ready, as far as his means would go, to advance them upon their scrip double the amount offered by the speculators, he holding the scrip as security, subject to redemption, should the men desire it. He concluded by reiterating his advice, that they should hold fast to their certificates.

Contrary to Morgan's expectations, a number of the soldiers soon gathered around him, and stating their pressing need of money, importuned him to make good his generous offer. He was thus induced to receive as many of their certificates as the amount of funds he had on hand enabled him to accept.

This circumstance was instantly seized by the speculators, who, disappointed of their prey by the interference of Morgan, sought revenge in attributing to him the heartless selfishness by which they themselves had been actuated. They labored diligently in all directions, in charging him with the baseness of speculating upon the necessities of his own soldiers, and of exercising his influence as their commander, in obtaining their certificates for the smallest considerations. When the proneness of the human mind to receive the impressions of calumny, is duly considered, it will not appear surprising that these efforts should have proved measurably successful.

These false reports at length came to the ears of Washington, with whom, it may be remarked here, no combination of ennobling qualities could compensate for the absence of probity. He was so much offended at the unworthy part which Morgan was said to have acted, that he ceased to correspond with him, in one or two instances was heard to express his want of confidence in him, and at length, upon an occasion when they met, treated him with marked reserve. Morgan, equally grieved and mortified at conduct, the reasons for which he divined, but which he felt to be

18

undeserved, lost no time in requesting an explanation.   His conjectures proved correct. Washington promptly told him that his
conduct could not be friendly towards any man, who labored under
the charge of having profited by the distresses and necessities of the
soldiery.   Morgan's plain statement of the facts of the case, supported by the evidence of a number of the soldiers themselves, and
of corroborating circumstances, speedily convinced Washington
that he had been deceived.   He expressed himself perfectly satisfied, and admitted his regret at having given credence to a story,
the plausibility of which made him forget that it affected the
character of a man, hitherto high in his esteem, whose version of
the matter was, moreover, yet to be heard.   The friendly regard
which had previously existed between Washington and Morgan,
immediately revived, and was thenceforward strengthened by time,
until death interposed between them.

The reconciliation between Washington and Morgan, with the
attending circumstances, speedily became known, and contributed
not a little to silence the clamor which slander had raised against
the latter.   Not only this, it produced a reaction in the public
mind in his favor, which resulted in giving him a higher place in
the popular regard, than he had ever before occupied.*

The course of conduct adopted by Morgan towards his calumniators, from first to last, had the effect, perhaps, of aiding their
efforts.   He disdained to stoop to the defence of a character which
he supposed was sufficiently well established in the estimation of
his countrymen and friends, to render it invulnerable to such
assaults.   The only public manifestations of his feelings towards his
assailants which were ever given, were those in which he chastised
two or three of the number who had been particularly malignant,
and who had been luckless enough to throw themselves in his
way.

This was a mode of vindication, however, that was ill-calculated
to disarm his enemies: it was by no means acceptable to his

* MSS. Dr. Hill.

friends; nor was it likely to produce a conviction of his innocence, in the the minds of those unacquainted with the parties and the circumstances. Among the remonstrances which some of his difficulties of this kind elicited from his friends, is one one from Col. Charles M. Thurston, contained in a letter from that distinguished gentleman to Morgan, under date of August 22d, 1783. "I really am glad," observes this gentleman, "that your affair with * * * * * * is at an end. I never heard the particulars of it, nor of the warrant, until a few days ago. But why will you contend with people so much below you? You are placed now on an eminence, and should suffer the little people to pass by you in silence. * * * * * * * * If you expect to escape the tongue of malevolence and the shafts of envy, you expect more than falls to the lot of mortal man. There is, indeed, one way for it. Become obscure—undo your great actions, and be poor. No meddler will then think it worth his while to level his pop-gun at you. Despise the little petulance of the day, and you blunt its edge. Like new opinions in religion, it gains ground by opposition; and I would see the authors d—d before I would notice anything not spoken immediately in my presence. For, let me tell you, sir, your situation is much altered. Your reputation, fortune, and present station in life, demand of you to conduct yourself with greater complacency, affability, and condescension to all, in the same proportion that these have increased and improved." *

Without subscribing to the wisdom of a course of conduct, such as that recommended by Col. Thurston, which, as it appears to us, is calculated to render calumny successful in most cases, it must be admitted that the steps which Morgan took, were much more objectionable, and less likely to free him from the misrepresentations of his enemies.

* In a letter from President Washington to Col. Thurston, written in 1794, the following passage occurs: "I have a great regard for Gen Morgan, and respect his military talents; am persuaded, if a fit occasion should occur, no one would exert them with more zeal in the service of his country than he would."—*See Sparks's Washington's Writings*, vol. **5.**, p. 427.

CHAPTER XX.

Morgan in private life—Becomes wealthy, and rises in consideration—His younger daughter married to Major Heard—He obtains the Cowpens medal—Indian war—Defeat of
St. Clair, followed by preparations for a new campaign—Morgan appointed a brigadier
general—The excise law, and the consequences of its execution—Gen. Neville—
Appointed inspector—Resistance to the law assumes the form of rebellion—Meetings of
the insurgents—Gen. Neville's house attacked, and destroyed by fire—He and other
persons obnoxious to the insurgents obliged to flee—Meeting at Braddock's field—The
President resolves to maintain the laws—Sends commissioners to confer with the insurgents, and calls 15,000 men into service—The Convention at Parkinson's ferry—Morgan's opinion of the conduct of the insurgents—Is appointed major general of the
Virginia militia—His alarm for the safety of his daughter and her children—Prepares to
go to Pittsburg, but is dissuaded therefrom—Letter from Col. Neville—The alacrity with
which the Virginians obeyed the President's call for aid—Letter to the President—The
reply—Letter from Col. Hamilton—The militia advance into the theatre of disturbance
—Morgan marches to Pittsburg—Termination of the "whisky insurrection"—The
troops return home.

THE succeeding ten years of Morgan's career were spent in the
bosom of his family, and in the increase of his means and the
cultivation and improvement of his farm. It is not in the quietude
of domestic life that the reader will look for those stirring incidents
and those developments of character, the sum of which forms
the hero's claim upon the recollection of posterity. A brief
review of the leading events which marked this portion of his
life, will, it is presumed, be deemed sufficient.

The habits of saving industry which distinguished Morgan
during his early career, had not been forgotten. He labored
diligently and judiciously in removing the embarrassments which
had gathered around his affairs during the war, and in rendering
his property productive. He had obtained from government, and

had acquired by purchase, titles to large quantities of land on both sides of the Ohio and on the head waters of the Mononga-hela rivers. In the year 1796, he owned not less than 250,000 acres of land. Thus he soon acquired the additional considera-tion which wealth seldom fails to confer even upon the great.

His family mansion was now the resort of people of the first rank in society. He had so far cultivated his mind and improved his manners, as to be at ease among men of talent and refinement. The amiability of his wife, and .the beauty and accomplishments of his daughters, contributéd largely to the consideration which attached to the family. The elder of his daughters, as has been already mentioned, had intermarried with Col. Presley Neville. The younger, Miss Betsey, was married to Major James Heard,* of New Jersey, during the year 1786. Both Mrs. Neville and Mrs. Heard resided with their parents several years subsequently to their marriage.

It was not until the year 1790 that Morgan obtained the Cow-pens medal.† The pecuniary difficulties of the Treasury Depart

---

* Major James Heard was the son of an English gentleman, who emigrated to America, and settled in New Jersey about the year 1755. At the opening of the revolutionary war, the major was the only member of his family who espoused the cause of the colonists. He joined the standard of his country at an early stage of the conflict, and continued in the service to the close of the war. At first, he held a commission of lieutenant, in one of the regiments composing Maxwell's brigade. He was subsequently promoted to a cap-taincy, and finally to a majority. He shared in the campaigns of 1777 and 1778 in Penn-sylvania and New Jersey. During this period he formed the acquaintance of Col. Morgan. The latter, upon retiring from the service in 1779, invited Major Heard to spend a few weeks with him at his residence in Virginia. The major, soon afterwards availing him-self of this invitation, saw and became attached to the colonel's younger daughter. From this time until his marriage, he was a frequent visitor at "Saratoga."

† When, in 1784, Col. David Humphreys proceeded to Paris, as secretary of the Ameri-can commissioners there, the execution of the Cowpens medals was confided to him. The colonel returning to America before much progress was made, it devolved upon Mr. Jef-ferson to superintend the completion of the medals. When the latter returned from France, he brought with him two complete sets, and delivered them to President Washing-ton, the one in silver for the President, and the other in gold and silver, as voted by Congress, for the officers. That to Gen. Morgan was of gold. Each die cost 2,400 francs, and the gold for the medal was four hundred francs as an additional charge. Congress had directed copies in silver to be presented to the different sovereigns of Europe, and to

ment had hitherto deferred his strong desire to obtain this testi-
monial of his country's regard. The medal was accompanied by
the following letter from the President.

NEW YORK, *March 25th*, 1790.

SIR: You will receive with this a medal, struck by order of the late
Congress, in commemoration of your much approved conduct in the battle
of the Cowpens, and presented to you as a mark of the high sense which
your country entertains of your services on that occasion.

This medal was put into my hands by Mr. Jefferson, and it is with singular
pleasure that I now transmit it to you.

I am, Sir, &c.,

GEORGE WASHINGTON.

GEN. MORGAN.

For the four or five years preceding the fall of 1791, hostilities
existed between the United States and the Indians on the Northwestern frontier. Generals Harmar, Scott, Wilkinson and St. Clair
had been successively sent against them. The results of these
expeditions were in every instance partial or unsatisfactory, and in

the Universities of that quarter and of our own. This part of the business was, however,
never executed.

This medal, at the death of Gen. Morgan, passed into the possession of his son-in-law, Col.
Neville; and when he died, it became the property of his eldest son, the late Major Morgan Neville. It was subsequently stolen from the Bank of Pittsburg, where, with other
valuables, it had been deposited. In the year 1836, an act of Congress was passed, directing that another medal be struck and presented to Major Neville. Much time was spent
in unavailing inquiries and search for the dies of the original medal, with which it was
designed to strike the new copy. Directions had been given to deposit them in the office
of Mr. Grand, the banker of the United States. It is believed that they were subsequently
transferred to the Treasury Department. In neither of these places, however, were they
to be found. In the year 1838, it was ascertained that the copy of the medal which Mr.
Jefferson presented to Washington was then in the possession of the Hon. Daniel Webster.
From this gentleman the copy referred to was obtained and sent to Paris, with directions
to Mr. Cass, then our minister to France, to have dies cut according to it. It was not,
however, until the year 1840, that the medal was ready for delivery. But in the meantime, Major Neville died; and the act authorizing the medal to be struck specially directing that it be delivered to him, some time was spent in determining what disposition should
be made of it. The difficulty was at length terminated by the Hon. Jno. Bell, Secretary
of the Treasury, who, on the 11th of September, 1841, transmitted the medal, with a letter
appropriate to the occasion, to the eldest son of the deceased, Morgan L. Neville, Esq., of
Cincinnati, who died recently.

that of General St. Clair, most disastrous. In the defeat which this officer sustained at the Miami villages, on the 19th of November, 1791,* General Butler, formerly Morgan's lieutenant-colonel, was among the slain.

The news of this defeat was followed by the passage of an act of Congress, authorizing the enlistment of three additional regiments of infantry, and a squadron of cavalry.† The resignation of Gen. St. Clair, called for the appointment of another officer to take the command of the army, which, it had already been resolved, should be organized and sent against the Indians without delay. Among the officers spoken of by the President in connection with this command, was Gen. Morgan.‡ It was conferred upon Gen. Wayne, an officer equally worthy of the trust, as was proved by his previous no less than by his subsequent successes.

About the same time Morgan was appointed a brigadier general,§ with reference to a command in the army under Wayne. He would in all probability have participated in the campaign which, two years afterwards, terminated in the overthrow of the Indians at the Miamis, had it not been that in the meantime, a different direction was given to his services. This change had relation to matters, deemed at the time of great moment, the facts and circumstances of which will now briefly be considered.

* Marshall's Washington, vol. ii., p. 218.   † Ibidem, p. 223.
‡ Sparks's Writings of Washington, p. 243.

§ WAR DEPARTMENT, *April 12th*, 1792.

SIR : I have the honor to inform you that the President of the United States, by and with the advice and consent of the Senate, has appointed you a Brigadier General in the army of the United States.

You will please immediately to signify your acceptance or non-acceptance of this appointment ; in case of your acceptance, you will for the present give every stimulus in your power , to further on the recruiting service in your quarter.

In order that you may judge of the pay, rations and emoluments for the commissioned and non-commissioned officers and privates in the service of the United States, I enclose you the act of Congress relative to the military establishment.

I have the honor to be, &c.

H. KNOX.
Secretary War.

GEN. DANIEL MORGAN.

On the 3rd March, 1791, Congress passed an act, imposing duties upon foreign and domestic distilled spirits. That portion of the act which laid a duty upon domestic spirits was strenuously opposed by most of the representatives from the southern and western States, and by the people generally in those sections of the Union, it was regarded in a very odious light. In the western counties of Pennsylvania and the country adjacent, particularly where the political bias and the private interests of the people united in rendering the law very objectionable, there was manifested from the outset, a determination to evade or refuse a compliance with its obnoxious provisions.

It would be foreign to the object of this work to enter into the details of the consequences, which, for a period of nearly four years, followed the adoption of the policy, embodied in what was termed at the time " the excise law." At first, opposition to the law was confined to public expressions of hostility to its objectionable features, to the extension and organization of public sentiment against its enforcement, and to such other legal expedients as were calculated to bring about its repeal. An opinion which subsequently became current, that the law would be repealed or greatly modified at the coming session of Congress, allayed public excitement for a time. But the disappointment of this expectation by the passage of the act of May 8th, 1792, rekindled into a flame fiercer than ever, the smouldering embers of popular discontent. The law, and the influences to which its passage was ascribed, were denounced in the fiercest terms, a refusal to comply with its obnoxious provisions was openly proclaimed, and its unconditional repeal was earnestly demanded. To defeat its operation no expedient was left untried, and those citizens who persisted in holding offices under it, and in carrying out its requirements, were shut out from the fellowship of their neighbors, and held as outcasts from society. A forcible opposition to the law was now openly recommended, and speedily carried into effect. In fact, resistance at length assumed all the forms of rebellion.

The President had, from the first, doubted the expediency of the law,* and finding that its operation was very unpalatable to the people of the western and southern States, he took pains to see that its execution was not enforced with unnecessary rigor. Though greatly moved at proceedings, which it appears were regarded by a majority of his cabinet as indicative of hostility to the constitutional compact which the States had recently formed, he determined to carry forbearance and conciliation to their utmost limits, before he resorted to force. Congress, under a sectional influence which had not hitherto manifested much regard for the west, displayed in the several measures passed during this period, in relation to the law of 1791, and the disturbances to which it had given rise, a spirit more threatening than conciliatory. The acts amendatory of this law, which were passed, preserved unimpaired the obnoxious provisions of the original law, while those passed about the same time for organizing and calling out the militia, with a view to " the execution of the laws," and " the suppression of insurrection," had an unmistakable reference to the scene of discontent.

Among the means employed by the President to induce the people in the disaffected counties of western Pennsylvania to acquiesce in the execution of the law, was the appointment of those charged with that duty, from the most influential and popular of their numbers. In pursuance of this policy, Gen. John Neville †

* Sparks's Writings of Washington, vol. x., p. 250.

† Gen. Neville had been one of the most zealous patriots of the revolution, a man of great wealth and unbounded benevolence. From his own resources alone, he had organized, equipped, and supplied a company of troops, including his son as an officer, which he had marched at his own expense to Boston, to reinforce the command of Gen. Washington, in support of the declaration of independence. During the " starving years," of the early settlement on the upper Ohio and Monongahela, he had contributed greatly to the relief and comforts of the destitute and suffering pioneers, and when necessary, he had divided his last loaf with the needy. In seasons of more than ordinary scarcity, when his wheat matured, he opened his fields to those who were destitute of bread. By blood and marriage he was related to some of the most distinguished officers of the revolutionary armies; and such was his popularity in the west, that, had it been possible for any one to have enforced this odious law, Gen. Neville was the man. *Monette's Valley of the Mississippi*, vol. ii., p., 205.

18*

was appointed inspector for western Pennsylvania. In the mind of this patriotic citizen, the sense of public duty was too strong for the suggestions of prudence, and in disregard of the perils, losses, and mortifications which he clearly foresaw the office would bring in its train, he promptly accepted it.

His first step, after entering upon the duties of his office, was to select his deputies from among the most popular and worthy of his fellow-citizens. He then proceeded in a spirit of forbearance, to put the law into execution. Against the perpetrators of some of the outrages which had been committed, bills of indictment had been found by a court of the United States. Process was accordingly directed to issue against these persons, and also against a number of non-complying distillers.[*]

In the execution of this duty the marshals were met by force and violence. Disregarding the warnings to desist from their purposes, some of these officers were beaten, others were tarred and feathered, and one was waylaid on the road by a body of armed men, who fired upon him, fortunately without effect.

General Neville now became the object upon whom the infuriated community sought to wreak its vengeance. His patriotism, his moral worth, his benevolence to the poor, and his services to the country, were all forgotten in the present causes of resentment against him. On the morning of the 16th of July, a party of the insurgents attacked his dwelling. Fortunately, he was apprised of the danger in time to prepare himself. His defence was so resolute as to oblige his assailants to retire.[†]

Justly apprehending that this attack would be repeated, General Neville applied to the militia officers and the magistrates of the county for protection. But the spirit of disaffection had become so general, that the few who remained free from its influence, were afraid to array themselves in opposition to its progress. The answer to General Neville's application, was that "owing to the too general combination of the people to oppose the revenue

* Marshall, vol. ii, p. 341.   † Ibid.

GENERAL DANIEL MORGAN. 419

system, the laws could not be executed so as to afford him protection : that should the *posse comitatus* be ordered out to support the civil authority, they would favor the party of the rioters."

He next applied to the commanding officer at Fort Pitt, and, on this occasion, he was more successful. That officer sent eleven of his garrison to guard the general's premises. These were soon after joined by Major Kirkpatrick, an old and worthy soldier of the revolution, and an intimate friend of General Neville, and his family.

Immediately following the issue of the process already referred to, public meetings were held by the insurgents in all the towns and settlements within the disaffected region. On the same day that General Neville's house was attacked, a meeting of the insurgents assembled at Braddock's Field, where it was resolved that the attack should be renewed, the general seized, and measures taken to compel him to resign his office, and to give up his papers.

With these objects in view, the insurgents, to the number of 500, assembled on the evening of the same day, at the appointed rendezvous, and thence proceeded to the house of General Neville. On their approach, the general, yielding to the importunities of Major Kirkpatrick, withdrew from the house and retired to Pittsburg. The major then assumed command of the soldiers, together with four or five male domestics, who had armed themselves ; and with this little force, he determined to resist the expected attack. In due time, the insurgents arrived. A parley was held, during which they demanded that the inspector and all his papers should be delivered to them, and that the party in the house should march out and ground their arms. To the first demand, Major Kirkpatrick replied that the inspector was not on the premises ; and to the second he gave a positive refusal. The assault hereupon commenced. The contest was warmly maintained for some time ; when the leader of the insurgents, Major

* Marshal, ii., p. 341.

McFarlane, being shot down, and several of his followers being wounded, the remainder, finding the fire of the garrison too hot for them, retired.*

At first, it was supposed the assailants had abandoned their design. But in a short time it was discovered, by the blazing outhouses,that they had merely changed their mode of attack. Major Kirkpatrick, desirous of saving the main building from the flames, and perceiving that it was useless longer to contend against a force so formidable in numbers, and desperate in purpose, surrendered. But the demon of destruction was unchained, and beyond control. The splendid mansion was first rifled, and then the torch was applied, which soon reduced it to a heap of ruins. †

For some time prior to these events, Mrs. Neville, the wife of Col. Presley Neville, and the elder daughter of Gen. Morgan, had been on a visit to the house of her father-in-law. At the first indications of danger, she, with her children, and the other female members of the family, were removed to the house of a friend in Pittsburg. Colonel Neville was at this place, when information reached him of the contemplated attack upon his father's house. While on his way thither, in company with the United States marshal, they were both arrested by the insurgents. The colonel, though held under restraint for a few hours, experienced no other indignity. The marshal was treated with extreme rigor, however, and obtained his liberty, only by solemnly promising to serve no more processes on the western side of the Alleghany mountains.

The insurgents, emboldened by the success which had hitherto attended their outrageous proceedings, soon after deputed two of their number, one of whom was a justice of the peace, to proceed to Pittsburg, and to demand of the marshal a surrender of all his processes, and of the inspector, a resignation of his office, threatening, in case of refusal, to attack the place, and seize their persons. The marshal and the inspector refused to comply with these demands. Unwilling, however, to subject the town to an attack, they left their families to the care of the inhabitants, and descending the Ohio, escaped the danger which threatened them. They were accompanied by Major Kirkpatrick, Colonel Neville, and several other persons, who had been proscribed by the insurgents.

Soon after this event, a number of the inhabitants of Pittsburg were obliged to flee from their homes, in consequence of the discovery that they had written to Philadelphia, and other places, disapproving of the conduct of the insurgents. To the enormities already committed by the latter, that of rifling the mail was now added.

The insurgents were now governed by the impression that they had achieved a complete and lasting triumph over the "Excise Laws," and that it only required an organization and display of their numbers, to intimidate government into an acquiescence in their demands. They seemed resolved that there should be no neutrals in the country. Many of those who had hitherto joined in denouncing the excise law, and in countenancing resistance to its execution, were not prepared to carry opposition to the extent of insurrection. Meetings were proposed by the friends of order, for the purpose of concerting measures for their own security. But so much time was lost in deliberation, that in the meantime, the insurgents became too strong to be resisted.

Soon after the destruction of Gen. Neville's house,* a general meeting of the insurgents was held at Braddock's Field to decide upon the measures which should thenceforward be taken in relation to the excise. About four thousand assembled, and an attorney named Bradford, was appointed to the command. A committee was appointed to report a plan of future action, of which H. H. Breckenridge, a distinguished lawyer of Pittsburg, and an opponent of the excise law and of other measures of the administration, was a member. Contrary to the expectations of the more violent of the assemblage, Mr. Breckenridge took ground

* American Pioneer, p. 209.

in opposition to forcible resistance. He succeeded in dissuading the committee from recommending unlawful measures, and urged a course of modei ation until the effect of their past resistance should be known. The report of the committee was in accordance with these suggestions. It merely recommended the holding of a convention, by delegates from the several towns in the disaffected region, at Parkinson's Ferry, on the evening 14th of August.

On receiving this report, much dissatisfaction was manifested by a considerable part of the assemblage.* It was adopted however, and therefore, the meeting adjourned. The more orderly of the insurgents immediately returned to their homes. The remainder, to the number of about 2,000, marched towards Pittsburg. After parading through the streets for some time, a large number proposed to set fire to the town. Being dissuaded from this design by the others, they contented themselves with burning the mansion of Major Kirkpatrick, and then departed.†

From this time, until the assemblage of the convention at Parkinson's Ferry, many of the more active and reckless of the insurgents, freed from all the restraint of law, and rendered desperate from the fear of failing successfully to resist it, traversed the country to ensure the election of delegates to their liking, and to intimidate the well-affected. Yet, in the face of this danger, † many of the towns sent delegates to the convention, who were disposed to submit to the law and its administration.

The crisis had at length arrived, which presented to the President the alternative, either to submit to lawless resistance, or to crush it. He met the emergency with that firmness which formed so conspicuous a feature in his character. The wisdom of the measures he adopted was proved by the gratifying results which they produced.

As a last effort at conciliation, before a resort was had to force,

* American Pioneer, p. 209.
† Ibid. p. 210.

three commissioners were appointed by the President, with directions to go to the disaffected region, and to offer pardon to all offenders who should abandon their evil practices and submit to the law. A proclamation was issued at the same time, warning the insurgents, that unless they should disperse before the 1st of September, the law empowering him to call out the militia would be put into execution.

The commissioners reached the disaffected region in time to confer with the convention, then in session at Parkinson's Ferry. Their efforts were so far successful, as to elicit from this body the admission, that it was in favor of submission to the laws. Not having been authorized by the people to make any terms with the general government, a majority of the convention declined to act, however, and referred the question back to the primary town meetings.*

On the 2d of September, a proclamation was issued by the President. He likewise made a requisition upon the governors of New Jersey, Pennsylvania, Maryland, and Virginia, for their respective quotas of militia, to form an army which ultimately numbered 15,000 men.

With this lengthy, but, it is believed, not unnecessary episode, we return to Morgan, whose active and prominent participation in the events subsequently brought about by the insurrection, will will now engage attention in connection with the events themselves.

Morgan was not an unconcerned spectator of the disorders, an outline of which has just been given. He marked their growing magnitude with feelings of surprise and indignation, that were referable to his admiration of the infant institutions of the country, his respect for the laws, and his regard for their chief administrator. While sharing in the belief, so generally but errone ously entertained by the members of the federal party at the time, that these disorders were the preliminary steps to a meditated separation of the territory west of the mountains from

* Marshall's Washington, vol. ii., p. 348.

the Union, he warmly coincided in the wisdom of asserting, peace-
ably if possible, but forcibly, if necessary, the sovereignty of the
laws, and the integrity of the national compact.

During the preceding December, Morgan was appointed by the
authorities of Virginia, major-general * of the militia of that State.
His attention was thereafter diverted from the military operations
against the Indians, to those which, it was already foreseen, would
ultimately have to be resorted to against the insurgents, as the
only means of suppressing their lawless proceedings.

But strong as were his feelings upon this subject, they were as
nothing, when compared with those he experienced upon being
informed of the more recent proceedings of the insurgents.
Before the actual circumstances which attended the destruction of
Gen. Neville's property became known to him, rumor had imparted to them a much more sanguinary coloring than they deserved.
At first he was led to believe that his old and valued friends, Gen.
Neville, and Major Kirkpatrick, his much-loved son-in-law, Col.
Presley Neville, and his favorite daughter, the colonel's wife, and
her children, had fallen a sacrifice to the fury of the insurgents.
The anguish of mind which this impression produced, was associa-
ted with feelings of the liveliest indignation, and an intense desire
to visit the supposed murderers with the severest chastisement.

His mind was soon after relieved from impressions so painful,
by receiving a correct version of the circumstances, in which his
feelings as a friend and a father were so deeply involved. Learning,
however, that his daughter and her children had necessarily been left
at Pittsburg, upon the compulsory departure thence of her husband,

---

* THE COMMONWEALTH OF VIRGINIA.

To DANIEL MORGAN, ESQ.: Know you that the General Assembly, having, from their
confidence in your fidelity, courage, and good conduct, appointed you major-general in
the militia, our governor, with advice of council, pursuant to the power vested in him by
law doth hereby commission you, the said Daniel Morgan, as major-general.

In testimony whereof, these our letters are sealed with the seal of the Commonwealth,
and made patent. Witness, Henry Lee, Esq., our said governor, at Richmond, this
eleventh day of December, one thousand seven hundred and ninety-three.

HENRY LEE

and apprehending that she was in danger from the animosity whicl
the insurgents evinced towards Gen. Neville and his family, Morgar.
determined at once to embody as many of his friends and former
associates in arms as would follow him, and proceeding to Pittsburg, bring her and her children back with him to Frederick. He
was with difficulty dissuaded from a purpose, which, it was represented to him, might create the danger which was then only
imaginary, would certainly fail in the execution, and perhaps cost
him his life. The history of the American people furnishes no
instance in which their exasperations have extended to defenceless
women and children. Parental solicitude may have blinded him
to a fact, so creditable to his countrymen, and so irreconcilable
with his misgivings. But the receipt at this juncture, of a letter
from Colonel Neville, allayed his fears for his daughter's safety,
and induced him to abandon his design.

An extract or two from this letter may be introduced here.
After a brief detail of the events which transpired, from the
burning of his father's house and his escape from Pittsburg until
his arrival at Philadelphia, where the letter was written, Colonel
Neville observes: "But to relieve your anxiety, I come immediately to the point, and inform you that Nancy and the children
are well; that she behaved with resolution and dignity during
the business; and, indeed, evinced a fortitude and strength of
nerves that I did not expect, especially as she had not been very
well. *   *   *   She is safe at Pittsburg, respected by
the people, and if necessary, will be protected by the military.
*   *   *   I know she is safe, beyond the reach of danger
and of insult, and very well; yet there is no circumstance in life
could affect me like leaving such a family in such a situation."
A little farther on, the colonel remarks: "I yesterday received
a letter from a gentleman in that country. He writes me that
they have heard you are to command the Virginians. It had
also been mentioned that you intended to go out and look
after my family. He begged me, in the most earnest terms,

to prevent your going, as they would most assuredly insult and even destroy you, and that it might put my family, who are now safe, in a dangerous situation."

Immediately upon the promulgation of the President's proclamation, and the issue of the consequent orders,* calling out the militia, those of Virginia displayed the greatest alacrity and zeal in assembling. In Frederic and Berkley counties, particularly, where Morgan's influence was felt and acknowledged, the men all volunteered. From the want of arms, however, and the delay occasioned in transporting them from New London, the men, after being twice assembled, were as often permitted to return to their homes.† A commendable spirit was likewise evinced by the militia of the other States, in responding to the summons of the President.. At first, it was feared that in Pennsylvania, from the unpopularity of the law which had caused the disturbances, and from the distaste for a service, which might involve the obligation of spilling kindred blood, the militia would not assemble. But the proceedings of the legislature of that State, seconded by the personal influence and exertions

---

* The orders to Morgan were contained in the following letter from the Secretary of the Treasury :—

WAR DEPARTMENT, *Sept.* 18, 1794.

SIR: I am instructed by the President to express to you his wish that every particular exertion may be made to accelerate the assembling of the militia at their appointed place of rendezvous, Winchester, and the vicinity of old Fort Pleasant, alias Moorefield. You are probably informed that a junction of the Virginia and Maryland troops at Fort Cumberland has been contemplated. You are at liberty to hasten to that point all such as may be ready, and which you judge it advisable should move that way. But if you think that those who are to assemble at Moorefield had better proceed by a route different from that of Fort Cumberland, they may continue at Moorefield till further instruction.

With consideration and esteem,

I am, Sir, your obedient servant,

A. HAMILTON.

P.S.—It will be well to have runners sent into the insurgent counties to ascertain what they are about, the degree of unanimity and probable strength. Colonel Carrington will furnish the means.

MAJOR-GEN. MORGAN.

† Letter to the Sec. of War, Jan 26, 1795.

of Governor Mifflin, soon brought into the field the quota of men required.

In reference to this and other circumstances just mentioned, and in illustration of the views and feelings with regard to the insurrection, which governed both Washington and Morgan at this time, the following letters which passed between them are inserted:

WINCHESTER, *Sept.* 24, 1794.

SIR : I am sorry to understand the difficulty experienced in the State of Pennsylvania to raise the quota of men, to suppress that horrid insurrection on their frontiers. The State of Virginia seems to be unanimous and determined to suppress it : and it is my opinion that we shall in a very few days have men enough at this post to do that business. For my part, I wish I was at Morgantown at this time with 2,000 men, which would be as many as I could ask with what would join me at that place, to bring these people to order. They are very much alarmed at this time. This I have from the best intelligence.

We have been greatly disappointed with respect to arms. Only 400 stand have yet arrived, and those came from Philadelphia. We have been expecting 1,500 stand from New London, and have applied to the executive of Virginia for 3,000 stand. Those and the arms from New London will, I expect, arrive nearly the same time, which will be about the last of this month.

I wish an accommodation may not be patched up with these rioters, under an apprehension of not getting troops to suppress them. Virginia could and would furnish an army sufficient for that purpose. A young man, a brother to Colonel Heth, gave me the best account of these people that I have had. He was at Braddock's Field, and says there were not four thousand men of all descriptions assembled there ; that there were not more than one thousand guns among them ; and if the ammunition had been divided among them, he does not suppose there would be more than one round a man.

For my own part, I think it a very easy matter to bring these people into order. I don't wish to spill the blood of a citizen ; but I wish to march against these people, to show them our determination to bring them to order and to support the laws. I took the liberty to write you this, lest your intelligence might not be so good, or that this might throw some light, or be of some service.

I have the honor, &c.,

DANIEL MORGAN.

His Excellency the President of the United States.

CARLISLE, *October* 8, 1794.

DEAR SIR: On the moment I was leaving the city of Philadelphia for this place, your letter of the 24th ultimo, was put into my hands.

Although I regret the occasion which has called you into the field, I rejoice to hear you are there; and because it is probable I may meet you at Fort Cumberland, whither I shall proceed, as soon as I see the troops at this rendezvous in condition to advance. At that place, or at Bedford, my ulterior resolution must be taken, either to advance with the troops into the insurgent counties of this State, or to return to Philadelphia, for the purpose of meeting Congress the 3rd of next month.

Imperious circumstances alone can justify my absence from the seat of government whilst Congress are in session; but if then, from the disposition of the people in the refractory counties, and the state of the information I expect to receive at the advanced posts, should appear to exist, the lesser must yield to the greater duties of my office, and I shall cross the mountains with the troops; if not, I shall place the command of the combined force under the orders of Governor Lee, of Virginia, and repair to the seat of government.

I am perfectly in sentiment with you, that the business we are drawn out upon, should be effectually executed, and that the daring and factious spirit which has arisen (to overturn the laws, and to subvert the Constitution), ought to be subdued. If this is not done, there is an end of, and we may bid adieu to, all government in this country, except mob, or club government, from whence nothing but anarchy and confusion can ensue. For, if the minority—and a small one, too—is suffered to dictate to the majority, after measures have undergone the most solemn discussion by the representatives of the people, and their will, through this medium, is enacted into laws, there can be no security for life, liberty, or property; nor, if the laws are not to govern, can any man know how to conduct himself with safety; for there never was a law yet made, I conceive, that hit the taste exactly of every man, or every part of the community. Of course, if this be a reason for opposition, no law can be executed at all without force; and every man or set of men will, in that case, cut and carve for themselves. The consequences of which must be deprecated by every class of men who are friends to order, and to the peace and happiness of the country. But how can things be otherwise than they are, when clubs and societies have been instituted for the express purpose (though clothed in another garb), by their diabolical leader, G————t, whose object was to saw sedition—to poison the minds of the people of this country, and to make them discontented with the government of it, and who have labored indefatigably to effect these purposes.

As arms, &c., have been sent on from Philadelphia, in aid of those from New London, I hope and trust your supplies have been ample. I shall add no more at present, but my best wishes and sincere regard for you, and that   I am, dear sir,

Your ob't serv't,
GEO. WASHINGTON.

MAJ. GEN. MORGAN.

At length, the necessary supply of arms and ammr ..:on having been received, the volunteers, who for the third time had assembled at Winchester, were organized into a brigade of infantry and a regiment of cavalry. The other division of the Virginia troops had in the meantime assembled and been organized at Moorefields. The quota of Virginia had been for some days in readiness to march, when the President's proclamation of the 25th September appearing, the troops were put in motion.*

The forces of Pennsylvania and New Jersey were directed to rendezvous at Bedford, Pa., and those of Maryland and Virginia, at Cumberland, Md. The Governors of Maryland, New Jersey, and Pennsylvania, and General Morgan, now senior major general of Virginia, were at the head of the troops of their respective States. The command of the expedition had been conferred upon Governor Lee, of Virginia.*

Late in October, the troops from Eastern Pennsylvania, and New Jersey, being well advanced towards Bedford, the Virginians marched towards Cumberland, whither also the Maryland troops

* Marshall's Wash., vol. ii., p. 347.

were tending. Upon the arrival of the troops at their respective rendezvous, they were inspected by the President. Perceiving, from the great strength of the army, that it must necessarily look down every thing like opposition; and judging from the information which had reached him, that the insurgents were prepared for unconditional submission, he relinquished his preconceived design of crossing the mountains, and returned to Philadelphia.

While a part of the Virginia troops were advancing towards Cumberland, Morgan, at the head of a division which included the whole of the light troops, and a regiment of cavalry, marched towards Uniontown, which place he reached about the close of the month. Here Gen. Lee promulgated his plan of operations. The Pennsylvania and New Jersey troops, who composed the right wing of the army, were directed to take position, with their left towards Budd's ferry, and their right towards Greensburg. The Virginians and Marylanders, who formed the left wing, were ordered to occupy a line between the Monongahela and Youghiogany rivers, with their left towards the former and their right towards the latter. A few days were passed in carrying these dispositions into effect, when Morgan with the light troops and cavalry advanced into Washington county. While the main divisions were in advance upon the disaffected region, Morgan with his command accompanied by Colonel Hamilton* and a *corps judicial* crossed the Monongahela and arrived in the neighborhood of Pittsburg on the 16th November. In Gen. Morgan's train were also a number of those who had been forced to fly beyond the reach of the insurgents, including, among others, Gen. John Neville, Col. Presley Neville, and Major Kirkpatrick.

The people of Pittsburg had from the first been free from the moral infection which prevailed so virulently in the surrounding country. During the height of the disturbances, they had been intimidated by the numbers and the violence of the malcontents, into an acquiescence in their wishes. Latterly, however, encouraged by

* Col. Hamilton ; Writings of Washington p., 451.

the prospect of protection from the government, and by the orders which had been sent to Colonel Butler, the commander of Fort Pitt, to afford the Pittsburg people every assistance and protection in his power, they had made a public declaration in favor c᷑ the laws, had associated and armed themselves against the insurgents, and had invited back their exiles. They received the Virginia troops with every demonstration of joy, and proffered their assistance in pointing out and arresting those, who had made themselves conspicuous in the recent outrageous proceedings.

Before the requisition of the President for a militia force was complied with, the moral sense of much the larger portion of the people in the disaffected region had received a startling shock from the outrages which had been committed upon the persons and property of Gen. Neville and others. But although they discountenanced a farther resort to force, and evinced a disposition to confine their opposition to the excise law, to the legal means calculated to bring about its repeal, still a violent and unreflecting minority remained, who were only to be checked by fear or force. The news of Wayne's victory over the Indians, which reached the disaffected region about this time, admonished the lawless, that the reign of anarchy must speedily cease, if they would avoid the advance upon them of the general and his victorious troops. But when the militia marched from Cumberland and Carlyle into their country, a general panic siezed the malcontents; Bradford and a few of the most obnoxious leaders of the disaffected, fled to the country on the Mississippi, and the last remnant of resistance disappeared.

Thus happily terminated, without the·spilling of a drop of blood or the firing of a hostile shot, the event in our national history popularly known as the " whisky insurrection."

As it has already been observed, the assembly of the militia at their appointed rendezvous put an end to open opposition to law in the disaffected region. Their subsequent advance was recommended, only for the moral effect which the presence of such an imposing force would naturally have on the minds of those who were not as yet sufficiently impressed with the enormity of their offence, nor with the power of the government to punish them. The troops had not occupied the position assigned them more than two or three days, when they were ordered homeward. The Virginians moved by way of Morgantown to Winchester; the Marylanders through Uniontown towards Williamsport and the Pennsylvania and New Jersey troops, by the old Pennsylvania route to Bedford.

CHAPTER XXI.

NOTWITHSTANDING the triumph which the laws had achieved in the termination of all opposition to their enforcement, it was manifest that the spirit of resistance was still secretly cherished by a large number of the people in the disaffected region, and that, without the presence of a considerable body of troops to keep this spirit down, it might revive again. Such a force was doubly necessary, when the reign of law and order was to be re-established, and when those who had made themselves conspicuous in the recent disorders were to be apprehended and punished. Accordingly, before Gen. Lee returned to Virginia, he directed Morgan, with the volunteers from Frederic and Berkley, to remain in the disaffected country, until authority should be obtained to raise a corps to serve in that quarter during the winter, which corps he was also to command.

Congress expressed its sense of the conduct of the militia on the late occasion, by a resolution of thanks, a copy of which was transmitted to Morgan, together with a complimentary letter from the

Secretary of War. * That body also passed a bill, authorizing the establishment in the disaffected district, of a military corps, to serve for six months. The enlistment of this corps commenced in anticipation of the legal authority; too long after the departure of the different divisions of militia, however, to enable the recruit-ing officers to fill its ranks as rapidly as was desired. When at length, the enlistments were completed, the organized corps num-bered about six hundred infantry and two hundred cavalry, and a company of artillery, with two pieces.

This force was soon after removed to a position on the Monon-gahela, near McFarlane's Ferry, where Morgan established his camp, and where he caused huts to be erected for the accommo-dation of his men during the winter.

In the meantime, the judicial tribunal instituted by Col. Ham-

---

* The resolution, and all of the secretary's letter having reference thereto, are appen-ded.

DEPARTMENT OF STATE, *Dec. 6th*, 1794.

SIR : Learning that his excellency, Gov. Lee, has departed for Virginia, permit me to address myself to you as the commanding officer of the troops to be posted in the western counties during the present winter.

It affords me great pleasure to be the channel whereby to communicate the enclosed resolve of the House of Representatives, so highly honorable to the militia comprehended therein. You will please to cause this to be published in orders, and upon the parades.

* * * * * * * * * * * * *

I have the honor to enclose you a copy of the law, authorizing the troops in the west-ern counties.

I have the honor, &c.,

MAJ. GEN. MORGAN.   H. KNOX,
                                                                              Sec. War.

CONGRESS OF THE UNITED STATES.

IN THE HOUSE OF REPRESENTATIVES, *Thursday, 4th Dec.*, 1794.

Resolved, unanimously, That the thanks of this House be given to the gallant officers and privates of the militia of the States of New Jersey, Pennsylvania, Maryland and Virginia, who, on the late call of the President, rallied round the standard of the laws; and in the prompt and severe services which they encountered, bore the most illustrious testimony to the value of the Constitution, and the blessings of internal peace and order; and that the President be requested to communicate the above resolution of thanks, in such manner as he may judge most acceptable to the patriotic citizens who are its objects.   *Attest.*

                             Signed   JOHN BUCKLEY,
                                                              Clerk.

ilton for the trial of the insurgents, had made considerable progress. A list of the names of the ringleaders having been made out, it was put into the hands of the marshal and his deputies, who, supported by detachments of the military, succeeded in a short time in arresting a large number.

Col. Hamilton returning soon after to the seat of government, the prosecution of this business devolved upon Gen. Morgan. The measures taken by him were of a milder character than those which had previously been pursued, and their good effects were speedily perceptible. A short time elapsed, after the appearance of a proclamation promulgated by him about this time, when a number of the principal insurgents emerged from their hiding places, and gave themselves up to him. Among these, as appears in one of Morgan's letters, were Arthur Gardner, George Parker, Ebenezer Golohan, John Colecraft, John Mitchell, Benjamin Parkinson, and Daniel Hamilton. All these men were permitted to depart to their homes on parole, upon condition that they would surrender themselves when required. His representations of the unjustifiable nature of their recent conduct, and his assurances of the merciful disposition of government towards them in the event of their abandonment of all designs of an unlawful character, were attended with the best effects. Few of these men violated their parole, and many of their companions in error, following their example, gave themselves up.

The difficult and delicate task of at once controlling and conciliating the people over whose conduct he was left as a guard, was well performed, as was subsequently acknowledged with thanks by the government. The apprehension, expressed by a few, that his natural "fierceness," added to his sense of the injuries which had been inflicted upon his relatives and friends, would render him unfit for the responsible station, were not justified by the event. So far from this, it appears that he became very popular among the people : the best proof that could be presented, perhaps, that his measures towards them were mild and conciliatory. We have, however, the additional evidence of these facts, which is furnished in his own letters, and in those of his friends. In one of the former, written to the President in the latter part of December, he says: " I am dealing very gently with them, and am becoming very popular, for which I am very happy, as it has been my opinion *from the first of this business*, that we ought to make these people our friends, if we could do so without lessening the dignity of government, which, in my opinion, ought to be supported at any risk."

In a letter to the Hon. Timothy Pickering, then Secretary of War, under date of the 26th January, 1795, Morgan observes: " With respect to affairs in this country, I have the pleasure to inform you, that appearances are favorable. The people are gradually becoming convinced of the impropriety of their conduct, and seem anxious to retrieve their character.   *   *   *   *
I spare no pains to obtain from them the most unequivocal proofs of their returning sense of duty. To effect this, I mix with them myself occasionally, and have generally some of my family among them, who, by reasoning with them, often make converts. I anticipate an issue the most honorable to the laws, from the measures which government have adopted."

Evidence of the sentiments of the people in the " disaffected region," regarding Morgan's conduct towards them, is furnished in many of the letters of his friends. In one of these occurs the following passage: " Mr. Johnston has been two weeks through the country, during which he heard nothing but the highest encomiums respecting your conduct in every particular."

Nor would it be just to Gen. Morgan to regard these evidences of his judicious conduct and its gratifying consequences, as the results of a calculating policy merely. They originated in the suggestions of a heart full of generous impulses, and extremely susceptible of pity for the unfortunate. Of the large number of the malcontents who were taken into custody, the major part were dismissed with an admonition, upon their promising good behavior for the future. The individuals most conspicuous in the recent outrages, were, however, sent to Philadelphia for trial, in accordance with directions from government. These, after a detention of several months in prison, were at length tried, nearly all found guilty, and condemned, some to different periods of imprisonment, and one, John Mitchell, found guilty of stopping and rifling the mail, was sentenced to die. The assurances which many of these unfortunate men received from Gen. Morgan, upon surrendering, that he would exert his influence to obtain their pardon, were not idly given. No one stood forth more prominently as the advocate of a merciful policy towards the accused than he did; and his repeated intercessions in behalf of this or that individual of the number, fully attest the fact. His representations in behalf of Mitchell, the man whose enormities pointed him out as the solitary mark for capital punishment, drew the following reply from the President, in a letter to Morgan, dated March 27th, 1795. "The interest which you have taken in the safety of John Mitchell, as expressed in your letter of the 19th of January, would be an inducement to me to go as far in relieving him as public propriety would admit. But the attorney-general having made a report, of which the enclosed is a copy, I think it advisable to postpone the further consideration of the matter until his trial shall have taken place." Mitchell and the other prisoners were eventually pardoned and discharged. If a policy, at once so wise and benevolent, was not contributed to by the influence of Gen. Morgan—an admission which we are very far from making—it is certain that its adoption was warmly recommended by him, and commanded his best exertions.

Early in January of this year, Morgan was announced as a candidate for Congress, for the district in which he resided, then composed of the counties of Frederic and Berkley. The party lines of federalist and republican had long since been clearly defined, and political feeling was already running high. During the two preceding years, this district had been represented in

Congress by Robert Rutherford, Esq., a prominent member of the republican party. Gen. Morgan had, from the first, adopted the views and principles of the federalists. He had subsequently shown much zeal and activity in promoting the success of his political friends; and at this time, he was considered the most popular and influential man of his party in the district. Mr. Rutherford having been announced as a candidate for re-election, Morgan consented to be placed in nomination as the opposing candidate.

In the beginning of the month of February, Gen. Morgan left the camp at McFarlane's Ferry, having obtained leave of absence, and returning to Frederic, started on an electioneering tour. During the three weeks preceding the election, he traversed the district in every direction, and put in requisition those faculties which, on sterner occasions, had never failed to win him the hearts of men. But equally active was his opponent, who, besides being a public speaker of some note, was considered unequalled in the business of electioneering. The result was, Morgan was defeated.

On his return to camp, he quickly discovered that public feeling in that quarter had undergone an unfavorable change during his absence. On inquiry, it appeared that the soothing policy which he had pursued with so much success towards the people there, had not been observed while he was away. The military, unrestrained by the presence of their chief, had been rather overbearing in their conduct, and at length committed some indiscretions, which subjected them to the civil law. As may be supposed, it needed but little provocation to re-arouse in the breasts of the people, those angry feelings to which the excise laws gave rise, and which Morgan had been so successful in allaying. Besides, many of their numbers were eager to avail themselves of an opportunity of presenting to the lips of the agents of government the bitter cup of mortifications which they had been compelled to drain to the dregs. Indictments were accordingly issued against a number of the cavalry officers, for alleged violations of the rights of certain individuals. One of these officers, having entered a man's house and seized a pair of pistols and a rifle, and another having taken by force a quantity of forage, without paying therefore, warrants were obtained for their arrest. The execution of these warrants was resisted, and the *posse comitatus* was called out to enforce them. A collision of a still more serious nature between the civil and military authorities was prevented, only by the opportune return of Gen. Morgan.

Majors Prior and Armstead were in command of the detachment during Morgan's absence. The former writing to the secretary of war, in relation to the foregoing circumstances, makes the following observation : " Gen. Morgan's presence is certainly very necessary in this country ; some from fear and others ⸫ om affection respect and obey him. The change during his absence is but too visible."

General Morgan at once employed himself in arranging, as far as it was possible, the difficulties which had unfortunately arisen. But some of these had already been made the subjects of counter-representations to the government. Washington's strong sense of justice is forcibly illustrated in the following letter, which these unpleasant circumstances elicited from him to Morgan.

PHILADELPHIA, 27*th March*, 1795.

DEAR SIR : The interest which you have taken in the safety of John Mitchell, as expressed in your letter of the 19th January last, would be an inducement to me to go as far in relieving him as public propriety would admit. But the attorney general having made a report of which the enclosed is a copy, I think it advisable to postpone the further consideration until his trial shall have taken place.

It has afforded me great pleasure to learn that the general conduct and character of the army has been temperate and indulgent, and that your attention to the quiet and comfort of the western inhabitants has been well received by them. Still it may be proper constantly and strongly to impress upon the army, that they are mere agents of civil power, that out of camp they have no more authority than other citizens ; that offences

19*

against the laws are to be examined, not by a military officer, but by a magistrate ; that they are not exempt from arrests and indictments, for violations of law ; that officers ought to be careful, not to give orders which may lead their agents into infractions of law ; that no compulsion be used towards the inhabitants in the traffic carrying on between them and the army; that disputes be avoided as much as possible, and be adjusted as quickly as may be, without urging them to an extreme ; and that the whole country is not to be considered as within the limits of the camp.

I do not communicate these things to you for any other purpose than that you may weigh them ; and without referring to any instructions from me, adopt the measures necessary for accomplishing the foregoing objects. With great regard and esteem, I am, dear sir, your affectionate humble servant.

GEO. WASHINGTON.
MAJ. GEN MORGAN.

The letter which follows is in reply to the foregoing. The sentences omitted are of a personal nature, the publication of which could serve no useful purpose.

CAMP McFARLANE'S FERRY, *April 9th*, 1795.

SIR : On the 4th instant, I was honored with the receipt of your letter of the 27th ult., and for the hints it contained I return you my sincere thanks.

Your approbation of my conduct and that of the army under my command, affords me peculiar satisfaction, which is heightened by the great coincidence of opinion between us, relative to the intention for which an army was stationed in this country.

To impress upon the army a due respect for the laws, and to urge the necessity of an uninterrupted harmony between it and the citizens, was my first care, and what I have uniformly practised. To promote this good understanding I found rather an arduous task, owing not so much to a licentiousness in the troops, as to an unaccommodating disposition in the people, which I find but too prevalent among a great part of the community. In my absence, while attending the election in Berkley and Frederic, some little bickerings took place, and some suits were brought by certain individuals against a part of the army.   *   *   *   *

It is a flattering consideration, however, that notwithstanding these things, I have it to observe, that affairs in general are in a pretty good train. It shall be my business to settle all disputes as amicably as possible.

I have already, since my return, terminated some of them, and shall use every precaution in my power, to prevent such misunderstandings in future. I have the honor, &c.

DANIEL MORGAN.

His Excellency, PRESIDENT UNITED STATES.

From this time forth, and until every cause of complaint was removed by the repeal of the excise law, the conduct of the people of western Pennsylvania was such as to relieve the government from all anxiety on their account. About the beginning of May, a large proportion of the forces on the Monongahela were, at the instance of Gen. Morgan, induced to enlist in the regular army. The remainder after occupying the post at McFarlane's Ferry till the latter part of the month, when their term of service expired, were paid off and discharged.

With this tour of service terminated the military career of Morgan. Although occasions subsequently arose, which threatened a resort to arms, and in which his counsel was invited and his aid counted upon, he was never destined again to draw his sword at the bidding of his country.

He was now once more at home, surrounded by all the members of his family, and actively engaged in attending to his private affairs. At this time his daughters and their husbands were included in the family circle. Mr. and Mrs. Heard had resided with the general from the time of their marriage ; and when Colonel Neville returned to Pittsburg with the army, he immediately sent his wife and children to " Saratoga." But the removal soon after of Colonel Neville and Major Heard, with their families, to Pittsburg, left the general and his wife alone. " Saratoga " being too large an establishment for two persons, and an advantageous offer being made to General Morgan about this time to sell this place : these reasons with the desire of being nearer to a house of worship, induced him to dispose of it, and to remove back to his former residence, called " Soldier's Rest."

Here he resided in perfect tranquillity for nearly two years, when the importunities of his friends induced him to try his fortune once more in the field of politics. The occasion was that, the chief result of which was the election of John Adams to the Presidency. Again the prize was the representation in Congress of the district in which he resided ; again his competitor was Mr. Rutherford. If, since that period, party spirit has occasionally been more imposing in its demonstrations, never, perhaps, has it displayed the same degree of bitterness and intolerance. The people of Frederic and Berkley were not exempt from the controlling influence which was then exercised by politics over the minds of their countrymen generally, in all parts of the Union. The district was so nicely divided in opinion between the opposing parties, that success depended, in a great measure, upon the popularity, influence, and exertions of the respective candidates : a circumstance well calculated to render more intense the party feeling where it occurs. Morgan's mortified pride at his former defeat, and his zealous desire for the success of his party, united in determining him on making extraordinary exertions on this occasion. For three or four weeks previously to the election, he gave himself wholly up to the business of electioneering ; and before the day of trial came, he had canvassed the whole district. His opponent had been equally active and untiring : so that, even up to the last hour, the result of the contest was considered doubtful. There were many more votes polled on this occasion, than on any previous one in the district. A considerable majority of them, however, were cast for General Morgan,* and he was declared duly elected.

General Morgan's career as a member of Congress was undistinguished by anything saving his zealous support of the administration of Mr. Adams, and his assiduous attention to the duties of his station. He attended the special meeting of Congress called in the summer of 1797, by the President, to take into consideration the unfriendly state of affairs which existed at that time between France and the United States.

* MSS. Dr. Hill.

While at the seat of government during the regular session of the following year, he was taken sick. The change from the pure air of the mountainous region in which he had passed nearly all his life, to the confined atmosphere of a legislative chamber, had first debilitated him, and afterwards revived those distressing maladies from which he had previously so suffered much.

His health continuing bad, and being fearful of encountering the hot weather in the city, he left Philadelphia before the session closed, and much enfeebled, returned to Frederick in the month of June.

From this time until the close of his life, there was a manifest yielding of his bodily strength and vigor of constitution. Although he soon afterwards recovered sufficiently to be abroad, and to give grounds for the hope that his health was re-established, he never again was destined to enjoy that greatest of blessings. Upon reaching the seat of government the following winter, he became so enfeebled that he remained there but a short time, and returned home in a state so low, as to inspire fears of his speedy dissolution.

The rumor of his impending death, which spread abroad about this time, was soon magnified into the actual occurrence of that event, and in this shape found its way into the newspapers. In relation to this rumor, the following passage occurs in a letter from Washington to General Morgan, written at Mount Vernon on the 10th April, 1799. "I assure you, my dear sir, it gave me not a little pleasure to find that the account of your death in the newspapers was not founded in fact: and I sincerely pray that many years may elapse before that event takes place; and that in the meantime you may be restored to the full enjoyment of your health, and to your usefulness in society."

The conduct of the French republic towards the United States, had been, for some time prior to this, of a nature so unfriendly, as at length to justify our government in taking measures in anticipation of a war with that power. A regiment of artillerists and engineers were added to the regular army. The President was authorized to raise twelve additional regiments of infantry and one regiment of cavalry, to serve during the continuance of the existing differences with the French republic, if not sooner discharged. He was also authorized to appoint officers for a provisional army, and to receive and organize volunteer corps. Immediately following these and other vigorous proceedings, Washington was appointed lieutenant-general and commander-in-chief of the armies of the United States.*

Gen. Morgan was named in connection with a high command, in the event of a war with France. The judgment and courage, with the happy union of caution and enterprise which had ever distinguished his conduct in the field, marked him as one eminently fitted to lead his countrymen against the soldiers of France. Happily, the occasion for his services never arrived, and had it been otherwise, his failing health would have forced him to be absent from the ranks of his country's defenders.

The preparatory organization of the officers of the eventual army by the government and the commander-in-chief, furnished the latter with an occasion for writing the following letter to Gen. Morgan:

MOUNT VERNON, *May* 10*th*, 1799.

DEAR SIR: I have just received a letter from the Secretary of War, in which (after giving it as the opinion of the President of the United States, that officers for the twenty-four additional regiments ought to be had in contemplation; that in case the exigency of our affairs should require them, greater dispatch might be used in the formation) is the extract which follows:

"The selection of officers for the eventual army appears to be an object of primary importance, requiring all imaginary circumspection and care; their characters ought, if possible, to be such as to inspire a general and well-grounded confidence that the fate of their country may be safely intrusted to them.

"I have, therefore, to request that you will accord your full attention to the subject, and furnish me as soon as practicable with a list of such char-

* Marshall's Washington, pp. 429, 436, 434.

acters in your State, to fill the annexed military grades, as in your opinion are best qualified and willing to serve in case of an actual war, which will render it indispensable to recruit men for the army.

"Every cautionary measure is necessary to guard against errors in appointments, which too frequently results from the ease with which recommendations are generally obtained, the partialities of friends, and the delusive hope that men of bad habits, by being transplanted into the army will become good men and good officers.

("The officers proposed to be drawn from the State of Virginia are, viz. :—

Four colonels,	One colonel,
Eight majors,	Two majors,
Forty captains, and	Eleven captains, and
Eighty subalterns of infantry.	Twenty-two subalterns of cavalry.)

"In making the selection, it will be proper to allow, if fit characters present themselves for a choice, a due proportion of captains and subalterns to the several counties, according to their respective population, as well with a view to facilitate the recruiting service as to give general satisfaction; this rule, however, is not meant to be so invariably observed as to exclude great superiority of talents by too strict an adherence.

"As circumstances may exist at the time of the President's making the appointments, which may render it proper to make some changes in the list with which I may be furnished, you are requested not to give the parties recommended such positive assurances as will render a change impracticable, without wounding too sensibly their feelings."

Having given you these extracts so fully, but little remains for me to add, further than to request your aid in carrying the secretary's views into effect, conformably to the principles he has laid down ; and that you will consider my application to you as an evidence of my confidence in your knowledge of character (especially of the old and meritorious officers of the Virginia line), of your patriotism and willingness to form a respectable corps of officers for our native State.

I have no objection to your conversing with Col. Parker, or others in whom you can place reliance, on this occasion—letting it be clearly understood, however, that the inquiry and selection here proposed is eventual only, not as a thing actually resolved on, but preparatory, in case the President, in the recess of Congress, should, from the aspect of things, deem it expedient to carry the law for raising twenty-four regiments into effect.

That you may be enabled better to understand that part of the secretary's letter which relates to the distribution of officers to counties, I
enclose you the inspector-general's allotment of the State into divisions
and subdivisions, for the convenience of recruiting and rendezvousing in
each.

Hoping that you continue to improve in your health, I remain, with
very sincere esteem and regard,

Dear Sir,

Your most obedient and

Very humble servant,

GEORGE WASHINGTON.

GEN. MORGAN.

A subject more important than all others combined—the subject of religion—chiefly engaged Morgan's attention during the
remainder of his days. It was about this time that he became,
to the great joy of his pious wife, a communing member of the
Presbyterian church.*

For some years prior to the period at which we have arrived,
he had been a constant attendant on public worship. Subsequently, he became by degrees more and more an observer of the
requirements of the Christian belief. To be nearer the society of
religious people and to a place of worship formed the chief
motives for his removal from "Saratoga" to "Soldier's Rest."
Mrs. Morgan had been, for a length of time, a professor of
religion, and had supported a consistent and exemplary character
as a Christian. Her influence and example were well calculated
to produce good effects upon the mind of a husband devotedly
attached to her, and predisposed, from the promptings of his own
heart, to follow her counsellings. To her praiseworthy efforts
with this object were joined those of the worthy pastor of the
Presbyterian church in the neighborhood, the Rev. Wm. Hill,
between whom and Morgan a warm friendship commenced about
this time. From the day that he made a profession of religion
until that of his death, nothing was observable in his life and con

*Dr Hill.

duct that was not becoming the character of a humble follower of the Saviour.

It may be remarked here, that during the wildest and most irregular period of Morgan's life, he always professed and manifested the greatest respect for religion. In illustration of this trait in his character, one or two anecdotes are told of him that are worth repeating. When, on the morning of the assault on Quebec, the word was given for the troops to form, Morgan was was asleep under a shed. Upon awaking, his mind became suddenly so impressed with the fearful nature of the enterprise in which he was about engaging, that he shivered through his whole frame, and for a time, felt quite unequal to the task which duty and honor imposed upon him. In this state of mind, he sought out a secluded spot, where, kneeling down, he prayed most fervently for protection for himself and his men, and for a triumph for his country. When he arose, his courage and confidence had revived, and with cheerfulness he took his position at the head of his command.

On one occasion, Morgan related this anecdote to the Hon. James Mackin, of Virginia. " General," said Mackin to Morgan, " I expect you prayed like a man I once knew, who led a very wicked life ; but when in great tribulation, he was driven to pray too ; and in his prayer he said : " O Lord ! thou knowest that I have very seldom troubled thee with my affairs. But if thou wilt help me now, and extricate me out of my present difficulties, I promise not to trouble thee again for a long time." To this Morgan replied : " No, Mr. Mackin, I never used mockery of that kind, nor ever treated religion disrespectfully. I always believed in the truth and importance of religion, and knew that I was a great sinner for neglecting my duty to my God. If I ever prayed in earnest, it was upon that occasion, when I was committing myself into the hands of the Almighty, and imploring his protection. Having done so, I arose from my knees, dismissed my fears, and led on my men to the assault. I verily believe that it was entirely owing to an overruling Providence, in which I reposed confidence, that I was so mercifully protected, and brought off safely from the dangers through which I passed that morning."*

When the battle at the Cowpens was over, and all the enemy and prisoners were flying, Morgan rode across the fields offering to the Almighty thanks, which were audible to many of his men as he passed.

In the summer of 1800, his infirmities began to increase upon him. Unable longer to devote any portion of his time to business, and desirous of having readier access to his physician and his friends, he removed about this time from "Soldier's Rest," to a house belonging to him in Winchester.

During the closing year of his life, he was confined almost entirely to his house, and at last exclusively to his bed and easy chair. For the six or eight months prior to his death, he became so feeble as to require the attendance, night and day, of some person at his bed-side. Having gradually sunk under the pressure of his infirmities, he at length expired on the 6th of July, 1802.

An eloquent and impressive sermon was preached over the body by the Rev. Mr. Hill. His funeral was attended by the largest concourse of citizens ever seen in Winchester upon such an occasion. The military escorted the corpse to the grave, and buried it with the honors of war. In the procession were seven members of the rifle company which Morgan raised and marched to Boston in 1775. It might be truly said, that none in that sad cortege, were sincerer mourners than these men. They carried their war-worn rifles with them, and fired over his grave their last military farewell.

Morgan's mortal remains lie interred in the Presbyterian burying ground at Winchester. His monument is a horizontal slab

* Dr. Hill

raised a few feet above the ground, whereon is the following inscription, written by Gen. Presley Neville:

MAJOR GENERAL DANIEL MORGAN.

DEPARTED THIS LIFE

ON JULY THE 6th, 1802,

IN THE 67TH YEAR OF HIS AGE.

PATRIOTISM AND VALOR,

WERE THE PROMINENT FEATURES IN HIS CHARACTER;

AND THE HONORABLE SERVICES HE RENDERED TO HIS COUNTRY,

DURING THE REVOLUTIONARY WAR,

CROWNED HIM WITH GLORY,

AND WILL REMAIN IN THE BREASTS OF HIS COUNTRYMEN,

A PERPETUAL MONUMENT

TO HIS

Memory.

Gen. Morgan's family and descendants may justly claim a few words of notice before we close our narrative.

Mrs. Morgan, soon after the general's death, removed from Winchester to the residence of her son-in-law, Colonel Neville in Pittsburg, where she remained for some time. Subsequently she removed to Russelville, Kentucky, in which place Major and Mrs. Heard had previously settled, and with whom she passed several years of her life. She died in the year 1816, at the country seat of her grand-daughter, Mrs. Matilda O'Bannon, near Russelville, and was buried in the family cemetery at that place.

Colonel Presley Neville continued a resident of Pittsburg until the year 1817, when he removed with his family to Neville, Ohio. He died in that place in the year 1823. In the year following,

Mrs. Neville removed to Cincinnati, where she remained until her death, which occurred during the year 1831. They had had fifteen children : nine sons and six daughters. The eldest of the sons was the late Major Morgan Neville, of Cincinnati a name proudly associated with the worth and literature of the west. Another son Frederick, is a lieutenant in the United States Navy.

In the year 1803, Major and Mrs. Heard removed to Russel-ville, Kentucky. In the year 1813, Mrs. Heard died suddenly of apoplexy. Major Heard survived his wife many years, but died while on a visit to his sister, at New Brunswick, New Jersey, in the year 1827. Their children were three daughters and two sons. The elder son, Daniel Morgan Heard, was a member of the medical profession, having graduated at the Philadelphia Medical school in the year 1816. Morgan Augustus Heard, the youngest of this branch of the Morgan family, was a student of law when the war of 1812 commenced. He took up arms on that occasion, and was a lieutenant in the army under General Harrison which operated on our northern frontier. He subsequently served in the Florida war of 1817, under Gen. Jackson, during which he was appointed one of the general's aids, with the rank of major.

Our task is nearly completed. That it may not prove unworthy of the subject is all we desire. Should it recommend itself to the reader, from having familiarized him with the character, and intro-duced him, as it were, to the acquaintance of one, whose name and deeds are associated with such proud recollections, our utmost expectations will be more than realized.

The relations of cause and effect are presented in their most attractive, if not their most instructive shape, when they serve to illustrate the moral afforded by a life, such as that we have been recording. In the present instance, it is strikingly shown, that there is no condition, however humble and uninformed, that is not susceptible of improvement; that when the will unites with the desire to be advanced, advancement follows as a certain conse-quence ; and that the road to distinction presents no impediment however great, which cannot be surmounted by genius and perseverance. Fortune, it is true, occasionally invests the undeserving with honors. But let not this fact be a discouragement to him, who would shake off the trammels that bind him to the earth, and rise above the circumstances which surround him. The mere favorite of the fickle goddess can seldom boast of her constancy through the devious paths of a long life. Sooner or later he is left to discover, in the elevation far above him, of those whose success resulted from laborious, patient perseverance, the consequences of his misplaced devotion. Neither should the envy, and rivalry, and other obstacles which the aspirant to distinction must necessarily encounter, deter him from resolutely pushing forward in the path pointed out at once by interest and duty. General Morgan was less indebted to the adventitious aids afforded by birth, education, friends, and fortune, than perhaps any other man that ever lived to acquire a like degree of distinction. To these impediments to his advancement were added those, arising from bad associates and youthful indiscretions. Even the high military reputation which he subsequently earned, checked for a time his progress, by arousing a jealousy which caused his just claims to promotion to be disregarded. Yet, in spite of considerations, which, at the outset of his career, seemed to forbid even hope, he obeyed the promptings of a mind, eminently aspiring and vigorous, and persevered in the improvement of his condition. Happily, the circumstances of the times laid open to him an ample field for the display of his peculiar genius. The result is furnished in the fame with which his name is associated in the mind of every American citizen. Yet, such were the high qualities of his head and heart, that had he received an education, such as is now within the reach of the humblest, circumstances similar to those which favored his pursuit of distinction in the field, would have made him equally distinguished in the council.

General Morgan was a man of very large proportions. He was upwards of six feet high, and although never fleshy, seldom weighed less than two hundred pounds. To an iron constitution were added great powers of strength and endurance. Before he was visited by those ailments which embittered the evening of his days, his physical energies seemed unbounded. Few men of his time could compare with him in his ability to withstand the effects of hunger, cold, or fatigue; and when duty subjected him to these severe tests, no one encountered them with more alacrity. His person was well developed, and his movements and gestures indicated both vigor and grace. His face was handsome, and remarkably expressive of the emotion of the moment, whether gentle or violent. It is said that when dressed in uniform, a more imposing figure than that he presented, was seldom to be met with.*

His mind was solid, and comprehensive, yet acute and discriminating. Long before he attained the meridian of life, its vigor and activity had largely compensated for the want of early cultivation. Fully impressed with the conviction, that the improvement of his mind was an indispensable pre-requsite to his advancement, he was an early and diligent student. At a later period of his life, he possessed a better knowledge of history, ancient and modern, than is usually acquired by those who enjoy the advantages of a liberal education. But perhaps the most striking illustration of his mental improvement is furnished in his correspondence. At first, his style of writing was exceedingly inaccurate. His improvement, through a long series of years, was, however, progressive, and plainly perceptible. In proof of this, we need only refer to those of his later letters which have been introduced in this work, some of which, for strength of thought, and elegance of expression, would do no discredit to one who had acquired a reputation upon the achievements of his pen.

His knowledge of human nature was an inherent gift, the extent of which was displayed in the mastery it enabled him at all times to exercise over the minds of his associates. Although subject

* Dr. Hill.

to violent gusts of passion, when his unconquerable will was thwarted, such ebullitions had never more than a momentary control over his actions. His courage was of a peculiar quality, if we are to credit his oft-repeated declarations regarding it. When beyond the reach of danger, or of any exciting cause, he was accustomed to admit his sensibility to the impressions of fear. Just previous to some of the most glorious occasions of his life, those feelings are said by himself to have come upon him like an apparition, shaking for a moment his inmost soul. But at the crisis of battle most trying to human fortitude, when death presented itself on every side, and danger flew thickly around, no such weaknesses were ever exhibited. Perils which appalled ordinary men, only seemed to raise his spirit still higher, and to stimulate and bring into more active exercise, all the faculties of his mind. His fearlessness, under such circumstances, was the consequence, not so much of a dull perception of danger, as of the behests of a will, which, like a mountain-torrent, knew no stop, but rose and grew stronger by opposition. Yet, his courage was tempered by a prudence and a circumspection, which the superficial observer would consider bordering on timidity. Throughout his long military career, during which the most cautious officers were occasionally caught off their guard, he never experienced a surprise, although the nature of the service on which he was chiefly engaged, subjected him constantly to such a contingency. Decision and firmness were always displayed both in the combination and the execution of his plans. These at all times evinced a sound and far-reaching judgment, and seldom disappointed his expectations. In fine, he possessed that faculty, which is, perhaps, the rarest and most valuable of those which enter into the position of a great commander—that by which he was always enabled to conciliate the respect and regard of those who were placed under his command, and to inspire them with a share of his own confidence and resolution.

Morgan's heart was full of every generous and ennobling principle. He was a fond and devoted husband and father, a warm friend, and a zealous and active citizen. Before he adopted religion as the guide of his actions, his conduct was regulated by the most rigid notions of honor. He was remarkable through life for his candor. Whether the occasion for the exercise of this quality was agreeable or not to his hearers, seemed all the same to him. He was never known to sacrifice truth to conventionality. He abhorred the character of a hypocrite or dissembler, and never took any pains to conceal his contempt for the dishonest, the treacherous and the cowardly. Hospitality was regarded by him as duty; and his house and purse were ever open to the distressed and unfortunate. His resentment, though easily provoked, had nothing malignant in it, and was short-lived, even in cases where it was aroused by injuries. However strong his reasons might be for the indulgence of revengeful feelings, yet when such existed, they never withstood the first appeal to his magnanimity. It needed only an unfortunate change in the circumstances of those who had provoked his ire, to render them eligible claimants upon his sympathy and assistance.

At all stages of Morgan's life, he was industrious and economical. One of the natural results of the operation of these qualities was, his accumulation of a handsome property before he died. Yet he was far from being parsimonious; on the contrary, he was lavish of his means when an appeal was made to his patriotism or his friendship. His manners were simple and unobtrusive, devoid of everything calculated to attract notice. His intercourse with strangers was marked by a politeness that made up in heartiness what it wanted in polish. Good-humored familiarity marked his conversations with his friends and acquaintances. His disposition was naturally cheerful and obliging. His appearance and conversation would at first indicate a character unusually grave. Yet he possessed a lively sense of the ridiculous, and a fund of rich humor—faculties which he missed few opportunities of exercising. His early excesses had a short-lived existence, and were abandoned during his military career. He retained, however, a rational fondness for the society of his friends around the festal board, to the convivialities of which, few could contribute so largely and so well.

If Morgan had enemies—and who is he, worthy of notice, that has had none?—their numbers were inconsiderable when compared with those of his friends. His frank ingenuous manners, his sociability, and his higher qualities of the head and heart, were well calculated to win for him the regard of all who came within the scope of his acquaintance. By none was he more beloved than by the officers and soldiers who served under him. He was indebted for much the greater part of his enemies to political considerations. When parties were first formed, under the Constitution of 1789, he joined the Federalists. Subsequently, his apprehensions for the newly formed Union, threatened as he honestly thought it was by the Republicans, aroused in its defence feelings of a nature more patriotic than partisan, and made him regard political opponents as little better than personal enemies. In this way, he was drawn to the arena of party strife, from which few escape without injury, none without detraction.

APPENDIX.

APPENDIX A.

COPY OF A WILL DRAWN BY GENERAL MORGAN IN 1773.

In the name of God, amen.

I, DANIEL MORGAN, of Frederick county, Virginia, being in my proper senses, and calling to mind the uncertainty of life and the certainty of death, do make this my last Will and Testament, hereby revoking and dis-annulling all former wills and codocils of wills, heretofore made by me the aforesaid Daniel Morgan.

And in the first place it is my will and desire, and I do hereby constitute and appoint my loving and affectionate wife Abigail Morgan, the whole and sole executrix of this my last Will and Testament, of all and every part of my estate, both real and personal.

Item. It is my will and desire that all my just debts be honestly and punctually paid, and that the remainder or residue of my estate (after the discharge of those my debts) be appropriated to the use and for the benefit of the said Abigail, my dear and loving wife ; and that the same continue to be at her disposal, during her natural life and widowhood.

Item. It is my will and desire, that after the decease of the aforesaid Abigail (or in case she should intermarry after my decease) that the whole and sole of my estate, both real and personal, be equally divided between her two daughters, named Nancy Morgan and Betsey Morgan ; and in case of the decease of either of them, that then the whole and sole of my estate aforesaid be appropriated to the use and benefit of the survivor, or survi-ving sister.

Item, it is my will and desire, and the intent and meaning of this, is that my loving wife Abigail have the use and benefit of all my estate aforesaid, as aforesaid specified, only excepting against, and prohibiting her from disposing of any part thereof to defraud the two children aforesaid, to wit, Nancy Morgan and Betsey Morgan. In witness whereof, and in testimony of my approbation of this my last Will and Testament, 1 have hereunto set my hand and affixed my seal, this 17th day of April, in the year of our Lord one thousand seven hundred and seventy-three.

DANIEL MORGAN.

Signed sealed and delivered in the presence of

BAYLIS EARLE,   ELIJAH ISAACS, .

JOHN McGUIR,   SAMUEL PRICE. | SEAL. |

COPY OF GEN. MORGAN'S LAST WILL.

  I, DANIEL MORGAN, of Winchester, in the county of Frederic and Commonwealth of Virginia, possessing fully the powers of recollection and all the usual faculties of my mind, but being weak in body and knowing that all men must die, do make this my last Will and Testament, hereby revoking all former Wills or Testaments heretofore made by me, and allowing this only to be my last Will and Testament.

  First, I recommend my soul to the Omnipotent Creator of all things, trusting for salvation in his mercy and the atonement of my blessed Lord and Saviour Jesus Christ. I desire that my body may be decently interred at the discretion of my family and as to my worldly affairs I make the following arrangement and distribution.

  Having by two deeds of trust bearing date the sixteenth day of March in the present year of our Lord one thousand eight hundred and one, conveyed to certain trustees in the said deeds named the place called Saratoga, containing two hundred and fifty-five acres of land with its appurtenances; and also four hundred and seven acres of land more or less, adjoining the lands of Thomas Bryarly, the heir of John Bell deceased, Richard K. Mead and Alexander Henderson, which I purchased of Nathaniel Ashby; also three hundred and eleven acres of land adjoining Saratoga, which I purchased of Col. Nathaniel Burwell, late of Isle of Wight county, deceased, also one hundred acres of land which I purchased of Nathaniel Burwell, Esq., of Frederic county, adjoining Saratoga, all of the said lands being in the county of Frederick, and Commonwealth of Virginia, also all the stock, slaves, household stuff and furniture, on the said place called Saratoga, and in the mansion house thereon, to hold in trust for the benefit of my well beloved daughter Betsy Heard wife of James Heard, according to the tenor of the said deeds, which it is my desire may be fully executed and complied with in every particular, and in addition to the property aforesaid I now give, devise and bequeath to my said daughter Betsy Heard all my land in the State of Kentucky, whether granted for military services or otherwise, and whether in my own name or procured by purchase, computed to be about ten thousand acres, to hold to her the said Betsy Heard, her heirs and assigns forever; and I do hereby empower and authorize Major James Heard to make sale of the said lands in Kentucky or any part or parcel thereof, and upon such sale being made to make good and sufficient titles to the purchaser, and apply the purchase money to the use of the family, provided my said daughter Betsy shall consent to such sale. I also give, devise and bequeath to my said daughter Betsy Heard five thousand acres of land in the State of Tennessee on Crow Creek, purchased of Major Armstead for five thousand dollars to her, her heirs and assigns forever.

I give, devise and bequeath to my beloved wife Abigail the tract of land I purchased of Samuel Bell, containing two hundred and seventy-eight acres, to her, her heirs and assigns forever, to be by her sold and the money applied to such uses and purposes as she may think proper.

I desire that my executors hereafter named, may with all convenient speed after my decease collect all debts due to me, and out of the moneys so collected pay all my just debts and funeral charges, and being conscious that I owe no just debts of long standing, I desire that if any such should be brought against my estate the statute of limitations shall be pleaded in bar of such claims. All my military land in the northwestern territory I give, devise and bequeath to Presley Neville, my son-in-law, to be disposed of at his discretion to him, his heirs and assigns forever.

All the rest, residue, and remainder of my estate real, personal or mixed, I give, devise and bequeath unto my beloved wife Abigail, for and during the term of her natural life, and after her decease, I give, devise and bequeath the same to my well beloved daughter Nancy Neville, wife of the aforesaid Presley Neville, to her heirs, executors, administrators, and assigns, forever.

And lastly, I do hereby appoint my beloved wife Abigail Morgan and my son-in-law Presley Neville, executrix and executor of this my last Will and Testament.

In witness whereof I have hereunto set my hand and seal this seven-

teenth day of March in the year of our Lord one thousand eight hundred
and one.

                                            DANIEL MORGAN.

Signed, sealed, published, pronounced and declared
   by the said Daniel Morgan as and for his last will
   and testament in presence of us, who in his pre-   [SEAL]
   sence and in the presence of each other, have sub-
   scribed our names as witnesses.
         JOHN WALTERS,
         JACOB HARMER,
         OBED WAITE.

Whereas, I Daniel Morgan of Winchester, in the county of Frederic
and Commonwealth of Virginia, on the seventeenth day of March in the
year of our Lord one thousand eight hundred and one, did make and pub-
lish the foregoing will and testament, contained on three pages of this
sheet of paper, and bearing date on the aforesaid seventeenth day of
March 1801, which said will and testament I do hereby ratify and confirm
in all and every article thereof, except the alteration hereinafter mentioned
in this present writing, which I make and add as a codicil to my said last
will and testament, and to be taken as part thereof, that is to say, whereas,
in and by the said last will and testament, I did among other things give,
devise and bequeath unto my well beloved daughter Betsy Heard, wife of
James Heard, all my lands in the State of Kentucky whether granted for
military services or otherwise, and whether in my name or procured by
purchase, computed to be about ten thousand acres, to hold to her the said
Betsy Heard, her heirs and assigns forever, and did empower Major James
Heard to make sale of the said lands or any part thereof and apply the
money arising from such sale to the use of his family, provided the said
Betsy should consent to such sale being made, and I did by the same will
devise to the said Betsy five thousand acres of land in the State of Ten-
nesee on Crow Creek, purchased of Major Armstead for five thousand dollars,
to her heirs and assigns forever, now it is hereby declared to be my will and
desire that instead of said lands going and being devised as aforesaid, that
my four grandchildren Matilda Heard, Nancy Morgan Heard, Daniel Morgan Heard, and Morgan Augustus Heard, children of the said Betsy Heard,
have the same to be equally divided among them, share and share alike
as to quantity and quality, and I do hereby devise the same to them, the
said Matilda, Nancy Morgan, Daniel Morgan, and Morgan Augustus Heard,
their heirs and assigns forever, to be equally divided as aforesaid.   In

witness whereof I have hereunto set my hand and seal this seventeenth day of March, 1802.

DANIEL MORGAN.

Signed, sealed, published and pronounced, and declared by the said Daniel Morgan, as a codicil to his
last will and testament, in presence of
    OBED WAITE,
    HAMILTON COOPER,
    JOHN KINGAN.

| SEAL |

At a Superior Court composed and held, for the district composed for the counties of Frederic, Berkley, Shenandoah and Jefferson, at Winchester, the 30th day of September, 1802. This last will of Gen. Morgan, deceased, was proved by the oaths of Jacob Harmer and Obed Waite, two of the witnesses thereto, and the codicil thereto annexed was proved by the oaths of Obed Waite, and John Kingan, two of the witnesses thereto, and ordered to be recorded. And on the motion of Presley Neville, one of the executors therein named, who made oath according to law, certificate is granted him for obtaining a probate thereof in due form, giving security whereupon he with John Peyton, Hugh Holmes and Joseph Tidball, his securities, entered into and acknowledged bond in the penalty of one hundred thousand dollars conditioned for his due and faithful administration of the said decedant's estate. Abigail Morgan the executrix therein named in open court, refused taking upon herself the burthen of the execution thereof.

By the court,
J. PEYTON, C. W. D. C.

A copy: Teste, J. Kean, clerk of the circuit Superior Court of Law and Chancery for the county of Frederic in the State of Virginia, and as such, keeper of the records of the former District Court, composed of the counties of Frederic, Berkley and Winchester.

APPENDIX B.

To give my history in the war: I must begin with 1774, when I served a very active and hard campaign under Lord Dunmore. We had beaten the Indians, brought them to order, and confirmed a treaty of peace; and on our return home, at the mouth of the river Hockhockin, we were informed of hostilities being offered to our brethren, the people of Boston. We, as an army victorious, formed ourselves into a society, pledging our words of honor to each other to assist our brethren in Boston, in case hostilities should commence, which did on the 19th of April ensuing, at Lexington. I was appointed a captain by Congress on the 22nd of June, 1775, to raise a company of riflemen, and march with haste to Boston. In a few days, I raised ninety-six men and set out for Boston—reached that place in twenty-one days from the time I marched, bad weather included, nor did I leave a man behind. I remained at that place inactive for six weeks, as the enemy was shut up in Boston; when, with my own consent, detached to Quebec with the command of three rifle companies, viz.: my own, and two from Pennsylvania, under the command of Captains Smith and Hendricks. The latter fell at the attack on the garrison. I was under the command of Gen. Arnold, with whom I marched through the woods and led the van. For a description of that march, I refer to a journal kept by Col. Heth, who was a lieutenant in my company. We reached Canada, I think, on the 3rd of November, in a most shocking condition—destitute of provisions and of every comfort. We marched to Point Levi, recruited the troops, and on the night of the 13th, by the means of some small craft that we found drew up in the guts, and some bark canoes that we purchased from the Indians, crossed the river between two men-of-war, and within point-blank shot, slipping through undiscovered. Here I led the forlorn hope—·went up Gen. Wolfe's cove, and formed on the plains of Abraham, where I expected to be attacked, but was not discovered. We then proceeded on to Caldwell's house. The enemy had a strong guard in the building, which we attacked and carried sword in hand. Here I also commanded the forlorn hope. We then besieged the place for several days; but finding our ammunition was wet, we raised the siege, and marched to Point Auxtrembles, twenty miles distant from Quebec. Finding there that the rifle powder was dry, I marched back with the three rifle companies under my command, and renewed the siege. On my return, I took several prisoners. I kept up the siege until Gen. Montgomery arrived, when an attack upon the town was determined upon, and in a few days carried into effect. Here I was again appointed to the command of the forlorn hope, on the river St. Charles, under Gen. Arnold. The general having been wounded in the leg while under the walls, and before we got into the town, I sent him off in the care of two of my men, and took his place in the command. For although there were three field officers, they would not take the command, alleging that I had seen service and they had not, which reflected great credit on their judgment. I had to attack a two-gun battery, supported by Capt. McCloud and fifty regular troops. The first gun that was fired missed us—the second flashed, when I ordered the ladders, borne on the shoulders of the men, to be raised. The order was immediately obeyed; and for fear the business might not be executed with spirit, I mounted myself, and leaped into the town. The first man among Capt. McCloud's guard who was panic-struck, made a faint resistance, and run into a house that joined the two-gun battery and platform, where the guard was posted. I lighted on the end of a great gun, which hurt me very much, and perhaps saved my life, as I fell from the gun on the platform, where the bayonets were not directed. Col. Charles Porterfield, who was a cadet in my company, was the first man that followed me, and all the men came after him as fast as they had room to jump down. All this was performed in a few seconds. I ordered the men to fire into the house, and follow up with their pikes (for in addition to our rifles, we were also armed with long espontoons), which they did, and drove the guard into the street. I went through a sally port at the end of the platform; met the retreating guard in the street, and ordered them to lay down their arms if they expected quarters. They took me at my word, and every man threw his arms down. We then made a charge on the battery, and took it sword in hand—and pushing on, took everything that opposed us at the point of the bayonet till we

arrived at the barrier gate. Here I was ordered to wait for Gen. Montgomery, and a fatal order it was. It prevented me from taking the garrison, as I had already made half the town prisoners. The sally port
through the barrier was standing open; the guard had left it, and the people
were running from the upper town in whole platoons, giving themselves
up as prisoners, to get out of the way of the confusion which might shortly
ensue. I went up to the edge of the upper town *incog.*, with an interpreter, to see what was going on, as the firing had ceased. Finding no person in arms at all, I returned and called a council of what few officers I
had with me, for the greater part of our force had missed their way, and
had not got into the town. Here I was overruled by sound judgment and
good reasoning. It was said, in the first place, that if I went on I should
break orders; in the next, that I had more prisoners than I had men, and
that if I left them they might break out, retake the battery we had just
captured, and cut off our retreat. It was further urged that Gen. Montgomery was certainly coming down along the river St. Lawrence, and
would join us in a few minutes, and that we were sure of conquest if we
acted with caution and prudence. To these good reasons I gave up my
own opinion, and lost the town. For Gen. Montgomery, having cut down
an out picket, was marching up to the two-gun battery, when an unlucky
shot put an end to his existence, killing at the same time Capt. Cheseman,
Major McPherson, and some others of his good officers. Upon this Col. Donald
Campbell, the quarter-master general, undertook to order a retreat. We
were then left to shift for ourselves, but did not yet know the extent of
the misfortunes which had occurred, or it was still in our power to have
taken the garrison.

*　　*　　*　　*　　*　　*　　*　　*

APPENDIX C.

THE ORIGINAL ACCOUNT OF THE BATTLE OF THE COWPENS.

CAMP NEAR CAIN CREEK, *Jan.* 19*th*, 1781.

DEAR SIR: The troops I have the honor to command have been so fortunate as to obtain a complete victory over a detachment from the British army, commanded by Lieut. Col. Tarleton. The action happened on the 17th inst., about sunrise, at the Cowpens. It, perhaps, would be well to remark, for the honor of the American arms, that although the progress of this corps was marked with burning and devastation, and although they waged the most cruel warfare, not a man was killed, wounded, or even insulted, after he surrendered. Had not Britons during this contest received so many lessons of humanity, I should flatter myself that this might teach them a little. But I fear they are incorrigible.

To give you a just idea of our operations, it will be necessary to inform you, that on the 14th inst., having received certain intelligence that Lord Cornwallis and Lieut. Col. Tarleton were both in motion, and that their movements clearly indicated their intentions of dislodging me, I abandoned my encampment on Grindall's Ford on the Pacolet, and on the 16th, in the evening took possession of a post, about seven miles from the Cherokee Ford, on Broad river. My former position subjected me at once to the operations of Cornwallis and Tarleton, and in case of a defeat, my retreat might easily have been cut off. My situation at the Cowpens enabled me to improve any advantages I might gain, and to provide better for my own security should I be unfortunate. These reasons induced me to take this post, at the risk of its wearing the face of a retreat.

I received regular intelligence of the enemy's movements from the time they were first in motion. On the evening of the 16th inst., they took possession of the ground I had removed from in the morning, distant from

the scene of action about twelve miles. An hour before daylight one of
my scouts returned and informed me that Lieut. Col. Tarleton had advanced
within five miles of our camp. On this information, I hastened to form as
good a disposition as circumstances would admit, and from the alacrity of
the troops, we were soon prepared to receive him. The light infantry,
commanded by Lieut. Col. Howard, and the Virginia militia under the command of Maj. Triplett, were formed on a rising ground, and extended a line
in front. The third regiment of dragoons, under Lieut. Col. Washington,
were posted at such a distance in their rear, as not to be subjected to the
line of fire directed at them, and to be so near as to be able to charge the
enemy should they be broken. The volunteers of North Carolina, South
Carolina, and Georgia, under the command of the brave and valuable Col.
Pickens, were situated to guard the flanks. Maj. McDowell, of the North
Carolina volunteers, was posted on the right flank in front of the line, one
hundred and fifty yards; and Maj. Cunningham, of the Georgia volunteers,
on the left, at the same distance in front. Cols. Brannon and Thomas, of
the South Carolinians, were posted in the right of Maj. McDowell, and Cols.
Hays and McCall, of the same corps, on the left of Maj. Cunningham.
Capts. Tate and Buchanan, with the Augusta riflemen, to support the right
of the line.

The enemy drew up in single line of battle, four hundred yards in front
of our advanced corps. The first battalion of the 71st regiment was
opposed to our right, the 7th regiment to our left, the infantry of the legion
to our centre, the light companies on their flanks. In front moved two
pieces of artillery. Lieut. Col. Tarleton, with his cavalry, was posted in the
rear of his line.

The disposition of battle being thus formed, small parties of riflemen
were detached to skirmish with the enemy, upon which their whole line
moved on with the greatest impetuosity, shouting as they advanced.
McDowell and Cunningham gave them a heavy and galling fire, and
retreated to the regiments intended for their support. The whole of Col.
Pickens's command then kept up a fire by regiments, retreating agreeably
to their orders. When the enemy advanced to our line, they received a
well-directed and incessant fire. But their numbers being superior to ours,
they gained our flanks, which obliged us to change our position. We
retired in good order about fifty paces, formed, advanced on the enemy,
and gave them a fortunate volley, which threw them into disorder. Lieut.
Col. Howard observing this, gave orders for the line to charge bayonets,
which was done with such address, that they fled with the utmost precipi-

tation, leaving their fieldpieces in our possession. We pushed our advantages so effectually, that they never had an opportunity of rallying, had their intentions been ever so good.

Lieut. Col. Washington having been informed that Tarleton was cutting down our riflemen on the left, pushed forward, and charged them with such firmness, that instead of attempting to recover the fate of the day, which one would have expected from an officer of his splendid character, broke and fled.

The enemy's whole force were now bent solely in providing for their safety in flight—the list of their killed, wounded, and prisoners, will inform you with what effect. Tarleton, with the small remains of his cavalry, and a few scattering infantry he had mounted on his wagon-horses, made their escape. He was pursued twenty-four miles, but owing to our having taken a wrong trail at first, we never could overtake him.

As I was obliged to move off of the field of action in the morning, to secure the prisoners, I cannot be so accurate as to the killed and wounded of the enemy as I could wish. From the reports of an officer whom I sent to view the ground, there were one hundred non-commissioned officers and privates, and ten commissioned officers killed, and two hundred rank and file wounded. We have now in our possession five hundred and two non-commissioned officers and privates prisoners, independent of the wounded, and the militia are taking up stragglers continually. Twenty-nine commissioned officers have fell into our hands. Their rank, &c., you will see by an enclosed list. The officers I have paroled: the privates I am conveying by the safest route to Salisbury.

Two standards, two fieldpieces, thirty-five wagons, a travelling forge, and all their music are ours. Their baggage, which was immense, they have in a great measure destroyed.

Our loss is inconsiderable, which the enclosed return will evince. I have not been able to ascertain Col. Pickens's loss, but know it to be very small.

From our force being composed of such a variety of corps, a wrong judgment may be formed of our numbers. We fought only eight hundred men, two-thirds of which were militia. The British, with their baggage-guard, were not less than one thousand one hundred and fifty, and these veteran troops. Their own officers confess that they fought one thousand and thirty-seven.

Such was the inferiority of our numbers, that our success must be attributed to the justice of our cause and the bravery of our troops. My wishes would induce me to mention the name of every sentinel in the corps I have the honor to command. In justice to the bravery and good conduct of the officers, I have taken the liberty to enclose you a list of their names, from a conviction that you will be pleased to introduce such characters to the world.

Maj. Giles, my aid, and Capt. Brookes, my brigade-major, deserve and have my thanks for their assistance and behavior on this occasion.

The Baron de Gleabuch, who accompanies Major Giles with these dispatches, served with me in the action as a volunteer, and behaved in such a manner as merits your attention.

I am, dear sir, your obedient servant,

DANIEL MORGAN.

Our loss was very inconsiderable, not having more than twelve killed and about sixty wounded. The enemy had ten commissioned officers and upwards of one hundred rank and file killed, two hundred rank and file wounded, and twenty-seven officers and more than five hundred privates which fell into our hands, with two pieces of artillery, two standards, eight hundred stand of arms, one travelling-forge, thirty-five wagons, ten negroes, and upwards of one hundred dragoon horses.

Although our success was complete, we fought only eight hundred men, and were opposed by upwards of one thousand British troops.

APPENDIX D.

{ SENATE ROOM UNITED STATES,
  PHILADELPHIA, *Jan. 20th,* 1795.

DEAR GENERAL: Since I last saw you in Philadelphia, which I think was in 1791, a gentleman has undertaken to write the history of Georgia. Your address to the Georgia refugees, published at Pacolet, in South Carolina, being in my hands, I gave it to him among other materials for insertion. The same gentleman, a Mr. Langworthy, has applied to me for other documents, and particularly to know if any Georgians were at the Cowpens. None of the authors who have written, have mentioned them in that action, nor did the account given by your aid-de-camp, Maj. Giles, to Congress, notice them, or any officer belonging to the State, although the officers of the other States were very generally mentioned, and their militia applauded. The Georgians have imputed this to the loss of your dispatches, and not of any intention of yourself, who have always been one of their favorite commanders; but they think hard of the silence respecting them in that celebrated action, and which did you the honor of turning the tide of affairs in favor of the United States.

My object in writing at present is to request, if you see no impropriety in it, your giving a certificate under your hand of their being present—three companies. The detachment was small; but, if you recollect, you placed them in front of the whole ; and they strictly obeyed your orders in keeping up a warm fire and gradually retreating. I could wish your expressing that they behaved as well as the other militia in the field. The officers commanding, if you choose to say anything of them, were Maj. Cunningham and Capts. Samuel Hammond, George Walton, and Joshua Inman, who all behaved well ; and the latter was particularly serviceable to you in advertising you of the enemy's approach and skirmishing with their advance.

The detachment was under my immediate command and direction, although I acted also as brigade-major to all the militia present. It is with difficulty I mention myself; but having the honor of introducing Maj. McArthur, the commander of the British infantry, a prisoner on that occasion, *taken by myself*, and having run the utmost risk of my life, in an attempt to seize the colors of the 71st regiment in the midst of it, on their attempt to form after they were broken, being saved by an exertion of Col. Howard's, and for which I had the honor of your thanks on the field of battle, I think it a duty to my children, as the history of my State is to be told, to have some insertion, *even of my conduct*, in that well-fought battle. You, sir, were rendered immortal by the action. My ambition is, to let my descendants and the citizens of Georgia know that I was present, and contributed my mite to your glory. Gen. Pickens has already certified to the requests of this letter fully. But whilst you are alive, his certificate is not the best evidence, and your testimony will be grateful to the citizens of Georgia.

I am sorry to break in upon the important business of your present command, and should have waited until the next session of the Federal Legislature, where we hope to see you a member, but for the pressing request of Mr. Langworthy to have the necessary papers.

I am, dear general, with the highest repect and esteem,

Your old fellow-soldier and most obedient servant,

JAMES JACKSON.

If you could favor me with an answer, previous to the rising of Congress about the 1st of March, it would highly oblige me.

BRIG. GEN. MORGAN.

GEN. JAMES JACKSON TO GEN. MORGAN.

PHILADELPHIA, *Feb. 9th*, 1795.

SIR : I did myself the honor of writing you about a fortnight since, respecting the service of the Georgians under you at the Cowpens. Lest two observations of mine in that letter should be misunderstood, I beg leave to correct them. The first was, that I was brigade-major to all the militia present. I since recollect that you had militia from Virginia. The second, that I had your thanks. I meant not by this, your thanks in orders, but verbally for my conduct, which a hundred living evidences could prove was creditable to myself, and deserving of your approbation. Colonel McDowell, now in Congress, and who commanded the North Carolina

militia on that day, is one of them. General Pickens's written testimony,
I informed you, I was possessed of, and under him I was acting. A circumstance I will take the liberty of mentioning will serve to revive your
memory. You had placed a sergeant over a cask of wine. After my return
with General, then Major McArthur, and who I had left in custody of Col.
Washington, I came across this man, and found him dealing the wine out
to all in his way. A wounded militia-man at some distance requested me
for a drop to revive him, which the sergeant refused on my application,
and I then ordered the men with me to drive him off and take possession
of the cask. He went and complained to you, and you came very angry,
and I expected would have struck me. Feeling myself injured, I explained
to you the conduct of the fellow, and could not help adding that my conduct had deserved a better return, mentioning to you my leaving the British officer commanding their infantry with the Colonel (Washington). It
was then that you made the sergeant beg my pardon on his knees, and
gave me your verbal thanks, which were repeated when we stopped on the
borders of North Carolina, and where we (Gen. Pickens and brigade) took
the prisoners under charge, and you parted from us. Maj. Giles mentioned
at Charlotte, on his tour to Congress, my name, as one who had distinguished himself; and considering the responsibilities of my station, and
the risks I ran that day, I had some right to expect to be named. I con
fess I was chagrined when the account came. I, after this, ran the utmost
risk of my life at Torrens's, when the British crossed the Catawba, and
believe, that in some measure, owing to my exertions with a few officers
and men, the slaughter was not so great as it otherwise would have been.
At Salisbury, where you had reached, it was believed by Gen. Pickens and
yourself, that I was killed. When I arrived, I had the honor of being
received by you and him with friendship and satisfaction. At the Yadkin
we parted, and I had the happiness after, to have my conduct signally
approbated by that great officer Gen. Greene, who appointed me to the
command of a State legion.

I have been thus particular, lest so long a lapse of time should have
made those circumstances escape your memory; and which, not being
necessarily connected with the principal events, and only concerning an
individual officer, are not likely to be retained. I had the honor, however,
in 1791, to have the principal circumstances recognized by you.

I shall leave this in about a fortnight for Savannah. Should you not see
it proper to give a certificate as to myself, I shall be happy to have your
approbation of the conduct of my countrymen.

I am, sir, &c.,   JAMES JACKSON.

Feb'y 9th, 1795.

APPENDIX E.

Paris, le 28 *Novembre*, 1847.

Je dois commencer, Monsieur, par vous demander pardon d'avoir été si longtemps sans vous répondre. J'avais toujours espéré que j'arriverais à découvrir le moyen de vous aider à remplir la pieuse et utile tâche que vous avez entreprise, et le désir que j'avais de ne vous adresser qu'une réponse satisfaisante, pourra peut-être me valoir vôtre indulgence pour un silence qui sans cela serait tout à fait inexcusable.

Malheureusement, je n'ai rien pu trouver de relatif aux temps sur lesquels vous auriez besoin d'être renseigné, dans les papiers de mon père. Cela vous paraîtra bien extraordinaire, et il est très simple que vous vous en étonniez; voici l'explication de cette singuliére circonstance. Assurément vous ne pouvez pas douter que mon père en revenant des États-Unis n'eut conservé, avec bien des soins, toute sa correspondance de la guerre et de la révolution Américaine. Elle était trop précieuse pour lui, pour qu'il ne la recueillit pas scrupuleusement; mais des circonstances indépendantes de sa volonté l'ont privé de la retrouver à son retour de sa prison d'Olmutz, et par conséquent, de celui de nous la transmettre. Vous n'ignorez pas, Monsieur, qu'en 1792, mon père fut proscrit; que par suite de cette proscription, ses propriétés furent confisquées. En 1793, au moment où la France gémissait sous le régime de la terreur, tous les papiers de mon père déposés à Chavaniac, lieu de sa naissance en Auvergne, furent saisis et brulés, sous les yeux de ses enfans, dans la cour du château; et au retour de sa prison, il ne retrouva que ceux de ces papiers si précieux pour lui, que des amis à leur risques et périls avaient pu enlever à la vigilance des hommes qui s'en étaient emparés. Ce n'est donc que dans ce petit nombre de papiers et dans les communications faites à d'autres qu'à nous, que mon père a pu retrouver les documents relatifs aux événements de la guerre d'Amérique, qui ont été publiés par nous, après lui, dans ses mémoires.

J'espérais pourtant dans ce qui nous reste entre les mains, retrouver peut-être quelque chose qui se rattacherait à la correspondence avec l'honorable Général Morgan, dont j'ai si souvent entendu parler à mon père ; mais mon espérance à été déçue. Je suis donc obligé, je le répète, de finir cette lettre comme je l'ai commencée, en réclamant vôtre indulgence pour mon trop long silence.

Ma vénération pour la mémoire des compagnons d'armes du père que je pleurerai toute ma vie, ne saurait être douteuse ; ma respectueuse reconnaissance pour les États-Unis, ma seconde patrie, ne saurait l'être davantage. Permettez moi d'espérer, Monsieur, que vous ne doutez pas, non plus, du desir que j'aurais, de pouvoir être agréable à un citoyen de ce beau et bon pays, auquel je suis tout dévoué, et du regret que j'éprouve de ne pouvoir accomplir le vœu de mon cœur, en vous procurant les renseignements dont vous avez besoin. Croyez bien que si des recherches nouvelles pouvaient me procurer les renseignements dont il s'agit, je ne tarderais pas un moment à vous les transmettre.

Veuillez agréer, Monsieur, l'expression de ma considération la plus distinguée.

Signé   GEORGE W. LAFAYETTE.

A Monsieur
    JAMES GRAHAM,
        A la Nouvelle Orléans,
           États-Unis d'Amérique.

CPSIA information can be obtained at www.ICGtesting.com
Printed in the USA
BVOW08s0500040815

411723BV00001B/89/P

9 781429 021333